Stability and Change
in
Revolutionary Pennsylvania

George David Rappaport

Stability and Change
in
Revolutionary Pennsylvania

Banking, Politics,
and
Social Structure

The Pennsylvania State University Press
University Park, Pennsylvania

Library of Congress Cataloging-in-Publication Data

Rappaport, George David.
    Stability and change in Revolutionary Pennsylvania : banking,
politics, and social structure / George David Rappaport.

        p.   cm.
    Includes bibliographical references (p.   ) and index.
    ISBN 0-271-01531-4 (alk. paper)
    1. Bank of North America—History.   2. Banks and banking—
Pennsylvania—History—18th century.   3. Pennsylvania—History—
Revolution, 1775–1783—Influence.   4. Social structure—
Pennsylvania—History—18th century.   5. Pennsylvania—Social
conditions.   I. Title.
HG2613.P54B45   1996
332.1'09748'09033—dc20   95–35472
                                                                 CIP

It is the policy of The Pennsylvania State University Press to use acid-free paper for the first printing of all clothbound books. Publications on uncoated stock satisfy the minimum requirements of American National Standard for Information Sciences—Permanence of Paper for Printed Library Materials, ANSI Z39.48–1992.

Contents

Acknowledgments vii
Introduction xi
Abbreviations xvii

PART ONE The Social Structure of Revolutionary Pennsylvania

1. The Capitalist Question 3
2. Traditional or Modern? 43
3. The Associational System 63
4. Politics, Conflict, and Parties 81
5. Politics: A Class Analysis 109

PART TWO The Bank of North America and the
      Problem of Change

6. The Birth of a Bank 137
7. The Seeds of War 159
8. Destroying the Monster 179
9. The Bank Reborn 199

Afterword 223

Appendixes 231
  A. Analysis of the Discount Ledger of the Bank of North
    America, January 7, 1782, to February 6, 1783 233

B. A Note on the Methodology Used to Analyze the
    Discount Ledger of the Bank of North America,
    January 7, 1782, to February 1783   237
C. English-Language Newspaper Articles and Pamphlets
    on the Bank of North America Published in
    Philadelphia, 1784–1787   239

Bibliography   245
Index   269

Acknowledgments

The last happy chore in writing a manuscript that has taken virtually all of my professional career is to acknowledge the assistance I received. My wife and friend, Susan Grabel, has read and criticized every draft of every chapter. Whatever clarity has been achieved owes her an enormous debt. Even more important, she tolerated long periods of scholarly withdrawal and never stopped believing in me. My son, Matthew, and my daughter, Julie, made demands that took me away from the book but enriched my life, and my brother Andrew Rose has become a loving friend and adviser. My parents, Tilly and Herman, brought me up in an environment that respected creativity and encouraged critical thinking.

Herman E. Krooss steered me through the dissertation shoals. I regret his untimely death and wish he could read the final product. I would also like to express my thanks to Brooke Hindle, the best teacher I had at New York University, who also read portions of the manuscript, and to John Hope Franklin, one of our great historians. His warmth and acceptance helped an awkward undergraduate at Brooklyn College and inspired him to become a historian.

Several friends made important contributions to this book. Ron Glassman encouraged my experiments with historical sociology and taught me much of what I know of Max Weber. Robert Kaczorowski strengthened my understanding of legal history and the development of corporations, and Allan Schiffmann challenged and deepened my understanding of Marxism. Each read and commented on earlier drafts of the entire manuscript, and each played a significant role in my intellectual development. Of all the readers of this manuscript, Peter Potter of Penn State Press stands out. His editorial work was meticulous, but even more important he understood what I was attempting to do and guided the project in the direction I wanted it to go. Peggy Hoover, also of the Press, did an exemplary job as style editor. Special thanks are due to James Henretta. I am deeply grateful for his sensitive reading of the manuscript. He provided sorely needed support and encouragement, and his critique enormously strengthened the manuscript. Allan Kulikoff also read the entire manuscript and offered praise and helpful criticism.

Billy (William) Cohen, whom I have known since childhood, read portions of the manuscript and offered a reality test. It is a pleasure to acknowledge his help. Others read portions of the manuscript, offering praise and useful criticisms. I would like to thank Robert Anderson, Mordechai Rozanski, Leonard Bernstein (his premature death was a grievous loss), Maarten de Kadt, Eric Foner, Julie and Laura Gordon, Don Krug, and Owen Ireland, who not only read my work but generously shared his own research with me. The members of the Philadelphia Center for Early American Studies, especially Marianne Wokeck, Richard Dunn, and P. M. G. Harris, as well as the members of the Columbia University Seminar in Early American history, offered a variety of useful and stimulating comments on portions of the manuscript. The camaraderie and intellectual stimulation offered at these seminars helped sustain my scholarly energies. Elaine Crane provided useful help in identifying eighteenth-century Philadelphians. I am particularly grateful to Jerry Grabel for his labor-intensive computational efforts that resulted in Appendix A, to Mary Ann Zinacola, who typed early drafts, and to Myra Farrell for entering the footnotes and appendixes and portions of the manuscript onto a word processor.

All studies like this require institutional support. Wagner College generously provided me with several sabbaticals and several study grants. Richard Palumbo and Mitchell Dakelman of Wagner College's Horrmann Library provided invaluable assistance in my research. I would also like to express my appreciation for the assistance provided by the librarians and archivists at the New York Public Library, the New York Historical Society, Columbia University, New York University, the University of Pennsylvania, the American Philosophical Society Library, the Connecticut Historical Society, the Pennsylvania State Archives, the Rutgers University Library, the West Chester Historical Society, and the Library of Congress. Peter Parker, at the Historical Society of

Pennsylvania deserves special mention; his command of the Society's manuscript collections was invaluable. John Catanzariti, Elizabeth Nuxoll, and Mary Gallagher at the Robert Morris Papers provided friendship, professional courtesy, and a great wealth of knowledge.

Introduction

This study grew out of the hopes and assumptions of a social historian. At the moment, the historiography of the Early National Era is dominated by those who focus on ideology and by those who place Americans on an agrarian-localist and commercial/cosmopolitan polarity. As an alternative, I offer a historical analysis built around the concept of social structure. The discussion assumes that societies have organizational patterns and that these patterns or social structures constitute both the arenas within which action occurs and the patterned constraints that channel action. An examination of the social structure can enrich our understanding of the past by clarifying the contexts of action and by helping us to understand the finite range of choices open to individuals in specific historical circumstances.

Part One of this book undertakes a description and an analysis of the social structure of Revolutionary Pennsylvania. Chapters 1 and 2 establish the general societal type that existed in the Quaker province. Chapter 1 enters the debate about whether early America was capitalist and concludes that, whatever definition is used, Pennsylvania did not have a capitalist economy. The prominent social actors were not maximizers, and neither markets nor capitalist social relations dominated. Merchants were traditional social figures of the type that has existed since the emergence of large-scale organized societies, while artisans and most farmers are best understood as petty-commodity producers. Chapter 2 looks at the rhythm and nature of social change and finds that modernization was not occurring. The slow pace of change and the predominant organizational (social) form—simple and unspecialized—mark Pennsylvania's social structure as traditional.

Chapters 3, 4, and 5 shift the focus from the general to the particular. Chapter 3 looks at the unusual integrative pattern that emerged in the Quaker province, which I call the "associational system." The system was built around voluntary associations and a set of supportive norms and values. These associations played an unusually important role in Pennsylvania because of the simplicity of the social system and because of the weakness of hierarchical institutions and ascriptive restraints. Political institutions are the focus of Chapter 4. At the center of the political sphere was a fully developed party system whose organizational framework was derived from the associational system. Chapter 5 focuses on the distribution and organization of power. The stratification system was built around the interaction of three politically active social classes—urban merchants and petty-commodity-producing farmers and artisans. At its apex was an urban ruling class that managed to establish and maintain itself despite the absence of coercive institutions like the European church, state, and military.

Part Two, Chapters 6 through 9, offers a case study. The analytic framework or model developed in Part One is used to examine the processes of change in a traditional society in the early stages of the transformation to capitalism and modernity. The focus shifts from exploration of the social structure to the actions and motives of individuals and social groups.

The establishment of the Bank of North America—America's first commercial bank—in 1781, and the bank war, also America's first, that followed are examined in detail. Chapter 6 describes the creation of the bank by Congress and its incorporation in Pennsylvania. Despite Robert Morris's nationalist predilections, the bank was created in large part as an entrepreneurial venture designed to support the economic interests of Pennsylvania's mercantile elite.

In 1783 and 1784 the bank was tested by prosperity and then by the postwar economic crisis. Chapter 7 describes the bank's successful campaign to protect its local monopoly and its rejection of the General Assembly's request for economic assistance to fight the consequences of hard times, a rejection that triggered the creation of a land bank. In turn, increased public understanding of the nature of the Bank of North America, the class biases revealed by the bank's resistance to the land bank, and the imperatives of the party system combined to spark an attempt to destroy the bank.

Chapters 8 and 9 provide a detailed narrative of the Constitutionalist Party's abolition of the act incorporating the Bank of North America and the successful campaign led by Robert Morris and the bank's directors to survive the loss of the charter and then restore it. Throughout the discussion, the tension between noncapitalist and capitalist social relations, the strain exerted by the appearance of a powerful modern organization, and the demands of the political parties are made clear. Furthermore, a comprehensive description of the first public debate on the nature and significance of commercial banking helps clarify the perceptions and motives of the participants.

The writing style in Part Two differs from that adopted in Part One. The difference is deliberate, reflecting the different purposes of the two parts. In Part One, my attempt to create a model of the social structure by exploring a series of analytic problems is best served by an analytical and expository writing style. In Part Two I use narrative to describe the establishment of the bank and to portray a sense of the unfolding of events and the actions of individuals.

Other disciplines deal with similar problems and routinely use similar techniques. Sociologists and psychologists frequently begin monographs with extended theoretical discourses, which they follow with case studies written in the narrative form.

Yet although Parts One and Two have different purposes, the entire book rests on the assumption that human action must be understood contextually, and that the social structure is the key arena in which agency is exercised. The primary importance of the social structure is that it channels choice and limits options.

A second purpose underlies this project. When I finished graduate school in 1970, the historical profession was dramatically different from what it is today. For the overwhelming majority of historians, historical methodology consisted of finding and critically reading primary sources, constructing narratives, cultivating objectivity, and eschewing theory. This methodology was married to an insistence on the uniqueness and diversity of the human experience, a stance that further protected against the development of generalizations that could be used in theoretical work. While Marxists, Freudians, and a few maverick quantifiers railed against the establishment, their efforts had no discernible impact.

More than a century ago, Charles Darwin charmingly criticized the antitheoretical position.

> About thirty years ago there was much talk that geologists ought only to observe and not theorize; and I well remember someone

saying that at this rate a man might as well go into a gravel-pit and count the pebbles and describe the colours. How odd it is that anyone should not see that all observation must be for or against some view if it is to be of any service![1]

Darwin was right. Mainstream historical methodology resulted in a single-minded focus on technique. An unfortunate result of this emphasis has been a disciplinary tendency toward hyperfactualism. No more devastating critique can be imagined than that offered by a panel of historians:

No profession has set greater store by data—all kinds of data, big, small, important, trivial. Every little bit counts. Hence the respect of the historian for erudition—for the ubiquitous foot-note, for the obscure reference, for the long array of variant texts. Hence also the goal of the definitive work, which is not the last word in interpretation (that, never!) but the last word in research.[2]

Today the intellectual assumptions of traditional historical methodology lie in shambles. The internal challenge mounted by Carl Becker and Charles Beard, and the intensification of this challenge by Thomas Kuhn; the broadening of the historical canvas by the inclusion of an ever-increasing number of disciplines, such as environmental demography, economics, sociology, and anthropology, to help study a widening array of human activities; and the importation of theoretical techniques and methodologies from these disciplines have combined to weaken the ramparts between history and the social sciences.

It no longer seems possible to argue that we can find and organize evidence without drawing on theory, or that we can explain the past without using theories about human language, motivation, culture, the distribution and use of power, and the relationship between economics, technology, culture, and ideology.

Nevertheless, the hold of traditional methodological assumptions remains strong. Historians still manage to keep social theory at arm's length. History remains the only scholarly discipline characterized by covert theorizing, which is done in prefaces, introductions, appendixes,

---

1. Quoted in Finley, *Ancient Slavery*, 65.
2. Landes and Tilly, eds., *History*, 18.

and footnotes—anywhere but in the main body of the text. Even so, some progress has been made. In recent decades, historians have made a start at learning and using theory. The blurring of disciplinary lines and the influence of the social sciences has seen to this. However, additional steps need to be taken to break the hold of disciplinary assumptions and style.

This book works hard at integrating theoretical considerations into the center of the historical discourse, and particular attention is paid to the need to learn to "think theoretically." To accomplish this, we must explore the nature and limitations of theory.[3]

Theories are either explanatory tools or heuristic devices. They consist of clusters of related concepts, models, definitions, and propositions. Theories specify forces, structures, and systems, and also the relations between them and variables. They also help explain, which is their most important function. They explain by using analogues and metaphors, by revealing patterns, by facilitating the development of generalized descriptions, and by specifying models and causal mechanisms.[4]

Theoretical explanation is very different from our everyday, ordinary explanation. We normally explain in terms of our personal experiences, but when we use theory we try to explain everyday experiences abstractly "in terms of something of which we do not and cannot have any direct experience at all and it is at this level that theory really tells us something new about the world."[5]

Theories are not empirical generalizations. They are not fact patterns or tendencies we can observe in the data. Theories are conceptual tools that help us explain empirical generalizations. This means that we will not have a theory about an event. To explain an event, we develop causal generalizations and then explain those generalizations theoretically.[6]

The basic theoretical tool used in this book is the typology. In

3. Craib, *Social Theory*, 5. A fine example of historians experimenting with the use of theory is Ellis and Wildavsky, "Cultural Analysis."

4. Giere, *Explaining Science*, 79–86; Hanson, *Patterns*, 90; Harre, "Role of Models"; Harre, *Philosophies of Science*, 23, 115–18, 172–75; Hesse, "Models Versus Paradigms," 7–9; Suppe, ed., *Structure*, 122–24.

5. Craib, *Social Theory*, 7.

6. Turner, "Ideographic vs. Nomothetic," 274; Willer and Webster Jr., "Theoretical Concepts"; Kocka, "Theories and Quantification," 170–72. There is an important debate over whether theories are real (realist) or simply tools (instrumentalist). For the purposes of this discussion, it is not necessary to navigate these troubled waters. The point here is simply that, whether or not theories refer directly to reality, they have to be used and their use requires training and skill.

Chapters 1 through 5, typologies of capitalism, modern and traditional societies, voluntary associations, parties, and classes are constructed, explored, and used. These typologies are constructs or models that identify the basic "features (qualities, propensities, location, etc.) of some social entity, be it a person, a class of persons (e.g., politicians, businessmen, priests), or a collectivity or institution (the government, a corporation, a church)." They represent general or theoretical categories rather than specific individuals.[7]

As numerous scholars have noted, such typological constructs are "neither typical nor ideal." They are analytic constructs that are logical and precise "statements of possible relationships" and organizational patterns. They cannot be falsified, and they are not true. There is no such thing as pure capitalism, pure modern society, or pure rational bureaucracy. Still, types are essential tools for studying the dynamics of social structures. They also facilitate comparisons. In fact, types and other theoretical constructs are as useful and as necessary to the work of historians and other social scientists as manuscript collections and databases are.[8]

Even though ideal types frequently generate academic heat, they have a long and honorable history in the natural and social sciences. Scientific concepts like id, mass, and electrical resistance, and historical concepts like epoch, state, feudalism, republicanism, proletariat, social class, and free market capitalism, are ideal types. They are ubiquitous and necessary for the writing of history.

Perhaps the most difficult lesson is that theories cannot be applied mechanically. Theories are neither templates nor puzzle boards with convenient slots into which we fit empirical data. The working relationship between theory, analytic arguments, and evidence is complex.

Thinking theoretically involves developing new skills, and creating the best possible fit between theory and social reality. In this book, theorizing is assumed to be a legitimate and important part of the historical enterprise. Part One carefully spells out, examines, and uses the relevant social theory, and then uses it to construct a model of Pennsylvania's social structure. The narrative case study developed in Part Two is constructed on that foundation.[9]

7. Sabia Jr. and Wallulis, eds., *Social Science,* 14.

8. Abrams, *Historical Sociology,* 79–81. See also Papineau, "Ideal Type"; Roth, "Typological Approach"; Shiner, "Tradition/Modernity"; Tiryakian, "Typologies."

9. For a description of the way historical sociologists use theory, see Bonnell, "Uses of Theory."

Abbreviations

AA	*American Anthropologist*
AAAPSS	*Annals of the American Academy of Political and Social Science*
ABS	*American Behavioral Scientist*
AER	*American Economic Review*
AH	*Agricultural History*
AHR	*American Historical Review*
AJS	*American Journal of Sociology*
APSL	American Philosophical Society Library, Philadelphia
APSR	*American Political Science Review*
ASR	*American Sociological Review*
BHR	*Business History Review*
CHS	Connecticut Historical Society, Hartford
CL	Clements Library, University of Michigan Ann Arbor, Michigan
CP	*Comparative Politics*
CSSH	*Comparative Studies in Society and History*
D	*Diogenes*
DAB	*Dictionary of American Biography,* ed. Allen Johnson and Dumas Malone, 20 vols. (New York, 1928–80).
DH	*Delaware History*
EDCC	*Economic Development and Cultural Change*
Hamilton Papers	Harold C. Syrett, Jacob E. Cooke, et al., eds. *The Papers of Alexander Hamilton* (New York, 1961–87).
HSP	Historical Society of Pennsylvania, Philadelphia

HT	*History and Theory*
IESS	*International Encyclopedia of the Social Sciences,* ed. David L. Sills, 16 vols. (New York, 1968).
JAH	*Journal of American History*
Jefferson Papers	Julian P. Boyd, Charles T. Cullen, John Catanzariti, et al., eds., *The Papers of Thomas Jefferson* (Princeton, N.J., 1950–).
JEH	*Journal of Economic History*
JIH	*Journal of Interdisciplinary History*
JPE	*Journal of Political Economy*
JPS	*Journal of Peasant Studies*
JSH	*Journal of Social History*
JTSB	*Journal for the Theory of Social Behavior*
LC	Library of Congress
Madison Papers	William T. Hutchinson, Robert A. Rutland, et al., eds., *The Papers of James Madison* (Chicago, 1962–).
Morris Papers	E. James Ferguson, John Catanzariti, Elizabeth M. Nuxoll, et al., eds., *The Papers of Robert Morris, 1781–1784* (Pittsburgh, 1973–).
NLR	*New Left Review*
NYHS	New York Historical Society, New York City
NYHSQ	*New York Historical Society Quarterly*
NYPL	New York Public Library, New York City
PA	*Pennsylvania Archives,* Series I, ed. Samuel Hazard (Philadelphia, 1853).
Pa. Min.	*Minutes of the General Assembly of the Commonwealth of Pennsylvania,* Sessions 6 and 7 (Philadelphia, 1781) and Sessions 8–14 (Philadelphia, 1783–90).
PH	*Pennsylvania History*
PMHB	*Pennsylvania Magazine of History and Biography*
PP	*Past and Present*
PS	*Peasant Studies*
PSA	Pennsylvania State Archives, Historical and Museum Commission, Harrisburg
QJE	*Quarterly Journal of Economics*
RAH	*Reviews in American History*
REH	*Reviews in Economic History*
REHC	*Working Papers from the Regional Economic History Center,* Eleutherian Mills–Hagley Foundation
RHR	*Radical History Review*

RRPE	*Radical Review of Political Economy*
RS	*Rural Sociology*
RUL	Rutgers University Library Manuscript Section, New Brunswick, New Jersey
SA	*Social Analysis*
SP	*Sociological Perspectives*
SR	*Sociological Review*
SSH	*Social Science History*
VAR	*Voluntary Action Research*
WCHS	West Chester Historical Society, West Chester, Pennsylvania
WMQ	*William and Mary Quarterly*
WP	*World Politics*

PART ONE

═══

The Social Structure
of
Revolutionary Pennsylvania

1

The Capitalist Question

The first step in exploring the social structure of late-eighteenth-century Pennsylvania is to ask some questions about the nature of the social landscape. Before we can examine the region's integrative systems, institutions, and stratification system, or an event like the establishment of the Bank of North America, we must deal with issues of a more general nature. We need to ask: Was the regional economy capitalist? What was the nature of the social forms and organizations that populated the various social spheres? And what were the characteristics of the rhythm and pace of change?

The answers to these questions will help establish the general type of society that existed in this part of the Middle Atlantic region. In turn, these questions presume that we can generalize about types of societies, that we can profitably talk about pastoral, early horticultural, and capitalist societies. Finally, the argument assumes that we must establish an abstract framework before we analyze the concrete and the historical.[1]

In this chapter we ask whether Pennsylvania in the 1780s can be

1. Bottomore, "Structure," 159–71, esp. 160.

understood as predominantly capitalist. This is currently the subject of a fierce debate. At stake is our understanding of the basic nature of American history. Was America capitalist from the beginning? If so, American history can be understood in terms of continuity and unfolding, which is the view that predominates. Scholars have portrayed every aspect and every era of American history as capitalist. Carl Degler's famous aphorism "Capitalism Came in the First Ships" captures the spirit of the consensus.[2]

Most students of eighteenth-century Pennsylvania find this view congenial. Pennsylvanians from all walks of life, from the countinghouse, the mechanic's shop, the farm, have been portrayed as property owners operating family businesses in a speculative, competitive, and profit-oriented social environment. The commercial nature of the Philadelphia trading area, with its ties to international markets, has also been highlighted.[3]

However, this dominant view has been subjected to searching critique. At the core of this second interpretation is the sense that American history involved a radical transformation from traditional, noncapitalist social relations to a capitalist present. Many of the scholars making this argument have directed their analyses at rural life and portrayed farmers as focusing on family needs, as embedded in noncommercial exchange networks, and as resisting commercialization. Others have looked at merchants and artisans and found a similar resistance to commercialization.[4]

Both sides of the debate have proved adept at gathering evidence to buttress their positions. The settlement of British North America was part of the commercial revolution. From the very beginning, Americans bought and sold goods and participated in international markets, and private property was widely owned and socially desirable. At the same time, as discussions of mentalité and local exchange networks make clear, there were aspects of rural and urban life that are inconsistent with the commercial interpretation. Theoretical and definitional issues have been even more troublesome. Capitalism appears to have almost as many meanings as there are scholars writing about it. Common

2. Degler, *Our Past*, 1.
3. Lemon, *Poor Man's Country;* Warner Jr., *Private City;* and Schweitzer, *Custom,* are representative.
4. Influential early criticisms were offered by Henretta, "Families and Farms"; Merrill, "Cash Is Good"; and Foner, *Paine.*

usages include the activities of businessmen, an ideology, a mode of production, a market system, a social system, a global economic system, and a historical epoch.[5]

This will not do. The issues surrounding evidence and definition are related. Starting from different vantage points, scholars have looked for different types of evidence and interpreted their findings differently. It is no small testimony to the complex nature of reality that both sides have been able to build plausible cases. Further complicating matters has been the historian's traditional reluctance to engage in explicitly theoretical discussions. Discussants generally try to establish their positions by accumulating more evidence, and as a result underlying assumptions remain largely unexamined and the existence of analytic problems has been ignored.[6]

To chart a course around the present impasse, I shall begin with a substantial discussion of the major definitions of capitalism—not to argue that one definition is superior to another, but to lay bare the theoretical implications embedded in each definitional stance and to make clear the kinds of evidence it would take to prove each position.

The three main definitions of capitalism focus on the capitalist, the market, and the mode of production. The first definition—the entrepreneurial—was developed by such writers as Werner Sombart, Max Weber, and Joseph A. Schumpeter. They stressed the development and spread of a capitalist ethos through the rise to dominance of the bourgeoisie. Schumpeter said:

> Here was a class that saw business facts in a different light and from a different angle; a class, in short, that was *in* business, and therefore could never look at its problems with the aloofness of the schoolman. . . . [Moreover,] it is more essential to realize that quite irrespective of the assertion of his *interests,* the businessman, as his weight in the social structure increased, imparted to society an increasing dose of his *mind* just as the knight had done before him. The particular mental habits generated by the work in the business office, the schema of values that emanates from it, and the attitude to public and

5. Lane, "Meanings of Capitalism."

6. Recent studies exhibit a greater comfort with explicit theorizing. See Headlee, *Political Economy;* Kulikoff, *Agrarian Origins;* Merrill, "Self-Sufficiency"; Rothenberg, *Market-Places;* Osterud, *Bonds of Community.*

private life that is characteristic of it, slowly spread in *all* classes and over *all* fields of human thought and action.[7]

The entrepreneurial definition has three core assumptions: (1) that buying and selling for profits is the essence of capitalism, (2) that a capitalist social system emerges when businessmen become the dominant class, and (3) that capitalists, as the dominant class, impart their values—especially the drive to acquire and accumulate wealth—to society.

The last assumption requires further explication. According to Max Weber, capitalism developed when maximization became an end in itself. But Weber was careful to make clear that maximization did not mean avarice. Avarice, he asserted, does not distinguish the modern era from earlier ones: "The notion that our rationalistic and capitalistic age is characterized by a stronger economic interest than other periods is childish. The moving spirits of modern capitalism are not possessed of a stronger economic impulse than, for example, an oriental trader."[8] According to Weber, maximization means a willingness to sublimate such economic passions as avarice and greed to legitimate economic activity. Encouraged by religion to treat work as a calling, capitalists maximize by the efficient and rational and devoted performance of work. Weber also insisted that maximization involved an ascetic avoidance of the use of income for personal gratification. Instead, capitalists reinvest in search of ever-larger profits.[9]

Thus, the entrepreneurial definition stresses the rise to power of businessmen who focus on the legal accumulation and reinvestment of wealth. As the bourgeoisie achieves power and legitimation, its ideas circulate and act as an example for other social groups, who also learn to maximize. The result of this process is the emergence of a capitalist society.

The second definition of capitalism derives from neoclassical economic theory. Capitalism is understood to be a society with a fully developed market economy. To the economist, markets refer not to places but to

---

7. Schumpeter, *Economic Analysis*, 78–79. There are substantial differences between Schumpeter and Weber. The discussion that follows reflects current usage as exhibited in influential or typical works. This is *not* an attempt to explore what such writers as Marx or Weber meant by capitalism.

8. Quoted in Abrams, *Historical Sociology*, 94.

9. For Weber on capitalism, see ibid., 87–107; Brubaker, *Limits of Rationality*, ch. 1; Collins, *Weberian Theory*, chs. 2, 5; Giddens, *Capitalism*, 124–32.

social situations with specific norms, mind-sets, and social relations. As Alfred Marshall said, "economists understand by the term *market,* the whole of any region in which buyers and sellers are in such free intercourse with one another that the prices of the same goods tend to equality easily and quickly."[10]

Markets transform services, processed goods, capital, labor, and land into saleable items (commodities) with prices. In economies governed by markets, changes in the prices of one commodity affect the prices of others. Prices also regulate the supply and the demand of all commodities. It is significant that prices operate as if they were commodities; they too are part of the market mechanism. Finally, markets for goods (product markets), markets for the factors of production (land, labor, and capital), and prices are entwined in a systemic relationship. The result is that a change in part of the system has an impact on the whole. This is the reason economists such as Walter C. Neale talk about the "self-equilibrating mechanism" when they use "the term market."[11]

For a market economy to exist, capital, land, labor, and the fruits of labor must be treated as things (commodities) that are saleable. The result is that economic and social relations are treated as if they were atomistic, impersonal, and decentralized. Traditional ascriptive restraints (social roles mandated by birth) cannot play an important role in a capitalist society.

As traditional social relations cease to regulate economic behavior, the resulting fragmentation leads to the development of the profit motive as an integrative mechanism. At this point, the second definition merges with the first. The market system cannot function unless people translate social relations into prices and act rationally in a Weberian sense. Economic man is not a fabrication. Capitalism legitimates, and in fact insists, that people devote themselves to work, investment, and economic gain. As this norm is universalized, it operates as "a powerful tool for *allocating* [societal] *resources*" and for encouraging acceptance of an unequal distribution of private property.[12]

Not until market dynamics come to predominate in the economy can we talk of capitalism. Such societies are unique. Until recently there has been no economy directed even theoretically by market mechanisms.

10. Quoted in Rothenberg, "Massachusetts Farmers," 300. See also Ellis, *Peasant Economics;* Hodges, *Primitive and Peasant Markets.*

11. Fraser, *Economic Thought,* 131–33; Neale, "Theory and History," 359.

12. Heilbroner, *Economic Problem,* 70–73; Lane, "Meanings of Capitalism," 10; Dorfman, *Price System,* 38–42.

Historically, general economic relations and markets have been submerged in broader integrative patterns that are primarily political in character, such as reciprocity and redistribution.[13]

To facilitate the operation of the pricing mechanism, the economy is first isolated from other social spheres and then encouraged to predominate. As Karl Polanyi says: "Control of the economic system by the market is of over-whelming consequence to the whole organization of society: it means no less than the running of society as an adjunct to the market. Instead of the economy being embedded in social relations, social relations are embedded in the economic system."[14]

The third definition of capitalism—the Marxist definition—shifts the analytic focus from entrepreneurs and the sale of commodities to production. On the most general level, Marx believed that the process of production he called the labor process was composed of four elements—human labor, raw materials, technology, and a coordinating agency such as management—when large numbers of people are involved.[15] Central to his analysis of the elements that constitute the labor process is the concept of a mode of production. This concept expresses a duality. Frank Roosevelt tells us that according to Marx, a mode of production "appears as a double relationship: on the one hand as a natural, on the other as a social relationship." The natural or material aspects of production are the processes that involve the transformation of nature into goods for human consumption. The social aspects of the labor process are the relationships that are concerned with the ownership of the means of production and the unequal distribution of the social product so that classes are formed.[16]

The social aspects of production loom so large in Marx's analytic framework that he categorized societies in terms of class structures and the corresponding forms of exploitation. Thus, Marx insisted that "the essential difference between the various economic forms of society, between, for instance, a society based on slave-labour, and one based

13. Dorfman, *Price System*, 3; Polanyi, *Transformation*, ch. 6. Reciprocity involves "material gift and counter gift-giving induced by social obligation derived typically, from kinship" (Dalton, "Economic Theory," 9–10).

14. Polanyi, *Transformation*, 57.

15. Roosevelt, "Cambridge Economics," 3. The following passages, and my understanding of Marxism, owe a great deal to discussions with Alan Schiffmann. Also useful were Hindess and Hirst, *Modes of Production;* Althusser and Balibar, *Reading "Capital";* and Dobb, *Studies*.

16. Roosevelt, "Cambridge Economics," 3. According to Maurice Dobb, a mode of production is "the way in which the means of production were owned and the social relations between men which resulted from their connection with the process of production" (*Studies*, 9).

on wage-labour, lies only in the mode in which . . . surplus labour is in each case extracted from the actual producer, the labourer."[17]

When Marx shifted his attention from modes of production to historical analysis, he made use of an additional concept: the social formation, which he understood to refer to the totality of social relations that exist at any particular moment. In the Marxist tradition, this translated into a focus on classes and class systems. Maarten de Kadt provides an illustration of the use of these concepts: "U.S. capitalism of 1978 is a social formation. The mode of production is capitalism, but that is an abstraction. The social formation is an attempt to describe a specific period of history more concretely. Elements of several modes of production can coexist in a single social formation even though one usually—though not always—dominates."[18]

A capitalist mode of production is one in which capitalist relations predominate in both the natural and the social aspects of production. The material aspects of production are organized so that control and execution are separated. In particular, the producer is not allowed to participate in the process of production without being subject to the supervision and control of the capitalist and/or management. The result is alienated labor.[19]

Marx saw alienated labor as a defining characteristic of capitalism and as a human tragedy. According to Marx, alienated labor is constituted by

> the fact that labor is *external* to the worker, i.e., it does not belong to his essential being; that in his work, therefore, he does not affirm himself but denies himself, does not feel content but unhappy, does not develop freely his physical and mental energy but mortifies his body and ruins his mind. The worker therefore only feels himself outside his work, and in his work feels outside himself. He is at home when he is not working, and when he is working he is not at home. His labor is therefore not voluntary, but coerced; it is *forced labor*. It is therefore not the satisfaction of a need; it is merely a means to satisfy needs external to it.[20]

For alienation to predominate, a small minority of capitalists must own and control the means of production. As this occurs, a process of

17. Marx, *Capital*, 1:216–17.

18. Private communication from Maarten de Kadt, January 13, 1978; see also Hindess and Hirst, *Modes of Production*, 13–15.

19. Roosevelt, "Cambridge Economics," 14.

20. Marx, *Manuscripts of 1844*, 74.

commodity exchange comes to characterize the labor process. In this process, capitalists buy the means of production and items of personal consumption from other capitalists. Capitalists also purchase labor power from workers who in turn use their wages to buy their own subsistence.[21]

At the heart of the process of commodity exchange is the connection between labor and capital produced by wages. Wage labor is the mechanism through which profits emerge and through which capitalists expropriate the surplus value produced by labor. The act of expropriation involves exploitation and results in antagonism, so in addition to profits the wage relationship also accounts for alienation and the creation and perpetuation of social classes and class struggle.[22]

Thus, wage labor is central to Marxist analyses of the capitalist mode of production. According to Perry Anderson,

> capitalism is the first mode of production in history in which the means whereby the surplus is pumped out of the direct producer is purely economic in form—the wage contract: the equal exchange between free agents which reproduces, hourly and daily, inequality and oppression. All other previous modes of exploitation operate through *extra-economic* sanctions—kin, customary, religious, legal or political.[23]

With these three definitions in hand, let us turn to Pennsylvania in the 1780s and ask whether the region was capitalist. The discussion begins by applying the first definition to the region's export-import merchants, artisans, and farmers. Afterward, I utilize the second and third definitions.

The obvious fact about Philadelphia's export-import merchants is that their major economic activity was buying and selling. They dealt in international and local markets and bought and sold in bulk. Merchants sold everything that had a market. The same firm might sell haberdashery, housewares, liquor, sugar, and even hardware. It was not unusual

---

21. Hindess and Hirst, *Modes of Production,* 10, 21, 101–3, 128–30; Althusser and Balibar, *Reading "Capital,"* 212–16; Marx, *Capital,* 1:167–70. The portion of the product used for the laborer's subsistence is the necessary-product; the rest is the surplus-product. Surplus-value is the monetary form of the surplus-product. See Mandel, *Introduction,* 7–10.

22. Roosevelt, "Cambridge Economics," 13–14; Friedmann, "World Market," 556–58.

23. Anderson, *Lineages,* 403.

for advertisements to list as many as 100 to 200 items.[24] In their search for profits, however, merchants played a role that went far beyond buying and selling. Merchants were the region's major suppliers of capital. They lent to other merchants, retailers, manufacturers, land speculators, governments, friends, and neighbors. They also dealt in foreign currencies and bills of exchange, acted as insurance underwriters, brokers, and collection agents, and provided information about the local market to their correspondents. They rented space in their warehouses for storage. They owned vessels, earnings from which were a major source of mercantile wealth. A few invested in industries related to commerce, such as flour-milling, shipbuilding, distilling, and iron production. And they invested heavily in real estate.[25]

Under the tutelage of its mercantile community, Philadelphia and its hinterland developed into America's largest commercial center. More flour was exported from the city than from all the mainland colonies combined. The city also led in exports of masts, iron, and cooperage materials. As a result, Philadelphia handled more goods than any other American port.[26]

Despite the impressive performance of the Philadelphia mercantile community, the economic environment imposed substantial limitations on the growth of commerce. Populations, and markets, were small and dispersed. Transportation and communication technology was primitive. Sailing was slow and heavily weather-dependent. Trips between Philadelphia and the West Indies took three to four weeks, and difficult weather could double the time involved. Once in port, it was necessary to unload and dispose of cargoes and to procure return cargoes. The fact that a ship's cargo was composed of several merchants' goods was an additional complication, as was the practice of firing the crew when they arrived in port. It was not unusual for a vessel to spend months in port between voyages.[27]

Merchants also had to deal with an inadequate monetary system, capital shortages, and the absence of ancillary business service institu-

24. Berg, "Organization," 168; Doerflinger, "Farmers," 166, 174. Also, consult the ads in any Philadelphia newspaper in the 1780s.

25. Doerflinger, *Vigorous Spirit*, 64–65, 67, 85, 131–32, 151–56; Cochran, *Business*, 23–24; Krooss and Gilbert, *American Business*, 54–55; Anderson, "Wharton," 49–50, 59, 69, 72–73, 76, 81–83.

26. Crowther, "Shipbuilding," 208; Duvall, "Maritime Commerce," 6–10.

27. Krooss and Gilbert, *American Business*, 71; Bruchey, *Oliver*, 144–45; Cole, *Enterprise*, 189–90; Cole, "Tempo," 289; Egnal, "Changing Structure," 157.

tions (management consultants, debt collectors, market researchers, bankers, investment brokers, public relations specialists, employment agencies, etc.). As a result, merchants faced severe limits on the scale of the business operations they could undertake.

These limitations translated into a relatively light workload. The best studies we have of eighteenth-century mercantile practices focus on New England, but it is reasonable to assume that there was little variation in the way merchants from different ports carried on their enterprises. What we do know is that successful merchants like Boston's Thomas Hancock averaged fifteen sales a week, some two or three a day. The rest of Hancock's workload was correspondingly light. He mailed only sixty-two business letters a year, although the typical number of letters sent by merchants in the late colonial period was apparently four to six a week. No wonder Thomas C. Cochran's discussion of Philadelphia's merchants concludes: "Between the dispatch or reception of shipments, there were many days or weeks during which the clerk could run the office while the proprietor inspected his real estate holdings or lived the life of a country gentleman."[28]

With relatively few sales and few other pressing tasks, work in the countinghouse was not arduous. Typically, the merchant arose at 8:00 or 8:30, said morning prayers with his family, and enjoyed the first meal of the day. After attending to his wardrobe and powdering his hair, he walked to his countinghouse. Sometimes he detoured, stopping at the market to purchase supper and send it home with a servant. Arriving at work around ten o'clock, the merchant worked for three or four hours, a stiff rum in mid-morning punctuating his labors. Finished for the day, he walked to the London Coffee House or the newer City Tavern and traded business information and gossip with friends until hunger drove him home. The midday meal was the largest of the day and was usually followed by a nap. Unless he had a ship in port or some other urgent business, the merchant did not return to his countinghouse. During the late afternoon and early evening, he attended to his other investments or participated in social, political, or community activities.[29]

This daily routine does not reveal the merchant to be an economic maximizer. It is not surprising that the "structural limitations" that shaped business were reflected in behavioral norms and values. As

28. Cole, "Tempo," 279–84; Cochran, *Pennsylvania*, 27.

29. Doerflinger, *Vigorous Spirit*, 18; Cole, *Enterprise*, 131–32; Cole, "Tempo"; Warner Jr., *Private City*, 20; Bridenbaugh, *Cities in Revolt*, 71.

Stuart Bruchey notes, "the slow information and transport flows of an age of sail imposed sluggishness on the motions of the market and opened vistas of leisure for other activities." Thus, by modern standards, merchants did not see their work as a calling and did not reinvest as much of their profits as we might expect from a modern capitalist.[30]

Studies of colonial accounting point in the same direction. They suggest that merchants were not encouraged about keeping profit accounts and did not bother to strike balances to determine their profits and losses. In addition, family and business expenses were commonly mixed in the account ledgers. Such practices raise questions about the extent to which merchants conceived of business as a goal in and of itself.[31]

The mixing of family and business concerns points to a particularly important aspect of mercantile practice. Commerce was impersonal, often hostile, and uncontrollable. Faced with these unpleasant realities, merchants responded sensibly. When they needed advice, information, storage, transportation, loans, consignments, insurance, agents, partners, or apprentices, they turned to family, friends, and dependents.[32]

Thomas Wharton provides a perfect example. The eldest son of a wealthy and respected Quaker merchant, Thomas began his business career in 1751 at the age of twenty-one with family capital. His countinghouse and wharf were also family property, and his first commercial contact in England was made with the advice of an uncle. Thomas trained his younger brother Isaac in the trade, and Isaac served a full four-year apprenticeship, living in his brother's house. After completing his apprenticeship, Isaac entered the firm as a full partner. When Thomas Wharton chose a business agent—full partner or limited partner—it was a relative or someone recommended by an acquaintance, and frequently a member of the Society of Friends. He engaged in numerous business deals with his father, at least three of his brothers, and two of his cousins.[33]

As the example of Wharton suggests, the kinship network was

30. Bruchey, "Economy and Society," 305.
31. East, "Business Entrepreneur," 24–25; Baxter, "Accounting," 279–81; Cochran, *Business,* 22; Krooss and Gilbert, *American Business,* 67–68; Parker, "Printer," 33–35, 45–46. For more sanguine views of colonial accounting, see Bruchey, *Oliver,* 135–41; and Harrington, *New York Merchant,* 95–97.
32. Doerflinger, *Vigorous Spirit,* 47–49; Berg, "Organization," 158–60, 169. See also Bailyn, "Communications," 383–84; Cochran, *Business,* 22; East, "Business Entrepreneur," 19–20; Bruchey, *Oliver,* 122–36; Harrington, *New York Merchant,* 52–56, 185–87, 194–227.
33. Anderson, "Wharton," 31–32, 48–49, 52–53, 55–58, 60.

extended and buttressed by ties of religion and ethnicity. The Philadelphia mercantile community was composed of overlapping groups of Quakers, Anglicans, Presbyterians, and Jews, and of Englishmen, Scots-Irish, Irish, Germans, and Frenchmen. Families and their allies, who were given the status of partial relatives, provided partners, staff, capital and credit, business information and advice, training through apprenticeships, wharves and countinghouses, and even business itself. In such circumstances, therefore, it is not surprising that family and business were entwined.[34]

Was the Philadelphia merchant a capitalist? Can we from the vantage point of the entrepreneurial definition portray the merchant as being absorbed in business, as comprising an upper class, as spreading the drive to maximize and accumulate wealth throughout the social order? Clearly, as Schumpeter so aptly put it, merchants constituted a class "that saw business facts in a different light and from a different angle: a class, in short, that was *in* business." They bought and sold goods and services, and sought profits, and constituted an important and highly visible element of the provincial upper class—and as such played an enormously important cultural role in the life of the community.[35]

But a simple yes will not do. The Philadelphia merchant was not a maximizer. Merchants contributed to the process of commercialization, but their example also served to strengthen noncommercial values and social patterns. The merchant's unhappiness with impersonal markets, his focus on family, his attempt to personalize business, his relaxed attitudes toward work and reinvestment all lend plausibility to Arthur H. Cole's comment that business "had not become so much an end in itself, and success in business did not become so adequately a basis for self-satisfaction, as was to become the case in the next centuries." It is probably fairest to say that the merchant was a capitalist, albeit a primitive one, and that his ability to serve as a vehicle for commercialization was weakened by the ambivalence of his stance.[36]

The region's second major socioeconomic group, numerically the largest, were farmers. From the standpoint of the entrepreneurial definition, the key issues relating to the farmer are those that deal with rural production and the extent to which it was oriented toward markets and the farmer's attitudes toward the accumulation of wealth. The most

---

34. Doerflinger, *Vigorous Spirit*, 55, 59–61; Berg, "Merchants," 3, 6; Tolles, *Meeting House*, 89–92; Cochran, *Pennsylvania*, 21–22.

35. Schumpeter, *Economic Analysis*, 78–79.

36. Cole, "Tempo," 293.

influential discussions about the Pennsylvania farmer have argued that he was profit-oriented and eager to enter available markets.[37]

William Smedley of Middletown, Chester County, exemplifies these entrepreneurs. A farmer-artisan whose account book spanned the years between 1751 and 1766, Smedley farmed and sold produce from his farm; rented a shop to a weaver; purchased such goods as worsted yarn and finished cloth from local craftsmen, probably the same weaver who was his tenant; hired live-in wage laborers to help with tasks like plowing and harvesting and chores like spinning tow; and leased several (probably three) small farms to cottagers, some of whom were craftsmen themselves. Smedley also earned a substantial income as a builder-carpenter building and improving several dozen "houses, barns, shops, stables and springhouses." When that trade went sour, he shifted to brick-making, a highly capital-intensive craft. Later, Smedley and several helpers produced more than 58,000 barrel staves. The busy "farmer" also dabbled in the local real-estate market.[38]

Smedley's activities reveal the broad range of business activity in which many farmers engaged. Flour, bread, and flaxseed were the key exports, but virtually everything produced on the farm was sold: "Rye, barley (for malting), oats, hay (and other fodder crops), wool, meat, and hides all figured in local sales or went to the expanding urban market. Farm wives added to the market surplus by making cheese and butter, and their daughters spun wool and flax."[39]

In 1800 more than half of Chester's landowners worked at a variety of nonagricultural pursuits. Rural families wove cloth, constructed and repaired buildings, hauled goods, and sold firewood and lumber, stone and minerals, barrel staves, bricks, and wood shingles.[40]

In addition to selling materials, goods, and services, eighteenth-century farmers also purchased a wide assortment of services and goods. They bought tea, coffee, molasses, chocolate, sugar, rum, condiments, tobacco, yarn, thread, cloth, buttons, needles, bows, shoes, pottery, glassware, pewter, books, candles, gunpowder, and a variety of metal utensils, such as guns, axes, plows, and scythes. Gristmills, sawmills, smiths, wheelwrights, coopers, tanners, masons, shoemakers, carpenters, weavers, tailors, ministers, lawyers, teachers,

37. The clearest examples of this position are Lemon, *Poor Man's Country,* and Clemons and Simler, "Rural Labor."
38. Clemens and Simler, "Rural Labor," 121–26.
39. Ibid., 110–11.
40. Ibid., 112–14.

and merchants were also patronized. Most important of all, however, farmers bought land—better and more land for themselves and their children.[41]

The rural economy depended on a complex labor force made up of substantial landowners, tenant farmers who rented farms with commercial possibilities, small holders who rented or owned farms that were too small for commercial agriculture, male and female lodgers, apprentices, indentured servants, slaves, and everyone's children. This work force was organized around the needs of wheat, the region's most important commercial crop, which required intensive labor during the spring, when fields were prepared, and during the fall harvest. These periods of intensive labor lasted less than three months of the year, but the response of farmers to good wheat prices and the skewed demand for labor was ingenious. They developed nonagricultural occupations and diversified their agriculture, making it possible themselves to work productively throughout the year.[42]

The portrayal of the Pennsylvania farmer as an entrepreneur has merit, but it is one-sided. Although farmers did enter markets and seek profits, these activities must be understood in context. It is important to recall that the most important market crop in the region, wheat, "was normally cultivated on only one third of the acreage devoted to the production of grain, most of which was corn that was consumed by livestock. The 'surplus' wheat exported to foreign markets thus remained a relatively small part of total production (15–20 percent), even for commercially minded family farmers." The impact of the market was further moderated by the fact that the crop was edible. Unlike farmers who grow rubber or cotton, wheat farmers can eat their profits when faced with poor markets. So wheat functioned both as an attractive commodity and as a buffer against poor markets.[43]

The presence of businessmen like William Smedley is a significant discovery, but other types of farmers were part of the rural economy. We need a framework that encompasses both commercial and noncommercial farmers. Because the family farm was the most important rural institution, it is a good place to start.

The farm is not a typical capitalist firm, because it is a family enterprise. As a household, it is necessarily concerned with the con-

41. Danhof, *Change*, 3–4; Lemon, "Household Consumption," 67–69; Loehr, "Self-Sufficiency"; Shammas, "How Self-Sufficient?"
42. Simler, "Landless Worker," 166–67.
43. Henretta, "Families and Farms," 14–20 (quotation on p. 17).

sumption needs of a family. But the farm is also an economic institution, a business, and as such it has investment needs. Thus, the family farm was driven by two sometimes contradictory imperatives. An exploration of the interplay of these needs will help unravel the confusing mélange of commercial and noncommercial behavior that existed in the countryside.[44]

Farm families faced the fact of isolation. They had irregular contacts with nearby hamlets and more-distant urban centers, and prolonged absences had to be carefully planned because chores needed to be done and travel was difficult. Bad weather turned dirt roads into bogs and made streams impassable, but if the weather was good and the roads were in reasonable shape and the streams were placid and wagons and animals avoided mishap, twenty-five miles was achievable. A round trip from Christiana to Philadelphia with a stopover, a journey of eighty-five miles, could take a week.[45]

Although those who lived near a navigable river or stream had an easier time traveling, two of the three largest rivers in the area posed problems for travelers. The Susquehanna was rocky and treacherous, and below Middletown it moved away from Philadelphia. The Schuylkill was navigable only in the spring, when thaws and rains raised the water level. Only the Delaware offered reliable transportation most of the year.[46]

The combination of dispersed settlement and poor transportation forced farm families to rely on their own efforts, but the degree to which farm families were self-sufficient has engendered controversy. It is clear that farm families were able to meet a substantial portion of their needs through their own efforts. They produced and processed cereals, poultry, meat and animal products, vegetables and fruit, sweeteners such as honey and maple sugar, and various alcoholic beverages. Cloth and articles of clothing were made from homegrown wool, flax, and hemp. Farmers built, repaired, and improved buildings, house furnishings, sheds and other outbuildings, and an assortment of utensils.[47]

44. Galeski, *Basic Concepts*, 10–12, 27; Nash, *Primitive Systems*, 23–25, 91; Mendres, *Vanishing Peasant*, 76–92; Osterud, *Bonds of Community*.

45. Walzer, "Transportation," 68, 84–86, 170, 279; Buck and Buck, *Planting*, 236–37, 240–241; Wolf, *Urban Village*, 25.

46. Lemon, *Poor Man's Country*, 37.

47. Bidwell and Falconer, *History*, 115–16, 123, 126–29; Cheyney, "Thomas Cheyney," 339; Lemon, *Poor Man's Country*, 156–68, 216; Loehr, "Farmers' Dairies," 318; Rutherford,

Still, practical considerations limited self-sufficiency. The investment required to purchase the necessary "land, livestock, seed, and equipment (including plow and field tools, dairy utensils, a cider mill, equipment to manufacture apparel, soap and candle-making utensils, a carpenter and cooper tools)" was beyond the resources of many families. In Chester County only 10 percent of the households had sheep shears, 15 percent had carding "cards," and 60 percent had spinning wheels. Moreover, many of these tasks were too difficult and time-consuming for all families to engage in. For example, the production of woolen cloth involved at least eleven different steps.[48]

Our present knowledge of the percentage of a farm's product consumed by the typical farm family, and the percentage sold, is sketchy. The distance to market, the quality of the land, the farmer's skills, values, and temperament, the size and composition of the family, and the size of the harvest all had an impact on behavior. The best estimates are that farmers who had good land and reasonable access to urban markets sold only 20 to 40 percent of their farm's production, although many sold less and larger farms may have sold a bit more. What is clear is that farm families consumed a great deal—probably most—of what they produced.[49]

Consumption needs structured the kind of agriculture practiced in the region. One indication of this is that farmers engaged in diversified agriculture. The pattern held true on large and small farms and does not seem to have varied significantly with location—that is, farmers who were located close to markets had the same crop mix as those who were distant. One might explain this by suggesting that diversification maximized the available labor supply and thereby facilitated participation in a variety of markets, but diversification can also be understood as a safety-first strategy that put the families' consumption needs ahead of a greater emphasis on such crops as wheat and flaxseed, which offered the best chance for profits. In fact, these interpretations are not mutually exclusive. They reflect different aspects of the farm—the

---

"Notes on the State of New Jersey," 81, 87; Schmidt, *Agriculture*, 96, 98–100; Schoepf, *Travels*, 1:130–31; Osterud, *Bonds of Community*, 205–10, 212–14.

48. Jensen, "Churns," quoted in Shammas, "Self-Sufficient," 252, 247–72; Ulrich, "Friendly Neighbor," 393–94, 392–405; Waggoner, "Women"; Hood, "Textile Manufacturing," 84, 88, 96.

49. Lemon, "Household Consumption," 60; Danhof, *Change*, 13; Wharton Jr., "Subsistence Agriculture." See Wright, *Political Economy*, ch. 3, for the impact of family needs on agriculture.

consumption needs of a household and the investment needs of an enterprise.[50]

Technology also encouraged diversification. Tools like the plow, the sickle, and the flail were similar to tools used in eighth-century Britain. They created bottlenecks in production, especially during harvest. When the impact of these tools is added to the almost equally archaic transportation technology and the limited labor supply, the result was to reinforce an emphasis on diversification as the safest way to satisfy the consumption needs of the family.[51]

Farmers showed little interest in escaping what to some scholars has appeared to be an economic trap. Somewhat bemused, James T. Lemon notes that "before 1800 few farmers sought to improve wheat yields," that they were not interested in new rotations or improved seed and did not fertilize grain fields. But although many farmers did not dung their wheat fields, they did fertilize their gardens and orchards. And despite the painful inefficiency of the tools they used, they did not quickly adopt laborsaving devices. The cradle scythe, for example, was introduced into Concord, a Chester township, probably in 1757. Even though it was much more efficient than the traditional hand sickle, which made harvesting "back-breaking" and "labor-intensive," acceptance was slow. As late as 1832 it was reported: "Two-thirds of the wheat in some townships of Chester County was still harvested with the sickle." Because the same farmers eagerly adopted Conestoga wagons and improved rifles, their lack of interest in tools that might improve the yields of their fields is noteworthy. Apparently, most farmers were satisfied with their yields and with the diversified agriculture they practiced.[52]

It is significant that the portion of the farm product that was sold was called a "surplus," because it was not needed by the family. Not until commercial agriculture dominated did the production of saleable commodities become the primary purpose of farming. The difference between surpluses and commodities defines the distance between social systems.

50. Lemon, *Poor Man's Country*, ch. 2. For the argument that farmers' adaptation of diversification is evidence of a market orientation because it enabled them to enter more markets, see Clemens and Simler, "Rural Labor," 131.

51. Krooss, *Economic Development*, 108; Schmidt, *Hunterdon*, 64, 102.

52. Case, *Prosperity*, 1:78; Cheyney, "Thomas Cheyney," 339; Lemon, *Poor Man's Country*, 156, 169–70, 175, 178–79; Lemon, "Rural Geography," 318–19, 343–46; Schmidt, *Hunterdon*, 78.

As late as the post–Civil War era, the farm press was still attacking the older view. In 1868 the *Prairie Farmer* argued: "The old rule that a farmer should produce all that he required, and that the surplus represented his gains, is part of the past. Agriculture, like all other business, is better for its subdivisions, each one growing that which is best suited to his soil, skill, climate and market and with its proceeds purchase his other needs."[53]

There is a certain irony to the belief that eighteenth-century farmers were capitalists and businessmen. In the nineteenth century, elites and intellectuals were forced to expend considerable energy selling capitalism to northern farmers. For almost a century, educational societies, fairs, and a flood of publications were employed in an intensive propaganda campaign. Reformers labored to persuade farmers to improve their tillage techniques and their seed and stock, to adopt laborsaving devices and cost accounting, and in general to act as if they were in business. The task was not easy. The stubborn resistance to the suggested improvements suggests that something fundamental was at stake, that a transformation was occurring.[54]

Even though farmers were more than willing to sell their goods and services, they did not conduct their affairs as if they were in business. Production was geared to the family's consumption and investment needs, and those needs could be met without maximizing commercial relations and profits. Visions of life as a competitive struggle for wealth were not pervasive in the eighteenth-century countryside. In terms of the entrepreneurial definition, farmers were not capitalists.

The third major social type to consider is the artisan, or craftsman or mechanic. Like merchants and farmers, eighteenth-century artisans bought and sold goods and, like farmers, produced goods that entered into the stream of local, regional, and international commerce. Arguing that artisans were often shopkeepers with a retail trade, many scholars treat them as small-scale businessmen. According to Sam Bass Warner Jr., the craftsman "shared entrepreneurial experience and goals with the shopkeeper and merchant." Edwin J. Perkins agrees: "[the artisan] usually had a sizable investment in equipment and tools, managed his own work schedule, and kept his own accounts. Most artisans owned sufficient property to qualify as voters in municipal and provincial elections."[55]

53. Danhof, *Change*, 17–18. For the quotation, see Johnstone, "Identification," 39.
54. Abbott, "Agricultural Press," 40–41; Buley, *Old Northwest*, 1:171, 175, 190–99; Johnstone, "Identification," 38–39; Ross, "Retardation," 11–17; Throne, "Book Farming."
55. Perkins, *Economy*, 82; Warner Jr., *Private City*, 9.

Some artisans engaged in commerce. The *Philadelphia Directory* of 1785 listed eight tailors who labeled themselves "merchant-tailor." Caleb Attmore, a hatter, stocked and sold large amounts of the materials he used in his trade, as did Direk Cooper, a painter, who sold oil and colors. The inventory of tailor John Holliday included "Chesire cheese, an assortment of European dry goods, and a compound designed to remove superfluous facial hair." Others—a rope-maker, for example— developed ties to the country merchants they supplied. Some, such as farmer William Smedley, were engaged in a number of occupations. Thomas Affleck, a cabinetmaker, had a logyard and a sawmill behind his shop, while Robert Kennedy, a copper-plate printer and engraver, also did some house-painting and glass-fitting.[56]

At the same time, artisans were preindustrial manufacturers engaged in small-scale craft production. They were specialists trained to under-stand the properties of their raw materials, the use of their tools, and the conduct of their trade, and they were able to conceptualize the entire process of production, including design, and to perform all the necessary operations, many of which were extremely difficult and time-consuming. Acquiring the requisite craft skills and knowledge took years and involved an apprenticeship. This investment gave mechanics a virtual monopoly, and therefore control, over the process of production. The combination—apprenticeship, acquisition of skill, and control of the labor process—put its mark on the craftsmen. It gave them pride and made their lives meaningful.[57]

The point is an important one. Like farmers, craftsmen derived satisfaction and a sense of identity from the labor process. The products of their labor were needed by the larger community and in their own eyes gave them status. They had an identity as artisans and as members of a craft and a community of craftsmen. These communal bonds engaged their social and political energies. Furthermore, the ambitions of the vast majority of artisans encompassed only modest competency and a good standing within the crafts community, not commercial success.[58]

Some worked alone or with family. Wives, sons, and daughters helped with production and tending the shop, and many took on apprentices, journeymen, indentured servants, or slaves. When the craftsman's labor force was expanded, the individual generally lived in the master's home

56. Olton, "Philadelphia Artisans," 86–92, 94–96, 98, 100–105.

57. Rule, "Property of Skill." For a description of the craftsman as a social type, see Shorter, "History of Work," 3, 6–16.

58. Northrup, "Decomposition," 136–43; Schultz, *Republic,* 6–14.

and was absorbed into a web of kinship and household relations that were further strengthened by the living arrangements and by intermarriage within the craft community.[59]

The small size of the labor force reflected the small scale of the production—exceptions being mostly in Philadelphia, with its international markets and enormous hinterland. There artisans produced such goods as shoes, buttons, hats, cloth, clothing, furniture, and ironware in sizable quantities. It was not unusual for urban mechanics to "build up small inventories for sale to browsing shoppers," and a few attempted to increase the scale of their operations—for example, Philadelphia's John Bedford, who employed twenty to twenty-four men in his boot and shoemaking shop.[60]

The great bulk of artisanal production was small-scale, however. In the countryside and the smaller towns, local markets were so small that many mechanics were forced to farm part-time and practice more than one craft. James Scott of Bucks County, for example, worked at four crafts. These men produced primarily custom-made or "bespoke" goods. In the larger towns and in Philadelphia, the scale of operations was somewhat larger, but even in those communities most craftsmen produced particular items for specific customers.[61]

The size of the market was not the only thing that determined the scale of operations. The nature of craft production, and the norms and values that were part of the artisanal life-style, deemphasized the commercial aspects of the mechanics' life and discouraged them from maximizing. Like merchants and farmers, artisans were not willing to allow the market to determine the structure of their lives. They worked to maintain a decent competency, to become masters and set up for themselves, to maintain a good standing in the craft and their trade networks, and to maintain the control over their time, skill, and labor that they prized. They exerted themselves to support their families and settle their children. And they aspired to social respectability.[62]

Thus, it is doubtful that the three major social groups can be described as capitalists according to the entrepreneurial definition. Merchants and

59. Northrup, "Decomposition," 110–24; Moss Jr., "Master Builders," 146–51.

60. Bridenbaugh, *Craftsman*, 129, 148–49; Laurie, *Working People*, 5–7.

61. Bridenbaugh, *Craftsman*, 80–81, 126–27. For rural craftsmen, see Hummel, *Hammer in Hand*, 215–16, 221, 227, 230–34, 238–39; Martin, "Craftsmen," 20–23, 33–40; Hood, "Textile Manufacturing," 14, 37–44; and Cox, "Woodworkers."

62. Foner, *Paine*, 36–37; Northrup, "Decomposition," 136–38; Schultz, *Republic*, 6–14; Rosswurm, *Arms*, 14–18.

craftsmen were indeed in business, but the way they operated their enterprises and lived their lives does not reveal evidence of maximization. Farmers, who constituted the great bulk of the population, were further removed from the sphere of commerce and the inroads of commercialism. For both the artisan and the farmer, competence and independence, not wealth, were major life goals.

The second main definition of capitalism focuses our attention squarely on the development of markets. An enormous amount of scholarly energy has been expended on unearthing evidence of markets and market-oriented behavior. From the vantage point of a later day, it is clear that the second half of the eighteenth century was a period of market development, in which markets ran the gamut from nascent to imperfect to fully formed. Because many markets were only partially developed, the pricing system was not fully operational and markets could not dominate economic behavior.

The product markets of the 1780s follow this pattern, and the flax market can serve as an example. In Ireland there was a strong demand for flaxseed, which a group of Irish-American Philadelphia merchants attempted to satisfy. They placed newspaper ads offering "ready money" for flaxseed, and over time the crop became the city's third largest export, behind flour and bread. The response of Chester County's farmers was typical: They increased their production of flax. In 1715–37 some 6 percent of the households grew flax, and by the mid-1770s the number increased to 16 percent, and to 20 percent by the end of the century.[63]

The farmers' response is interesting. Even though the offers of "ready money" were well publicized, and Chester County was in the most highly commercialized region of the Philadelphia hinterland, the reaction was modest. Over a seventy-five-year period there was a 14 percent increase in the number of farmers growing the crop. What happened was that farmers treated flax like shingles or butter or any other commodity and integrated it into the general pattern of diversification. As a result, the flax market was not a radical agent of change.

Income earned by exporting flax, flour, and wheat played a significant role in the late-eighteenth-century domestic economy, and much of it was used to purchase foreign imports. Like the flax market, retailing can tell us a great deal about the state of product markets. Their most

63. Hood, "Textile Manufacturing," 53–55.

striking characteristic was their primitiveness. Rural shopkeepers used signs, displays, credit sales, and flexible terms of payment to attract business. Sugar, tea, coffee, and alcohol were also used to win and hold customers. There was price competition, but it was not as intense as in the next century. Handbills, signs in stores, and newspaper ads were the most common forms of advertising. The latter consisted primarily of long lists—a 1789 advertisement in the *Pittsburgh Gazette* listed 143 items.[64]

Shipments of dry goods flowing from Philadelphia to rural retailers were mostly cloth—a full 70 percent, and sewing materials, handkerchiefs, hats, and hosiery constituted another 15 percent. The next largest category—at 3.6 percent—was groceries. Thus, 85 percent of the dry goods shipped from Philadelphia to rural retailers were cloth, sewing materials, and wearing apparel.[65]

The variety of items offered was staggering. Customers could choose from long lists of fabrics that included "superfine ratinets, common grazets, black padusoys, and single tandem silesias, . . . wide pompadour, purple and light grounds true Indian chintz morees." One merchant stocking a store in the "extreme northern frontier . . . included in the inventory twenty-seven different types of cloth and nine varieties of buckles."[66]

These inventories tell us a great deal about the nature of the market. Rural families were primarily concerned with procuring the means to make clothes and house furnishings. The huge selection also meant that small quantities of fabrics, buttons and bows, and needles were purchased. While farmers and their wives happily purchased consumer goods, these inventories indicate the slow pace of change and the limited impact of the consumer revolution.

Although merchants profited from the demand, they did not use fashion or style to organize the market. The contrast with England is instructive: "There by the end of the eighteenth-century, 'the competitive, socially emulative aspect of fashion was being consciously manipulated by commerce in pursuit of increased consumption.'" The behavior of merchants regarding consumption was similar to their behavior regarding production. Merchants were quick to take advantage of commercial opportunities but controlled neither consumption nor pro-

64. Doerflinger, "Farmers," 169–74.
65. Ibid., 178.
66. Ibid., 166–67, 174, 179–80.

duction. Thus, eighteenth-century rural Pennsylvania retail markets were growing, but they remained weak and had limited impact.[67]

If it is true that a consumer revolution was occurring and that, as Thomas M. Doerflinger says, "the dry goods trade of Philadelphia and other Northern ports is best understood as a commercial extension of the Industrial Revolution," then it is also true that the rapidity of the process must not be exaggerated. Changes of this magnitude proceed slowly, extending over decades and centuries.[68]

Wheat markets were the most important exception. Only three years after the province had been settled, Philadelphia merchants were selling wheat in Barbados, and over the next seventy-five years the West Indies served as the province's major export market. After 1750, additional markets opened up in southern Europe, Great Britain, and France. Despite fluctuations, wheat prices were buoyant—doubling between 1720 and 1770.[69]

Yet farmers did not grow more wheat. They insisted on continuing to fit the crop into their diversified agriculture. As a result, the growing demand created logistical problems, and specialized flour merchants appeared, filing the niche—in 1785, Philadelphia boasted fifteen. Levi Hollingsworth's network of 400 correspondents was easily the most extensive. The search for grain led traders as far north as Quebec, and to Maryland and Virginia in the south, but the bulk of the grain came from the city's productive hinterland.[70]

To support the growing demand, a transportation system developed. By the 1760s some twenty to thirty shallops were working the Philadelphia hinterland on regular routes, usually scheduled for one round-trip a week. These shuttles transported wheat, flour, and bread to Philadelphia, took orders from millers and general stores, and sometimes served as purchasing agents. While some shippers worked for flour merchants, independents also plied the local waters. Tramp shallops and flatboats without regular routes picked up farm produce and delivered it to the mills, and part-time teamsters carried goods on the country

67. McKendrick et al., *Consumer Society*, 43; Doerflinger, "Farmers," 182–84; Breen, "Empire of Goods."

68. Doerflinger, "Farmers," 182.

69. Egnal, "Development," 208–9, 217; Henretta, "Transition," 227; Doerflinger, *Vigorous Spirit*, 112–14, 122–24; McCusker and Menard, *British America*, 194–95, 197, 205.

70. Doerflinger, *Vigorous Spirit*, 113–14, 123–24. Another example of the development of product markets is provided by lumber. In the late 1780s twenty-four lumberyards were located outside Philadelphia, selling to exporters and to the local construction industry. They undoubtedly had networks of suppliers. See ibid., 124–25.

roads. By 1776, farmers probably carried less than 20 percent of their wheat and flour to Philadelphia. The demand for wheat also stimulated investment in gristmills. The local industry centered in Wilmington, Delaware, where the first gristmill was built in the late 1750s. In less than half a century, thirteen large state-of-the-art mills "clustered around the tidal basin of the Brandywine Creek."[71]

Even so, the attractiveness and power of the wheat market must not be exaggerated. Merchants and shippers took steps to gather wheat from farmers, and millers invested in new technology and expensive facilities, but farmers did not respond in the same way. Most farmers grew wheat but they did *not* specialize in the crop, increase acreage devoted to it, or make substantial investments designed to improve productivity.

Of the factors of production (land, labor, and capital), only land had a well-articulated market. The Penn family were careful to organize a land market even as the colony was being established. The widespread practice of speculating in rising land values is evidence that their efforts were successful, as is the widespread ownership of land.[72]

The contours of the eighteenth-century labor market are only now beginning to become clear. The market was composed of a confusing mix of bound and free labor, noncommercial labor relations and an innovative form of wage labor, combined with a highly mobile labor force.

Bound labor persisted into the nineteenth century, although as a less important component of the labor force. Slavery in Philadelphia was most important from 1691 to 1721, and especially from 1701 to 1710, when 17.4 percent of the city's population were slaves. Urban slavery began its decline well before the emancipation act of 1780. Some 15 percent of the city's households owned 1,481 slaves in 1767, but the number declined to 728 slaves in 1775 and to 55 in 1800. In the same period the population of the city grew dramatically from 26,460 in 1767 to 33,290 in 1775 and 67,811 in 1800.[73]

Rural slavery had a different history. While slavery was more important in Philadelphia than in the countryside during the colonial era, rural

71. Dauer, "Transportation Systems"; Walzer, "Colonial Philadelphia," 163; McCusker and Menard, *British America,* 323. For the quotation, see Welsh, "Merchants," 323; Welsh, "Brandywine Mills," 34–35.

72. G. Nash, *Quakers,* 15–21; Lemon, *Poor Man's Country,* 49–57, 98–109; Schweitzer, *Custom,* ch. 3.

73. Nash and Soderlund, *Freedom,* 7–9, 15–16, 18, and ch. 1.

slaves began to increase naturally after 1750. Consequently, slave owners in counties along the Maryland and Virginia borders were more successful than their urban counterparts and less willing to part with their property. In 1790, residents of these counties accounted for 44 percent of the state's population but held two-thirds of the remaining 3,760 slaves.[74]

The other important form of unfree labor was indentured servitude. It now appears that while wars and embargoes virtually stopped the flow of German servants, the market revived and survived into the 1830s. In 1817 more than 4,000 Germans arrived in Philadelphia, a number higher than that of any period since the migration of 1749–55, which averaged 5,755 per year. In untroubled years, servants poured into Pennsylvania at rates comparable to those of the colonial era. Therefore, unfree labor continued to be an important part of the labor force until well into the nineteenth century. Of course, because these servants arrived in a considerably larger population the impact of indentured servitude declined.[75]

While bound labor continued to make its presence felt, Pennsylvania's farmers were creating a labor supply that was free, skilled, available when needed, and self-supporting. Landholders (owners and tenants) of commercially viable farms rented plots of land and houses to free, landless male heads of families called "inmates" or "cottagers." For a fee, cottagers were also offered a variety of services, in return for which the landholder had the option of purchasing the labor of the cottager. The result was that landholders gained a work force they could use as needed, fire, and pay only for work done. It was, in other words, a wage-labor system shaped to the needs of the rural community. The system enabled landholders to increase production and, not incidently, to improve the value of their property.[76]

Cottagers also benefited. They got lodging, fuel, a chance to keep a pig and a cow and to grow some of their own food, as well as some flax. The family was promised work at harvest time and on scattered days the rest of the year, an arrangement that gave cottagers and their

74. Ibid., 4–5, 32–36, and ch. 1.
75. Brophy, "Indentured Servitude," 69–126, esp. 70–75, 80, 84 n. 64, 85–95, 97–99, 118–20; Grubb, "Immigrant Servant Labor," 249–52, 255–57, 272; Grubb, "Servant Auction Records," 156–57, 160, 165; Grubb, "Long-Run Trend," 167–240. For a contrary view, see Salinger, "Colonial Labor."
76. Simler, "Landless Worker," 165; Bordley, *Essays,* 387–93; Clemens and Simler, "Rural Labor," 112–14, 127.

families privacy and a chance to maintain their independence. They could change employers, live in a private house, and use their free time as they chose. The system appeared as early as 1750, in Chester County. Over time it flourished. Between 1760 and 1800, the number of cottager families in Chester County increased from 20 percent to 25 percent.[77]

In the second half of the eighteenth century the system flourished. More farmers, especially in the most commercial regions of the state, used cottagers. In addition, between 1760 and 1820 Chester cottagers worked more days for their primary employer. As the use of wage labor increased, the price paid for particular tasks was affected. "Wage rates for farm labor were seasonal. A 'common' wage was paid during the growing season. Harvest wages were higher. . . . Winter wages were lower through most of the eighteenth century; however, as the demand for farm labor became year-round, the distinction between common and winter wages became blurred and winter wages tended to rise." This is clear evidence that the market was being rationalized and that capitalist labor relations were developing.[78]

While capitalist labor relations made their appearance in the countryside, the signs of a similar development were fainter in urban Philadelphia. The city had the greatest concentration of independent artisans and journeymen in the region. Within the craft shops that dotted the city, work was infused with patriarchal ties. Apprentices and journeymen boarded and roomed with their master, and, for a price, masters provided additional services, loans, and such goods as clothing and tobacco. Still, because guilds were unable to take root the way they did in Europe, what Gary Nash calls "economic clientage" did not become a rigid system.[79]

One reason that economic clientage did not become a rigid system was the remarkable mobility of the American work force. Mobility was a fact of life in the countryside as well as in the urban areas. Samuel Wilson, a skilled stonemason who lived in Chester County's Sadsbury Township, hired forty men between 1780 and 1827. Only three were "regulars," most of the rest were young transients. The same pattern appears in Philadelphia's shipyards and smaller workshops. Joshua Humphrey hired more than thirty-five men between 1794 and 1797, only

77. Simler, "Landless Worker," 165, 192.
78. Ibid., 175 n. 33; see also 165, 177–80.
79. G. Nash, Crucible, 258–59; Moss Jr., "Master Builders," 143–46.

three of whom worked regularly for more than half the working days each month. Samuel Ashton had five positions in his cabinetmaking shop. In eight years, 1795–1803, he hired forty-nine journeymen for an average of 145 days each. The result was that many journeymen did not stay with masters long enough to establish close working or social ties.[80]

Gary Nash has found instances of craftsmen attempting to free themselves from patriarchal relations. During the prosperous 1750s, Benjamin Morgan and William Falk asked Isaac Norris for daily wages. Daily wages were higher, but they lacked the security of monthly or yearly contract. They also meant providing one's own living quarters and one's "own diet." However, Nash cites only two men who opted for the new arrangements, and they enjoyed unusually strong market positions. When the good times ended, one of them—William Falk—tried to get back into the more secure, traditional arrangement.[81]

Despite the course of action taken by Morgan and Falk, and the general pattern of mobility, it appears that the arrangements made between most masters and journeymen involved provision of room and board—more than half the forty-nine journeymen who worked for Samuel Ashton lived with him. Further, it would appear that hopes for long-term relationships were still the norm.[82]

Journeymen had practical reasons for holding on to economic clientage: the system provided security. After master builder Isaac Zane hired William Crage in 1754, he was injured, but even though Crage was unable to work for ten days "by a lame hand of which he Eate [sic] at my house 6 days," Crage was paid in full. Day laborers were not so fortunate.[83]

Labor markets in Pennsylvania during the 1780s were a confusing mix. Capitalist and noncapitalist labor processes coexisted in the countryside while in Philadelphia the situation was even more confusing. Day laborers worked for wages, as did some journeymen, but craft labor remained tied to economic clientage. At the same time, slavery and indentured servitude survived in rural and urban areas both, although unfree labor was more important in the rural areas. Finally, urban and rural labor was extremely mobile.

To complicate matters even further, approximately half the rural population owned farms. Family labor was important, but in rural

80. Lanier, "Wilson's World," 56–57, 64–67; Salinger, "Colonial Labor," 72–74.
81. G. Nash, *Crucible,* 258–60.
82. Salinger, "Artisans," 74.
83. Moss Jr., "Master Builders," 144.

neighborhoods labor was also bartered and exchanged. Such noncommercial exchanges were extremely important and are discussed later in this chapter.

If contradictory trends appeared in the regional labor markets, capital markets remained primitive. The major sources of capital were reinvestment of profits and the labor of people working with kin and neighbors. Trade was financed through an elaborate system of book credit for goods on consignment, while community projects like churches and colleges, hospitals, and internal improvements were often funded through lotteries. Of the modern financial intermediaries, only insurance and private banking had made their appearance.[84]

The first successful fire insurance company, "The Philadelphia Contributorship for the Insurance of Homes for the Loss by Fire," was established in 1752 by a group led by Benjamin Franklin. Marine insurance had appeared earlier. At least as early as the 1720s, Philadelphians were trying to market insurance, by the 1750s brokers were competing for business, and by 1783 there were enough brokers and underwriters in the city to support a semi-monthly newspaper that dealt largely with insurance. Still, the organization of the industry remained rudimentary. Insurance companies with permanent staffs and a capital stock did not yet exist, and the trade was carried on by brokers, like Thomas Wharton, who shopped long lists of business acquaintances to find people willing to risk small-to-moderate sums of money on a particular venture. Not until 1792 was a specialized marine insurance company able to maintain itself.[85]

Private banking was organized very much like marine insurance. Individuals who needed cash located individuals with surplus funds, generally the elderly. In Philadelphia and the larger inland towns, newspapers carried advertisements for money at 5, 6, and 7 percent. Merchants, like the Biddle brothers, engaged in private banking as early as 1764. In the country, local shopkeepers, millers, innkeepers, and well-off farmers lent to their neighbors. Like marine insurance, private

84. Krooss and Gilbert, *American Business*, 109–11; Krooss and Blyn, *Financial Intermediaries*, 12, 15–16. These institutions connect savers and investors. Their "assets and liabilities consist almost exclusively of financial instruments." Krooss and Blyn cite ten types of financial intermediaries: "commercial banks, investment banks, trust companies, mutual savings banks, savings and loan associations, life insurance companies, general insurance companies, noninsured pension funds, investment companies and credit unions" (ibid., 3). Other scholars include such public agencies as postal savings banks.

85. East, *Business Enterprise*, 23–24; Jensen, *Maritime Commerce*, 21–22; Krooss and Blyn, *Financial Intermediaries*, 14; Krooss and Gilbert, *American Business*, 62–64.

banking was unspecialized and organized informally. Not until the second decade of the nineteenth century did private banking emerge as a profession in its own right. With the exception of commercial banking, which began with the establishment of the Bank of North America in 1781, this was true of the other financial intermediaries. Savings banks, stock markets, life insurance, investment trusts, and building and loan associations all emerged in the nineteenth century.[86]

Private capital markets were so weak that colonial governments experimented with land banks that made loans secured by land and personal property, generally to farmers and small-scale entrepreneurs. These "banks" did not accept deposits or discount commercial paper. Land banks are best understood as "pseudo rather than genuine financial intermediaries, particularly as no prior act of saving was required." The key point, however, is that private markets were so poorly developed that public intervention was called for.[87]

Thus, with the exception of land and wheat, markets for commodities and the factors of production were either nonexistent or in the process of development, and, as such, imperfect. Given the unformed state of capital markets and the importance of subsistence activities and the fragmentation caused by the primitive transportation system, this is hardly surprising. While the direction of change was toward the increased importance of markets, a pricing system had not yet emerged in the last third of the eighteenth century.

While everyone participated in markets and sought ways to earn money, production, distribution, and the organization of work was not atomistic, impersonal, and decentralized. Everyone tried to personalize economic relations and protect themselves from the working of the market. Maximization occurred but was not typical. Economic relations had not been severed from social relations, and even entrepreneurs like William Smedley worked their neighbor's fields during fall harvest.[88]

As we shall see, family labor, kinship, neighborliness, production for use, and barter and exchange networks loomed large. Work in the countinghouse and the shop was infused with nonmarket ideals and behavior. These nonmarket relations and values coexisted with, had an impact on, and often superseded market dynamics. As Robert E. Mutch

86. East, *Business Enterprise*, 20–22; Krooss and Blyn, *Financial Intermediaries*, 15–17; Krooss and Gilbert, *American Business*, 61–62; Schweitzer, *Custom*, 142–45; Martin, "Craftsmen," 57.

87. Krooss and Blyn, *Financial Intermediaries*, 14–15.

88. Clemens and Simler, "Rural Labor," 122.

says, "market relations were not so pervasive as to determine what was produced and how much labor was to be allocated to producing any given commodity; markets, in short, did not determine social relations."[89]

The Marxist definition of capitalism is, similarly, inapplicable. Production was not organized so that control and execution were separate. Merchants, artisans, and farmers conceived and executed their tasks in a manner of their own choosing. Any constraints that existed were generally those imposed by nature, custom, or the needs of the family, rather than those growing out of markets or the relationship between owner and laborer. Alienated labor did not exist in the regional shops, countinghouses, or fields.

The people engaged in production controlled the process. Where this was not true, production was just as likely to be controlled by tradition or by the desires of neighbors as it was by markets or employers. When Sharon Salinger argues that wage labor was increasing and that the gap between masters and journeymen in post-Revolutionary Pennsylvania was widening, she may be correct. But there was no corresponding change in the organization of work that continued to be structured along craft lines. Masters and journeymen continued to control the labor process, and their labor remained unalienated.[90]

At the same time, the means of production was not owned by a small minority. Land, skills, and tools were owned and controlled by a majority of those engaged in production. If they existed, mercantile putting out systems did not play an important role in the region's manufacturing sector. Before 1780, Philadelphia merchants invested the great bulk of their capital in international commerce and real estate, so although they reinvested in their trade and speculated in land, merchants did not design policies to bring agricultural production under their control.

Part of the reason merchants did not attempt to control production is that its organization discouraged such attempts. The widespread ownership of the means of production, and the existence of noncommercial systems of subsistence, production, and exchange, limited their ability to control production. As Robert Mutch says, the merchant may have "appropriated the surplus, but only such as he found. No one

89. Mutch, "Yeoman and Merchant," 280; see also Hodges, *Primitive and Peasant Markets*, x, xii, 4, 8, 62–63.
90. Salinger, "Artisans."

was obliged to turn over their surplus to him, and he could not set production quotas."[91]

This analysis is consistent with classical Marxist theory, which holds that merchant capital does not constitute a mode of production. What merchants do is link communities. So too in Pennsylvania, where merchants connected the countryside to the major eastern cities, and the cities to the Atlantic trading centers.[92]

When we turn to an examination of the expropriation of the surplus-value from the social product, however, complications emerge. Was the economy characterized by a process of capitalist commodity exchange? Can one analyze existing economic relations as a series of processes that involve capitalists buying the means of production and items of personal consumption from other capitalists, and also purchasing labor power from propertyless workers who are forced to sell their labor so they can earn the means to ensure their survival? The question is crucial because of the importance placed on the labor process in Marxist analysis.

Wage labor in fact made inroads in late-eighteenth-century Pennsylvania and unfree labor declined in importance. While the transformation of urban artisans was hardly complete, the general direction of change was clear. Slavery was on the way out and wage labor was slowly increasing. In the countryside the situation was much less clear. The farmer-cottager relationship was a form of wage labor—farm owners paid cottagers and sold them services in order to gain access to their labor. However, the farmer-cottager relationship was only one ingredient in the rural labor process.

To this point, the discussion of farmers has focused on the consumption and investment needs of the farm family, but now our focus shifts from the family to the community. There is a considerable body of evidence that a noncapitalist rural labor process existed. Rural neighborhoods may have been dispersed, but they *were* communities, and the bonds that held them together—mainly noncommercial exchange networks and a variety of labor exchanges based on reciprocity—were powerful.

The most celebrated and least studied of these exchanges were the "bee" and the "frolic." When the rural population faced tasks that

91. Mutch, "Yeoman and Merchant," 296; Doerflinger, *Vigorous Spirit,* 67.
92. Marx, *Capital,* 3: chs. 16–20. See also Mutch, "Cutting Edge," 850–52, 858–59.

required large outlays of labor, they called on everyone in the community for help. These tasks included "breaking-out" snow-covered roads, pulling stones, chopping and rolling logs, splitting rails, "raising" homes, barns, and outbuildings, pulling stumps, plowing fields, clearing dung, processing and spreading lime, harvesting crops like wheat, hay, and flax, maple-sugaring, shucking corn, shearing sheep, fulling flax, kicking and soaping woolen cloth, butchering livestock, fishing, berry-picking and nutting, baking, apple-paring and drying, making apple butter and cider, spinning, sewing, weaving, quilting, and carpet making.[93]

Descriptions of rural life emphasize the importance of such occasions. John Hall, an English immigrant, wrote to his family that when a boy drowned a cry was raised and, "as all extraordinary things here are done by frolic, so was the search for the corps [sic]," and another letter-writer described a neighbor's plowing frolic, the second of the year to which nine teams had come. There were building projects, such as the one in Paxton Township to which 100 neighbors came to help James Burd erect a barn. Such heroic efforts were not unusual. In one case twenty wagons appeared on Saturday to gather and haul stones for the foundation of a new house. The following Monday a timber frolic was held, and a few days later the house was raised. Such community efforts were also noticeable during harvest time. Frolics, then, were regular features of the annual calendar, and they were not restricted to frontier regions. Two of the above-mentioned frolics occurred in Flemington, New Jersey, and Chester, Pennsylvania—well within the most commercialized area of Philadelphia's hinterland.[94]

Frolics combined work and festivity. Men, women, and children worked, feasted, gossiped, danced, sang, courted, and played games. Drinking and roughhousing were part of the scene. Cornhusking, "with the red ear penalties duly extracted" (kissing the partner of one's

93. Buck and Buck, *Planting,* 354–55; Fletcher, *Agriculture,* 137, 439–44; Loehr, "Farmers' Diaries," 322; Thayer, "Farmer," 49–50; Waggoner, "Producers"; Hubka, "Farm Family"; Weiman, "Families"; Faragher, *Sugar Creek,* 130–70.

94. John Hall to Jas. Choyce, August 30, 1793, Philadelphia, Capner-Exter-Hill Family Papers, RUL 4; Ann Capner (hurst) to Mary Exter, 31 August 1787, in ibid.; Ann Capner (hurst) to John Cotman, 13 November 1787, in ibid., 2. See also Sugar Diary, WCHS, 1794; Fletcher, *Agriculture,* 90; Ashmead, *History,* 181, 189; Doddridge, *Notes,* 131; Hanna, *History,* 146–47, 166–67. For the quotation on the "red ear," see Henning, "German Settler," 21–24, 26, 33–34. See also Johnson, *Letters,* 70–71; Van Voorhis, *Old and New,* 13; Plumb, *History,* 220, 224; Watson, "Account," 1:295–96, 299; Ulrich, "Housewife," 25, 30–31. Virtually all descriptions of neighborhood labor-sharing mention use of alcohol; see also the citations listed above in note 93.

choice) were combined with hoedowns and feasts. The greatest frolic of the year, according to a German farmer, occurred at butchering time. He recalled neighbors and young men and women gathering together in late November to slaughter and process meat. Huge fires and kettles worked the whole day, and at night there was feasting, dancing, singing, and some "sparking."[95]

While bees and frolics were the most visible examples of labor-sharing, they were not necessarily the most important. To fight the loneliness they faced and to lighten their workload, farmers adopted "the plan of 'neighboring,'" or what was later called the "borrowing system." People did not talk about "buying" or "selling," but instead "took" or "gave." Farmers and their families constantly shared chores and did favors for one another: berry-picking and gardening were done together, pregnant women were nurtured, the sick or disabled and their farms and families were cared for, food was shared and tools were borrowed, and those who did not own plow or wagons or oxen regularly relied on their more fortunate neighbors.[96]

It was not easy, and it was certainly unwise, to refuse to enter the network of labor-sharing and neighboring. Joseph Doddridge recalled: "At house raisings, log rollings and harvest parties everyone was expected to do his duty faithfully." The reason, as Reverend Hanna pointed out, was clear: "Families could not afford to be bad neighbors, because they were to a great extent dependent upon each other." It is important that we not idealize these communitarian practices. The cost of neighboring was the requirement to reciprocate.[97]

Frolics and bees and the plan of neighboring were aspects of a broader institutional pattern that included what Barbara Clark Smith calls "neighborhood exchange." People traded materials, goods, animals, skills, labor, and money in order to satisfy concrete needs, not to earn money or profits. A man might trade a calf to a neighboring woman for some linen, or shoes for honey. The distinguishing characteristic of these exchanges was the inclusion of labor and relaxed (noncommercial)

95. Ashmead, *History*, 181, 189; Hanna, *History*, 147, 166–67; Watson, "Account," 296, 299.

96. Hanna, *History*, 146–47; Ball, "Process of Settlement," 130; Faragher, *Sugar Creek*, 133–34; Osterud, *Bonds of Community*, 188, 198–99, 216–22; Ulrich, "Housewife," 25, 30–31; Clark, *Rural Capitalism*, 35. Clark mentions two Amherst farmer-neighbors who both owned oxen and plows (30). In September 1778 they worked four days, "together," plowing each other's fields.

97. Doddridge, *Notes*, 131; Hanna, *History*, 146–47.

terms of payment. While most of the exploratory work has been done on New England and Upstate New York, it seems clear that these networks existed in Pennsylvania too.[98]

In a study of Ulster County, on the west bank of the Hudson and midway between New York City and Albany, Mike Merrill explores the nature of these neighborhood exchanges. The dealings between Jacob Delameter, one of the richest men in Ulster, and his neighbor, wheelwright Jacobus Davis Jr., are illustrative. In 1768, Davis worked for Delameter for two days, and five months later Delameter settled about one-third of his debt with some bran. A year later Davis gave Delameter seven pounds of sugar, and one-and-a-half years later two small wheels. Jacob Delameter finally settled most of the debt with cash. "He had waited 56 months to pay for Davis's [two days of labor and] 44 months to pay for the sugar, and 27 months to make his first payment on the wheels." Four months later, in 1774, the account was finally balanced when Delameter gave Davis some corn. Between 1768 and 1791 the two men entered into 115 transactions. Their accounts were balanced at intervals of six years, four years, two-and-a-half months, four years, and eight years.[99]

Although cash payments were involved, the monetary notations in Delameter's account book were not cash. The notations served as standards of value and facilitated the exchange of items and services. The bookkeeping in this case functioned like a scorecard, as a record of who owed whom what. Money has a number of functions, one of which is to serve as a standard of value. But the exercise of this function alone does not indicate the presence of money. Evaluating services and goods in terms of money is not the same as purchasing them.[100]

The credit arrangements between Delameter and Davis were noncommercial. Interest was not charged, demands for prompt and regular repayment did not occur, and barter was part of the process. Thus, the exchange between Delameter and Davis was not commercial. Like frolics and bees, neighboring was part of a system of reciprocal noncom-

98. B. C. Smith, *After the Revolution*, 75; Clark, *Rural Capitalism;* Merrill, "Self-Sufficiency."

99. Merrill, "Self-Sufficiency," 262–70.

100. Ibid., 41–42. Money serves as a medium of exchange, a standard of value, a repository of value, and a standard of deferred payments. Schumpeter, *Economic Analysis*, 62–63, 297, 320–21, 1087–90. On barter, see Humphrey, "Barter"; Hart, "Barter," 196–98; Clark, *Rural Capitalism*, 33–35. See also Fullam, "Farm Account Book," 16–23, 47–50. For a different view of barter, see Merrill, "Self-Sufficiency," 146–53.

mercial exchange. Families did not participate in these exchanges to earn profits. The exchanges enabled people to support their families with the resources "they had at hand"—that is, with the skills and materials they possessed. Because these exchanges involved acquaintances and reciprocity, the "creditor" was obliged to take the "debtor's" ability to pay into account. This was also true about the timing and the nature of the payment.[101]

Sometimes the exchanges did lead to substantial (monetary) debts, which occasionally engendered litigation. A witness in a Delaware court testified that the parties involved "did neighbor with each other, by borrowing & lending, etc." Barbara Clark Smith's description of neighboring as "economic exchange in a social context" is apt.[102]

Neighborhood exchange was an important institution in Pennsylvania, even in the more commercial regions. In Chester County's Sadsbury Township, farmers and artisans exchanged cash and goods and services. Samuel Wilson, a stonemason, received "the season of [Alisha Hamble's] horse to a mare" as payment for work on his lime kiln. A local innkeeper paid for his services with a cow, and a shopkeeper "paid for his new house with cash, a Bible, velvet and checked fabric, sugar, and a mixture of goods from his store." In other exchanges, Wilson received wheat, a pig, and transportation to Philadelphia.[103]

According to Paul Clemens and Lucy Simler, Samuel Swayne and his wife, Hannah—Quakers who lived in East Marlborough, Chester County—were prototypical capitalist family farmers. Samuel engaged in the profitable trade of saddletree-making and also ran a successful apple and peach nursery. Hannah marketed butter and cheese. The Swaynes hired day laborers, live-in lodgers, and several cottagers.[104]

Between 1767 and 1781, Swayne had economic exchanges with fifty of his neighbors, a substantial cross-section of the community. His account books reveal that the payments he made were a combination of cash, goods, produce, and services. The payments the Swaynes received involved a similar mix. Cash constituted a smaller percentage of this exchange than the value of the goods, produce, and services. Thus, it seems clear that the Swaynes engaged in noncommercial neighborhood exchanges.[105]

101. Clark, *Rural Capitalism*, 69–70.
102. B. C. Smith, *After the Revolution*, 74–77.
103. Lanier, "Wilson's World," 2, 19, 49; Hood, "Textile Manufacturing," 70 n. 39; S. A. Martin, "Craftsmen," 37–38, 46, 55.
104. Clemens and Simler, "Rural Labor," 114–20.
105. Ibid., 114–16.

Three patterns of exchange existed in the countryside: a commercial system that was international in scope, and two local systems—one combining barter and commerce, the other built on reciprocity and neighboring. International commerce was built on money and motivated by profits. Promptness in payment was occasionally required, and legally enforceable contracts were part of the system. The fact that the commercial system and its norms were external to the rural economy made it possible for the rural economy to operate on different principles.[106]

Social relations in the rural communities were shaped by the needs of the family. To facilitate their survival, families participated in frolics, the borrowing system, and exchange networks with neighbors and kin. The rules governing these exchanges differed dramatically from those governing commercial markets. Cash and profits were not important, and although payment was expected the timing and form of payment were negotiable. The key to the system was that family needs had to be taken into account.[107]

The rural economy poses genuinely complex analytic questions, but that is no surprise. The family farm has long been the bane of social theorists. All the founders of modern social theory, including Marx, expected the family farm to go the way of the artisan's shop—and they were wrong. As the twentieth century comes to a close, family farms continue to play an important role in American agriculture. Steven Hahn reminds us of the "persistence of the household as the dominant productive unit in agriculture. As late as 1970, the ratio of family to hired labor in commodity production stood at 3 to 1."[108]

Equally striking is the survival of subsistence efforts and noncommercial communitarian labor-sharing practices well into the twentieth century. The literature is replete with examples, and an Ohio farmer's recollection is illustrative:

> Threshing required a dozen to twenty hands and was therefore a neighborhood cooperative project. Farmers "changed work" with each other, each furnishing a team and a wagon and one or more men. . . . It was always an occasion to catch up on all the neighborhood talk and for much gaiety and banter. . . . Now and

106. Clark, *Rural Capitalism*, 31–32.
107. Ibid.
108. Friedmann, "Family Enterprises," 41; Mooney, *My Own Boss?* 178; Osterud, *Bonds of Community;* Hahn, "Southern Yeomanry," 196.

then a farmer gained temporary unpopularity by raising a field of barley. The prickly awns from ripe barley beards penetrated the clothing. . . . No one liked to work on a barley threshing job, but to refuse would have been unneighborly.[109]

The appearance of an interdisciplinary body of studies on peasants, family farmers, and petty-commodity producers promises to end this theoretical embarrassment. A reading of this literature suggests that what we have in the Pennsylvania countryside are petty-commodity producers, not capitalists.[110]

Petty-commodity producers are farmers who own land and own or have access to the implements of production. Family labor constitutes their primary work force. Over the life cycle of the family, the labor process contains a structural requirement for wage labor. In Pennsylvania, this need was satisfied by a combination of cottagers and hired hands. Beyond this structural requirement, there were few internal requirements that compelled entrance into the market. These noncapitalist farmers needed money to pay taxes and buy land. They bought salt, sugar and rum, tea and coffee, cloth and hardware. The services of mills, artisans, and professionals were purchased, but if times were bad they could do without or satisfy family needs through the neighborhood exchange networks. Thus, petty-commodity producers can survive with little or no profits because they have greater flexibility than business farmers in reducing consumption. These advantages help explain why petty-commodity production continues to flourish in the twentieth century.[111]

The Swaynes of East Marlborough illustrate the labor pattern of the family farm. Their family was large—eight children survived their father. More distant kin, including Hannah's father, were part of the household. Expenditures for hired hands and wage labor rose and fell in an obverse

109. Quoted in McMillan, *Ohio Farm*, 87, 92, 94, and chs. 4, 7; Adams, "Decoupling," 458, 461; Culbertson, "Pennsylvania Boyhood," 81–82; Friedmann, "Family Enterprises"; Faragher, *Sugar Creek*, 131–38; Hubka, "Farm Family," 13–19; Kimball, "Rural"; Osterud, *Bonds of Community*, 212–14; D. Smith, "Middle Range Farming," 358–59, 362, 364.

110. For useful introductions to this literature, see Buttel et al., *Sociology of Agriculture;* Ellis, *Peasant Economics;* Friedmann, "Family Enterprises"; Shanin, ed., *Peasants;* and Scott, ed., "Rethinking."

111. Adams, "Decoupling," 454; Bernstein, "Capitalism," 18–19; Goodman and Redclift, "Capitalism," 25–27; Harrison, *Marxist Economics*, ch. 2; Kahn, "Marxist Anthropology," 112–21; Kelly, "Independent Mode," 40–46; G. Smith, "Reflections," 100–101; Weiman, "Families."

relationship to the size of the family. The Swaynes entered labor markets in a cycle that depended on a number of considerations, which included market conditions, but the single most important factor shaping the Swaynes's use of wage labor was the life cycle of the family and the investment requirements of the farm.[112]

Petty-commodity producers have existed in a variety of societal settings, including slavery and serfdom, but they fare best when they are free. Because of their compatibility with different modes of production, the bonds that integrate them into specific social formations are important to understand. In Pennsylvania these linkages were both commercial and noncommercial. Farmers were tied to commercial markets by the services, products, and credit offered in general stores and local mills and by their powerful desire to own land and their need to pay taxes and wages. At the same time, they were embedded into rural neighborhoods by a variety of noncommercial reciprocal institutions.[113]

If their desire to own land (property) does not mark Pennsylvania's petty-commodity producers as capitalists (clerics and lords want property too), it did link them to the cultural strain we know as possessive individualism. This tendency was reinforced by the powerful currents of individualism inherent in Protestantism. The result of this combination was to limit the potential appeal of egalitarian and communitarian principles. Eighteenth-century family farmers advocated a society in which all were small-property owners, but eventually the form of equality espoused by most would be the opportunity to possess property.[114]

At the same time, the presence of large numbers of petty-commodity producers imparted a powerful sense of egalitarianism to the culture. These producers built institutions like the borrowing system and the noncommercial exchange networks that were especially important in nourishing this egalitarianism. The result was a constellation of communitarian norms, values, and ideas that often proved to be fiercely anticapitalist.[115]

Because it included communitarian, noncapitalist elements and also individualistic, property-oriented values and behavior, the resulting

112. Clemens and Simler, "Rural Labor," 116–20.
113. Kelly, "Independent Mode," 39–43; Kahn, "Marxist Anthropology," 114–15; C. Smith, "Reconstructing," 29–38; G. Smith, "Reflections," 100–104.
114. Friedmann, "Family Enterprises," 52–55.
115. Ibid.

cultural mix was dynamic and unstable. Over time, it changed in response to its own internal dynamics and to external influences. In Pennsylvania, petty-commodity producers provided fertile ideological ground for an amalgam of republicanism, egalitarianism, and democracy on the one hand, and possessive individualism and liberalism, on the other. The combination enabled family farmers to behave like businessmen and also to take communitarian stances.

One of the most fruitful developments in the entire discussion over the place of capitalism in American history has been the recent proposals of interpretive frameworks that encompass large portions of American history. The analyses of Christopher Clark, Mike Merrill, James Henretta, Allan Kulikoff, and Winifred Rothenberg, to name the more prominent, span a century or more. All these interpretations are built around the concept of a transformation to capitalism, and as we combine these larger frameworks with studies that have a narrower focus, it becomes clear that at any specific point in time we can find variations in social development and individual behavior between and within communities.[116]

If we apply the logic of this insight to Pennsylvania in the 1780s, we can see that although capitalism had made inroads in some communities and on some individuals, capitalism as a social system had not yet emerged. Thus, the appearance of wage labor in the countryside, and the presence of entrepreneurs like William Smedley, were harbingers of things to come and denote the beginning of a long, slow, and difficult process. They do not provide evidence for the existence of a new order.

What did happen, though, was the appearance of the conditions for the transition to capitalism. By the middle of the eighteenth century, Pennsylvania had a clearly articulated and successful mercantile sector. Money was important and entrepreneurial talent was plentiful, and as the century wore on, the vigor and vision of Philadelphia's mercantile community intensified. One consequence of this growth was the establishment of the Bank of North America. All these developments were inextricably connected to the increasing desire exhibited by consumers, which was the demand side of the changes in productive capacity occurring concurrently in Britain.

Since property rights were central to Anglo-American culture, most Americans and Britains were committed to the principle that ownership

116. Clark, *Rural Capitalism;* Merrill, "Anticapitalist Origins"; Henretta, "Transition"; Kulikoff, "Transition to Capitalism"; Kulikoff, *Agrarian Origins;* Rothenberg, *Market-Places.*

conferred absolute control. Encouraged by this view, an entire body of property and contract law was developed and institutionalized. Because guilds had never successfully rooted themselves, occupational mobility was easier. Finally, ascriptive restraints on labor were rapidly disappearing. Slavery was a relic of the past, and wage labor was slowly making its presence felt.[117]

Independence lifted the heavy hand of British restraint and opened the door to new possibilities—perhaps the most important of which was capitalism. But if independence eased the way for development of an indigenous capitalism, it also created opportunities for groups like Pennsylvania's petty-commodity producers, who would become opponents of the new order. Many if not most of the major political questions of the day—including the controversies over slavery and the Bank of North America—are best seen as part of a transition to capitalism that would not be completed, in the Middle Atlantic region, until the mid-nineteenth century.[118]

The easiest way to understand the complex brew of tendencies and social groups that constituted Revolutionary Pennsylvania is to see it as a social formation in which a ruling class of merchants coexisted with artisans and a class of numerically dominant petty-commodity producers. Widespread ownership of land, easy access to occupational skills, a frontier location in the Atlantic trading community, the commercial and consumer revolutions, the Anglo-American colonial heritage, and unbreakable ties to the rapidly developing British capitalism all combined to shape the culture and social structure of the region and usher in capitalism.

117. Lemon, "Early Americans," 119–25; Ely Jr., *Guardian,* ch. 2; Salinger, "Artisans."
118. Kulikoff, *Agrarian Origins,* ch. 4; Merrill, "Anticapitalist Origins."

2

Traditional or Modern?

Because America was created, and the act of creation involved utopian impulses, many observers have seen America as exceptional. Alexis de Tocqueville's suggestion that Americans were born free exemplifies this view. So pervasive is this idea that it has come to constitute a major component of the culture. The tenacity of the view that America was capitalist at birth is at least partly attributable to this cultural heritage. Exceptionalism has also manifested itself in the view that by the time of the Revolution the New World was already significantly modern. Those who hold this view portray Pennsylvania and the Middle Atlantic region as the most modern region in British North America.[1]

The second step in exploring the social structure of late-eighteenth-century Pennsylvania is to examine the kinds of social forms and organizations that existed and the nature of change in the Quaker province. Again, this discussion revolves around the assumption that we can generalize about types of societies. How would one test the thesis that by the 1770s Pennsylvania had already begun the shift to a modern society? A common tactic has been to focus on evidence of

1. A full rendition of this thesis can be found in Bonami, "Middle Colonies."

change and then show that its consequence was to bring the region's social forms closer to the shape of the present.

Most often, scholars have pointed out that the region was transformed from a series of wilderness settlements into a bustling colonial province and then into a proud republic, all in less than a century. The problem with this approach is that it assumes something still to be proven. The concept of modernity is not a blank check. It has a well-defined history and refers to a clearly defined body of social theory. In this chapter, I begin by summarizing the historical literature as it deals with changes in the province, especially in the regional economy, and then use modernization theory to evaluate the historical discourse.

Underpinning discussions of social change and modernization in the region is an awareness of the enormously impressive population growth. Pennsylvania's early years were the success story of English colonization. Learning from previous mistakes, the Quakers avoided a "starving time" and established reasonably congenial relations with the indigenous population. Agriculture and commerce flourished, and successful efforts were made to attract both English and non-English immigrants.[2]

Established in the early 1680s, Pennsylvania saw its population increase dramatically from 17,950 in 1700 to 85,637 in 1740 and to about 327,000 in 1780. In the first forty years of the eighteenth century the population grew 4.7 times, while in the next forty years, slowed by war and revolution, it grew another 3.8 times. The result was the most heterogeneous population in North America. In 1790 some 92 percent of the population were English, German, and Scots-Irish; the rest were an amalgam of Welsh, Scots, Africans, Dutch, French, and Swedes.[3]

Population growth increased the level of social complexity, as the number of towns, churches, gristmills, and so on, grew rapidly. The presence of many ethnic and religious groups further complicated social relations. Pennsylvanians were forced to deal, often intimately, with people they might have preferred to exclude or treat as foes. Language and sex, cooking and clothing, and economic, political, and religious behavior all reflected the diversity.[4]

Another form of complexity engendered by population growth was

2. The best study of the establishment of Pennsylvania remains G. Nash, *Quakers*.

3. Population statistics are computed from *Historical Statistics*, 756; and Potter, "Colonial Period." The percentages of the three main ethnic groups are English 35.3, German 33.3, and Scots-Irish 23.1. The remaining 8.3 percent was divided as follows: Dutch 1.8, French 1.8, Swedish 0.8, and the ubiquitous "others" 3.9. See *Historical Statistics*, 756.

4. Harper, "Town Development."

social stratification. The pattern was the same everywhere. On the western frontier, in the well-developed agricultural regions, in towns, and in Philadelphia, most of the community's wealth was held by a small minority. Over the Allegheny Mountains in the newly settled west, the richest 10 percent of the taxpayers owned 25 percent of the land in 1782–85, while the poorest 10 percent held only 2 percent, and 38 percent of those living on the frontier did not own any land. In Westmoreland County in 1786, the richest 10 percent owned 31 percent of the county's wealth, while the poorest half had a bit less than 16 percent. Bedford County was even more skewed. In 1783 the wealthiest 10 percent owned just over 38 percent, and the poorest half had 24 percent of the taxable wealth.[5]

Closer to Philadelphia the distribution of wealth was even more skewed. In prosperous Chester County, the top tenth of the taxpayers held one-third of the county's wealth in 1782, while the bottom half held only 14 percent. In 1789, in Chester's Concord Township, the richest 25 percent owned 62 percent of the wealth, and the poorest half owned 14 percent. Similarly, in Berks County in 1785, just under 40 percent of the wealth was in the hands of the wealthiest one-tenth, while the poorest half owned only just over 11 percent. The wealthiest 10 percent of the residents of Lancaster, America's largest inland town in 1788, owned 50 percent of the town's wealth, compared with only 12.5 percent held by the poorest 60 percent.[6]

The greatest disparity in the province existed in Philadelphia. Between 1756 and 1774 the richest 10 percent increased their share of the taxable wealth from 47 percent to 72 percent. When we take into account that Philadelphian's per capita wealth was significantly higher than that enjoyed in the countryside, the position of the urban elite appears even more impressive. Although the fortunate prospered, the plight of the poor was pitiable. In 1772 almost one-quarter "of the city's mariners, laborers, sawyers, and carters were receiving some form of poor relief."[7]

5. Harper, "Class Structures," 36, 45–46, 54, 79; Schweitzer, "Elements," 9–10.

6. Case, *Prosperity*, 151; Lemon and Nash, "Distribution"; Schweitzer, "Elements," 9–10.

7. Wood, *Conestoga Crossroads*, 166–79; G. Nash, "Urban Wealth," 550–51; G. Nash, "Up from the Bottom," 64; Warner Jr. notes that mercantile inventories and money on loan were not taxed. As a result, therefore, mercantile wealth was understated (*Private City*, 9 n. 14), and Jones, "Wealth Estimates," concludes that in 1774 the poorest 50 percent owned 13 percent of the wealth, while the richest 10 percent held 40 percent. B. Smith, "Inequality"; B. Smith, *Lower Sort*, 84–89, 224–29; G. Nash, *Crucible*, 325. See also Wolf, *Urban Village*, 120–26.

Stratification began almost immediately. As early as 1710 a provincial elite made its appearance. By 1720, Quaker oligarchs, tied together by blood, marriage, religion, commerce, wealth, and outlook, were in firm control of the province. In the second quarter of the century they were challenged by the rise of Presbyterian, Anglican, and proprietary elites. The newcomers eventually surpassed the Quakers in wealth, numbers, and social prestige. Thus, the eighteenth century was marked by the rise of a group of wealthy Philadelphia entrepreneurs with diverse religious and ethnic backgrounds and an urban-cosmopolitan outlook.[8]

The tendency toward social complexity and stratification was encouraged by the impressive growth of Philadelphia. The city possessed a safe, deep port and an enormous and productive hinterland. A combination of navigable rivers, streams, and roads gave most of Pennsylvania, all of Delaware, and large parts of New Jersey and Maryland easy access to the city's markets and services.[9]

Philadelphia's hinterland was huge. The trading area encompassed some 20,000 square miles, a realm half the size of England and one-fifth the area of the thirteen mainland colonies. Despite its enormous size, one-sixth of the hinterland's residents lived only a day's journey from Philadelphia. Another one-sixth lived half a day from water transport to the metropolis. Thus, one-third of the region's population lived no more than a day's journey from the city.[10]

Export markets also shaped the regional economy. The commercial development of England and its empire provided the context, and conveniently located West Indian markets were the key. Specializing in the production of sugar and rum, West Indian planters were more than willing to purchase the foodstuffs, forest products, and manufactured items produced in Philadelphia and its hinterland.[11]

Commercial expansion was greatly aided by the activities of the British navy's successful campaign against piracy. It is difficult to exaggerate the economic impact of piracy. In 1723, marauders closed Philadelphia's port for more than two months, but by the 1730s decisive action by the British virtually eliminated the problem. As a result,

---

8. G. Nash, *Quakers*, 321–31; Tolles, *Meeting House*, ch. 3; Brobeck, "Changes in Composition," ch. 3.

9. Walzer, "Transportation," 2; Walzer, "Colonial Philadelphia"; Bridenbaugh, *Cities in Revolt*, 49–51; Doerflinger, *Vigorous Spirit*, 74–76, 113–15.

10. See works cited above in note 8.

11. Egnal, "Development," 191–222; Lydon, "Commercial Expansion"; Lemon, *Poor Man's Country*, 27–32, 219–27.

shippers were able to hire smaller crews, use fewer cannon, leave port more quickly, and save money on insurance. Increased safety was an important reason for the growth of international trade.[12]

Given a good location and exploitable markets, capable entrepreneurs appeared and shaped the character of the region. A few arrived on the first boats: Quakers with the requisite attitudes, skills, connections, and capital. Their presence helped Pennsylvania avoid the pitfalls of the southern development. In the South, entrepreneurs channeled most of their capital, skills, and energy into the production of export crops. The result was a pattern of unbalanced economic development dominated by commercial agriculture. Philadelphia's merchants created a more diversified economy.[13]

The search for profits and economic security led merchants to invest widely. They lent money, speculated in foreign currencies and bills of exchange, sold insurance, bought real estate, financed construction, and invested in ways they thought would strengthen the export trade. Merchant capital flowed into flour-milling, distilling, iron production, and shipbuilding.[14]

These investments expanded the labor force and improved its skills. The construction of one sailing vessel, for example,

> required a year's work of at least thirty craftsmen, including shipwrights, joiners, ropemakers, blockmakers, sailmakers, carpenters, riggers, caulkers, carvers, cabinetmakers, smiths, founders, braziers, glaziers, painters, coopers, tanners, and bricklayers. . . . The entire operation could occupy more than a hundred workers, and, on average, one or two lesser-skilled men assisted every skilled craftsman employed in a shipyard.[15]

Artisanal production triggered increased demands for tools and raw materials, new wharves and warehouses were eventually needed, and additional hands were required to staff, provision, and maintain the new vessels. Thus, the shipyards and carrying trade were part of a regional

12. Shepherd and Walton, *Shipping*, ch. 5, esp. 80–85; Lydon, "Commercial Expansion," 416.

13. Tolles, *Meeting House*, ch. 2.

14. For the role of local entrepreneurs, see Crowther, "Shipbuilding," 6–15, 180–82. For an introductory discussion of entrepreneurial behavior, see Krooss and Gilbert, *American Business*, 1–20.

15. B. Smith, *Lower Sort*, 78.

economy that created work and profits for merchants, clerks, bookkeepers, and lawyers, as well as for retailers, landlords, farmers, craftsmen, and laborers.

As the economy of the city grew and became more complex, occupational specialization increased. By the 1780s the export-import trade had been reorganized. Smaller mercantile firms had "generally" chosen to specialize. The provision and dry goods trades were separate and clearly defined. Shipping on the Atlantic and in Philadelphia's hinterland had become a specialized trade, as had the procurement of flour and lumber. General retail establishments declined, while more specialized drug, dry goods, and grocery stores multiplied. Peter Thompson's China Emporium and the Wistar brothers' button and glass shop exemplified this trend. Coffeehouses and taverns also showed signs of specializing, catering to specific ethnic groups, social classes, occupational groups, like-minded individuals, and neighborhoods. The James Coffee House, for example, catered to artists, while the city's bibliophiles met at the Library Tavern.[16]

Specialization was most pronounced in the ranks of the artisans. Trades underwent a significant fragmentation—for example, woodworking divided into coopering, stave-making, box-making, crate-making, rough carpentry, joining, turning, carving, and cabinetmaking. Other woodworkers built homes, vessels, furniture, coaches, and wagons, and still others produced buttons, coffins, picture frames, looking-glass frames, tools, and bowls and dishes. The more than 100 percent increase in the number of crafts practiced in Philadelphia between 1745 and 1771 is dramatic testimony to the inroads of specialization.[17]

The emergence of Philadelphia as a business center, the establishment of its enormous hinterland, and its export markets combined to further the commercialization of the region. In the city and in the countryside, families owned more and more possessions. As the eighteenth century went on, an increasing percentage of these goods and services were purchased—most were produced locally but an increasing number were not.[18]

Considerable change had occurred. Population growth resulting from a healthful environment and a reasonably well fed and well cared for

16. Doerflinger, "Specialization"; Bridenbaugh, *Cities in Revolt,* 156–62, 276, 279; Bridenbaugh and Bridenbaugh, *Rebels,* 21–22; Thompson, "Philadelphia's Taverns."

17. Bridenbaugh, *Cities in Revolt,* 76, 272–74; Bridenbaugh, *Craftsman,* 75–81 (for other crafts, see 84–104); Olton, *Artisans,* 4–5; Quimby, "Apprenticeship," 30.

18. Michel, "In a Manner."

population, plus a large number of immigrants, was impressive. An important consequence of population growth was greater social complexity, furthered by stratification and a maturing mercantile sector. In less than a century, Pennsylvania developed from a series of primitive wilderness settlements into a bustling province with a world-class urban center.

Many historians see these changes as evidence of the existence of an emergent modern, pluralistic society, at least in the early stages of modernization. But concepts like modernization are not neutral. They are theoretically grounded and do not refer to all types of change. Certainly Pennsylvania had changed dramatically, but it remains to be seen whether those changes are those experienced by societies undergoing modernization.

Contemporary theories of social change and modernization are built on the work of the great nineteenth-century social theorists Karl Marx, Max Weber, and Emile Durkheim. The founders of modern social theory were fascinated by the sweeping societal changes they witnessed. While they all accepted evolution and developmentalism, each explained the process differently. Marx stressed class conflict, Weber stressed rationality, and Durkheim emphasized structural differentiation.

Because the Bank of North America was the first commercial bank to be established in the hemisphere, America's first private corporation, and arguably eighteenth-century America's most powerful private enterprise, we have an opportunity to explore the impact of the development of new social forms. The organizing principles of the bank, its power, structure, and ethos, differed in fundamental ways from the organizing principles of Pennsylvania's social structure. Durkheim's work, with its focus on social institutions, organizations, and roles, offers a rich theoretical framework within which to examine the impact of the bank.

Durkheim saw society as an organic system of autonomous but interdependent elements in which the whole was greater than the sum of its parts. He focused on the institutions and norms that make up societies and regulate the behavior of individuals. Durkheim was particularly concerned with the functions of these institutions and norms and with the way societies were integrated, an approach that led him to emphasize processes internal to particular societies.[19]

19. Burke, *History*, 130–35; So, *Social Change*, 17–20; Jaffee, *Levels*, 3–6; Alexander, "Introduction—Differentiation Theory," 3–4; Alexander, "Durkheim's Problem," 179–86; Etzkowitz and Glassman, "Introduction," 6–11; Haritos and Glassman, "Emile Durkheim," 75–80, 87–88.

Like many nineteenth-century scholars, Durkheim was heavily influenced by evolutionary thought. He believed that societies grew and decayed, and he adopted the popular nineteenth-century traditional/modern typology: traditional societies were static, agricultural, superstitious-magical, and relatively undifferentiated, while modern societies were their polar opposites—dynamic, industrial, scientific-rational, and increasingly differentiated. He saw the transition from traditional to modern as a linear process—as societies modernized they became less traditional. Finally, Durkheim's vision of modernity, like that of many of his peers, was Eurocentric.[20]

All major theories of social change possess master trends. For Marx, history involved class development and struggle until a classless society was achieved, while for Weber the master trend was rationalization. The core of Durkheimian differentiation theory is the insistence that the most significant aspect of social change is the process in which multifunctional social structures are replaced by more-specialized social roles, organizations, and institutions. The new specialized social forms are more efficient and increase the adaptive capacity of the social system or subsystem.[21]

Specialization is the process during which a new social unit separates into two or more units. "The new social units are structurally distinct from each other, but taken together they are functionally equivalent to the original unit." The process involves division, compartmentalization, simplification, and standardization.[22] The major institutional expression of specialization in modern societies is the proliferation of social units that are deliberately constructed to accomplish specific goals. In traditional societies, people lived their lives in a small number of unspecialized kinship and neighborhood groupings, but today we routinely frequent thousands of specialized organizations run by strangers.[23]

But the most important manifestation of specialization has been the spread of powerful bureaucracies—which are not necessarily a new phenomenon, but modern societies have more of them serving more functions for more people than ever before. Because all the major institutional spheres have come to be dominated by bureaucracies, it

20. See sources cited above in note 19.

21. Colomy, "Recent Developments," 291; Colomy, "Conclusion," 466–67. Ironically, the best explanation for the drive toward specialization is offered by Marxists. See Braverman, *Labor*; and Brenner, "Social Basis."

22. Smelser, "Mechanisms of Change," 35.

23. Levy Jr., *Modernization*, 60–62.

does not seem to be an exaggeration to speak of an organizational revolution.[24]

As Durkheim showed, an important consequence of specialization was a decline in the self-sufficiency of the new specialized units and roles. The problems created by this dependency are typically solved by creating specialized integrative units and mechanisms to coordinate and regulate the interaction between the new specialized units. Specialized factories gathered artisans, laborers, and peasants (men, women, and children) and transformed them into machine-tenders, a new social class defined by its role in the division of labor. Subsequently, the proletariat working in a new setting and living in new neighborhoods created a culture and elective affinities of its own—and such organizations as trade unions which served to integrate them into the new industrial world.[25]

Modern integration also involves development of broad mechanisms that operate at the societal and global levels. Among the most prominent of these are written languages, money, citizenship rights, and inclusive legal systems. Ideologies like nationalism, rationalism, progress, and populism have played a similar role.[26]

World War II and the onset of the Cold War revived interest in the problem of social change. The collapse of the European colonial empires, and the appearance of an apparently unending stream of Third World nations in the late 1950s and early 1960s, intensified interest in development. Predictably, the search for explanatory frameworks led scholars back to Marx, Weber, and Durkheim and their emphases on evolution, stages of development, and the traditional/modern polarity.[27]

Talcott Parsons captured the moment by reviving Durkheim and placing differentiation at the center of structural functionalism. According to Parsons, when functional needs were not satisfied, social strains developed. The resulting tensions would be eased by the creation of more efficient, specialized social arrangements. As Parsons's influence spread, Durkheimian offshoots like the hugely popular modernization theory of the 1950s emerged.[28]

Yet if the influence of Durkheim and Parsons was pervasive, the work

24. Hays, "Introduction"; Presthus, *Organizational Society*.

25. Durkheim, *Division of Labor*.

26. Eisenstadt, *Modernization*, 38–40.

27. Eisenstadt, "Studies of Modernization," 225–27; So, *Social Change*, 17–18; Wiarda, "Rethinking," 66–68.

28. So, *Social Change*, 18–23; Jaffee, *Levels*, 86–101; Sanderson, *Social Evolutionism*, ch. 6; Simmons, *Perspectives*, 13–19; Harrison, *Sociology of Modernization*, 29–41.

on modernization encompassed tremendous theoretical diversity, a diversity that many critics conveniently ignored. In fact, in the early 1960s a number of scholars working within the functionalist tradition, such as S. N. Eisenstadt and Manfred Halpern, labored to enrich their explanatory model.[29]

While they continued to adhere to the Durkheimian master trend by insisting that the most important changes ushered in by modernization involved specialization and integration, Eisenstadt and Halpern went on to suggest that the distinguishing characteristic of modernization was the tendency of modern social systems to transform themselves at a breakneck pace. "System transformation" as Halpern called it, was "the first revolution of mankind [that] . . . requires an enduring capacity to generate and absorb persistent transformation. . . . To maintain such a capacity for transformation constitutes both the uniquely modern opportunity and the uniquely modern requirement."[30]

Inherent in the concept of system transformation was a sensitivity to the dark side of modernization. The process was inherently wrenching. Breakdowns and the possibility of failure were no chimera. S. N. Eisenstadt made the point clearly: "The very fact that modernization entails continual change in all major spheres of a society means of necessity that it involves processes of disorganization and dislocation, with the continual development of social problems, cleavages, and conflicts between various groups, and movements of protest, [and] resistance to change."[31]

One reason modernization has been so explosive is the appearance and spread of societal modern "centers." Edward Shils describes centers as "zones"—or "realms" in which the values, beliefs, and actions "which govern the society" are created and acted out. Traditional societies restrict access to the cultural and institutional centers to elites. Modernization has, so to speak, opened the door. As a result, modern centers have proved to be particularly powerful integrative mechanisms that encourage participation and intensify interaction among the various

29. For a sense of the diversity in the early modernization theory, see So, *Social Change*, chs. 2–3; Harrison, *Sociology of Modernization*, 41–57; and Sztompka, *Sociology*, 129–35. For Eisenstadt, see his "Modernization and Conditions"; "Social Change," 375–86; "Breakdowns"; "Transformation"; *Tradition;* "Studies of Modernization"; and "Reappraisal of Theories."

30. The quotation is from Halpern, "Rate and Costs," 21–23. See also Halpern, "Toward Further Modernization"; Halpern, "Revolution of Modernization," 39; and Eisenstadt, *Modernization*, 40–43.

31. Eisenstadt, *Modernization*, 20.

social groups. Discourse is encouraged and, inevitably, so is conflict. Participation in the center increases self-awareness. To the extent that this occurs, other groups are seen as competitors, a development that eventually intensifies the level and scope of conflict.[32]

Integration structures conflict in another way. Modernity has proved conducive to the creation of social movements. The absence of traditional restraints, the appearance of modern societal centers with participatory norms, and the spread of various integrative ideologies, such as populism and nationalism, have created the necessary conditions for the spread of these movements. Political disagreement over the utility of the Bank of North America was transformed from debate and interest politics into appeals that suggested the future of humanity was at risk. And despite the survival of the bank, antibanking spread outside the region of its birth and moved to other states and to the national arena. In the process a social movement(s) was created.

Eisenstadt also paid serious attention to the rise of popular demands for increased participation and equal rights. Populism, which has manifested itself in a number of ways, is largely responsible for creating the modern view of citizenship. Sex, race, birthplace, occupation, and class are no longer absolute barriers to citizenship. Moreover, the rights and responsibilities associated with citizenship have seen a steady expansion. Finally, citizens are expected to participate in the public arena, and failure to do so is treated as a social problem.[33]

The appearance of large, bureaucratic organizations and the rise of populism has been an especially explosive mix in the American context. The attack against the Bank of North America, Jackson's crusade against the Second Bank of the United States, the railroad riots of 1877, the subsequent attacks against big business and Wall Street toward the end of the nineteenth century, and the recurrent fears of a too powerful government are all examples of this tendency.

Modernization also created new possibilities for dealing with the stresses and strains unleashed by development. The new organizational forms are often more efficient. New technologies and techniques facilitate repression and manipulation, and new forms of integration create powerful communal bonds. Modern societies also manage conflict by allowing and often encouraging social protest, and at times by responding to the needs and demands of their citizens. Moreover, modern social

---

32. Shils, "Centre and Periphery."
33. Coleman, "Development Syndrome," 76–78; Worsley, *Third World,* 164–67.

roles have become so complex that they tend to blur and confuse the lines of conflict. Workers, for example, are members of gender, age cohort, class, and specialized occupational and ethnic groups, as well as religious groups, residential neighborhoods, and families.

This, then, constitutes the version of modernization theory developed primarily by Eisenstadt and adopted here. Modern societies are social systems capable of a rapid and continuous transformation in which three related processes are involved. First, social units are subject to differentiation, and the major expression of this is bureaucratization. Second, integrative institutions, roles, and ideologies are created to facilitate communication and exchange between the specialized social units. In the process, traditional centers are expanded and opened to broader participation. Finally, modernization unleashes explosive tensions and conflicts and at the same time provides the means to deal effectively with these problems.

In the late 1960s a powerful critique against modernization theory was launched from the left. Latin Americanists introduced dependency theory, attacking the theoretical orientation and moral rectitude of modernization theorists. The battle raged for a decade. In the mid-1970s, world-system theorists entered the fray, and the result was a steady decline in influence of both modernization theory and structural functionalism.[34]

Some attacked the ideal typical polarities (traditional/modern) of the theory, arguing that the theory reified the polarities and treated them as unitary and stable historical end-states. Others disliked the tendency to treat modernization as an inevitable unilinear process exemplified by the Western experience. Critics also rejected the view that tradition was the polar opposite of modernity and an impediment to development.[35]

Particularly heavy criticism was aimed at a number of theoretical omissions. States and their interests and conflicts did not play a major role in formulations of the theory—which is a puzzle, considering the tendency of theorists to focus on the internal development of particular societies and its popularity among political scientists. In addition, scholars had developed strategies that attempted to ignore Marx, class theory, and exploitation. Like those of states, the interests and strug-

34. So, *Social Change*, chs. 5, 8; Simmons, *Perspectives*, 19–23. For early critiques, see Bendix, "Tradition and Modernity," 294–303; Huntington, "Change to Change"; Cockcraft et al., eds., *Dependence;* and Tipps, "Modernization Theory." Recent critical summaries are Evans and Stephens, "Development"; and Roxborough, "Modernization Theory."
35. Tipps, "Modernization Theory"; Shiner, "Tradition/Modernity."

gles of social classes are simply too important to be left out of the equation. Finally, it became clear that development could not be explored without locating nations and classes within the context of the regional and global political economy.[36]

Despite decades of heavy criticism, modernization theory has not disappeared and is not likely to. The tide of criticism was diverted and blunted as dependency and world-system theorists encountered theoretical difficulties of their own. Furthermore, appeals to stop using the concept are not likely to succeed because it is rooted too deeply. The notion dates back to the fifth century, when Christians used it to distinguish their era from the pagan past. Since the Enlightenment, some version of the concept of modernity has played a role in virtually all the major discussions of social change.[37]

More important, the concept is not likely to disappear because it is useful. Raymond Grew, a critic of modernization theory, reminds us that the modern era does differ from earlier ones. The concept of modernization helps us deal with the fact that "many similar changes—in demography, modes of production, technology, urbanization, communication, political mobilization—have occurred (at different rates and in different degrees) throughout most of the world since the eighteenth century."[38]

Much of the criticism leveled against modernization theory was based on a badly truncated time frame—a decade or two. If we compare developments in the Third World since World War II with the long and often bumpy trajectory of Western history from the seventeenth century, the plausibility of the model is strengthened. Moreover, the remarkably successful economic development in China and the Asian rim during the last few decades is consistent with predictions made by modernization theorists. The even more recent turn to democracy in Central America, South America, Eastern Europe, and Russia, although incomplete and clearly fragile, offers additional corroboration.[39]

Modernization theory has survived partly because it has been strengthened and legitimated by a neo-Durkheimian revival. The rebirth began in the 1980s and shows no signs of slowing. According to Jeffrey

36. Evans and Stephens, "Development."

37. For a convenient summary of the problems faced by dependency and world system theorists, see So, *Social Change;* Habermas, "Modernity," 141–43.

38. Grew, "More on Modernization," 181.

39. Wiarda, "Rethinking," 75–80; Hadenius, *Democracy,* ch. 5; Morris and Adelman, *Comparative Patterns;* Reynolds, "Spread."

C. Alexander, the revival stems from the cooling off of the ideological climate, the emergence of a new generation of scholars, and the reappearance of interest in Europe in social theory (including Parsons). Out of this mix, the broad intellectual tendency Alexander calls neo-functionalism appeared. Scholars working in this "tendency" are critical of some of the basic tenets of the earlier model and have incorporated elements from Marx and Weber. Finally, "this neofunctionalist tendency is manifest in a variety of often competing developments rather than a single coherent form."[40]

While the core element of the theory continues to be the Durkheimian master trend's focus on the "replacement of multifunctional structures by more specialized institutions and roles," the simplistic optimism is gone, as is unilinear evolution. Picking up on the work Eisenstadt did in the early 1960s, scholars like Paul Colomy now talk about "blunted, unequal, and uneven differentiation and dedifferentiation" in specific institutions and role structures within the social structure. "Traditional" and "modern" are no longer treated as polar opposites. In fact, traditions can play positive roles in modernization, and/or the two may coexist. Finally, the dark side of modernization is now integrated into the theory. Colomy insists that the successful establishment of more differentiated institutions and roles "invariably produces a cultural-ideological struggle centered around the legitimacy of the new structure."[41]

Despite the fierce attacks against the ideal typical elements of modernization theory and the traditional/modern polarity, both survive, albeit in a more nuanced fashion. It is apparently impossible for such theories as Durkheimian differentiation and Weberian rationalism to avoid using ideal types. This is *not* a weakness. Ideal types are well established in scientific and social scientific methodology. Concepts like id, mass, electrical resistance, historical epoch, social class, and capitalism are ideal types that have proved their heuristic utility.[42]

In short, modernization theory is attractive for this study because it offers a nuanced theoretical approach for an analysis of social structures and the impact that different types of social forms can have on behavior.

40. The quotation is from Alexander, "Introduction," 10–11. See also Alexander, "Neofunctionalism"; Ritzer, *Sociological Theory*, 602–6; Sztompka, *Sociology*, 136–41.

41. For the quotations, see Colomy, "Uneven Differentiation," 120, 122; Colomy, "Conclusion," 473. See also the older Eisenstadt, *Tradition*.

42. For an effective use of the traditional/modern polarity, see Crone, *Pre-Industrial Societies*.

Ironically, the Eurocentric character of modernization theory, which remains something of an embarrassment, poses no handicap for this study and should ease doubts about the relevance of the theory.[43]

A neo-Durkheimian approach influenced by Eisenstadt is used in this essay to help study the impact of the Bank of North America, a powerful corporate, semi-bureaucratic institution on a society whose dominant organizational forms were dramatically different. It is no small matter that modernization theory also makes the pace of change theoretically significant.

The question before us, then, is whether the types of change that characterize the history of Colonial and Revolutionary Pennsylvania indicate the presence of modernization. More specifically, was the economy of eighteenth-century Pennsylvania structured by the processes of specialization, integration, and conflict peculiar to system transformation or uneven differentiation? The answer would seem to be no.

As we have seen, the major sources of economic change in the Quaker province were brought about by natural causes like weather and disease, and man-made causes like war, population growth and movement, stratification, and economic growth. It seems clear that some of these processes, such as warfare and epidemics, have nothing to do with modernization, but others, such as population growth and stratification, are problematical.

The demographic history of the region was determined by a number of factors, which included a productive agriculture; a climate that avoided extremes of cold, heat, and moisture; a relatively disease-free rural environment; large-scale immigration; and the relative absence of serious problems with the Native American population. None of these (food, weather, health, immigration, peace) had anything to do with modernization. After all, a respectable number of traditional societies achieved populations much larger than those in Pennsylvania with no hint that modernization was occurring; India and China are obvious examples.

Similarly, *all* large-scale societies are stratified. The process is related to such phenomena as the production of a food surplus and the

43. Few American historians have made use of modernization theory. Notable among them are Brown, *Modernization;* and Wiebe, *Search for Order.* See also Cmiel, "Destiny and Amnesia."

emergence of priestly and warrior social groups. Like population growth, stratification provides no evidence for the existence of modernization.[44]

Nevertheless, population growth and economic growth pose questions related to scale that will not disappear so easily, and at a certain point there do seem to be correlations between size and specialization. Given a large enough population, people begin to organize their activities in different ways. The growth of Philadelphia and the filling up of parts of the countryside did encourage people to specialize in such occupations as the production of cheese, buttons, and rope or in such services as bookkeeping and transportation. Is this increase in specialization an instance of Durkheimian modernization? Perhaps a better way to ask the question would be to ask whether all specialization indicates modernization?

To answer the question of whether the growth in scale and the related specialization that occurred in the region reveal the presence of modernization, we need to pause and look at the types of organizations that dominated the regional economy. A study of the colonial economy from the vantage point of economic development concludes:

> The fundamental characteristics of the early agrarian and commercial economy were its small-scale production for local or regional markets and its relatively small capital requirements for production, with the consequent ability of noncorporate forms of business enterprise to assemble the capital sums required. Partnerships and individual proprietorships were the common forms of enterprise, and relationships between employers and their workers tended to be personal. In agriculture the small family farm was everywhere typical. . . . In comparison with later years, markets were small and the pace of business a leisured one; [and] institutional forms and techniques of administration were relatively simple.[45]

Although this description of the late-eighteenth-century economy is clearly too simple, it is not without merit. In the last third of the eighteenth century, the social form of economic units in rural Pennsylvania was traditional and small-scale. Productive techniques and marketing

44. Crone, *Pre-Industrial Societies*, chs. 2–3.
45. Chandler et al., *Changing Economic Order*, 2–3.

practices were primitive. Economic relationships primarily involved neighbors, friends, and family. Transportation was crude, and market information was scanty and outdated. Markets existed, but they did not drive the economy to the extent that they would do so in the next century. Urban and rural sectors were so poorly integrated that it is reasonable to talk about a bifurcated economy.

In the countryside, the isolated family farm dominated, but there were substantial numbers of artisans, many of whom farmed part-time. Other rural occupations were miller, tavern keeper, and retailer, and there was a scattering of professionals and laborers. Property and skills were widely distributed, and the needs of the family were preeminent.

Despite their isolation, rural homesteads were integrated into communities. Families were tied together by commerce and patterns of dependency created by institutionalized labor-sharing and reciprocity. Rural goods and produce were marketed in local retail outlets, in the small towns that dotted the countryside and in Philadelphia. In return, Philadelphia and the towns, aided by rural artisans and professionals, provided goods and services the rural population needed.

The second sector was urban. In many ways, Philadelphia was more closely tied to the Atlantic seaports than it was to the hinterland. The city did, of course, gather the rural surplus and funnel it to distant markets, and it did export goods and services to the rural population.

Nevertheless, Philadelphia faced outward, toward the sea and foreign markets. The urban economy was dominated by commerce, the trade was managed by merchants. As Porter and Livesay note, Philadelphia's merchants "dominated the commerce of this extension of Europe, just as they had dominated European commerce since their supplanting of the petty capitalism of traveling merchants and peddlers in the late Middle Ages." In the preindustrial economy of the eighteenth century, merchants both stood astride the flow of goods and also controlled the great bulk of the community's capital. The organizational shape of economic activity in the urban sector resembled in significant ways that of premodern cities like Leiden and Lille.[46]

Like earlier commercial centers, Philadelphia was poorly integrated with its hinterland. A substantial portion of the rural population had no direct contact with the city, and many who dealt with urban merchants engaged in what amounted to a one-way trade; they sold their produce,

---

46. Porter and Livesay, *Merchants and Manufacturers,* 5–6; DuPlessis and Howell, "Reconsidering."

but primitive transportation and the way business was organized limited the flow of goods and services to the hinterland.

Philadelphia was much more complex than the hinterland. The size of the city, the number of people, the noise and variety were attractive, bewildering, and frightening. Visitors, including some from abroad, were impressed by the number and quality of the markets, which were complemented by a profusion of shops and shipyards, inns and taverns. The city also boasted a work force that included export-import merchants, retailers, numerous lawyers, bookkeepers, and clerks, the largest assortment of what were perhaps the best artisans in America, sailors, carters, a large number of wage laborers, apprentices, indentured servants, and a rapidly shrinking number of slaves.[47]

One striking change was the increase in specialization in the rural and urban sectors. In manufacturing, the more than 100 percent increase in the number of crafts practiced between 1745 and 1771 provides dramatic testimony to the rapid and significant specialization that had occurred. But the specialization had not transformed either the labor process or the institutional character of the manufacturing sector. The work force retained its artisanal character. A craftsman who specialized in making buttons or clocks or picture frames remained a craftsman in status, in outlook, and in practice.

Specialization in the manufacturing sector of traditional preindustrial cities was common but, as Gideon Sjoberg put it, it "occurs in product, not in process." So long as the organization of manufacturing was not transformed by whatever specialization was occurring, the class structure and social relations and the norms and values of those engaged in production remained unchanged.[48]

The most likely sources of specialization in manufacturing were located in the growth of international commerce and the related increases in consumer demand and wage labor, but these tendencies were in the early stages and, as a result, had not achieved any significant intensity. Not until the nineteenth century was well under way would capitalism and the industrial revolution bring about the modernization of the manufacturing sector.

The characteristic forms of the modern economy had not yet begun to appear in Revolutionary Pennsylvania. Single-purpose businesses,

47. Bridenbaugh and Bridenbaugh, *Rebels,* 5–12; Hawke, *Midst,* 36–42; Lemon, *Poor Man's Country,* 129. See also, especially, G. Nash, *Crucible,* 387–91 (table 1), "Occupational Structure of Philadelphia and Boston, 1685–1775").
48. Sjoberg, *Preindustrial City,* 197.

like commercial banks and factories, corporations, and large-scale bureaucracies, had not yet begun to supplant families and their exchange networks as the primary economic units in either the countryside or the city. Specialization and integration had not transformed economic roles, norms, or values. The economy, and the social structure in which it was embedded, was not characterized by the types of change characteristic of system transformation. When development and change occurred in Pennsylvania, it did so in response to ecological conditions, disease, natural disaster, population growth, politics, and war.

The pace of change was slow. In an important discussion of economic modernization and its absence in the colonial economy, Stuart Bruchey notes: "The relatively slow rate of economic growth is the key link in the causal chain. Slow growth evoked relatively minimal structural change, whether defined as occupational differentiation of the labor supply, pull of rural resources into the commercial sector, industrialization, or urbanization." The pattern Bruchey delineates can be discerned in Pennsylvania during the 1780s. In the context of modernization theory, the leisurely pace of change is further evidence that change was not generating change, that system transformation had not yet impacted on the regional economy.[49]

With the exception of the deep, unbreakable ties to the emergent British capitalism, the forces shaping and guiding the regional economy were the forces that have always structured traditional societies. Like preindustrial Europe, and Africa, Asia, and Latin America before European domination, the Quaker province experienced change. "But the characteristic changes which moved people and restructured social, political, and economic life were principally ravages of nature and ravages of man." As a result, Pennsylvanians did not have to deal with the more-or-less constant transformation of the various social spheres.[50]

The Revolution, of course, did occur, causing significant dislocation and substantial change. Lives and property were destroyed, Tories left, republican constitutions were written, the polity was politicized, and new groups demanded the right to participate. Once in, those groups formulated demands and agitated for their own programs. Slavery was abolished in the North. Beyond this, there is scanty evidence for important socioeconomic change.[51]

49. Bruchey, "Economy and Society," 307.
50. Dalton, "Introduction," 17.
51. For a different interpretation, see Kulikoff, *Agrarian Origins,* ch. 4.

The only other significant development occurring in the immediate aftermath of the Revolution was the adoption of the corporation for new purposes. The establishment of Pennsylvania's Bank of North America was the first such instance. The bank was also an example of an enormously powerful, specialized, semi-bureaucratic organization whose power, norms, and operating principles differed from the dominant existing forms of social organization. They were not only different but also posed a threat to the traditional values and behavior that most Pennsylvanians espoused. When the nature of the bank was understood, America's first bank war erupted.

3

The Associational System

If Pennsylvania's economy was noncapitalist, the pace of change slow, and organizational forms simple and traditional, what of the region's institutions and associations? Here the experience of the Quaker province differed sharply from that of Europe. The European social order was dominated and shaped from the top down. At its center was a stratification system with estates and social classes. The position of social elites was enhanced by the presence of powerful institutions—church, army, and state—which they dominated and operated in their own interests. Although Pennsylvania had an ordered social universe, an examination of the institutions that dominated the European experience—church, army, and state—finds them missing, weak, or so constituted that they functioned differently in the New World.

A first, quick glance suggests similarities between the religious institutions of Europe and Pennsylvania. Quakers had close ties to the government, and for virtually the entire colonial era Quakers and their allies controlled the province. The Quaker party was so strong that it continued to dominate the Assembly and the province long after the Penn family converted to Anglicanism.[1]

1. Murrin, "Political Development," 438–40.

Quaker power was also exercised within their fellowship. Members were expelled for drinking, swearing, cursing, lying, and loose sexual behavior. They could also be kicked out for excessive gestures, speech, apparel, and furniture. Marrying outsiders, failure to attend meetings, selling liquor to the Native Americans, and owning slaves were also grounds for expulsion. The resulting discipline carried over to the political sphere and was a factor in the political success of the Quakers.[2]

Still, if Quakers exercised considerable power and influence in Pennsylvania, their policies led in new directions. Belief in religious toleration encouraged a campaign to attract non-Quaker immigrants. The campaign succeeded, and the province became the home of the greatest number of religious and ethnic groups of any province in the British Empire. In the township of Reading, for example, there were Lutherans, Reformed, Anglicans, Quakers, Catholics, Mennonites, Presbyterians, Baptists, and Jews.[3]

The different ethnic and religious groups that poured into Pennsylvania were forced to develop new relationships with one another and with the provincial political institutions. Religious toleration and pacifism prevented heresy from becoming an important weapon and limited the development of state-controlled instruments of coercion.

Although the ability of religious institutions to exercise coercive power was limited, a professional military did not even exist, and public opinion ensured that independence would not change that. During the colonial era, the military was an imperial responsibility; the British assumed colonial support, but Pennsylvania, under Quaker domination, did not comply. Whiggish fears of a professional army also mitigated against a state-supported military, so the sole indigenous military force was the militia. Because the militia was voluntary and the officers were elected, and because unruly elements were recruited, the militia itself was a source of strife, disorder, and violence.[4]

Because the sovereign power resided across the Atlantic, colonial governments lacked a tradition of effective power and legitimate authority. Pennsylvanians had a charter and a frame; they had a government

---

2. Forbes, "Quaker Tribalism," 148.

3. Becker, "Diversity," 197. See also Bonami, "Middle Colonies," 68–71; Butler, "Spiritual Tower"; Rothermund, *Layman's Progress.*

4. Martin and Lender, *Respectable Army,* esp. ch. 2. For attitudes toward the military, see Pocock, "Machiavelli"; and Bailyn, *Ideological Origins,* 36, 48, 61–63, 115–21. For the militia as a destabilizing force, see Foner, *Paine,* 63–66; Alexander, "Fort Wilson"; and the important Rosswurm, *Arms.*

but did not control the state—the British did that. The primary "administrative, legal, extractive and coercive" organizations that governed the empire resided in Britain. Independence seemed to exacerbate the problem. By elevating the people to the sovereign authority, the Constitution of 1776 raised the specter of democracy and, according to the dominant political thought of the day, instability. In the eyes of many observers, the events of the next decade, like the attack on the Bank of North America, confirmed these fears.[5]

Beyond questions of sovereignty and legitimacy, Colonial Pennsylvania, like most of the colonies, lacked effective government, but this issue has been clouded by the strength and effectiveness of the Quaker-dominated Assembly. However, if one shifts attention from the legislature to the delivery of services and the mobilization of community resources, a different picture emerges.

Counties were governed by an astonishingly few men. The most important county officials were a prothonotary, a sheriff, a coroner, three commissioners, six assessors, a treasurer, a recorder of deeds, a registrar of wills, a surveyor, a sealer of weights and measures, and a collector of excise taxes. These eighteen were supplemented by several justices of the peace and a few legal clerks. The counties were subdivided into townships that were serviced by another half-dozen or so officials, including two road supervisors, an assessor, a tax collector, a constable, an overseer of the poor, and an inspector of elections. Each borough also had a number of burgesses, councilmen, and clerks.[6]

The larger villages and towns were incorporated and had their own government, and of these Philadelphia was by far the most important and the most poorly governed. The city was chartered in 1701, and membership in the corporation was limited to freemen—a privilege too expensive for most. Administrative supervision was by committee, and all decisions required action by the full council. There were no full-time officials and only one salaried official: the recorder. All other city officials were paid from the numerous fees they levied.[7]

Fees were ubiquitous because the legislature refused to grant Philadelphia the power to tax, on the grounds that the Corporation was not representative. Without adequate resources, the Corporation was unable to provide even the most rudimentary services. Whether it was

5. Skocpol, "Bringing the State Back," 7–12, 20–22.
6. Bockelman, "Local Government," 224, 226, 216–26.
7. Diamondstone, "Government," 242–46.

the night watch that occasionally preyed on the people they were paid to protect, or poor relief, or the construction and maintenance of city streets, or fire protection—all were equally inadequate.[8]

Faced with an impotent Corporation, citizens turned to the Assembly for relief, and at times the legislature tried to meet their needs. Thus, in 1750 the legislature created the "Wardens of the Watch," an independent, popularly elected body supported by local taxes. Of course, to the extent that community needs were satisfied through Provincial intervention, the power and legitimacy of the Corporation was eroded.[9]

The combination of a virtually absent military, grossly inadequate local police forces, and undermanned administrative agencies meant that the capacity of Provincial authorities to execute policy depended to a significant degree on popular compliance. Nothing in Pennsylvania's history suggested that the situation would change easily.

Given the absence of a powerful and coercive church, military, or state, and given the widespread distribution of the means of production, a European-style, ascriptive class system did not emerge. Most adult males in the countryside owned or rented farms or were self-employed. In the developed agricultural counties of Chester and Lancaster, between 65 and 75 percent of the population owned land. In the frontier counties the pattern was similar: approximately 62 percent were landowners. Not all the rest were economically dependent. Many were sons of property owners, renters of substantial farms, or skilled artisans.[10] Similar patterns prevailed in Philadelphia and in the small towns that dotted the region. In the city, the one-man shop was ubiquitous; approximately one-third of Revolutionary Pennsylvania's residents were artisans who had their own shops. Merchants, shopkeepers, innkeepers, and professionals also had property and skills that gave them some independence.[11]

While considerations of class influenced Pennsylvanians, the widespread distribution of property inevitably affected norms and values. These developments, plus the absence of powerful hierarchical institutions, largely explain the failure of an indigenous aristocracy to emerge.

8. Ibid., 246, 253–56.
9. Ibid., 250–51.
10. Lemon and Nash, "Distribution," 10; Harper, "Class Structure," 38.
11. Warner Jr., *Private City*, 5–7.

Finally, independence ended any possibility that an ascriptive class structure would be imposed from Britain.[12]

Developments in the countryside intensified the weakness of traditional coercive and integrative institutions. Abundant and easily available land, extensive agricultural techniques, the institution of private property, and the relative absence of an Indian threat, coupled with a deeply rooted desire to own land, resulted in a highly dispersed population. The failure of the rural hamlet to become the predominant pattern of settlement further weakened ties to place and magnified the problem of social integration and control.[13]

The fact that European-style institutions and class structures were not replicated in Pennsylvania does not mean that the region lacked a social structure. In fact, as Tom Bottomore put it, every society has "a particular relational structure, . . . exhibits a certain order, a specific interconnectedness of the diverse elements, or spheres, of social life."[14]

Social structures are best thought of as the organizational framework of a society. They are composed of social groups, institutions, associations, and a stratification system. Interactions between the component parts acquire characteristic patterns that help distinguish one social structure from another. Moreover, social structures have boundaries that distinguish them from other social structures.[15]

The configuration of the social structure is determined by the arrangement and relationship of the social units that compose it. The component parts are not autonomous, but must be understood in relation to one another. Functional interdependence and interaction constitute the main integrative elements of the system. Interactions between component parts may be conflictual, as well as benign. For example, capitalist class relations are constituted so that they simultaneously involve both interdependence and conflict.[16]

The key to understanding the social structure in late-eighteenth-century Pennsylvania lies in shifting the analytic focus from coercive and

12. Berthoff and Murrin, "Feudalism."

13. Brown, *Modernization*, ch. 3; Lemon, *Poor Man's Country*, 98–117, 219–20; Lemon, "Spatial Order."

14. Bottomore, "Structure," 159–68, esp. 160; Blau, "Parameters"; Leach, "Social Structure"; Bottomore, *Sociology*, ch. 7; Porpora, "Four Concepts."

15. Smelser, "From Structure," 36.

16. Bottomore, "Structure," 160; Smelser, "From Structure," 35–36; Smelser, "Social Structure," 103–5; Warriner, "Levels," 179–81; Blau, "Structures," 43–46.

ascriptive institutions to a set of personal and intimate groups and associations. Social development in Pennsylvania occurred in an undeveloped colonial frontier with a large land mass and a relatively small Anglo-European-American population. Given the absence of powerful hierarchical institutions as well as bureaucratic and specialized organizations, the result was a strikingly simple social order. In turn, the result of simplicity was that the social groups, institutions, associations, and organizations that did exist took on a heightened importance.[17]

Families and family motives, for example, penetrated and played a role in all the major social groups and institutional spheres. This is true in all societies, but the absence of social alternatives gave Pennsylvania's families a more important role than usual. In the economic sphere, for example, families were the basic unit of production, and consumption and rural exchange networks based on familial reciprocity virtually defined communities. Even merchants, those archetypes of commercial individualism, created networks of kin and friends to buffer themselves from the impersonal marketplace.

Social simplicity shaped the social structure. Its major consequence was the development of new forms of integration. In the countryside, the necessary social glue grew out of the actions of families, ethnic and religious groups, and communities. Despite the pattern of dispersed settlement, people were tied together by bonds of kinship and patterns of reciprocity and neighborliness. In these intimate and personal groupings, people learned how to play, court, marry, parent, work, pray, and participate in the larger community. The fact that work was done in or near the home by and for families and neighbor's families reinforced the integrative powers of the intimate groupings and the exchange networks.

The situation in Philadelphia and in the region's towns was more complex. Inadequate local government caused people to rely on their own resources to an unusual extent. Kinship, religion, ethnicity, and community continued to integrate, but Philadelphians deprived of effective government seized on the voluntary association as a device to solve their particular problems and needs.[18]

Eventually, the city was crisscrossed by networks of clubs and associations, and although we do not yet know when the first rural exchange networks appeared, Philadelphia's first voluntary association

17. Tully, *Penn's Legacy,* 60–63.
18. Diamondstone, "Government," 253–54.

was apparently a club organized by a group of bachelors sometime in the late 1720s. Following this,

> in 1729 Welshmen of the town organized the "Society of Ancient Britons" to observe St. David's Day, promptly precipitating formation of a similar organization of Englishmen to give due honor to St. George's Day. Sportsmen formed themselves into fishing clubs, the first of which was the Colony in Schuylkill. . . . The Colony was complete with governor, sheriff, and even a coroner, at its courthouse on the west bank of the Schuylkill . . . and was famous as the home of Fish House Punch. The prerevolutionary membership included such mayors of the city as Thomas Lawrence, William Plumstead, and Samuel Shoemaker. Having been founded on May 1, 1732, when what were to become the London Clubs were still public coffeehouses, the State in Schuylkill holds claim to being the oldest organized men's club in the English speaking world.[19]

Sociologists describe such organizations as voluntary associations. Nonprofit and nongovernmental, they are created to accomplish certain purposes that, according to sociologists, must be unrelated to making a living. Voluntary associations have formal criteria for membership, explicit leadership roles, stated goals, rules of conduct, and regular meetings. Most of the members are unpaid. Participation is part-time and usually occurs during leisure time. Convivial activities frequently play an important role in the activities of associations.[20]

An important characteristic of voluntary associations is the ability of members to join and quit voluntarily, but in practice this freedom is limited. Philadelphia's fire-fighting clubs restricted their membership to male residents of particular neighborhoods. Club membership was further delimited by class, ethnicity, and religion. Wealthy and prominent men like Thomas Willing, Francis Hopkins, and Dr. Benjamin Rush joined the Hand-in-Hand Fire Company, while shoemakers organized

---

19. Bronner, "Village," 55.

20. Broadly speaking, all nonstate organizations are voluntary associations. Sociological practice is more restrictive—churches, even when not established, and political parties are treated as separate phenomena. See Bottomore, *Sociology,* ch. 6; Hoebel and Frost, *Cultural,* 233–40; Lowie, *Social Organization,* chs. 1, 13; Sills, "Voluntary Associations"; and Smith and Freedman, *Voluntary Associations.* For a historical perspective, see Anderson, "Voluntary Associations."

the Cordwainers Fire Company. Almost the entire membership of the Hibernia Company was Irish, and the members of the Queen Charlotte Company were Lutheran.[21]

Compared with primary institutions, such as family and occupation, formal voluntary associations are of secondary importance. Nevertheless, even though it is not the purpose of voluntary associations to satisfy the basic needs of members, they do enable people to accomplish a great variety of tasks—some, like fire-fighting, of considerable importance. From an organizational standpoint, the great advantage of voluntary associations lies in their flexibility. Sherwood Fox describes them as "interstitial" social mechanisms filling gaps between the major social institutions.[22]

The Hand-in-Hand and Hibernia fire companies illustrate Fox's point. They were shaped by and embedded in social class, ethnicity, and community, and as a result they served a variety of purposes in the mix of ethnic, religious, and occupational groups, in neighborhoods, and in the stratification and institutional systems.[23]

Benjamin Franklin's energy, ambition, and talent played a large role in the development of Philadelphia's network of formal voluntary associations. Franklin is a perfect example of what Eisenstadt calls "institutional entrepreneurs." In 1727, Franklin organized the Junto, first known as the "Leather Apron Club." Some of the dozen members were young artisans, others came from well-to-do families. They met at a tavern on Friday evenings for fellowship, food, beverage, intellectual discourse, and the chance to improve themselves. Meeting in secret, they discussed books and the essays each member was required to write. They also had picnics and once a year held a gala dinner. The Junto became so successful that an increased number of applications threatened to destroy its intimate nature. The solution was to create a number of subordinate clubs under the sponsorship of the original group.[24]

Franklin's energies were not contained by the Junto. In 1730 he suggested that the members pool their books and hold them in common,

21. K. W. Warner, "Conceptual Elements," 72–73; Neilly, "Violent Volunteers," 19–21; Gilbert, "Patterns," 13.

22. K. W. Warner, "Conceptual Elements," 73. For the reference to Sherwood Fox, see Smith and Freedman, *Voluntary Associations,* 3, 136.

23. Smith and Freedman, *Voluntary Associations,* 131.

24. Van Doren, *Franklin,* 73–78; Clark, *Franklin,* 50–52. For the reference to Eisenstadt, see Colomy, "Conclusion," 477–78.

an idea that galvanized the group and struck a responsive chord in the larger community. Fifty citizens agreed to invest in the purchase of new books and committed themselves to annual membership fees for what eventually became the Library Company. The public was permitted to use the collection for rental fees. At first the collection was kept in the Junto's quarters, but this quickly proved inadequate and separate lodgings for the library were found. The idea caught on, and other reading rooms and lending libraries were organized.[25]

That same year, after a fire at Fishburn's wharf threatened to destroy a large portion of the city, a public discussion ensued. Various expedients were experimented with, including the purchase of three fire engines, but none proved satisfactory. The solution involved creating yet another voluntary association. Benjamin Franklin was, of course, involved. He also helped organize the Union Fire Company—in 1736. Its thirty members were volunteers. They purchased their own equipment and met eight times a year for dinner and discussion. At the meetings, minutes were kept and reports were made on the condition of the company's equipment. Fines were levied for missed meetings and other infractions of the constitution. As with the lending library, the idea caught on, and additional fire-fighting companies were organized. The resulting system made Philadelphia the envy of other American cities.[26]

A decade later, in 1747, the organizational principle was applied to the defense of the Quaker province. Mid-century Imperial diplomacy brought England into an alliance with Austria and a war with France. The French threat was real, but the Quaker-dominated Assembly refused to vote money for defense. Again, Franklin seized the initiative and proposed a volunteer force. The resulting militia—or "Association," as it was called—almost immediately enrolled some 10,000 men throughout the province. They provided their own weapons and proceeded to organize themselves into companies that chose their own officers and drilled weekly.[27]

As the organizing principle became familiar, voluntary associations were established for a widening array of purposes. There were convivial groups, such as the Mount Regale Fishing Company; "glutton" clubs like the Beef-Stake Clubbe; a Dancing Assembly, for the city's elite; and three Masonic Lodges. Associations were also formed to provide

25. Van Doren, *Franklin*, 104–6.
26. Ibid., 129–30; Neilly, "Violent Volunteers," 14–17.
27. Van Doren, *Franklin*, 183–88; Clark, *Franklin*, 94–98.

social services and solve social problems. Prominent among these were the private fire companies and several societies that fought crime, like the Association for Southwark for Suppressing Vice and Immorality. Public health was the concern of the Pennsylvania Hospital and the Philadelphia Dispensary for the Medical Relief of the Poor, which focused on inoculating the poor against smallpox. Other associations included the Magdalen Society, the Philadelphia Society for Alleviating the Miseries of Public Prisons, and the Abolition Society and its companion organization, the Committee for Improving the Condition of Free Blacks.[28]

A substantial number of voluntary associations concerned themselves with the plight of immigrants. The first such society to be established, in America, was Philadelphia's Society of Ancient Bretons, which was created in 1729 to aid needy Welsh immigrants. Others imitated them. In 1749 the Saint Andrew's Society of Philadelphia was founded to help needy Scots, while the Irish organized the Hibernian Club in 1759 and the Friendly Sons of Saint Patrick in 1771. Not to be outdone, the English organized the Society of the Sons of Saint George in 1772 to help "Englishmen in Distress."[29]

Among the most ambitious and effective of the immigrant aid associations was the German Society of Philadelphia (1764), which was formed to lobby for legislation to improve conditions on board vessels engaged in carrying immigrants. The society also involved itself in providing food, clothing, and money to destitute German immigrants. They also aided Germans who were serving indentures, and offered legal assistance and schooling to adults and children, especially orphans.[30]

Charity was offered by an even larger variety of associations. Various "friendly" societies, most founded in the decade before the Revolution, such as Saint Andrew's Society, the Society of the Sons of Saint George, the Gentlemen of the British Society, the French Society, the Sons of Saint Tammany, the Friendly Sons of Saint Patrick, the German Society, and the Saint Thomas African Church offered aid to the impoverished

28. Alexander, *Render Them*, 67–71, 81, 132, 135, 137; Baltzell, *Puritan Boston*, 152–53 (table 10.1, "The Founding of Philadelphia Institutions in the Age of Franklin"), 162–65, 169–71; Bridenbaugh and Bridenbaugh, *Rebels*, 22–25, 86–92, 183–84, 136–252, 322, 334–39; Cabeen, "Sons of Saint Tammany," 10–22, 339–40; Geib, "History of Philadelphia," 40–42, 220–25; Gilbert, "Patterns," 9–15, 17, 23; Neilly, "Violent Volunteers," 15–22; Scharf and Westcott, *History*, 2:1092, 1464–67.

29. Risch, "Immigrant Aid," 15–18; Alexander, *Render Them*, 125, 136–37, 144; Bridenbaugh and Bridenbaugh, *Rebels*, 238.

30. Risch, "Immigrant Aid," 18–21, 23, 25–28.

of their nationalities. Religious groups also operated extensive relief programs for the poor. Quakers established an Almshouse in 1704, the Bettering House in 1766, and the Philadelphia Society for the Relief of Distressed Prisoners in 1776. Moravians and the Episcopalians were active as well. Occupational groups organized voluntary associations, such as the Society for the Relief of Poor Decayed Masters of Ship Carpenters, which provided charity for their own needy. Episcopal ministers, pilots, printers, stonecutters, barbers, and bricklayers also organized societies to provide relief to impoverished members and their families.[31]

The American Philosophical Society, the Philadelphia Society for the Promotion of Agriculture and Agricultural Reform, the Moravian Collegium Musicum, the Orpheus Club, and the several lending libraries provided arenas and stimulation for intellectual and cultural activity for adults. The College of Philadelphia, Quakers, Episcopalians, the African Methodist Episcopal Church, and the German Society were among the many groups to form associations to educate needy children.[32]

The need for Pennsylvania's families and communities to solve problems with local resources, and the pervasiveness and importance of patterns of reciprocity, combined with the absence of powerful hierarchical institutions to make voluntary associations extraordinarily useful organizational devices serving an almost unlimited number of purposes. At the same time, their effectiveness in mobilizing the population was simply astonishing. The greatest testament to their organizational capacity can be seen in the fact that during the Revolutionary era the total membership of Philadelphia's political clubs was roughly equal to the number of voters.[33]

While voluntary associations were primarily an urban phenomenon, the price-fixing campaign of 1779 provides an example of rural adaptation of voluntary associations. In 1779, military exigency, inflation, and food shortages created a crisis. Congress and the state governments faced the impossible choice of taxing or fixing prices. Their first response, naturally, was hesitation. Exploding with frustration, Philadelphia's popular forces seized the moment and created a committee to regulate prices. Philadelphia, Chester, and Lancaster counties rapidly followed their example, as did the towns of Reading and York. The movement

31. Alexander, *Render Them*, ch. 7.

32. Ibid., ch. 8; Bridenbaugh and Bridenbaugh, *Rebels*, 156, 334–39; Ellsworth, "Philadelphia Society."

33. Geib, "History of Philadelphia," 220.

spread beyond the boundaries of Pennsylvania, only to fail almost as rapidly as it had begun. The important point in this context, however, is the applicability of the voluntary association to areas outside of Philadelphia.[34]

Thus, Pennsylvanians responded creatively to the absence of clearly defined, powerful hierarchical and integrative institutions. Need, convenience, and inclination spawned numbers of loosely organized part-time groups for a variety of purposes. The resulting combination of voluntary associations and informal groupings was a unique integrative system I shall call the "associational system." The key to the system was the willingness of the population to join together in informal clubs for a variety of purposes. Popularized by their flexibility and legitimated by deeply rooted participatory norms, the system proved to be an extraordinarily successful way to mobilize the population.[35]

The success of the associational system in Pennsylvania is not surprising. As Alan Tully reminds us, Pennsylvanians "accepted the premise that individuals and families should have the widest possible choice of building up personal associations and should be able to choose whether, or in what degree, they would participate in larger community activities."[36]

Politics in Revolutionary Pennsylvania offers an instructive illustration of the associational system in operation. The 1770s saw the adoption and spread of the extralegal committees of correspondence. According to Charles Thomson, the ability of the New England towns to communicate, because of the committees, was so obvious that the expedient was copied—first in Philadelphia, then in the towns, and finally in many rural districts. Where population density allowed, as in Philadelphia, each ward had a committee and a representative on the citywide central committee. Over time, organizational skills improved. News was able to travel astonishingly fast, and, Thomson noted approvingly, the system was paid for by the people involved.[37]

The main virtue of the committees was their ability to mobilize

34. Buell Jr., "Committee Movement of 1779," 154–59; Foner, *Paine*, 158–78.
35. For discussions of voluntary associations in the larger context of American history, see G. Nash, "Social Evolution," esp. 138–42; Schlesinger, *Paths*, ch. 2; Brown, "Emergence"; Boylan, "Woman in Groups"; and Singleton, "Protestant Voluntary Associations."
36. Tully, *Penn's Legacy*, 63.
37. Ammerman, *Common Cause*, ch. 8, esp. 104–5; Brunhouse, *Counter-Revolution*, 19, 28; Col. Andrew Boyd to Col. James Young, 29 December 1779, *PA*, 2d ser., 3:340; Charles Thomson to Dr. David Ramsay, 4 November 1786, "Thomson Papers," 218–19; Ryerson, "Political Mobilization."

and channel popular support. Richard Alan Ryerson, historian of the Philadelphia committees, notes:

> [The committees] had no significant professional politicians, almost no treasury, and only insignificant civil service and public contract resources. . . . [T]he resistance committee system was oriented toward mass politics; its representation was by neighborhood or ward, by ethnic-religious group, by occupation, and by relative economic standing. On each index it was radically inclusive by the standards of its day. In just three years, from the tea affair to Independence, Philadelphia's committee movement broadened the leadership base of the city's politics by a factor of several times, thereby generating an intense identification with the cause of the resistance among heretofore ignored nationalities, creeds, and occupational classes.[38]

The committee system also proved to be superbly flexible. Clubs were easy to organize and could serve virtually any administrative function. For example, committees of correspondence set prices, encouraged manufacturing, inspected customs houses, questioned suspected Tories, enforced an embargo, regulated morals, and at various times engaged in or forbade the use of violence. After the provincial government collapsed in 1776, the committees virtually ran Pennsylvania.[39]

Other techniques designed to mobilize and manage people were grafted onto the associational system. Circular letters were sent through associational channels. In 1764, for instance, the convention of Presbyterian ministers and elders meeting in Philadelphia wrote to every Presbyterian congregation in the province and recommended union. Organizers were also sent out, frequently pretending that they were on pleasure trips or traveling to gather information. Petition campaigns became an important political technique. Often involving thousands of signatures, petitions came to be important in the political campaigns to make the province a royal colony, to change the Constitution of 1776, to repeal the Test Acts, and to remove and to reinstate the charter of the Bank of North America. And public gatherings were used to

---

38. Ryerson, *Revolution*, 250.
39. Ammerman, *Common Cause*, 110–24; Ryerson, "Political Mobilization," 582; Schlesinger, *Colonial Merchants*, 498–502, 586–87. Once the committee system was understood, it was widely adopted. Foner's discussion of price-fixing in 1779 nicely illustrates the process; see Foner, *Paine*, 168–69.

generate and channel mass support. Christopher Marshall's diary recounts the striking frequency with which town meetings were called in the early 1770s. Before the end of the next decade the Harrisburg Convention and the Federal Procession (celebrating the adoption of the new national constitution) signaled the addition of conventions and parades to the tactical arsenal of political activists.[40]

To these organizational techniques Pennsylvanians added improvements in the print media that amplified the integrative potentials of the associational system. This development has been clearly described by historians, and any student of the eighteenth century soon becomes aware of the importance of the broadsides, books, pamphlets, and newspapers that poured off the Philadelphia presses. In 1776 the city boasted of seven newspapers. A paper was published every day of the week except Wednesday and Sunday in editions that ranged from 500 to 3,000. While these numbers may seem small, Philadelphia's output accounted for approximately one-seventh of the entire American output. By the time Tom Paine was working in local printing houses, the media bore more than a faint resemblance to that of the modern era.[41]

The associational system was impressively flexible. Each organizational nexus within the social system provided a point at which the associational system might be brought into play. Religious and ethnic groups, for example, utilized the network to further their interests. In the early years of the colony the Quakers constituted a majority and almost completely dominated the political life of the province. At that time "the lines dividing the secular government . . . from the Quaker meeting structure were often obscure and at times nonexistent." When the Friends became a minority, the relationship between the meeting structure and the government changed. The Yearly Meeting, which met one week before the election for the Assembly, began to function as a caucus deciding political strategy and picking candidates. When the

40. For circular letters, see Samuel Purviance Jr. to Col. Burd, 20 September 1765, in Balch, ed., *Letters and Papers*, 208–10; Benjamin Rush to ———, 10 November 1784, in Butterfield, ed., *Letters of Rush*, 1:340. For organizers, see Brunhouse, *Counter-Revolution*, 19, 89, 192; Duane, ed., *Christopher Marshall*, 98–99; Foner, *Paine*, 168–69. For the petition campaigns, see Brunhouse, *Counter-Revolution*, 31, 58–59, 164, 174, 182, 212; Hutson, *Politics*, 124–29, 133–34, 167–68. For public meetings, see Brunhouse, *Counter-Revolution*, 6, 18–19, 31, 213–15; Duane, ed., *Christopher Marshall*, 5–8, 98–101, 218–22; Hutson, *Politics*, 126; Sellers, *Peale*, 170. And for conventions and parades, see Brunhouse, *Counter-Revolution*, 213–15; Bell Jr., "Federal Procession."

41. Bridenbaugh, "Press and Book"; Bridenbaugh and Bridenbaugh, *Rebels*, 72–79; Foner, *Paine*, ch. 3; Hutson, *Politics*, 124–27, 132–33; G. Nash, "Transformation," 616–19.

specter of war posed a real threat to Quaker rule and principles, the Yearly Meeting was unable to deal with the situation. In the crisis, a special standing committee was created.[42]

Among Presbyterians the process and structure of political involvement was different. The Indian conflicts of the 1750s and 1760s generated political activism among the Scots-Irish and aligned them actively against the Quakers. The Presbyterian church played a leading role in this process. Synod and church meeting proved to be superb organizational "sites" for political activity. Circular letters passed between congregations, and pulpits were used as political platforms.[43]

The associational system also served as a convenient vehicle to further class interests. Artisans, for example, traditionally deferred to their betters and played a passive political role. During the politicized 1770s they were caught up in the political ferment and recruited into the extralegal revolutionary committee system. In 1770 they created a standing Mechanics Committee and held the first public meeting restricted to themselves. Two years later, master craftsmen formed a "permanent" political club, the Patriotic Society. Calls for creating an independent artisan's electoral ticket appeared for several years until 1784, when the "Mechanical Society" for craftsmen was organized to defend the Constitution of 1776.[44]

So pervasive and successful were voluntary associations that when nonvoluntary institutions were politicized they adopted the techniques and tactics of the associational system to produce and mobilize support and press political demands. Thus, militia meetings provided an opportunity for political action. At times entire battalions would meet, discuss issues, vote on resolutions, and appeal to other battalions to follow their example. The militia also held public meetings and formulated demands. In the early stages of the war, the officers led and the rank and file followed. On at least one occasion a battalion was instructed by its officers on how to vote, marched en masse to the polling place, given ballots, and one by one released to vote. For many, such as the Germans and those from the lowest economic rank, the militia "served

42. Bauman, *Reputation*, 1, 65–69; G. Nash, "Transformation," 614–15.

43. Samuel Purviance Jr. to Col. Burd, 20 September 1765, in Balch, ed., *Letters and Papers*, 208–10; Hutson, *Politics*, 96–103, 155; Thayer, *Pennsylvania Politics*, 41–42, 100–101, 118–20.

44. Ammerman, *Common Cause*, 115; Foner, *Paine*, 61–63; Olton, "Philadelphia Artisans," 127, 286–87, 309–14; Olton, "Philadelphia Mechanics," 321–22; Schlesinger, *Colonial Merchants*, 280, 351; Thayer, *Pennsylvania Politics*, 149–51.

as a school of politics." Eventually, privates followed the example of their officers. A Committee of Privates composed of two men from each company was organized, and demanded the right to elect their officers, the right to vote, and either universal service or much severer penalties for those not serving. Later they agitated for price-fixing and the banishment of Tories (men, women, and children). They staged a number of demonstrations, including marches on the Assembly and the ill-starred "parade" past James Wilson's home in 1779, which resulted in bloodshed.[45]

Patterns of multiple membership increased the flexibility and effectiveness of the associational system. An individual might belong to the Constitutional Society, the Whig Association, the Sons of Tammany, the militia, the Presbyterian church, a fire-fighting company, a library, and a music or dancing society. When the organizational flexibility of the voluntary associations was combined with the pattern of multiple memberships and the mobilization techniques of the day, the result was the associational system and its extremely powerful integrative and mobilization potential.

Emerging in the second third of the eighteenth century, the associational system was produced by the confluence of a number of historical, cultural, and demographic developments. The colonial heritage and the struggle for independence, weak and often inadequate government, the Quaker presence and influence, religious and ethnic pluralism, and low population density, coupled with patterns of geographic mobility and the widespread possession of private property and the means of production, all contributed to the emergence, spread, and success of the associational system. At the same time, the absence of European-style hierarchical institutions—state, church, military, and bureaucracy—and the resulting weakness of the upper class enabled the associational system to fill the vacuum and become an important element in the social structure.

The associational system had an impact on every social group and institution. Appearing as networks of loosely articulated, part-time nongovernmental associations, clubs, and informal groupings, the system derived much of its power from the pervasive communitarian ethos, which encouraged participation. The fact that it was not tightly

45. J. K. Alexander, "Fort Wilson"; Brunhouse, *Counter-Revolution,* 105–6, 135–39; Foner, *Paine,* 63–66; Main, *Political Parties,* 184; Peale, "Autobiography," 68–76; *Pa. Packet,* 31 May and 12 June 1783; Sellers, *Peale,* 172–80; Thayer, *Pennsylvania Politics,* 183.

articulated meant that it was permeable to the influence of social classes, groups, and individuals. Circumstances and need, therefore, determined the usage, function, and the character of the system.

Historically, voluntary associations have played an important role in tribal societies. As large, complex traditional societies with urban centers and powerful states emerged, they declined in importance, only to reappear in the modern world, especially where they are encouraged by the state and permitted by the upper class.[46]

Only in America (outside the South) does the associational system appear to have played so important a role in the period before the modern epoch. James Shultz describes an ideal typical "voluntary society" as one that "achieves a high degree of integration, but which does this with a minimal reliance on force and money as organizing principles." Given the importance of rural dependency networks and patterns of reciprocity and the urban and rural voluntary associations, it is not farfetched to portray post-Revolutionary Pennsylvania as a "voluntary society."[47]

As is always the case, social forms like voluntary associations and bureaucracies carry along with them what Weber called elective affinities—norms and ideas that are "appropriate" to the particular social form. Weber developed the concept to help him explore the link between ideas and material reality. The concept of elective affinities, then, was designed to aid in the exploration of the process in which ideas and social groups or organizational forms "seek each other out." In late-eighteenth-century Pennsylvania the link between voluntary associations and broader social structure and culture must be sought in the fact that the associational system cut across class, religious, and ethnic lines, and in the fact that it encouraged participation, egalitarianism, and a sense of self-reliance. It should come as no surprise that the associational system should blossom in the relatively democratic and decentralized social environment of the Quaker province.[48]

As a new and more powerful state began to emerge in the 1780s, and as the Bank of North America was established, a different kind of political conflict came to Pennsylvania. This battle would involve conflict between the values and norms associated with different kinds of social forms, as well as ethnic, class, and ideological interests. America's first

46. Anderson, "Voluntary Associations."

47. Shultz, "Voluntary Society," 25.

48. Gerth and Mills, eds. and trans., *From Max Weber*, 62–63; Berger and Berger, *Sociology*, 35, 94–95.

bank war would be fought in a social environment in which voluntary associations played a prominent role in mobilizing and shaping political discourse and action. In fact, voluntary associations became the organizational basis for the first modern party system to appear in America.

4

Politics, Conflict, and Parties

Unlike the economy and the social structure, Pennsylvania's polity was an interesting mix of modern and traditional forms and behavioral patterns. In the crucible of revolt, deference waned. The revolutionary decades saw the emergence of a public that was politically aware and eager to exercise the rights of citizenship. The major institutional innovation of the era was the development of a party system. Parties played an important role in channeling and motivating the actions of the public. While parties injected a modern quality to the politics of the era, the existing mode of political organization was not modern. The associational system, with its loosely organized, unspecialized, and small-scale organizational mode and norms, defined the larger organizational environment within which the parties operated.

War and independence posed the major problems. The need to create and support an army meant that taxes and debts would become political hurdles. Because Pennsylvania was a major battleground, the regional economy was disrupted. Food shortages and hard times made matters worse. Independence, the British occupation of Philadelphia, and the presence of substantial numbers of Tories and Neutrals made it inevitable that loyalty would become a serious problem. Finally, because it touched on the legitimacy of the Revolution, the Constitution of 1776 became the central political issue of the era.

At the same time, the colonial heritage continued to affect political behavior. The eighteenth century saw the rise of the Quaker party. They controlled the province by the 1730s, and along with their allies the party was in power, with brief exceptions, until the Revolution. The Quaker party had a definable organizational structure, continuity of leadership, a loyal constituency, and a set of popular issues. They successfully implemented William Penn's vision of religious and political freedom and protected property rights against proprietary encroachment. The party's insistence on the Assembly's right to control taxes and the importance of keeping the voluntary militia also generated support. Quaker domination was furthered by their refusal to grant equal representation to western counties—in 1770, the eastern counties had twenty-four representatives, while the equally populated west had only ten. The strength of the Quaker party, however, did not enable it to survive the turmoil of the Revolution.[1]

Several factors account for the demise of the Quaker party in 1776. First, by 1750 the Quakers and their Anglican allies had become a numerical minority. Second, the party's relations with the west had always been uncomfortable; differences over representation and defense had exacerbated east-west relations. Still, if tensions existed, westerners saw the Quaker party as a bulwark against the proprietor and enthusiastically supported such Quaker policies as the loan office. Aware of their problems, the Quakers acceded to defense expenditures and in 1771–73 created three new western counties. Still, the potential for disaster existed and in the tumultuous days of the revolt it was realized. The Quakers blundered at the wrong time. Their campaign to have the colony taken over by the Crown in 1764 revealed how out of touch the party was with popular opinion. The party recovered, but did not learn the necessary lesson. When they opted for loyalism in the Revolutionary crisis, the Quaker party died.[2]

In the Revolutionary crisis, Scots-Irish and Germans joined with Whigs and radicals. Many of the radicals, like James Cannon and Tom Paine, had ties to the Committee of Privates. Moved by hope and animus, they had recognized the moment for what it was and used it. In

1. Tully, "Quaker Party," 75, 77–85; Ryerson, "Portrait," 107–8; Tully, "Ethnicity," 493–94, 527–29; W. Adams, *First Constitutions*, 43–44, 77–79.

2. Tully, "Quaker Party," 87–90, 99–104; Tully, "Ethnicity," 527–29; Ryerson, "Portrait," 132–34.

a real sense the Revolution was theirs. Scars from Indian wars and unequal representation combined with ancient grudges against England, Republican fervor, and class grievances to create revolutionary militants. They believed in God, Republican virtue, and equality, and they saw the world starkly, fearing traitors and British arms. In the crisis, they directed their animus against the old elite, whom they saw as selfish and anti-Republican.[3]

In power, the radicals wrote a new constitution. The Constitution of 1776 proved to be the most controversial frame of the Revolutionary era. While other states weakened the executive branch, Pennsylvania went the furthest. The governor was replaced by a Supreme Executive Council of twelve that did not have a veto. The judicial branch was also weakened; judges were appointed for seven years but could be removed by the General Assembly for "misbehavior." The unicameral Assembly of the colonial Frame of 1701 was retained, and its powers were increased. The Assembly was elected annually by a broad electorate, which included all free adult male taxpayers and the sons of freeholders (although loyalty oaths posed the possibility that many would be disenfranchised). Moreover, each county's representation in the Assembly would be equal until two years later, when a complete list of all taxable citizens would be completed and proportional representation would go into effect.[4]

The Constitution of 1776 did more than redress old wrongs. By giving equal representation to all counties, if only for two years, it underrepresented the older and more densely populated eastern counties and shifted power westward. The loyalty oath also disfranchised citizens. Members of the old elite and moderate Whigs were outraged. Almost all of the other state constitutions embraced the ideas of a mixed government and a balanced constitution, but the radicals marched to a different tune. They constructed a constitution built on the idea that legitimate power was derived from the people. Although the idea was widely held, Pennsylvania radicals applied it more systematically than most. Because America had no aristocracy, they insisted that bicameral legislatures and independent governors were dangerous expressions of distinction and privilege.[5]

3. Bockelman and Ireland, "Internal Revolution"; Ryerson, "Republican Theory," 103–7, 118–29; Hawke, *Midst*, ch. 9. The best study of ethnic tensions in Pennsylvania is Ireland, "Ratification."

4. "Constitution of Pennsylvania, 1776," 233, 221–39.

5. Wood, *Creation*, 229–31.

The democratic ethos that pervades the Constitution of 1776 can be seen in the omnipotent unicameral legislature, the broadened electorate, the principle of rotation in office, and the assumption that the people should oversee the legislative process. Section 15 provided that a proposed bill must be published so the people could consider it. Not until the *next* legislative session could the Assembly vote on the bill.[6]

More than political equality was involved. The men who wrote the Constitution were extremely conscious of the importance of the socioeconomic aspects of democracy. Section 35 of the Constitution insisted that public officials were entitled to a "reasonable compensation."

> As every freeman to preserve his independence, (if without a sufficient estate) ought to have some profession, calling trade or farm, whereby he may honestly subsist, there can be no necessity for, nor use in establishing offices of profit, the usual effects of which are dependence and servility unbecoming freemen, in the possessors and expectants; faction, contention, corruption, and disorder among the people.[7]

Conflict over the Constitution of 1776 surfaced almost immediately. When the Constitutional Convention submitted a draft of the proposed constitution to the public in the fall of 1776, an outcry was raised about the weakness of the governor and the absence of a second legislative chamber. The lack of an independent judiciary and the loyalty oath required of voters and elected officials were also criticized. Defenders of the Constitution insisted that the convention had acted legally and that the war required a quick end to the bickering.[8]

But the conflict never ended. As Gordon Wood says, during the political strife in the next decade "over the test oaths, the College of Philadelphia, the Bank of North America, the incorporation of Philadelphia":

> the future of the radical Constitution of 1776 remained a basic issue. However much the antagonists . . . may have temporarily shifted tactics and accepted or abused the Constitution for their

---

6. Ibid., 86–87, 229–33; "Constitution of Pennsylvania, 1776," 230–31.
7. "Constitution of Pennsylvania, 1776," 236.
8. Shaeffer, "Public Consideration"; Arnold, "Political Ideology," 80–98.

partisan purposes, the ultimate worth and durability of the Constitution was never long lost from debate.[9]

During this strife a two-party system emerged. The years 1775 to 1779 were years of formation. Other issues and factors were important in the creation of the parties, but the new constitution was central. Although party labels did not come into formal use until the spring of 1779 when the Republican and Constitutional societies were created, for the sake of convenience supporters of the Constitution will be identified as Constitutionalists and the opponents will be called Republicans.[10]

When the first Assembly convened in the fall of 1776, opponents of the new frame tried to bring the government down. They insisted that another constitutional convention be called, and when the majority refused, a number of assemblymen resigned. Opponents turned down appointments in the militia, seats on the bench, and administrative posts, and some officials refused to give up colonial records to the new administration. As if these problems were not serious enough, a taxpayer revolt was brewing, Tories and Neutrals were numerous and active, and British forces threatened to overrun the region.[11]

Government officials were frightened. Letters to Vice-President George Bryan reveal the depth of this concern. Archibald McClean described the situation in York as "deplorable" and worried that preparations for the election were not being made. The sheriff was doing nothing, and the election of inspectors "is not advertised nor attended to: we have no Constables who will take the Oath to qualify them to serve." Should the elections occur, the correspondent feared that less than one-fifth of the voters would participate. All the local notables were vehemently opposed to the new frame. "Under all these discouragements," complained McClean, "with what heart can a few raw and unexperienced Persons proceed?"[12]

At this juncture the British military threatened Philadelphia. The Assembly was not in session, and the Executive Council was immobi-

9. Wood, *Creation*, 438.

10. Ryerson, "Republican Theory," 97 n. 2; Arnold, "Political Ideology," 59–60.

11. Arnold, "Political Ideology," 69–80; Brunhouse, *Counter-Revolution*, 18–38; Hindle, *Rittenhouse*, 167–92; Rowe, "McKean," 113–16.

12. Alexander McDowel to V.P. Bryan, York, 1 June 1777, *PA*, 1st ser. 6:572; Archibald McClean to V.P. Bryan, York, 3 September 1777, in ibid., 5:575–77; Archibald McClean to V.P. Bryan, York, 11 October 1777, in ibid., 5:661–62; Rosswurm, *Arms*, 138–40.

lized when many of its members fled. Congress was forced to intervene and issue orders to the council. The invasion did not materialize, but the regime was badly embarrassed.[13]

When the legislature reconvened it was met by a "Proposal" demanding a new constitutional convention. Shaken by the failure to collect taxes, supporters of the new government, such as David Rittenhouse, backed the call for a new convention. The Assembly capitulated and issued instructions for another referendum. At this moment the feared invasion occurred, and this time the government rose to the occasion. Opponents realized that this was no time to carry on as if the situation were normal. Edward Biddle, who believed that the Constitution was "lamentably defective," expressed the new mood when he wrote: "There is a time when the manifest errors of a people must be submitted to, in order to take the proper advantage for rectifying these errors. Such I take to be our present situation." Despite the victory of Constitutionalist forces in the fall elections, the Assembly proceeded with the referendum on the new constitution.[14]

To save the Constitution, supporters launched a petition campaign and collected 14,000 signatures. Faced with this impressive show of strength, the legislature did what it wanted to: it aborted the plan for a new convention. For the moment, Republican hopes were crushed.[15]

British arms did more than thwart Republican hopes—they paved the way for several years of revolutionary violence and coercion. Worried about the large number of Tories and Neutrals, the Constitutional Convention of 1776 had required a loyalty oath, which divided the ranks of the Whigs. When the state was faced with a British invasion in the summer of 1777, a second and more stringent oath was imposed. All white males over the age of eighteen had to pledge allegiance to the state of Pennsylvania and reject the king. Refusal meant they would lose the right to bear arms, hold appointive office, vote and run for office, serve on juries, sue, and buy, sell, or transfer land. Moved by military exigency and fear, even Republicans supported the measure.[16]

13. Brunhouse, *Counter-Revolution*, 22–23; Hindle, *Rittenhouse*, 179–81.

14. Arnold, "Political Ideology," 76–77; Brunhouse, *Counter-Revolution*, 23–24, 30–33, 46, 57; Hindle, *Rittenhouse*, 181–87, 192, 203–4; Ireland, "Ethnic-Religious," 426. For the quotation from Edward Biddle, see Rowe, "McKean," 119.

15. Brunhouse, *Counter-Revolution*, 58–60; Duane, ed., *Christopher Marshall*, 210–11.

16. Violence is used here in its broadest sense, to encompass legal and illegal coercive actions. Arnold, "Political Ideology," 100–119; Brunhouse, *Counter-Revolution*, 16–17, 40–41; Ireland, "Ethnic-Religious Dimension," 429–30.

Toward the end of the summer, lists of suspected Tories were published, and some were arrested and jailed. After the invasion, pressure built up for even more repressive measures. The Assembly declared that those who were unwilling to take the oath would have to pay a double tax and lose more of their rights, including the use of the courts and such legal instruments as wills and the freedom to earn a living as a merchant or professional. When the British evacuated the state, the government was further burdened with the problem of dealing with the large number of Philadelphians who had cooperated with the enemy. Arrests were made and twenty were tried. Only two unimportant individuals were convicted and sentenced. Militants were enraged and violence flared.[17]

Republicans were appalled: law and order seemed to be collapsing. They appealed for tolerance and a relaxation of the Test Acts but the Constitutionalists sensed a political issue and, according to Owen Ireland, suggested that "opposition to the constitution was one of the principal reasons for refusal to take the loyalty oath." The Assembly asserted that those who did not take the oath by December 1779 would be barred from politics forever. By the end of the year, the purpose of the tests had been changed from shoring up security to banning those suspected of disloyalty from politics, and in the process loyalty had become an important political issue.[18]

Because the tests created a cycle of persecution and vengeance and removed large numbers of citizens from the body politic, the tests came to rival the Constitution of 1776 in political importance. With the onset of peace and the reduction of constraints on voters, turnouts increased. The new voters increasingly responded to Republican appeals and became part of the coalition that eventually buried the Constitutionalists.[19]

In addition to the Constitution and loyalty, economic problems proved to be the most troublesome. Confiscations, personnel shortages, poor harvests, and the breakdown of trade resulted in shortages and inflation. By the end of 1779, prices were seven times higher than they had been two years earlier. The winter of 1779 was grim. The prices of corn,

17. Brunhouse, *Counter-Revolution,* 42–43, 50; Geib, "History of Philadelphia," 137–41; Ireland, "Ethnic-Religious Dimension," 430–32; Rosswurm, *Arms,* 155–58; Foster, *In Pursuit,* 92.

18. Arnold, "Political Ideology," 108–9; Ireland, "Ethnic-Religious Dimension," 431–32.

19. Owen Ireland has done more than any other scholar to alert us to the importance of the tests. See Ireland, *Religion, Ethnicity, and Politics.*

wheat, and flour rose at a frightening pace, and hunger became a serious problem in urban areas.[20]

Everyone was unhappy about inflation, but that was the extent of the consensus. Republicans blamed the war, paper money, and legal tender laws and advocated free trade and an end to paper money. The more popular position, adopted by the Constitutionalists, was rooted in the old English tradition of "moral economy," which advocated regulation for the general welfare. They blamed profiteers: Tories, hoarders, middlemen, and the wealthy. To counter the disastrous rise in prices, the Constitutionalists advocated price-fixing, regulation of commerce, and vigorous action against profiteering.[21]

The situation was explosive: People were mobilized, and in the militia they had an institution to act through. In the spring of 1779 the issue was joined. The First Company of the Philadelphia Militia Artillery petitioned the Executive Council. In an angry message, they pointed out that each time they had been called to serve they returned to find their families "at the mercy of the disaffected, Inimical, or self Interested." They were also angry because the "rich and the 'disaffected' were escaping military service." Referring to abuses they had suffered in the past, the militia warned: "We had Arms in our hands, and know the use of them." No one mistook the threat.[22]

The Constitutional Society quickly organized a public rally and as the day of the meeting approached "threatening" handbills appeared. When one man tried to pull down a poster, he was seized by the militia, paraded about town, and jailed. On the day of the rally, the Germantown militia marched into Philadelphia and joined their urban allies. Groups of armed men forced shopkeepers to lower their prices.[23]

At the rally, the Constitutionalists proposed a schedule for lowering prices and the creation of two committees: one to supervise price reductions and one to investigate Robert Morris, who was accused of

20. Arnold, "Political Ideology," 125–26; Foner, *Paine,* 161–62; Geib, "History of Philadelphia," 91–95; Rosswurm, *Arms,* 166–71.

21. Arnold, "Political Ideology," 130–39; Baumann, "Democratic-Republicans," 34; Foner, *Paine,* 146–48, 162–65; Geib, "History of Philadelphia," 95; Thompson, "Moral Economy"; J. K. Alexander, "Fort Wilson," 593–94; Foner, *Paine,* 165; Rosswurm, *Arms,* 194–99. Rosswurm's is the best modern study of both the militia and the Fort Wilson affair.

22. For the militia's petition, see J. K. Alexander, "Fort Wilson," 593–95. See also Brunhouse, *Counter-Revolution,* 69; Foner, *Paine,* 165.

23. J. K. Alexander, "Fort Wilson," 595–96; Brunhouse, *Counter-Revolution,* 69–71; Geib, "History of Philadelphia," 99–102; Hindle, *Rittenhouse,* 205; Warner Jr., *Private City,* 36–37; Foster, *In Pursuit,* 152–53.

monopolizing food. Tom Paine, Charles W. Peale, Timothy Matlack, David Rittenhouse, and other well-known Constitutionalists dominated the committees. After the rally thousands of people marched to the river, calling for bread. Three accused of raising prices were jailed.[24]

Tensions subsided as the committees got to work. They set prices on thirty-two items and tried to prevent the export of foodstuffs. They questioned merchants and distributed bread and flour to the needy, but despite these efforts inflation continued unabated. Resistance to price-fixing intensified, and tempers flared again. In mid-summer a group of artisans protested the schedule of prices set for their trade, and in September eighty merchants argued that the regulations were against the "laws of property." Even members of the price-fixing committee, such as Tom Paine, came to believe that controls were impractical, and at the end of September operations were suspended.[25]

The response was sobering. The militia met and called for action against Tories. Captain Charles Willson Peale was asked to lead them, but he refused and tried unsuccessfully to quash the whole idea. The militia proceeded to reconstitute the Committee of Privates, and the committee announced a mass meeting of all militiamen to be held at Burn's Tavern on the morning of October 4. Radical officers like Peale, Colonel John Bull, Major Alexander Boyd, and Dr. James Hutchinson were invited; Colonel Bull was ill, but the others attended. Again, Constitutionalist activists refused to lead the militia and tried to quell the protest, and again, despite the rebuff, the militia acted.[26]

That afternoon the militia seized four men identified as Tories and ransacked a house in an unsuccessful search for a fifth. The captives were paraded around town escorted by the sound of drums beating the Rogue's March, during which General Thomas Mifflin, a Republican, spoke to their leader, Captain Ephrain Faulkner, and warned him that force would be used against the militia if they threatened James Wilson. In the course of the conversation, Matlock was "struck or pushed" with a musket. Another bystander spoke to the men about the rumor that they intended to attack the house of James Wilson, a prominent Republi-

24. J. K. Alexander, "Fort Wilson," 595–97; Foner, *Paine*, 164–68; Geib, "History of Philadelphia," 99–113; Hindle, *Rittenhouse*, 205–10; Warner Jr., *Private City*, 36–37. Paine was probably concerned about the lower prices artisans were getting.

25. J. K. Alexander, "Fort Wilson," 600–603; Brunhouse, *Counter-Revolution*, 75–76; Foner, *Paine*, 176–78; Peale, "Autobiography," 72–73; Rosswurm, *Arms*, 196–99, 209.

26. J. K. Alexander, "Fort Wilson," 600–602; Rosswurm, *Arms*, 209–11; Peale, "Autobiography," 73–74.

can lawyer who had defended Tories. He was told: "They had no intention to meddle with Mr. Wilson or his house, their object was to support the constitution, the laws, and the Committee of Trade."[27]

The marchers gave three cheers as they passed Wilson's house, where a number of armed "gentlemen" had gathered to protect their friend. We still do not know what happened, but as the parade proceeded past the house a shot rang out and a battle ensued. Several attempts to force the house were made before President Reed, Timothy Matlack, and two more men on horseback arrived. They were followed shortly by two full companies of horsemen. Order was quickly restored, and as the militia were taken to jail the authorities found themselves insulted and pelted with "large stones and bricks." Casualties were heavy: six or seven were killed, and fourteen to seventeen were wounded, including two bystanders—a black boy and a man.[28]

Led by angry militia officers, a volatile crowd gathered at the courthouse the next day. Captain Charles Willson Peale prevailed on General Matlock to release the twenty-seven men, and he did so when their officers promised bond for them. Officials were frightened. A public funeral was held, flour was distributed to the poor, especially to families of the militia, and the Assembly passed yet another law against "the evil practices of monopolizing and forestalling."[29]

Eight days after the violence the fall elections were held. Like James Wilson, Republican leaders hid—Wilson was in Robert Morris's country house—and the Constitutionalists won an overwhelming victory. Republican fortunes were at the lowest ebb of the entire decade, and events continued to widen the gap between the opponents and supporters of the Constitution of 1776. By late 1779, then, the political struggle had been broadened to include the issues of inflation, food, and law and order.[30]

During the first few years of the war, the Constitutionalists and Republicans developed distinctive programs, styles, and symbols. By 1780 the former were identified with a policy of exclusion, persecution,

27. J. K. Alexander, "Fort Wilson," 601–7; Geib, "History of Philadelphia," 123–25; Peale, "Autobiography," 74–75. For the quotation, see Rosswurm, *Arms*, 214; see also 211–15.

28. J. K. Alexander, "Fort Wilson," 607–8; Peale, "Autobiography," 75–77; Rosswurm, *Arms*, 215–17.

29. Brunhouse, *Counter-Revolution*, 76; Geib, "History of Philadelphia," 127–28; Rosswurm, *Arms*, 218–22; Warner Jr., *Private City*, 43–44. For the quotation, see Foner, *Paine*, 178.

30. Brunhouse, *Counter-Revolution*, 75–76.

and extralegal action aimed at enemies of the Republic. The Republicans were also concerned about the safety of the Republic, but they were more committed to protecting private property and the rights of individuals than their opponents were.

The programs and general stance of both groups were tied to their positions on the new Constitution. The Constitution of 1776 transcended the status of an issue. Contemporary political commentators invariably explained the era's politics in terms of the Constitution. As Alexander Graydon recalled, "The politicians were divided into *Constitutionalists* and *Republicans*. The first rallied around the constitution already formed, which was reprobated by the others." Because independence was involved, and because the issues that had impelled men to make the break were largely political, the Constitution of 1776 had come to symbolize the fruits of the Revolution. [31]

The tenor of politics was strikingly modern. The public had received a political education and participation had increased. The ability of the Constitutionalists to collect 14,000 signatures in defense of the Constitution, and the publication of large numbers of newspaper articles, pamphlets, and broadsides, points to the existence of a large and active public. Writers like Tom Paine were honing literary techniques that approached the modern in their ability to attract and arouse large numbers of readers. [32]

Time after time, activists and the press mobilized public energies and focused them on the political arena in general and on the Assembly in particular. The process increased the self-awareness of the social groups involved. For example, the urban poor were mobilized by the press, by revolutionary committees, by their own clubs and, especially by the militia. The fact that they saw themselves as a social group and consciously acted in their own self-interest, and had some success, encouraged others to emulate them. Finally, the General Assembly functioned like a modern institutional "center" that focused, intensified, facilitated, and created conflict.

Cutting across and shaping the polity was the organizational basis of politics. All social systems have an organizational structure with related values and norms that guide behavior. Standard treatments of politics in Pennsylvania have taken the position that political formations barely existed. Theodore Thayer argues: "The strength of political parties in

31. Arnold, "Political Ideology," 144–46; Littell, ed., *Graydon*, 331.
32. Foner, *Paine*, 82–87.

colonial days rested squarely upon the popularity of the individual politician. The parties, in no way formal organizations, consisted of a loose association of men drawn together by mutual likes and dislikes." Similarly, Robert L. Brunhouse insists that the parties of the era "were only loose, nebulous affairs and should not be confused with the highly organized political machines of the present time." But these evaluations misread the organizational structure that did exist, and by doing so are unable to come to grips with the political system.[33]

The problem grows out of a misuse of ideal types. Both scholars use the party of the 1840s or the late nineteenth century as the norm and then measure earlier political organizations against that standard—that is the proper way to use an ideal type. Because they take the modern, large-scale, single-purpose, highly organized, quasi-bureaucratic organization as a standard of measurement, Thayer and Brunhouse are able to assert that a difference exists. Unfortunately, however, Thayer and Brunhouse have assumed that such comparisons explain the past, but that is not the case. Instead, they make explanations possible. In effect, Brunhouse and Thayer have asserted that A is not B—a statement that is true and useful, but does not tell us what A is. Alerted by the ideal type that an analytic issue exists, we are in a position to ask whether the earlier era had its own organizational structure and how that structure affected the political process.

Comparative discussions of political organizations face additional problems. As Avery Leiserson notes, "the political party more than almost any other institution in society is not closed but permeable, subject to infiltration, influence, and control at all levels from other social structures and hierarchies." Political organizations exist in an environment that contains competitors. The military, church, communications media, government agencies, voluntary associations, and special interests operate in the political arena. One might add that class interests, ideological considerations, and peer pressure also affect political behavior.[34]

If political organizations do not have clearly defined boundaries—that is, are usually poorly institutionalized—this was especially true in the period under consideration. War, independence, civil strife, and the creation of new governments created turmoil. But Revolutionary America was not simply turbulent; it was also creatively experimenting with new political forms. In such periods, political organization is

33. Thayer, *Pennsylvania Politics*, 151; Brunhouse, *Counter-Revolution*, 9–10.
34. Leiserson, *Parties*, 177; Ware, *Citizens*, 16.

necessarily poorly institutionalized, and consequently a focus on the broader societal environment is especially important.[35]

Pennsylvania lacked powerful coercive institutions. It also had an upper class that lacked the tremendous accumulation of wealth that buttressed the position of the European aristocracy. Moreover, the provincial upper class had been disorganized and at least temporarily swept aside by the events of a decade that destroyed proprietary government and removed the Quaker-Anglican establishment from the political arena. The new political order that emerged in the troubled 1760s and 1770s was based on extralegal committees, town meetings, conventions, circular letters, organizers, petition campaigns, broadsides, newspaper essays, and a surprisingly effective communications system.

Let us return to the question posed by Thayer and Brunhouse. Were there political parties in Revolutionary Pennsylvania? The question is not an easy one. Kay Lawson reminds us: "There are now [1976] more than 500 political parties functioning in 100 nations. Furthermore, these 500-plus parties perform the widest imaginable range of political tasks." The range of these tasks is so great that Lawson is willing to say that the "domain of parties may be equal to the domain of politics itself, and every function that political systems perform *may* be performed by party."[36]

While diversity of context and function make defining parties a formidable chore, the problem is made even worse by the permeability of the political sphere. The chores accomplished by parties can and are accomplished through other social agencies.

> Schools, families, communication media, bosses, co-workers, and traveling sales people are all alternate sources of political education and information. Interest groups, even those not

35. Institutionalization involves the existence of clear boundaries distinguishing an institution from its environment; an internal organization characterized by a complex division of labor; and the use of universal criteria. The institution must have "a life—and goals—of its own," and it must be analytically separable from other institutions. See Zemsky, "Legislative Behavior," 690. The permeability of political organizations varies. Scholars distinguish between mass and class parties. The former tend to be more open than the latter. See Beer, "Comparative Method."

36. Lawson, *Comparative Study*, 1–2; Hodgkin, *African*, 16. Party studies that proved useful are Epstein, *Political Parties;* Eldersveld, *Political Parties*, esp. ch. 1; King, "Political Parties"; Shefter, "Party and Patronage"; Sorauf, *Party Politics;* Ware, *Citizens*, 16–23; Ware, ed., *Political Parties*.

overtly political, also bring together politically like-minded citizens, as do occupations, social events, and natural catastrophes. Newspapers, television, interest groups, city councils, and state and national legislatures frequently do the work of aggregating and articulating diverse interests. . . . Not all political leaders run for office on party labels; indeed, not all political leaders run for office.[37]

The problem is not insolvable. As Lawson says: "Only political parties openly claim to link the general public to political power by placing representatives of their organization in positions where they may exercise that power on behalf of that public."[38]

A definition that is built around this fact and that pays attention to the major analytical traditions in the treatment of party should be acceptable, and because the one proposed by William Nesbet Chambers meets these requirements and has played an important role in the discussion of early party development in America, that is the definition adopted here.

According to Chambers, a party is "a social structure which operates within the political arena, and which is directed toward exercising the power, filling the available offices, and shaping the general policies of government." He goes on to suggest that a modern political party is

a relatively durable social formation which seeks offices or power in government, exhibits a structure or organization which links leaders at the centers of government to a significant popular following in the political arena and its local enclaves, and generates in-group perspectives or at least symbols of identification or loyalty.[39]

This definition directs our attention to the characteristics of party that most political scientists feel are essential: form, purpose, and operation. Political parties, then, are organizations that join people who share political goals in political action. In the American context, parties operate in electoral systems. They represent the interests and desires of various groups and communicate world views and ideologies. In the complex political arenas of modern societies, political parties operate

37. Lawson, *Comparative Study*, 2.
38. Ibid., 3–4.
39. Chambers, "Party Development," 108 and 91–120. For the quotation, see Chambers, "American Mainstream," 5; Chambers, "Politics," 503 and 499–503.

as "linkage structures" integrating the public, interests, classes, and government. As Samuel Huntington says, "the function of the party is to organize participation, to aggregate interests, [and] 'to serve as the link' between social forces and the government."[40]

The period from 1776 to 1779 offers an opportunity to study party formation. As people were forced to deal with independence, war, the creation of a republic, a new government, and the problems of loyalty and inflation, new political groups emerged, and those groups organized and developed distinctive styles, symbols, and programs. Activists labored to cultivate followers all over the state. The effect was to spread political consciousness and intensify partisan feelings beyond elected officials and activists to the broader public.

Political organization was stimulated by the tensions and disagreements posed by the war and by the Constitution of 1776. Faced with a boycott by the old elite, government officials engaged in a recruitment campaign by using their power of appointment. These efforts were spearheaded by George Bryan, vice-president of the Executive Council. Aided by his son-in-law, Jonathan Bayard Smith, Bryan was responsible for recruiting such active Constitutionalists as Joseph Reed, William Moore, John Bayard, Thomas McKean, Charles Pettit, and the Rev. John Ewing.[41]

Once in office, the new recruits used their offices for party purposes. When J. D. Sergeant was installed as the attorney general, he chaired committees, wrote public statements, and defended party measures in court. Sergeant was a strong supporter of such Constitutional measures as the act divesting the proprietors, the attempt to destroy the Bank of North America, and the creation of the University of Pennsylvania. In the midst of the elections of 1781, he met with the militia officers of Philadelphia County and induced them to support the party slate. Sergeant also authored a number of vitriolic newspaper articles.[42]

Sergeant was not unique. In case after case, when candidates accepted an appointment to a government office they became party activists. This was true of Timothy Matlack, Thomas McKean, and Joseph Reed. In 1777 Reed was offered the position of Chief Justice, but he wavered and then rejected the offer, deciding to go along with the boycott. When he was offered the position of president of the Executive

40. Huntington, *Political Order*, 91–92; Eldersveld, *Political Parties*, 3–12.
41. Baumann, "Democratic-Republicans," 22, 24, 26, 78.
42. Brunhouse, *Counter-Revolution*, 79–80, 105–6, 143–44, 150–51, 154, 171, 267.

Council the temptation was too strong. He accepted and quickly became the titular head of the party. In one short year, Reed had shifted from opponent to party leader.[43]

Leadership was not restricted to government officials. One of the most important political developments of the Revolutionary era was the spread of political activism beyond the narrow sphere of government. Clubs were useful vehicles for this development—in fact, associational groups were at the heart of the politics of the day. The Whig Society, for example, began its life in the spring of 1777 as a group of "active Whigs" who wanted to discuss "precautions" that should be taken regarding "dangerous internal enemies many of whom were too open in avowing their attachment to the British." They were also concerned to defend the "constitution of Government just framed."[44]

The leadership of the Whig Society was composed of activists like David Rittenhouse, Thomas Paine, James Cannon, and Dr. Thomas Young. Like so many of the clubs and associations of the day, the organizational structure of the Whig Society was nebulous. Charles Willson Peale, an artist, wandered into a meeting and ended up chairing the meeting and eventually the society itself. The group had no constitution and no membership rolls, although it did issue a statement of principles. Meetings, usually held at the Philosophical Society, were open to the public. While members of the elite were associated with the club, they did not dominate. Composed, for the most part, "of mechanics, tradesmen, intellectuals, and men who in origin and spirit were closer to the mind of the common man than the respectable, mercantile leadership of the Republicans, the Whig Society" was a staunch defender of the new constitution.[45]

That a group composed largely of mechanics, tradespeople, and intellectuals could play a major role in the politics of the day tells us a great deal. Much of the Whig Society's power came from its ties to the militia companies, to local clubs like the Patriotic Association and the Society of Saint Tammany, as well as from the mobilization techniques of the associational system. The society discussed current events and issued numerous letters and memorials to the press in its own name. Members were encouraged to write letters and essays to the press on

43. Ibid., 14, 19, 22, 35, 56–57, 60–62, 77, 126–27, 166; Duane, ed., *Christopher Marshall*, 176; Secretary Matlack to Sub-Lieutenants of Philadelphia County, 1777, Lancaster, 10 October 1777, *PA*, 1st ser., 5:660–61; Rowe, "McKean," 108, 111–16, 255.
44. Peale, "Autobiography," 47–48.
45. For the quotation, see Hindle, *Rittenhouse*, 178–79; Sellers, *Artist*, 155–57.

their own. It is significant that the society formed a committee of correspondence composed of Peale, Rittenhouse, Cannon, Young, and Paine to establish ties with the rural counties to preserve "our common liberties." The society maintained close ties with the government and played a major and largely successful role in rallying public support behind the Constitution of 1776.[46]

For men like Peale, the clubs provided access into the political arena. The Whig Society introduced Peale to the leading political figures of the day. His first chores, beyond chairing meetings, involved writing letters and memorials to the press. When British forces threatened Philadelphia, Peale was appointed to a number of ad hoc committees. Between April and October 1777 he served on committees to ensure that useful provisions would not fall into the hands of the British, to collect supplies for the troops, to arrest a number of prominent recalcitrants such as John Penn, Benjamin Chew, Jared Ingersoll, and James Tilghman and to seize the personal property of traitors. He was later elected to the General Assembly on a Constitutionalist slate.[47] Opponents of the Constitution also organized. Benjamin Rush remembered: "soon after the British army left Philadelphia [June 1778] an attempt was made by a number of citizens to alter and amend the constitution of Pennsylvania, which had been formed in haste. These citizens united themselves into what they called a Republican Society. I became a member of it."[48]

The formation of the new society was announced in the local press along with a list of the eighty-two members and an "Address" stating their principles and goals. In addition to Rush, such notables as James Wilson, Robert Morris, Thomas Willing, George Clymer, and Thomas Mifflin were among the original members. Richard Bache, Benjamin Franklin's son-in-law, was the chairman.[49]

46. Baumann, "Democratic-Republicans," 19–21; Brunhouse, *Counter-Revolution*, 28; Foner, *Paine*, 142; Geib, "History of Philadelphia," 60–62; Hindle, *Rittenhouse*, 203–4; Sellers, *Artist*, 158; Sellers, *Peale*, 141–42. For a useful discussion of the Patriotic Association, which finds that their membership was composed primarily of artisans and some "lesser professionals and shopkeepers," see Rosswurm, *Arms*, 153–55.

47. Brunhouse, *Counter-Revolution*, 31, 140 n. 62; Hindle, *Rittenhouse*, 189–90; Peale, "Autobiography," 51–54, 65, 67; Scharf and Westcott, *History*, 1:343, 345–46, 370; Sellers, *Artist*, 165–66, 185, 194; Sellers, *Peale*, 141–43, 164–65.

48. Corner, ed., *Autobiography of Rush*, 158.

49. A.B., *Pa. Gazette*, 28 April 1784, says that the Republican society was formed in November 1778. See also Baumann, "Democratic-Republicans," 21; Brunhouse, *Counter-Revolution*, 9, 28; Ireland, "Ethnic-Religious Dimension," 440–42; Republican Society, "Address," *Pa. Packet*, 25 March 1779.

The Whig Society reacted by renaming itself the Constitutional Society and publishing a statement of its principles in the *Pennsylvania Packet*. Both clubs developed intimate ties with various groups, often creating "front" organizations to deal with particular causes and cement ties with specific social groups. In 1778, after the British evacuated Philadelphia, militants had been disappointed at the results of legal proceedings against suspected Tories and Neutrals. The Constitutionalists formed the Patriotic Association headed by William Bradford to organize a protest. Later, when commerce with the British was discovered, they created a Whig Association. The president, secretary, and a majority of the Executive Committee of the association were prominent party members. Meetings of the Sons of Tammany were held at the country home of Edward Pole, secretary of the Constitutional Society. The leadership of this patriotic society included prominent Constitutionalists such as George Bryan, Timothy Matlack, and William Moore. Constitutionalists also cultivated ties with societies like the Newly Adopted Sons of the United States and the Mechanical Society, an artisanal club, as well as with the state militia. Charles Willson Peale, president of the Constitutionalist Society, and militants like Dr. James Hutchinson and Daniel Roberdeau were active in the militia.[50]

The Constitutionalists were adept at organizing and using already existing committees of correspondence. These committees dated back to the 1760s. By the mid-1770s they had become the backbone of the resistance movement. When opposition to the revolutionary frame of 1776 had first appeared, many of the County committees were angered. The Whig Society had recognized this, and by organizing its own committee had hoped to tap the resentment. In 1779 the committees acted as the vehicle for the petition campaign. That same year they were active in the price-fixing campaign. Later, in 1783, the Constitutionalists tried to revive the rural committees. The proposed federal Constitution of 1787 led to another spurt of committee organization— leading, this time, to the Harrisburg convention.[51]

50. Brunhouse, *Counter-Revolution*, 4, 101, 192; Baumann, "Democratic-Republicans," 20–22; Carey, *Autobiography*, 13; Cabeen, "Sons of Saint Tammany," 21–22, 339; Geib, "History of Philadelphia," 139; Olton, "Philadelphia Artisans," 287, 309–10; Scharf and Westcott, *History*, 1:413; Sellers, *Artist*, 155; Sellers, *Peale*, 170, 172–73, 176, 178.

51. Baumann, "Democratic-Republicans," 119–20; Andrew Boyd to James Young, 29 December 1779, *PA*, 2d ser., 3:340; Brunhouse, *Counter-Revolution*, 9, 19, 28, 31, 59, 240 n. 62; Duane, ed., *Christopher Marshall*, 220–30; Foner, *Paine*, ch. 5; Walton, "Nominating Conventions," 263.

Although they were somewhat less active, the Republicans carried on similar activities. They founded the Philadelphia Society for the Encouragement of Manufactures and Useful Arts as part of a bid to reestablish the merchant-mechanic alliance of the 1770s. Republicans also had intimate ties with the Sons of Saint Patrick, a conservative Irish convivial club.[52]

Both camps had political coordinators. They spread propaganda and intelligence and sent advice and encouragement all over the state. Throughout the decade, Benjamin Rush labored in the Republican cause, and in 1777 he attempted to recruit General Anthony Wayne. In a series of letters filled with cloying flattery, Rush suggested: "A few letters from *you* to your friends in Chester county will put an end to its [the Constitution of 1776] existence forever." To a friend he sent a pamphlet and promised another. He also passed along news from Lancaster, where "many people who signed a petition against a Convention are now signing a counter petition." A few years later, Rush wrote to another friend that "fragments of the Republican party met at the city tavern . . . and agreed to recommend it to their friends throughout the state to set on foot petitions *indirectly* among the non jurors for a revision of the test law."[53]

The good doctor did not labor alone. Jaspar Yeates of Lancaster was active in the campaign of 1778 and wrote to a friend in Philadelphia asking him to have a pamphlet printed. Yeates was worried. It was difficult to get propaganda distributed, a substantial number of county residents had not taken the oath and could not vote, and many others were intimidated by the militia. Two weeks later Yeates wrote to another friend that he had

> been doing little for these ten days past but electioneering. . . .
> A ticket has been formed here this day, that will run well in the
> district. . . . Will not the people about Middletown vote? Be
> good enough to try. We have written to Col. Cox on the subject
> and enclosed him a ticket. . . . In the city of Philadelphia and

52. Brunhouse, *Counter-Revolution*, 4, 101.
53. Benjamin Rush to Anthony Wayne, 5 and 12 June 1777, Anthony Wayne MSS, 3:91, 104, HSP; Benjamin Rush to Anthony Wayne, 19 May and 13 July 1777, in ibid., 3:84, 113; Benjamin Rush to John Arndt, 31 March 1784, Gratz Collection, Case I, Box 20, HSP; Benjamin Rush to ———, 10 November 1784, in Butterfield, ed., *Letters of Rush*, 339–40.

other counties, every nerve will be strained to effect a change of men and measures.[54]

Thomas Hartley reported, in 1784, to another Republican activist that "exertions were not wanting at York and we are not idle at Lancaster." Anthony Wayne, whom Rush had successfully recruited, also shared in the effort. In 1786, he wrote John Hannum: "I am confident that you will exert every influence in your power to return Willing—I shall return to Chester where I will endeavor to keep things right."[55]

Men like J. D. Sergeant and John Nicholson, comptroller general, acted as coordinators for the Constitutionalists. Nicholson used his office to shape the Antifederalist campaign of 1788. He wrote pamphlets, spread propaganda and petitions throughout the state, received information from the outlying areas, and offered advice. From Carlisle a correspondent wrote that he had "received the petitions you sent me—I delivered the packets to the persons they were directed to." He described the local situation, sent along some articles for publication in the newspapers, and asked Nicholson to notify him "from time to time what measures you think most advisable." Another correspondent reported on the campaign in Shippensburg. And a third, who was a stranger to Nicholson, wrote that he had received a letter from the comptroller: "I found it contained a Petition. . . . I have coppyed it and . . . sent coppyes thereof to the Several Townships in the County."[56]

As the last letter to Nicholson reveals, political organization had gone well beyond the network of friends and kin. Lancaster Republicans went so far as to compose a formal recruiting letter, which they mailed to likely recruits. Moreover, as activists became known, strangers sought them out. Christopher Schultze wrote to Dr. Rush and inquired about the practicality of a petition against the Test Acts. He also asked advice about how to write and circulate petitions.[57]

54. Jasper Yeates to C. Biddle, Lancaster, 25 September 1778, Society Collections, HSP; Judge Yeates to Col. Burd, Lancaster, 10 October 1778, in Balch, ed., *Letters and Papers,* 267.

55. Thomas Hartley to Thomas Fitzsimons, 7 October 1784, Gratz Collection, Provincial Delegates, IV; Anthony Wayne to John Hannum, Waynesborough, 9 January 1786, Wayne MSS, XIX, 49.

56. Arnold, "Political Ideology," 263–64; Brunhouse, *Counter-Revolution,* 108, 133, 167, 204; Hindle, *Rittenhouse,* 236–39; Arbuckle, *Pennsylvania Speculator,* 46–47; John Jordan to John Nicholson, 26 January 1788, in General Correspondence Section of the Sequestered John Nicholson Papers, MG 96, PSA; Benjamin Blyth to John Nicholson, 11 February 1788, in ibid., R. Bard to John Nicholson, 1 February 1788, in ibid.

57. Jasper Yeates, Stephen Chambers, and Paul Lantzinger to Peter Grubb, Lancaster, 15

Political activists applied a battery of sophisticated techniques to electoral campaigns. Local political leaders developed the caucus system. First, they carefully picked popular candidates and then staged public meetings to rally the faithful. Christopher Marshall describes the process. On an evening in the fall of 1776, he "went to [the] Coffee House, being invited by letter to meet sundry of our citizens to appoint Inspectors and to think of six suitable persons to represent this City in General Assembly. This meeting was conducted with great unanimity and concord, and the proceedings referred to a larger meeting tomorrow evening."[58]

Only forty citizens showed up the next day, and the meeting was postponed "in hopes a larger company would attend." They did. "A large [and] respectable number of citizens" were present. A committee was appointed to "draw up the proceedings of this evening and have them printed in handbills and distributed through the City, before or on Election Day." The whole process was admirably suited to attract public attention and suggest a draft. As the political potential of the nominating process was realized, changes were made. When Republican leaders met in 1787 to choose a slate, leaders orchestrated the proceedings so that James Wilson and Benjamin Rush could address and inspire the faithful.[59]

Both sides used labels to advertise their party. In 1779 the Constitutionalists identified themselves as the Independent Constitutional Ticket. Until 1785 the parties were usually known as Constitutionalists and Republicans. After 1785 the changing political scene was reflected in the use of issue-related labels. Appealing to the nonjurors, Philadelphia Republicans called themselves Friends of Equal Liberty in 1785, and two years later they ran as Friends to the Federal Constitution. In 1786 the Constitutionalists ran on a University ticket. The point is an important one. From at least 1779, voters in Pennsylvania voted for slates of candidates whose ties to statewide political organizations was made clear by the use of labels.[60]

September 1785, Grubb Collection; Christopher Schultze to Benjamin Rush, 22 November 1784, Benjamin Rush Papers, XLIII, 106, HSP.

58. Brunhouse, *Counter-Revolution*, 9; Duane, ed., *Christopher Marshall*, 100–102. See also Baumann, "Democratic-Republicans," 137–38; Geib, "History of Philadelphia," 24–31.

59. Duane, ed., *Christopher Marshall*, 101–2; Brunhouse, *Counter-Revolution*, 204–5.

60. Baumann, "Democratic-Republicans," 73, 120; Brunhouse, *Counter-Revolution*, 177, 191–92, 202, 218; Sellers, *Peale*, 173. See also above, notes 50 and 52. It is worth noting that to one prominent political scientist the use of labels is itself sufficient to mark a political organization as a party; Epstein, *Political Parties*, 9.

Propaganda techniques were harnessed to the needs of party. Political activists organized mass meetings, initiated petition campaigns, used labels, and orchestrated a barrage of newspaper articles, broadsides, and pamphlets. Activists like Benjamin Rush, James Wilson, Charles W. Peale, and J. D. Sergeant wrote for their party. They also recruited new talent from friends or acquaintances, such as Pelatiah Webster, Tench Coxe, and Tom Paine. The resulting literature was rich in scandal, smear, and name-calling, as well as serious political discourse.

Party behavior continued after the elections. Both Republicans and Constitutionalists recognized the importance of controlling the Assembly, and the first days of each legislative session were marked by party strife. The elections of 1785 had resulted in a narrow victory for the Constitutionalists. Because much of their strength was centered in distant, rural counties, and because representatives from those districts were normally the last to arrive, the party was not at full strength at the beginning of the session. Moreover, the official election returns for four party members from Cumberland had been delayed, and they were not allowed to vote. The Republicans tried to take advantage of the situation by trying to organize the chamber as soon as a quorum was present. The Constitutionalists stalled. A few members absented themselves and prevented a quorum. When the errant election returns arrived, along with seven backcountry party members, the Constitutionalists organized the House. In the election for speaker and clerk they elected Thomas Mifflin and Samuel Bryan by identical margins of 33 to 29.[61]

As the events of 1785 show, the organization of the Assembly reflected the election returns. In 1779 when Constitutionalists dominated, the speaker and clerk of the Assembly were John Bayard and Tom Paine, while the president and vice-president of the Supreme Executive Council were Joseph Reed and William Moore. Three years later, when political fortunes reversed, Republicans chose Frederick Muhlenberg and Peter Z. Lloyd as speaker and clerk, and John Dickinson and James Ewing as president and vice-president. In addition, the composition of the delegations sent by the General Assembly to the Congress reflected the varying success of the parties.[62]

61. Brunhouse, *Counter-Revolution*, 176–79; Samuel Bryan to George Bryan, 3 November 1785, *PMHB* 42 (1918): 286–87; Samuel Bryan to George Bryan, circa 1 November 1785, George Bryan Papers, Box 2F3, HSP; Arthur Bryan to George Bryan, 3 November 1785, ibid.

62. Brunhouse, *Counter-Revolution*, 76, 123–24. For the role of parties in the choice of legislative officials, such as the Speaker of the House, see ibid., 56, 76, 90, 104, 123, 143,

Disputed elections reveal the same pattern of party behavior. On at least three occasions—1781, 1783, and 1784—party loyalty seems to have determined how representatives voted. After the 1781 election, during which J. D. Sergeant visited Philadelphia County and involved the militia, the returns were investigated by both the Assembly and the Council. According to Robert L. Brunhouse, "on almost every ballot . . . the house divided by a close vote, the Republicans favoring the petitioners and the Radicals [Constitutionalists] supporting the election as it was held." Even though the Republicans lost this battle, they publicized the event so effectively that John Bayard, whose seat was the one in question, was prevented from becoming president of the Executive Council.[63]

Partisan politics were also manifest in patronage appointments made by the Assembly and the Council. Positions like sheriff, prothonotary, judge, lieutenant, sublieutenant, auctioneer, collector of the port, and the various militia posts were all political plums. When John Bayard was defeated in the election of 1780, President Reed and the Constitutionalist majority on the Council appointed him auctioneer for the City of Philadelphia, probably the most lucrative government post in the state. Three years later, when the Republicans regained power, they replaced Bayard with a Republican.[64]

Bayard's experience was not unusual. The parties rewarded friends and punished enemies. When the Constitutionalists attacked the College of Philadelphia and reorganized it, the trustees, administration, and faculty were replaced. Most of the new appointees were party loyalists. The new board included the state's entire congressional delegation, which happened to be Constitutionalist, and such party notables as George Bryan, Timothy Matlack, and David Rittenhouse. James Cannon was recruited into the faculty, and Tom Paine was granted an honorary degree.[65]

165, 178, 194. For the election of the president and vice-president of the Executive Council, see ibid., 56–57, 76, 90, 104–7, 123, 179, 193–94. For the selection of the Assembly's clerk, see ibid., 63, 76, 161, 165, 178, 194, and Foner, *Paine*, 184. For the choice of the congressional delegation, see Henderson, "Constitutionalists"; Henderson, *Party Politics*, 162–63, 171, 176–77, 231–32, 248–49, 353–54; Brunhouse, *Counter-Revolution*, 25, 44, 56, 90, 146, 165, 194.

63. Brunhouse, *Counter-Revolution*, 106 and 103–7, 140–46, 164–65.

64. Ibid., 103–7, 118–19, 147–48.

65. Hindle, *Rittenhouse*, 220–22; Brunhouse, *Counter-Revolution*, 63, 77–79. For the general pattern, see Baumann, "Democratic-Republicans," 78, 593, 596; and Benjamin Rush to John Dickinson, 14 April 1786, in Butterfield, ed., *Letters of Rush*, 384–85. On the

Political activists had a well-developed sense of party, as illustrated by a letter from Benjamin Rush. The Republican doctor began by expressing sorrow at the election results in Lancaster and asking, "Why have our friends neglected to send down proofs of the frauds at Lebanon and Upper Paxton? We seem to content ourselves with acting *defensively* only." He went on to advocate an aggressive policy: "We must attack them for their public abuses and private vices"; if they could only present their "frauds and villanies . . . in the papers," it "would ruin them forever." Rush then described how the Republicans had met at the City Tavern and decided to initiate a petition campaign among nonjurors for a revision of the test laws. They had little hope that the petitions would influence the Assembly, which was controlled by the opposition, but it was hoped that "their refusal will serve to show their inconsistency, to rouse and irritate the sons and friends of the nonjurors, and above all to fix the dye of their infamy." He ended by requesting that the letter be passed on and noted that petitions were already circulating in the counties where Quakers and Mennonites lived. The letters of Rush, Francis Hopkinson, Anthony Wayne, Tench Coxe, John Nicholson, and the Bryans make it abundantly clear that activists understood the political universe to be populated by two identifiable opposing groups or parties.[66]

Elected officials were also aware of the existence of party spirit. When Charles Biddle entered the Supreme Executive Council, he found it "divided between what were then called Republicans and Constitutionalists." Biddle knew exactly where each member of the Council stood, and he left a neat list with the party affiliation of each member. Arthur and Samuel Bryan wrote a series of letters to their

---

appointment of prothonotaries, see Brunhouse, *Counter-Revolution*, 33, 44; on judges, see ibid., 76; on auctioneers, see ibid., 118–19, 147–48; on sublieutenants, see ibid., 81–82; and on the collector of the port, see ibid., 167. Republicans not only vilified Chief Justice George Bryan, who certainly gave as good as he got, they also cut his salary while giving raises to other judges. See Foster, *In Pursuit*, 105–6.

66. Benjamin Rush to ———, 10 November 1784, in Butterfield, ed., *Letters of Rush,* 339–40. See also Benjamin Rush to Charles Nisbet, 27 August 1784, in ibid., 335–39; Rush to John Montgomery, 13 November 1784, in ibid., 341–43; Rush to John Dickinson, 14 April 1786, in ibid., 384–85; Rush to John Montgomery, 21 January 1787, in ibid., 410–11; Francis Hopkinson to Thomas Jefferson, 21 April and 28 September 1785, in Boyd, ed., *Papers of Jefferson*, 8:98–100, 562–64; Anthony Wayne to John Hannum, Waynesborough, 9 January 1786, in Anthony Wayne MSS, xix, 49; Tench Coxe to James Madison, 28 September 1787, in Allen, ed., *Documentary History*, 4:304–6; Samuel Bryan to George Bryan, 3 November 1785, *PMHB* 42 (1918): 286–87; Samuel Bryan to George Bryan, circa 1 November 1785, Bryan Papers, Box 2F3; Arthur Bryan to George Bryan, 3 November 1785, in ibid.

father, who was traveling the circuit in the fall of 1785, about events in the Assembly. The letters assume the existence of two parties. Samuel wrote: "If I had before entertained any hopes [of being elected clerk] the appearance the first day must have destroyed them, for out of about 36 members who attended the Republican party counted 25." Arthur later told the senior Bryan: "You have already heard of Saml getting reinstated not withstanding the ungenerous attempts of many to put him out, the votes stood 33 Sam & 30 Lloyd, the Constitutionalists also carried the Speaker 33 to 29." And finally, "It was notorious," said assemblyman Dr. George Logan, that "the state was divided into two parties. Everyone that comes into the galleries sees we arrange our-selves on opposite sides in this house."[67]

Like activists and elected officials, the public exhibited high levels of partisanship. Letters, diaries, and virtually all contemporary published accounts of the politics of the era refer to Republicans and Constitution-alists. Thus, in 1782 John Wilson, accountant of the Bank of North America, happily noted to a former employer that the bank was "gener-ally approved of and encouraged not only by the merchants but the most Sensible part of the Community of every description and denomination, a few Constitutionalists excepted who do not wish any thing to prosper which has originated and is Supported by their opponents the repub-licans."[68]

Two years later the business agents of Jeremiah Wadsworth reported to him on the organization of a second bank in the city. They included a description of the stockholders that included comments like "3 are constitutionalists and early Whigs" and "Tench Coxe & Jeremiah Warder are professing republicans." Journalist Mathew Carey recalled: "At this period, parties ran as high in Pennsylvania as they have done at any time since. The denominations were Constitutionalists and Republicans."[69]

It seems clear that Constitutionalists and Republicans were parties in the sense that William Chambers meant. They were reasonably durable political formations. The Constitutionalists survived for about a decade,

67. Biddle, ed., *Charles Biddle*, 195, 202, 211; Samuel Bryan to George Bryan, 3 November 1785, *PMHB* 42 (1918): 286–87; Arthur Bryan to George Bryan, 3 November 1785, Bryan Papers, Box 2F3; Samuel Bryan to George Bryan, circa 1 November 1785, in ibid.; Main, *Political Parties*, 206 n. 87.

68. Rappaport, "First Description," 666.

69. John Chaloner to Jeremiah Wadsworth, 17 February 1784, Chaloner and White Letter-book, 251–53, HSP; Carey, *Autobiography*, 12–13. See also Brunhouse, *Counter-Revolution*, 59, 143, 256 n. 5; Main, *Political Parties*, 203–5; William Bradford to ———, 13 February 1784, Wallace Papers, HSP; and James Wilkinson Papers, 1779–99, I, HSP.

and the Republicans even longer. Faced with the collapse of the government, the Constitutionalists recruited personnel, organized an administration, and took steps to generate popular support. At the same time,
the Republicans shifted from an obstructionist stance to one of opposition within the constitutional framework. They too sought to create and
mobilize popular support.

Both parties had an organizational structure composed of networks of
clubs and committees of correspondence, as well as less-formal groups
that linked leaders and followers throughout the state. Individuals like
John Nicholson and Benjamin Rush served as party functionaries.

Each party developed a distinctive style. Constitutionalists adopted a
Calvinist-populist-democratic stance and utilized committees of correspondence whenever possible. This organizational tactic did not appeal
to the Republicans because it smacked of revolutionary activism. Republicans offered a combination of elitism, conservatism, protection of
private property, and a respect for the rights of individuals—a stance
that was strikingly similar to the conservative and Millsian liberalism of
the nineteenth century.

Republicans and Constitutionalists consciously strove to control the
government, and when they did they were successful in formulating
policies consistent with their general stances. The point is crucial.
Public policy was dependent on the fortunes of the party conflict.
Jackson Turner Main is correct when he says: "The outcome of an
election resulted not simply in the victory of one set of politicians or one
'faction' or another, but in major changes of policies."[70]

Voting patterns in the legislature between 1776 and 1790 support that
interpretation. Owen Ireland finds that "the vast bulk of the legislators
. . . grouped themselves into two relatively cohesive and opposed
blocs." Republicans and Constitutionalists consistently fought each other
over at least nine major issues, including the Constitution of 1776, the
Test Acts, the treatment of Tories, the College of Philadelphia, assumption of debts, and the Bank of North America.[71]

During elections, Constitutionalists and Republicans acted like political
parties. They used caucuses to choose candidates and labels to identify
themselves, and they both used rallies, petitions, newspapers, pamphlets, and broadsides to rally the faithful. Once in office, the two
political formations fought to control the legislature and the Supreme
Executive Council, and both made effective use of patronage.

70. Main, *Political Parties,* 206.
71. Ireland, "Political Development," 9–12.

The partisanship of the era is especially noteworthy. Aided by the climate of fear and hostility generated by war and independence, the parties generated intense loyalty. One of Owen Ireland's most striking findings in his study of voting patterns within the Assembly is that politically sensitive issues like disputed elections and the right of the Council to control patronage "produced internal bloc cohesion levels among the highest achieved on any policy issue." These levels varied "from 90% to 100%" and came close to "unanimity" most of the time. The fact that legislative voting patterns reveal two groups with consistent issue preferences, groups that are even more consistent on party questions, is strong evidence for the existence of parties.[72]

The relationship between politicians and the general public was complex. Elected officials and activists were frequently able to manipulate the public. Thus, when the militia erupted in 1779 the Constitutionalist Society stepped into the breach and tried to take charge of the movement to bolster their political fortunes. In fact, all mobilization techniques used by the parties—including petitions, mass meetings, parades, conventions, and propaganda barrages—were manipulative to one degree or another.

And yet while political elites tried to manipulate the public, Pennsylvania's polity was extraordinarily open to public initiatives. The associational system and organizations like the militia provided opportunities for large numbers of people to affect the course of events. The mobilization that occurred during the Revolution, and the success of the parties in increasing political participation, meant that the masses could not be safely ignored. They would at times act on their own initiative.

The price-fixing campaign of 1779, which had offered the Constitutional Society an opportunity to manipulate the public, was also a dramatic instance of initiatives on the part of the poorest members of the community. As it turned out, the Constitutionalists were unable to control their erstwhile allies and were placed in the uncomfortable position of attempting to distance themselves from their friends while offering them as much support as was politically prudent. The lesson was clear: Whatever their stance on certain issues, both parties were forced to take into account the desires of their constituents. Failure to do this could lead to disaster in an election or, even worse, to outbreaks of violence like the unfortunate Fort Wilson Affair.[73]

72. Ibid., 12–13.

73. The success of the parties in winning adherents and general public acceptance suggests that in the 1780s antiparty ideology was not particularly important in Pennsylvania. It is not

At the same time, despite the Test Acts, the jailing of Neutrals and Tories, and occasional outbreaks of political violence and intimidation, politics were generally characterized by a sense of fairness, by a belief that the "rules of the game" should govern. Elections continued, and although civil rights were threatened they survived and emerged even stronger.

The most significant institutional development of the era was the emergence of a modern party system governed by rules of fairness. Giving the political sphere an even more modern tenor was the persistence and strengthening of preexisting patterns of participation and conflict. At the same time, the organizational basis of the party system, with its clubs, societies, committees, and associations, conformed to the dominant organizational mode of the era, the associational system.

When an issue entered the political arena during the 1780s, whether it was loyalism, incorporating the City of Philadelphia, or reimbursing public creditors, it was almost inevitable that the political parties would play a role in setting public policy. This was certainly true in the case of the Bank of North America. Because Robert Morris, the bank's founder, and members of the board of directors were prominent in Republican Party circles, the bank was identified with the Republican Party. As a result, it was virtually inevitable that the fortunes of the bank would be tied to the ebb and flow of party politics.

surprising that the freest and most democratic political system in America was the least troubled by antiparty rhetoric.

5

Politics: A Class Analysis

Just as the associational system and political parties shaped politics in the province, the existence of social classes profoundly affected the operation of the associational system and the nature of politics. Classes exert their influence through all available channels. Their influence is felt in the economic, cultural, social, and political spheres. At the same time, the various institutional spheres and cultural impulses give expression to and shape the class system.

A successful class analysis of Revolutionary Pennsylvania is complicated by the fact that the region lacked European classes, with their ascriptive traditions and coercive institutions. Army, state, and church were either missing or too weak to play the same kind of roles they played in Europe. The large number of property owners in Pennsylvania, and the ability of citizens to move freely, to buy and sell property, and to enter a variety of occupations, resulted in a social order that was strikingly open compared with that in Europe.

Nevertheless, wealth and power were not distributed equally—all complex societies organize power hierarchically. There are no exceptions. When social scientists discuss the ways in which power is organized, they distinguish four types of stratification systems: slave, caste, estate, and class. Whatever the type, the strata always form a relational system that involves relations of status, privilege, domination, and exploitation.[1]

In slave, caste, and estate systems, social groups are tied together by cultural, legal, social, political, and economic bonds. For example, stratification in estate systems takes the form of an occupational hierarchy that is maintained by rigid rules, including codes of honor that regulate social relations. Ascription is a key component of such systems. People are born into social roles and occupations that are maintained in a variety of ways, including economic ties.[2]

Of all the types of stratification, a class system is the most open. Social classes, rooted in the economic sphere, are large-scale aggregations of individuals that are nominally open. Because they are not rigidly defined by law, age, custom, natural rights, ethnicity, or religion, the boundaries between classes are less precise than the boundaries between other types of strata. Moreover, class membership is less stable than membership in other types of strata, and mobility between classes is an important social dynamic.[3]

Precisely because they are not delineated clearly, classes are difficult to define. Do peasants doing seasonal factory work belong to more than one class? How about gentry who own factories? Compounding the difficulty is the fact that a variety of defining indices may be chosen. Income, occupation, and the perceptions of the social actors themselves have all been used to define class, and all have been found to pose serious analytic problems.[4]

The classical Marxist approach is built around property relations and the division of labor. It defines social class at the level of production and makes exploitation a central theoretical concern. Lenin's definition is representative:

> Classes are large groups of people which differ from each other by the place they occupy in a historically determined system of social production, by their relation (in most cases fixed and

1. Bottomore, *Sociology*, 185 and ch. 11; Worsley, *New Introducing Sociology*, ch. 10; Parkin, "Social Stratification," 599–601.

2. Worsley, *New Introducing Sociology*, 365–69; Berger, *Societies*, 105, 117; Bottomore, *Sociology*, 187–88.

3. Bottomore, *Classes*, 112; Giddens, *Class Structure*, 84, 106; Worsley, *New Introducing Sociology*, 369–75.

4. Reddy, "Concept of Class," 18.

formulated in law) to the means of production, by their role in the social organization of labor, and, consequently, by the dimension and mode of acquiring the share of social wealth of which they dispose.[5]

Although useful, this definition also has problems. Alvin Y. So warns that it is built around a static, architectural metaphor replete with rooms, walls, and foundations. He proposes, sensibly, that we conceptualize class structure "as a set of structured relationships that are enduring, recurring, and institutionalized."[6]

As we move from defining class to studying the dynamics of class, different issues emerge. Classes and class motives are always important, and that is true even if class members are not conscious of their interests. But when members of a class "become aware of and articulate their objective interests, organize themselves into a collectivity, and wage their struggle in class terms with their opponents," class consciousness and class struggle become important causal factors.[7]

At the same time, the social world involves more than social class. Other concerns and interests motivate action, the most important of which include religion, language, ethnicity, race, and gender. The environment and such issues as war and peace also generate problems around which people organize and struggle.[8] Furthermore, stratification systems involve more than relations of domination, exploitation, and conflict. As social groups emerge, they develop what Max Weber called elective affinities. Strata exhibit patterns of saving and consumption, work and play, courtship and marriage, manners and language, and of course political behavior. Strata also come to hold certain religious and political views as well as world views. Each stratum, as Marx and Weber held, is the carrier of a culture.[9]

It is important to remember that, in class societies, classes articulate themselves in relationship to other social classes and to status groups,

5. Quoted in Stavenhagen, *Social Classes*, 28; Worsley, *New Introducing Sociology*, 369–75; Parkin, "Social Stratification," 601–10.
6. So, "Class Struggle," 42–47; for the quotation, see 43. See also Calvert, *Concept of Class;* Elster, "Three Challenges," 141–61.
7. Quoted in So, "Class Struggle," 46; So and Hikam, "Class," 455–56, 463, 465; Kulikoff, *Agrarian Origins*, ch. 1; Giddens and Held, "Introduction," 94.
8. So and Hakim, "Class," 455–56, 463, 465; Giddens and Held, "Introduction," 94; Beynon, "Class."
9. Gerth and Mills, eds. and trans., *From Max Weber*, 62–63; Berger and Berger, *Sociology*, 35, 94–95.

and that these relationships give such stratification systems their inherent dynamism. The existence of such status groups as professionals and intellectuals raises the specter of class coalitions. In fact, political struggle in class societies always involves alliance between the major classes, class fragments, and status groups.

From the standpoint of stratification, eighteenth-century Pennsylvania was unusual. The absence of European-style ascriptive and hierarchical institutions shows that an estate system failed to take root. What did emerge was a stratification system based on social class.

To analyze the system, I shall use the classical Marxist definition constructed around property and occupation and emphasize class consciousness and meaningful participation in the political struggles of the day as limiting factors. There were three politically relevant social classes in eighteenth-century Pennsylvania—petty-commodity-producing farmers, urban artisans, and urban merchants—and each class was self-aware and entered into alliances with other social groups to struggle for their agendas.

The single most important characteristic about this stratification system, and the element that made it unusual, was the relative unimportance of exploitation, because the great majority of those engaged in production owned the means of production. The number of those owning land varied from county to county—between 40 percent and 70 percent were owners, and another 25 to 45 percent rented. And although some farmers and tenants were abysmally poor, the vast majority produced a great deal of what they needed; neighbors and markets made the rest available. Some 25 to 33 percent of the urban and rural population were artisans who owned the tools and had the skills required to practice their trade. While merchants were not engaged in production, their capital and skills enabled them to be autonomous. Thus, the great bulk of the population could reasonably aspire to independence.[10]

Production for markets and profits was important but did not dominate. Faced with the need to coax surpluses from the hinterland, merchants did not control production. Moreover, the deeply rooted desire to own property and achieve independence slowed the growth of markets, and although people were happy to purchase goods, they had not yet adopted a consumerist mentality. In such circumstances,

10. Harper, "Class Structures," 36, 45–46, 54, 79; Lemon, *Poor Man's Country*, 7–8; Lemon and Nash, "Distribution," 174; Simler, "Tenancy," 555; Schweitzer, "Elements," 8, 10–11; Olton, *Artisans*, 7–8; Olton, "Philadelphia Artisans," iii, 4–16.

exploitative class relations and the expropriation of the social surplus could not be at the heart of social relations.

Pennsylvania had a class system in which relations between social classes were predominantly relations of circulation. Each of the three classes engaged in the commercial exchange of goods and services, an exchange that defined merchants and, to a lesser extent, artisans. Farmers and rural artisans also engaged in a significant number of noncommercial exchanges. While the market capabilities of each class determined its wealth, the fact that the economy was not capitalist and that the social structure was not ascriptive meant that the coercive power of wealth was limited.

Pennsylvania's family farmers constitute the first social class. Their economy encompassed a duality. Driven by their hunger for land and the requirement that they pay taxes and wages, they entered local and international commercial markets for a variety of services, products, and markets. At the same time, they were embedded in reciprocal neighborhood exchange networks that operated separately from commercial markets.[11]

Although the family life-cycle forced them to use wage labor, petty-commodity producers relied primarily on the labor of their families and neighbors. Because of this, and because they owned land, they were able to survive for long periods with little or no profit—which is their great advantage over capitalist farmers. Because the state had a relatively small impact on their lives, family farmers could depend on their own resources and on their neighbors to protect their way of life. As it turned out, the major threat to the survival of these farmers in the eighteenth and nineteenth centuries was the growth of markets.[12]

The values of the family farmer reflected this institutional reality and helped sustain the family. What James Henretta calls "lineal values" was at the core of the farmer's world view. Farmers believed that their primary responsibility was to provide food, shelter, and clothing for their families. Almost as important was their desire to provide their children and heirs with the resources needed to support the next generation.[13] The ability of farmers to accomplish these goals depended on their access to land. Land and the life it made possible was at the heart of what Chester E. Eisinger calls the "freehold concept." At the

11. See Chapter 1, n. 110.
12. Ibid.
13. Henretta, "Families and Farms."

core of this concept was the belief that there is a natural right to own land. The power of this vision lay in the fact that it was achievable.[14]

Lineal values and the freehold concept combined to create a producer mentality. Despite the arduousness of farm labor, farmers got a sense of satisfaction and pride from the labor process, which in a literal sense was the direct cause of their family's well-being. The producer mentality was so strong that it became "an article of religious faith." Farmers believed that buying goods and services that "might be produced at home was . . . not only bad economy but also doubtful morality."[15]

Equally important to farmers was their autonomy and independence. The emphasis on the autonomous family farm was rooted in part in the fact of rural isolation. But the farmer's historical point of reference was a comparison between America and the Old World. The Europe they remembered was dominated by great lords and a rigid and often brutal ascriptive social system. Also fresh in memory was the fact that a great many had come to America as bound servants. Yet this concern with autonomy did not lead to a simple individualism. Exchange networks, neighboring, labor-sharing, and reciprocal exchanges produced powerful communal ties that pervaded rural life.[16]

Allan Kulikoff argues that American petty-commodity producers—he calls them yeomen—had created a set of ideals well before Pennsylvania had been established. Farmers believed that land ownership conferred citizenship and competency and guaranteed liberty. They insisted on maintaining the autonomy of their families along with their own patriarchal dominance. Family farmers also insisted on owning land and maintaining a "modest freeholder egalitarianism," and that translated into a desire for a standard of living a bit beyond the family's minimal needs, giving the children a good start in life, legal equality and citizenship, and respect for the dignity of human labor—popularly expressed as "competence, independence, and morality."[17]

Although rural petty-commodity producers had always prized their status as citizens and participated in politics, it was difficult for them to coalesce into a self-conscious class. Despite the importance of rural

14. Eisinger, "Freehold Concept"; Headlee, *Political Economy*, 2–4, 174.

15. Quoted in Bidwell and Falconer, *History*, 254. See also Kulikoff, *Agrarian Origins*, 35, 130; Danhof, *Change*, 15–18; Foner, *Free Soil*, 11–18, 21–23; Mooney, *My Own Boss?*, 66–67; Henretta, "Families and Farms," 14–32; Johnstone, "Identification."

16. Kulikoff, *Agrarian Origins*, 132; Sellers, *Market Revolution*, 12–16, 152–57. See especially Bushman, "Massachusetts Farmers" and "This New Man."

17. Kulikoff, *Agrarian Origins*, 132, 147; Burns, *Success*, 1–13, 24–25, 58–65.

neighborhoods, distance did translate into isolation. Deference also limited the activism of the lower classes. During most of Pennsylvania's first century, family farmers comfortably followed the lead of their betters, the Quaker party. Only on the Indian question did they strike out on their own.

The events of the 1760s and 1770s changed the situation. The Quaker party had been discredited in the royalization campaign of 1764 and by its discomfort with the nonimportation campaigns. News of the Boston port bill in 1774 led a group of radical Whigs to call a series of protest meetings in Philadelphia. As a result of these meetings, at least nine county committees were established. The committees proved so popular that many townships established their own. Politicized and mobilized, Pennsylvania's family farmers enthusiastically supported independence and the Constitution of 1776.[18] After independence, farmers supported low taxes, credit relief, and the loan office, and when their interests were threatened, as they were in the bank war, they unleashed a flood of class-based rhetorical attacks on their enemies, who were angrily portrayed as great men and aristocrats seeking to destroy already existing egalitarian social arrangements.

Philadelphia's artisans constituted Pennsylvania's second social class, and in 1772 they constituted virtually half of the city's taxable males. Their number, energy, and location in the regional hub gave them political importance.[19] The defining characteristic of this social class grew out of the nature of the labor process. A monopoly of skill and knowledge, and ownership of the necessary tools, gave artisans a measure of control. Working in small shops with a few men, they carried on a small-scale retail trade. Some were able to build up inventories, but even those operations were not large. Most artisanal production was "bespoke," or custom-made.

These men were proud of what they did and who they were. Henry Clark Wright remembered feeling "real satisfaction in being able to make a hat, because I loved to contemplate the work when finished, and because I felt pleasure in carrying through the various stages." To such men the quality of work reflected the quality of the man—in the late eighteenth century a day's work was not always a job.[20]

Encouraged by their cramped living conditions, craftsmen made

---

18. Ammerman, *Common Cause,* 104, 107–8.
19. G. Nash, "Artisans and Politics," 162.
20. Quoted in Hirsch, *Roots,* 9.

themselves at home in nearby workshops. What we would call leisure activities were woven into the fabric of work. They "kept up a steady flow of conversation on social, political, religious, and craft-related topics while they worked." Apprentices read the newspapers and broadsides aloud to relieve the tedium of the long day. (Benjamin Rush saw indigo dyers as "peevish and low-spirited" because they did not "hum a tune" while they worked.)[21]

Punctuating the workday was a series of social breaks. For example, Philadelphia card-maker and wire worker Nathan Sellers took breaks at 11:00 A.M. and 4:00 P.M. every day throughout his twenty-five-year career as a master. During their breaks, craftsmen visited other shops and taverns, and shop floors were rearranged to facilitate discussions, debates, singing, and cardplaying. Convivial activities continued, after work, on the streets and in neighborhood "taverns, grog shops, and oyster cellars."[22]

This socializing can be looked at in a number of ways. In addition to telling us something about the nature of the market and work norms, it was also a survival tactic. Large portions of the Philadelphia craft community barely made it economically. Winter, illness, and poor markets threatened them with serious hardship. To keep themselves afloat and meet unexpected emergencies, craftsmen created networks like those established by merchants and farmers. Socializing helped keep these "necessary" ties alive.[23]

Philadelphia artisans were more sharply divided by wealth and status than their country cousins were. Tailors, shoemakers, and coopers at the lower end of the social scale had a great deal "in common with merchant seamen and porters with whom they commonly shared low wages, uncertain prospects of advancement, and exclusion from the ranks of property-holders." Other craftsmen were well-to-do. "Brewers, bakers, sugarboilers and some construction tradesmen . . . blended into the ranks of shopkeepers, proprietors, and even real-estate developers," and a few like silversmiths and printers, flirted with the elite.[24]

Despite these divisions, Philadelphia artisans constituted a social class. Ronald Schultz has identified an artisanal world view, a small-

21. Quoted in Northrup, "Decomposition," 162–64.

22. Ibid., 173–76.

23. Ibid., 110–20, 142. A grim and convincing portrait of the standard of living of Philadelphia's laboring poor, including many of the city's artisans, appears in B. Smith, *Lower Sort.*

24. G. Nash, "Artisans and Politics," 162.

producer tradition, which helped unify the craftsmen. The tradition was built around a sense of pride in skill and in the utility of the items they produced. This tradition also made them militant egalitarian democrats. Moreover, artisans looked forward to achieving a competency that would bring them a "middling status" with "small comforts, a few luxuries and an abiding sense of self-esteem."[25]

A powerful sense of community tied the elements of the small-producer tradition—pride in work, a predilection for egalitarian democracy, and a goal of achieving competency—together. Living in artisanal neighborhoods, marrying daughters of craftsmen, working in small groups, socializing in the streets and taverns, Philadelphia's craftsmen "formed not only a social class but a genuine community," and this sense of community pervaded their lives and provided a vision.[26]

By the time of the Revolution, artisans had become a self-conscious, politically active class. The depression and the revolutionary agitation that followed the Seven Years' War were key events in their development. Except for the depression of the 1720s, Philadelphia's artisans had been prosperous between 1682 and 1760, but this changed after the war.[27]

Bad times were compounded by political events. The Quaker party's attempt, in 1764, to turn Pennsylvania into a royal colony called their stewardship of the colony into question. When the political and mercantile elite rejected nonimportation and then resisted independence, Philadelphia's artisans exploded, as they had in the 1720s.

The Stamp Act crisis set the stage. The by now traditional tactics were trotted out: outdoor rallies, voluntary associations, petitions, newspaper articles, broadsides and pamphlets, and "attacks on the wealthy as subverters of the community's welfare" energized the community. Soon newspaper articles began appealing to artisans as a "separate interest."[28]

Artisans struggled to bring the city's merchants into the nonimportation campaign, but the process was difficult and the experience was disillusioning. Nonimportation touched on constitutional questions and affected the economic interests of everyone. During hard times, the

25. Quoted in Schultz, "Small-Producer Tradition," 88. See also Schultz, *Republic*, 6–13; Northrup, "Decomposition," 136–41.

26. Schultz, "Small-Producer Tradition," 86–89; Schultz, *Republic*, 6–13; G. Nash, "Artisans and Politics," 164–67; Olton, *Artisans*, 12–13.

27. G. Nash, *Crucible*, 246–63; G. Nash, "Artisans and Politics," 164, 172–74.

28. G. Nash, "Artisans and Politics," 174–75.

artisanal community traditionally demanded some form of protectionism, and the 1760s were no exception. But it was just as clear to the merchants that protection was not in their interests. The crisis came in 1769, when the city's brewers refused to accept a cargo of malt and the Quaker Meeting responded by rejecting nonimportation.[29]

When importation resumed, artisans broke with their former leaders by calling a public meeting and organizing a "Mechanics Committee." The establishment of this committee and the creation of the Patriotic Society in 1772 were important events in the history of the Revolution and in the formation of a class. They signaled a weakening of deference and the unleashing of hostility toward merchants and the traditional upper class, and at the same time the emergence within the artisanal community of a leadership group determined to be an advocate for the interests of artisans.[30]

From this moment on events moved rapidly. Mechanics' tickets appeared in local elections, and artisans successfully demanded increased representation in the extralegal committee system. After Concord and Lexington, the Continental Congress intervened and the Philadelphia militia was organized. At the same time, a group of radicals, including Dr. Thomas Young, schoolteacher James Cannon, former retailer Timothy Matlock, and printer Thomas Paine, entered politics.[31]

The organization of the militia and the creation of the Committee of Privates were the decisive steps in the rise of Pennsylvania's radical egalitarians. These developments gave the new radical leadership a political base, expanded the political options of the artisanal community, and provided an opportunity for the community's poorest and most restive elements to play an active role in the political arena. That the militia was armed escaped the attention of no one.[32]

As the Revolution came to a head, the Committee of Privates played a central role in calling and directing the Constitutional Convention of 1776. Before the convention, radical appeals appeared in the press, attacking men of "rank" as petty tyrants and talking about an "aristocratical junto" that hoped to make "the common and middle class of people

29. Olton, *Artisans*, 42–47; Ryerson, *Revolution*, 31–33; G. Nash, "Artisans and Politics," 174–76; G. Nash, *Crucible*, 347–77.

30. Ryerson, *Revolution*, 33–34; G. Nash, "Artisans and Politics," 175–76; Olton, *Artisans*, 54–63.

31. Hawke, *Midst*, 102–6; G. Nash, "Artisans and Politics," 176–77; Olton, *Artisans*, 72–77; Rosswurm, *Arms*, 49–51.

32. Rosswurm, *Arms*, 52–72.

their beasts of burden." Philadelphia's slate of delegates was chosen at a meeting called by the Committee. The radicals counseled voters "to chuse no rich men, and few learned men to represent them in the Convention." At the convention, James Cannon unsuccessfully proposed a provision in the Bill of Rights limiting the amount of property a person could accumulate, on the grounds "That an enormous Proportion of Property vested in a few individuals is dangerous to the Rights, and destructive to the Common Happiness, of Mankind; and therefore every free State hath a right by its Laws to discourage the Possession of such Property."[33]

By 1776, Philadelphia's artisans had leadership, an organizational structure, and a program. They had coalesced into a self-conscious social class and entered the political arena to struggle for an agenda. As it turned out, these were the days when the power of the artisanal class was at its peak. Like the Parisian Sans Culottes, Philadelphia's artisans had the ability to have an impact on great events, but when normalcy returned their power would recede. As peace and a constitutional regime emerged, the artisans would play coalitional politics and their ability to lead would disappear.

Despite obvious differences, there were striking similarities between craftsmen and family farmers. Both were petty-commodity producers who were suspicious of capitalism and had a producer mentality and an egalitarian world view. Furthermore, both espoused independence and competency. Predictably, their main political differences came over prices and markets: Farmers wanted high prices for their produce and cheap manufactured goods, while the artisans wanted cheap farm produce and high prices for their goods.[34]

The third social class was the regional upper class—rich, urban, mercantile, and easily identifiable. Philadelphia's tax rolls revealed that the "top tenth of the wealthholders" held about 70 percent of Philadelphia's wealth. The estates of such men as Samuel Powel III were truly impressive. Reputedly the richest man in Philadelphia, Powel's grand tour abroad lasted a munificent seven years, and on his return he married the daughter of the wealthy merchant Thomas Willing. His estate included an opulent townhouse, a country seat near Gloucester,

33. For the appeals in the press, see Foner, *Paine,* 125; for the suggestions to vote against rich and educated men, see Olton, *Artisans,* 77; and for proposed additions to the Bill of Rights, see Rosswurm, *Arms,* 104.
34. Rosswurm, *Arms,* 13–18, and, implicitly, Kulikoff, *Agrarian Origins,* ch. 2.

New Jersey, more real estate in Philadelphia than anyone else, and some 15,000 acres in the countryside.[35]

The fact that this class was urban deserves to be underlined. Even though they purchased large tracts of land in the country and built opulent homes there, the elite retained its urban character. Philadelphia's "best," moreover, did not face powerful rural competitors. Some farmers, rural businessmen, politicians, and professionals were wealthy. They strove to develop ties with the elite whose life-style they emulated, but they did not approach the wealth or prestige of the urban group and they did not coalesce into a self-conscious group.[36]

To a striking degree, the upper class worked in the export-import trade. In 1775 more than 49 percent of the economic elite were merchants, and even twenty-five years later almost 48 percent still earned their income in trade. Allied with the merchants were a mix of independently wealthy gentlemen, professionals, retailers, and a few master craftsmen. Some of the gentlemen were retired merchants, while lawyers and retailers played important roles in the world of commerce. The occupational composition of the upper class was quite stable.[37]

Merchants bought and sold anything that had a market. They were the region's major money lenders, and also provided a wide range of business services, including storage, shipping, and market information. Like all traditional merchants, Philadelphia's exporters and importers had to deal with scattered markets, woeful transportation, and inadequate monetary systems. Primitive business conditions severely restricted the scale of their operations. The resulting workloads were light, economic ambitions were limited, and the time available for participating in the social, cultural, and political life of the community was ample.

35. Bridenbaugh and Bridenbaugh, *Rebels,* 210–12; Brobeck, "Changes in Elite Groups," 195, 210, 353–54; Brobeck, "Revolutionary Change," 425–26; Gough, "Towards a Theory," 225, 229–30; G. Nash, "Up from the Bottom," 64; Tatum, *Philadelphia Georgian,* 9, 16, 18.

36. Tully, *Penn's Legacy,* 74–76. Tully argues that a "genuinely province-wide elite" had emerged, but also notes that the rural segment had a much less "ostentatious" life-style (76).

37. Gough, "Towards a Theory," 202. For an interpretation similar to mine, see B. Smith, *Lower Sort,* 89 n. 55. Doerflinger, *Vigorous Spirit,* 16, 20, 31, differs; he argues that the upper class was not a "merchant aristocracy" because 50 percent of the upper class were not merchants and 85 percent of the merchants were not wealthy. Although the first assertion is factually correct, it ignores the predominance of merchants in the upper class and the fact that many of the rest—i.e., lawyers and gentlemen—were either their allies or retired merchants. The second assertion is simply not relevant. Poor artisans were not members of the upper class either.

Philadelphia's elite lived in an environment largely bounded by themselves. Mercantile apprenticeships were necessary to enter the trade. Merchants lent each other money, exchanged information, rented warehouses and vessels, and purchased goods, insurance, and real estate. And when businesses, such as the Bank of North America, were organized, merchants dominated their boards. Moreover, the lawyers and other professionals they dealt with understood their needs, shared their values, and were socially acceptable.[38]

Pennsylvania's upper class was a clearly defined, self-conscious group whose social characteristics grew out of the fact that they were colonials and a status group. It is no surprise that they sought to replicate what they believed existed in the heartland of the British Empire. That is what colonials have always done.

Adopting English standards of taste, behavior, and consumption, Pennsylvania's elite Anglicized themselves. Conspicuous consumption was the order of the day. Merchants wore powdered wigs, silver watches, and imported knee breeches. They built, rebuilt, decorated, and redecorated town houses. Carved wainscoting on hardwoods and ornate stucco designs of plants or musical instruments covered interior walls and ceilings. Marble chimneys and bath stoves, colored venetian blinds, and imported scenic wallpapers were popular. Even coats of arms made their appearance. Fine furniture, especially Chippendale, and silver objects decorated drawing rooms, dining rooms, and parlors.[39]

Wheeled carriages were an eighteenth-century status symbol, and the local gentry coveted them. In 1761 there were thirty-eight four-wheeled equipages and three of the more expensive coaches in the city, each of which cost the annual earnings of an ordinary citizen. By 1776 the total had grown to fifty-two chariots or post chaises, thirty coach wagons, and nine coaches. Outfitted with beautiful horses, livery, and footmen, carriages were driven proudly around the city and out to the country estates of the elite.[40]

The proliferation of country seats, with their formal gardens and

38. Illick, *Colonial Pennsylvania,* 106–7. Doerflinger concludes that it was easy to become a merchant and easy to fail in the business, and he is correct. At the same time, Billy Smith, also, correctly notes that "the vast majority of [Philadelphia's] laboring people" were unable to enter the trade. See Doerflinger, *Vigorous Spirit,* 57 and 47–55; Smith, *Lower Sort,* 148.

39. Alberts, *Golden Voyage,* 157–59, 162–63; Bridenbaugh, *Cities in Revolt,* 141–43, 336–37, 342; Bridenbaugh and Bridenbaugh, *Rebels,* 13–14, 181–82, 201–7; Harrington, *New York Merchant,* 23–30; Rasmusson, "Capital," 71–73; Rasmusson, "Democratic Environment," 164–67; Doerflinger, *Vigorous Spirit,* 21–32; Tatum, *Philadelphia Georgian.*

40. Bridenbaugh, *Cities in Revolt,* 146, 340–41; Oaks, "Big Wheels," 351–62.

carefully tended farms, is further evidence of the powerful appeal England held for the provincial gentry. By the 1760s more of these establishments could be found in the area surrounding Philadelphia than anywhere else on the continent. Some, such as Graeme Park, with its lakes, formal gardens, meadows, carefully planned vistas, and three-hundred-acre deer park, were in the grand manner. Most were smaller and not so grand, but all followed the English model.[41]

Once the country seat was established, wealthy men like William Allen followed the English example and dabbled in scientific agriculture. "Very few persons in this Country," he noted, "have made more experiments in the farming way than I have, and, in this latter Stage of my Life, my Books, and my little Farm are a great part of my Amusement." The demand for essays on agriculture was large enough for Bradford's *Journal* to advertise imported books on "Farming and Gardening." Predictably, when the Society for the Promotion of Agriculture was founded its membership was primarily upper class.[42]

The Anglicization of the Philadelphia elite extended in as many directions as possible. They sent their children abroad to cultivate personal ties, go to school, and develop sophisticated tastes. They also joined the Anglican church. Considering the history of the province and the prestige of the Quakers, the growth of the Anglican church is impressive testimony to the attractiveness of the British example.[43]

Richard L. Bushman pointed out that more was involved in the behavior of Pennsylvania's upper class than imitation or conspicuous consumption. Their actions, like those of their British counterparts, involved an attempt to cultivate gentility and personal refinement, and those ideals, which originated in the Renaissance, had three components. Individuals were encouraged to refine themselves. They learned correct bearing, manners, and the requisite skills, including dancing, riding, music, and drawing. Knowledge of science, history, language, and literature was also desirable. And it was necessary for those with the proper training to gather in small groups to cultivate and display

41. Bridenbaugh, *Cities in Revolt,* 144–45, 337–39; Bridenbaugh and Bridenbaugh, *Rebels,* 190–93, 215–20; Tatum, *Philadelphia Georgian,* 33–41; Tolles, "Town House."

42. For the quote, see Bridenbaugh and Bridenbaugh, *Rebels,* 191; for the reference to Bradford's *Journal,* ibid., 220. See also Ellsworth, "Philadelphia Society," 189–90; Lemon, *Poor Man's Country,* 169, 170–73.

43. Alberts, *Golden Voyage,* chs. 11, 12; Bridenbaugh, *Cities in Revolt,* 139, 152–53, 348–49; Bridenbaugh and Bridenbaugh, *Rebels,* 16–17, 182–84, 212–15, 223, 228; Tatum, *Philadelphia Georgian,* 9–11, 67; Chastellux, *Travels,* 1:132–36.

their refinement. Finally, the proper social environment was carefully crafted to properly display gentility. Town houses, country estates, formal gardens, and gala events provided the necessary stage.[44]

From a sociological standpoint, gentility is an aspect of stratification. Stratified systems rank people not only in terms of wealth and power but also in status hierarchies. Status distinctions are expressed in an individual's life-style, and particularly in the way income is spent. While status is often closely related to class and wealth and occupation, the correlation is not absolute; education, religion, and ethnicity also affect an individual's status.[45]

Anglicization, the propensity toward lavish expenditure and display, combined with the cultivation of gentility to give the upper class an unmistakable and unmatchable life-style, which created an enormous gap between the elite and the rest of the population. Deliberately created, social distance was carefully maintained. Class lines were drawn at teas, dinners, parties, visits, balls, and gala extravaganzas. For example, when young Polly Shippen visited Philadelphia, she plunged into the mandatory social whirl and in one week "attended a card party at Mrs. Mifflin's, the Assembly ball, Mrs. Washington's drawing room, dinner at Mr. Edward Burd's, a party at Mrs. Henry Livingston's, a play, the City Concert, and according to custom, in . . . free moments . . . engaged in the time consuming ceremony of morning visits." These activities were not only time-consuming and tiring but also prohibitively expensive.[46]

The social whirl was given structure by the familiar associational system. The upper class socialized in a large variety of clubs and associations that catered to every taste and inclination. There were convivial groups, like the Governor's Club and The Friends of the Young Sort, and gluttony clubs, including six fishing companies, the oldest and most prestigious of which was the Colony in Schuylkill. Among the others were the Philadelphia Dancing Assembly, a Jockey Club whose annual meet attracted sportsmen from the whole eastern seaboard, including George Washington, and, predictably, the Gloucester Hunting Club, America's first fox-hunting club.[47]

44. Bushman, "American High-Style," 349–62.

45. Worsley, *New Introducing Sociology*, 399–400, 460–63; Gerth and Mills, eds., *From Max Weber*, 191; and the classic Weber, "Class, Status, Party," in ibid., ch. 7.

46. For Polly's week, see Rasmusson, "Democratic Environment," 172, 171–73. See also Rasmusson, "Capital," 55–56.

47. Bridenbaugh, *Cities in Revolt,* 364–65; Bridenbaugh and Bridenbaugh, *Rebels,* 22–24, 220–21; Brobeck, "Revolutionary Change," 416; Miller, *Philadelphia,* 14.

The upper class also joined clubs to further a variety of intellectual, social, and cultural activities. They organized and managed the Hand-in-Hand Fire Company, the American Philosophical Society, the Agricultural Society, such schools as the University of Pennsylvania, the Pennsylvania Hospital, and the First Troop of Philadelphia Cavalry. Thus, if the associational system served the needs of party in the political sphere, in the social sphere it was put to the use of class.

The roots of the upper class stretched back into the seventeenth century. The major change in the configuration of the upper class in the second half of the eighteenth century was the decline of the Quaker elite and the rise of an Anglican faction. The proprietary faction not only survived the Revolution but emerged stronger than ever. By the late 1780s the upper class was richer, more powerful, and more united than it had been before the war.[48]

While a few prestigious families, like the Allens, failed to survive the revolutionary tide, most did. Many followed the example of John Dickinson and Robert Morris and labored in politics or fought on the battlefield. As always, there were opportunities for well-connected outsiders like John Swanwick and Charles Pettit. Others survived by keeping a low profile. For example, Edward Shippen, a wealthy supporter of the proprietor and judge of the British Vice-Admiralty Court, whose daughter Peggy was now Mrs. Benedict Arnold, retired to Chester County, where he managed his estate. In 1791, Shippen was appointed to the State Supreme Court, and eight years later he became the court's Chief Justice.[49]

Thus, although the Revolution affected factions, families, and individuals, it did not transform the upper class. According to Stephen Brobeck, the elite of the late 1780s was composed of thirty-seven men. More than half of them (twenty-two) were either members of the prewar elite or socially close to them before the war. At its core were nine wealthy merchants, who included Robert Morris, Morris's partner Thomas Willing, and William Bingham. In 1789, Morris and Bingham had the highest tax ratings in the city. All of the nine, except Bingham and Thomas Mifflin, were active members of the prewar upper class.

48. Brobeck, "Changes in Elite Groups," 31–33, 73, 111–43, 182–86, 212, 226–27, 239; Rasmusson, "Capital," 179; Brobeck, "Revolutionary Change," 431–33.
49. Brobeck, "Changes in Elite Groups," 211–12, 220–24, 226–27, 353, 371; Brobeck, "Revolutionary Change," 432; Brunhouse, *Counter-Revolution*, 220–21; Miller, *Philadelphia*, 25; Rasmusson, "Capital," 34. For the Shippen family during the war, see Klein, *Portrait*, 173–200.

Bingham simply was too young, while Mifflin had not yet made enough money.[50]

Still, events of the magnitude of the Revolution are likely to have a significant impact. Pennsylvania's prewar elite, including the Whigs, faced independence and blinked. Leaders like John Dickinson, Robert Morris, Thomas Willing, and James Wilson either vacillated or opposed independence. Their reluctance cost them dearly. When delegates to the Provisional Conference met in 1776 to write a new constitution, virtually the entire prewar elite was missing. The absence of the great proprietary and Quaker families was not surprising, but that of the leading Whigs was more important.[51]

Horrified by their exclusion from power and by the Constitution of 1776, the prewar elite returned to the political arena. The Republican Party was their chosen vehicle. Notables like John Cadwallader, George Clymer, Francis Hopkinson, and Robert Morris were charter members of the Republican Society. Eight of the nine richest members of the postwar upper class were among the party's leadership, along with such prominent professionals as James Wilson and Benjamin Rush. All were Philadelphians.[52]

An analysis of the leadership of the Constitutional Party in terms of class is complicated by the fact that it changed dramatically over the course of time. The party was organized and initially led by George Bryan, a merchant, and Bryan's son-in-law Jonathan Bayard Smith. They recruited party activists like Jonathan D. Sergeant and moderate Whigs like Joseph Reed. Radical proponents of the Constitution of 1776, such as Dr. James Hutchinson, Daniel Roberdeau, Frederick Kuhl, and David Rittenhouse, joined them. A rural contingent emerged in 1780. John Ewing died in 1783, and Joseph Reed died the following year. In the mid-1780s Peale, Bryan, Hutchinson, Smith, Sergeant, and Roberdeau withdrew from politics, while William Moore deserted to the Republicans. These losses were partly compensated for by new recruits and the maturation of men like William Findley and Charles Pettit.[53]

50. Brobeck, "Changes in Elite Groups," 218–19, 353–70; Gough, "Towards a Theory," 208, 266; Miller, *Philadelphia*, 20–26; Rasmusson, "Democratic Environment," 161–64; Doerflinger, *Vigorous Spirit*, 16, 20, 31.

51. Thayer, *Pennsylvania Politics*, 177–79, 181.

52. Brobeck, "Changes in Elite Groups," 224, 233, 237; Ireland, "Ethnic-Religious Dimension," 440–42; *Pa. Packet*, 25 March 1779. The Republican leadership was stable throughout the whole decade. The only major additions were Jacob Hiltzheimer, William Moore, and Anthony Wayne. Geib, "History of Philadelphia," 269–71.

53. Foner, *Paine*, 185; Geib, "History of Philadelphia," 269–71.

Constitutionalist leaders differed from their Republican counterparts in important ways. Except for William Moore, none had direct ties to the prewar upper class, and none were as wealthy. Stephen Brobeck found eight Constitutionalists who qualified as members of the postwar upper class, including Charles Pettit, Thomas McKean, Dr. James Hutchinson, and Jared Ingersoll. Only four Constitutionalist leaders appearing on the tax lists of 1789 were well-to-do, rated between £1,000 and £1,700, which compares with nine Republicans rated at between £1,900 and £6,185. The Constitutionalist leadership also included an important rural contingent of moderate means. The resulting difference between the wealth of Constitutionalist and Republican leaders was truly massive.[54]

The occupational structure of the urban leadership of both parties was similar: both included a significant number of merchants. Despite this similarity, however, the social backgrounds of party leaders were markedly different. Republicans were primarily Anglican, and Constitutionalists were mostly Presbyterian. Moreover, the Republicans were mainly of English stock and the Constitutionalists were English, Irish, and French. Finally, the Republican leadership came from older more established families, while a number of Constitutionalists, like Thomas McKean, Jared Ingersoll, Charles Pettit, and Jonathan D. Sergeant, moved into the province just before or during the War of Independence.[55]

At the leadership level, the struggle between the Republicans and the Constitutionalists was a struggle between different groups. The Republicans were primarily Philadelphia merchants, substantially richer, more established, and more prestigious. Religion and ethnicity widened the gap. These differences were partly muted by the fact that the Philadelphia Constitutionalists wanted nothing more than to be welcomed into the established inner circles of the provincial upper class. But they had to share power within the party with rural politicians of middling means and sharply different aspirations.

Party programs reflected these socioeconomic differences and the needs derived from them, and at the same time the needs and desires of their supporters. Once the political problems posed by independence were dealt with, new problems surfaced. Protection for manufactured

54. Brobeck, "Changes in Elite Groups," 227–29, 355–56; Main, *Political Parties*, 207–9.

55. Baumann, "Democratic-Republicans," 592, 595; Brobeck, "Changes in Elite Groups," 220; Brunhouse, *Counter-Revolution*, 353–54; Geib, "History of Philadelphia," 9–10; Ireland, "Ethnic-Religious Dimension," 442.

goods, state debts, the disposal of western lands, land banks and paper money, specie money, and commercial banking were the new issues. These issues reflected market relations and class interests.

Inevitably, class interests were contradictory. Merchants wanted low prices for goods they purchased, high prices for goods they sold, and open markets. Artisans demanded government protection and cheap farm produce, while farmers wanted cheap manufactured goods and high prices for farm produce. At the same time, the farmers' demand for land banks and a legal-tender paper currency conflicted with the merchant's desire for commercial banks and a specie-backed currency. Furthermore, while merchants wanted command, farmers and artisans had a deep fear of "great" men, and at the same time contradictory deferential urges.[56]

There was no easy way to bridge the gap. Both parties struggled with the problem. The Constitutionalists tried to rally artisans and merchants behind their banner by appealing to patriotism—hence their attacks on those whose loyalty was suspect. They also used egalitarianism to expand their support. The attack on the bank was part of this strategy, and that assault had considerable appeal in the urban business community, where many artisans and merchants feared the power of the new institution. The appeal of the Constitutionalist position, however, was limited by the antiurban, antimerchant, and antiprotectionist stance of the party.

The Republican answer to the Constitutionalists was to depict themselves as the defenders of freedom. They attacked the Test Acts, espoused free markets, and portrayed assaults on charters as attacks on property. The combination of a charismatic upper class defending freedom was eventually successful. Neither party was able to find a way to fully satisfy the class needs of the urban artisans who found themselves selling their favors.

The politics of class played an important role within the parties as well as between them. The situation was especially difficult for the Constitutionalists. The failure of the urban leaders to win elections in Philadelphia—they won only in 1779 and 1784—showed their weakness, and they were forced to share power.[57]

The Constitutionalist coalition was shaped by the historic situation it found itself in. In 1776 and 1777 the party had to generate support for

56. For a useful summary of the issues, see Main, *Political Parties*, 174–203.
57. Baumann, "Democratic-Republicans," 57–58.

the new government and for the war effort. It turned out that the strongest support for the new government came from regions that were primarily rural, noncommercial, and Presbyterian. The fact that the Constitutionalist leadership was also Presbyterian cemented the bond between the party and its rural followers.

As the rural wing of the party asserted itself, the party became a vehicle for rural petty-commodity producers, who were strongly egalitarian. Their rural backgrounds also predisposed them to take a variety of antiurban, antiartisan, and antimerchant positions, tendencies that were evident in attempts to move the capital from Philadelphia, to oppose tariffs, and to revoke the charter of the Bank of North America.[58]

While the Republicans also faced the problems involved in building a coalition, issues of class had less of an impact on their calculations. Wealthy urban merchants were unassailable within the party. By 1779 they had accepted the role of loyal opposition, and that determined their posture. In a few years they built a coalition that by 1786 would put them in firm control of the state. The Republican program was a shrewd amalgam of class appeal to merchants, artisans, and the more commercially minded farmers, an ideological demand for constitutional revision and a libertarian stance aimed at protecting nonjurors, whom they portrayed as victims of oppression.

Did Philadelphia's wealthy merchants constitute a ruling class, and if so how did they rule? In class societies the relationship between the classes and the state is frequently oblique. The existence of political, military, cultural, and intellectual centers of power, authority, and status creates complex relationships between the state and the social classes. But in Revolutionary Pennsylvania there was no ambiguity.

The small scale of the society and the low level of institutional development explains this clarity. In 1774 the entire mercantile community consisted of 329 men. The elite was much smaller. According to Thomas M. Doerflinger, during the 1780s "the great oaks of Philadelphia's merchant community" included only fifty-two merchants from thirty-seven businesses. The cohesiveness and class consciousness of the upper class owed a good deal to this fact.[59]

Before the Revolution, the elite had dominated the General Assembly and assumed aristocratic airs. That the elite was able to maintain an

58. Foner, *Paine*, 185; Ireland, "Ethnic-Religious Dimension"; Main, *Political Parties*, 207–9; Miller, *Philadelphia*, 21–24.
59. Price, "Economic Function," 178; Doerflinger, *Vigorous Spirit*, 20.

aristocratic stance and regain political power during a period of egalitarian activism underscores the significance of status distinctions. Manners, clothes, homes, and a lavish life-style created a glamour and an aura that in a Weberian sense constituted a form of manufactured charisma.[60]

Nevertheless, manufactured charisma, legitimacy, and deference are not enough to explain the power of the merchants. After all, the mechanisms that create and maintain charisma, legitimacy, and deference are not entirely cultural and ideological—power is also involved, and the more traditional sources of power were not available in Pennsylvania. So how were Philadelphia's merchants able to translate their wealth and social standing into effective power? The answer requires another look at the merchant's life-style.

Possessing ample resources of wealth and leisure, and encouraged by the ideal of gentility, merchants educated themselves. As a result, they became the intellectual elite of the province. While artisan intellectuals like Tom Paine are famous, they were not typical. Most books, pamphlets, and newspaper articles were written by merchants and their professional allies. It was men from the countinghouse, like Pelatiah Webster and Tench Coxe, and men from the courthouse, like James Wilson, who were responsible for most of the political writings that played such an important role in the politics of the day.

Wealth, leisure, education, high status, a tradition of service, the assumption that they should lead, and the broadening experience of travel and international commerce combined to produce the talents of men like Richard Morris, George Bryan, and George Clymer. Such men were typical, and their talents were diffused throughout the upper class. They held elective and appointive offices on the provincial and national levels, and they provided the cadres to organize and run political parties and grind out political propaganda.

The talents of these men were not limited to the economic and political arenas. They also constituted the social, cultural, and intellectual elite. The fact that *all* the major social spheres bore the imprint of the mercantile upper class is eloquent testimony to their talent. Influence in service and in cultural and political institutions was an important factor in the ability of the merchants to mobilize people and exercise power.

60. On the subject of deference, see Tully, *Penn's Legacy*, 79–86, 223–24 n. 1; Beeman, "Deference," 403–12, 423–28; Shils, "Deference," 104–5; Weber, *Economy and Society*, 1:212–15, 3:941–47. See also the excellent Newby, "Deferential Dialectic."

At the same time, however, the power of this class was limited. Farmers and artisans struggled, often successfully, to defend their interests. Their political activism was institutionalized by the appearance of modern centers of power, by political parties, and by the associational system. As a consequence, it was difficult for the ruling class to have its way. The attack on the Bank of North America and the loss of its charter exemplified this weakness. Despite this, and the fact that the elite had to struggle to have its way, the upper class achieved virtually all of its political goals. Whether it involved the Constitution of 1776, the Test Acts, price-fixing, rechartering the Bank of North America, or the federal Constitution, the upper class eventually had its way.

Pennsylvania's social structure was a mix of modern and traditional elements in an uneven, changing balance. A look at the economic sphere makes the point. The major economic figures were the export-import merchants, the artisans, and the farmers. Philadelphia's merchants were primitive capitalists. They entered markets and sought to make a profit, but they personalized economic relations whenever possible and organized their lives so that business was only one important activity among others. Resembling traditional merchants, they were unable to control either production or consumption, and thus were weak economic modernizers. The region's artisans were also traditional economic figures. Engaging in small-scale craft production, they resisted economic development and commercialization—they sold the articles they produced, but did not become entrepreneurs. Pride in skill, pride in product, and a desire for competence shaped the artisans' lives.

Farmers were the most complex economic figures in the region. Commercial farmers, who congregated near urban markets, were distinguished by their entrepreneurial efforts. They sold virtually everything they grew and produced on their farms. Some farmers owned businesses, such as mills, while others combined farming with artisanal activities. Those farmers created the cottager system—the rural wage-labor system. Many other farmers, however, were petty-commodity producers, especially those who were more removed from urban markets. Owning their farms, they relied on the labor of family and neighbors and were embedded in neighborhood exchange networks. These farmers bought and sold goods and services, but their commitment to markets was limited. It is significant that many of the noncommercial practices they developed, such as bookkeeping barter and the borrowing system, were used all over the state, even in the more commercial areas.

The same mix of noncapitalist and capitalist elements appears in the region's markets. Despite the existence of strongly institutionalized international commerce, most regional markets were incomplete or imperfect. Of the factors of production—land, labor, and capital—only land had fully developed markets. Labor markets were not nearly so well developed. While wage labor remained unimportant in the urban economy, the cottager system flourished in the countryside. However, the spread of wage labor in rural areas was mitigated by the continued importance of noncommercial "frolics" and "bees," the borrowing system, and barter. Labor markets were not fully developed.

Capital markets were extremely primitive. The credit networks of the international mercantile system were a significant source of capital, and the insurance trade had appeared, as had private banking. But the importance of land banks, noncommercial book credit, barter, and communal labor-sharing revealed the incompleteness of commercial capital markets.

Product markets existed but were also incomplete. A number of commodities like wheat, flax, lumber, and consumer items like cloth and tools had clearly articulated markets, but those markets did not dominate as they would seventy-five years later. Farmers, for example, would commit only one-fifth of their resources to wheat, the region's leading cash crop, and did not rush to adopt laborsaving devices to enhance their yields. The combination of primitive transportation and communication, the limited penetration of consumerism, cheap and available land, and neighborly reciprocity limited the appeal of commercial markets. In the long run the attractive power of international markets and British capitalism eroded the barriers created by petty-commodity production, but the transition was neither rapid nor easy.

Like the economy, Pennsylvania's social sphere was largely traditional. The presence of small, scattered markets and the limited capital requirements for most economic activities mandated loosely organized, small, unspecialized, and simple organizations. Social and economic relations were personalized and heavily influenced by the norms and values of household and community. Moreover, because economic development had not yet begun, the pace of change was slow; the careening rhythms of system transformation had not yet begun to alter organizational forms.

The powers of the government, the military, and the churches were so circumscribed that a rigidly ascriptive institutional social order did not emerge. Religious toleration and pacifism, and citizen soldiers, coexisted with a government that had too few officials to either administer or coerce its citizens effectively. In the resulting institutional arena, intimate groups and associations, which are neither traditional nor modern, played a vital role in integrating the social structure.

Voluntary associations were created to satisfy a wide range of public and private purposes. One characteristic of such associations is that they lend themselves to multiple membership. An individual could join the militia, the Constitutional Society, the Sons of Tammany, the Presbyterian church, and a fire-fighting company. Multiple membership combined with the flexibility of voluntary associations to give the network of voluntary associations much of its strength. And, when activists grafted the mobilization techniques of the day onto the network, the integrative potential of the associational system was magnified.

The political sphere was more modern than either the economy or the social arena. After 1760, participation increased, as did democratization, and political parties were created. The Constitution of 1776 was the most important issue of the day, while the development of political parties was the most significant institutional development of the Revolutionary decade. Between 1776 and 1779, political parties were organized and party politics was explored. During those years the parties developed organizational techniques, constituencies, programs, styles, and symbols.

In the 1770s and 1780s Pennsylvanians struggled through war and independence. They created a new state, two constitutions, two governments, experimented with political techniques, and developed a party system. The inevitable tensions produced by this experimentation were compounded by the economic hardships of the era and the presence of large numbers of Tories and Neutrals, which resulted in violence, the jailing of civilians because of their political positions, and the Test Acts.

Despite these difficulties, Pennsylvanians clung to constitutionalism and the need for fair elections. The political sphere was governed by rules of fairness and a modern party system. Participation was encouraged, and conflict was channeled into the realm of electoral politics. While civil rights were abused, they survived the travail of war and loyalty oaths. Yet if the parties and the electoral system they managed was modern, the clubs, societies, committees, and associations that constituted the organizational basis of the political sphere conformed to the dominant organizational mode of the day: they were loosely organized, unspecialized, small-scale organizations.

Largely unencumbered by the fetters of estates and slavery, Pennsylvanians created the socioeconomic classes that defined a modern stratification system. At the core of this system was the freedom to move, to buy and sell property, and to change occupations. Because so many owned land and tools, independence was within reach of a significant portion of the population. This fact was profoundly important for class relations, because it meant that relations between classes would not be defined in the realm of production and would not be shaped by exploitation.

Class conflict in Pennsylvania generally occurred as the major classes jockeyed for position in the realm of circulation. Thus, farmers wanted high prices for their produce and low prices for the goods and services they purchased. Artisans and merchants too had different priorities, each wanting high prices for the commodities they sold and low prices for the goods they purchased. The irony is that although Pennsylvania had a modern class system the major class actors were traditional economic figures.

There were three politically significant classes in Pennsylvania: petty-commodity-producing farmers, urban artisans, and export-import merchants. Farmers needed money to purchase land and consumer goods and to pay taxes. They entered commercial markets to earn the money they needed, but they remained embedded in neighborhood exchange networks driven by reciprocity. Deference encouraged them to follow the lead of their betters, but when aroused they turned and attacked great men and aristocrats. Mobilized during the 1760s and 1770s, they wanted land, good prices for their produce, cheap consumer goods, low taxes, and credit relief.

The region's urban artisans were the second politically significant class. The artisanal culture was shaped by the small-producer tradition. Artisans had the tools and the skills and were proud of their proficiency and the utility of their manufactured goods. They were also militant egalitarian democrats. Like farmers, they mobilized during the 1760s and 1770s. The establishment of the Mechanics Committee in 1769 and the Patriotic Society in 1772 were important events in their political development, as was the organization of the militia and the Committee of Privates in 1775. Both farmers and artisans were petty-commodity producers with a producer mentality, and, like the farmers, artisans wanted an economic equation that favored themselves: high prices for manufactured goods and low prices for agricultural produce.

Owning 70 percent of Philadelphia's wealth, the city's merchants were the region's upper class. Of English stock and members of the Church of England, they were proud of their wealth and the life-style they carefully created. As a class, they were driven by Anglicization, conspicuous consumption, and the cultivation of gentility. Philadelphia's merchants were able to sustain their aristocratic airs and their power well into the nineteenth century. Wealth was at the heart of their claim to power, but education, travel, a heritage of political and social service, and the awe created by their magnificent life-style also contributed, as did the leisure to cultivate cultural and intellectual talents. Men like Robert Morris rose to positions of leadership because they were genuinely talented. They ran successful businesses, held high elective and appointive office, and were active in party politics, as well as in the social, cultural, and intellectual spheres.

This, then, was Pennsylvania's social structure, the world into which the Bank of North America would be born. Each of the major constituent elements—the economic, social, and political spheres and the stratification system—contained traditional and modern elements in an unstable balance. In the late eighteenth century Pennsylvania was a flourishing traditional society, but the observer can see signs—faint in some places and stronger in others—that the balance would change in the direction of the dynamic, democratic, modern capitalist society that followed.

PART TWO

The
Bank of North America
and the
Problem of Change

6

The Birth of a Bank

The starting point for a discussion of historical change using the concept of the social structure is the functionalist notion that the social structure is a "system." In such systems the various components—the social groups and institutional spheres—fit together and exhibit a degree of compatibility. And changes in one component will have an impact on the rest of the system.[1]

If portions of the social structure change and become incompatible with the rest, adjustment and alterations would occur, and to the extent that elements of the system are able to adjust, the impact would be either great or small. Social structures change because of changes in the scale of the various units; changes in the nature of the various organizational forms, social groups, or institutional spheres; changes in the integrative mechanisms; changes in the external environment; and of course through the transforming hand of events, such as the American Revolution.

In eighteenth-century Pennsylvania, change had occurred in a number of ways. Population growth resulted in greater social complexity and

---

1. Worsley, *New Introducing Sociology*, 494–510.

increased stratification. As the population grew, the available land shrank and property relations changed. In the 1780s, however, a shortage of land was still only a possibility.

Mercantile developments were also a source of change. Commerce between Pennsylvania and the West Indies, Britain, Africa, southern Europe, and Asia increased the movement of people, goods, services, and ideas and created new opportunities for entrepreneurs. Expanding trade served as an engine for commercialization, which was slowly affecting attitudes and institutions ranging from consumption to religion to labor relations. Through the century these changes were incremental, and in the short run they did not destroy the social order, but helped a traditional mercantile society flower.

The creation of America's first commercial bank was an event of a different order. The bank did not resemble the other organizations in the region, nor did it behave like them. Contemporaries quickly became aware that the bank was an agent of change, and they reacted swiftly. As people came to understand commercial banking, and as they saw the bank change mercantile business practices and oppose popular measures in the Assembly, a traditionalist reaction erupted.

As the controversy intensified, it had an impact on the center of the political arena. In short order, the political parties, associational networks, and social classes mobilized. Given the simplicity of the social structure, it is not surprising that the impact was felt throughout the entire social order. Consequently, the early history of the Bank of North America is well suited to explore the nature of change through the lens of social structural analysis.

The Bank of North America was born in the midst of crisis, created by Congress to aid the flagging American cause. In late 1778 the British launched a major military thrust in the Deep South and easily carried Georgia and South Carolina, capturing or wiping out large American armies at Charleston and Camden. By August 1780 the Red Coats appeared to be on the verge of taking the Upper South.

American morale plummeted. The French were more interested in regaining their lost possessions than in helping Republican revolutionaries and the home front was an unmitigated disaster. Congress was mired in factional dispute. Congress and the states seemed to have exhausted their financial resources. The continental currency had all but ceased to circulate, and the winter of 1780–81 found the army on half rations, unpaid, poorly clad, and mutinous.

Even General Washington, that paragon of strength and optimism, was shaken. In a letter to Congress he mused, "We seem to be verging so fast to destruction that I am filled with sensations to which I have been a stranger till within this three months." Across the Atlantic, British hopes rose. Many believed they could bring the war to a successful conclusion before the year was out.[2]

The urgency of the moment finally communicated itself to Congress, and that august body began to stir. Congress abandoned the militia system and reorganized the army. An effort to give Congress the power to tax was begun, and administrative agencies were reorganized and centralized. Departments of war, foreign affairs, naval affairs, and finance were created.[3]

The Office of Finance was established on February 7, 1781, and the obvious candidate, Robert Morris, a wealthy, well-connected Pennsylvania merchant and Republican politician, was elected Financier. Shortly after he assumed office, Morris submitted a proposal to establish a bank: "Its immediate purpose was to assist his administration by enabling him to borrow money and anticipate his revenues." Morris had a grand vision. He hoped the bank would become "a pillar of American credit" and if it succeeded it would provide the nation with a circulating medium, strengthen the mercantile sector, and encourage business interests to support the national government.[4]

On May 27 the Committee on Public Finance reported the plan with a favorable recommendation and Congress approved it the same day. Only four of the twenty-four delegates opposed the measure, their opposition stemming from a concern that Congress was not empowered to grant charters of incorporation.[5] The plan Congress approved was simple. A capital of $400,000 would be raised by selling 1,000 shares of stock at $400 apiece. Only specie would be accepted as payment. Once the stock was fully subscribed, the bank would be organized under

2. Sumner, *Financier*, 1:258.

3. Ferguson, *Power*, 203–5; Rakove, *Beginnings*, chs. 11, 12; Studenski and Krooss, *Financial History*, 25–27; Carp, *To Starve*, esp. ch. 8.

4. Robert Morris to the President of Congress, 13 March 1781, *Morris Papers*, 1:17–19; Robert Morris to Benjamin Franklin, 13 July 1781, in ibid., 282–86; Diary, 17 May 1781, in ibid., 65; Saunders, *Evolution*, 129 and 128–32; *Journals*, 20:544–48; Ferguson, *Power*, 123. For the congressional discussions on the need for a bank, see Riesman, "Money," 137, and esp. Riesman, "Origins," 399–407.

5. Virginia Delegates to Benjamin Harrison, 8 January 1782, *Madison Papers*, 4:19; *Journals*, 20:544–48.

the title "The President, Directors, and Company of the Bank of North America."[6]

Having approved the plan, Congress proceeded to pass several supplementary resolutions providing that the bank would be incorporated as soon as the subscription was filled, the officers were chosen, and an application was made to Congress. In other words, Congress had committed itself only to receive a petition—the charter still had to be won. Congress also asked the states to grant the bank a monopoly during the war and to punish the counterfeiting of bank notes and embezzlement from it.[7]

Approval in hand, Morris undertook to organize the bank. The first task was to raise the necessary capital, and promotional literature poured out of his office. Even though the campaign was national in scope, the response was disappointing. As late as February 9, 1782, more than a month after the bank had opened its doors, only $60,499.87 had been collected. Banking was too new, and conditions were too unsettled, for the private sector to provide the necessary risk capital.[8]

An example of the lengths that Morris would go to in his campaign to raise the required capital is his overture to former investors in the Bank of Pennsylvania. In 1780 a number of Philadelphia patriots raised £312,500 to purchase supplies for the army. Calling the fund the Bank of Pennsylvania, the investors asked Congress to reimburse them. That body agreed but delayed payment. Morris intervened. He hoped that if Congress kept its promise the money would be invested in the new bank. Morris suggested that funds that had been collected to support the U.S. ambassador to Spain be released and turned over to the Philadelphians. Congress acquiesced, and $64,000 was delivered. The results were disappointing. The Philadelphia patriots invested only $16,400 in the Bank of North America on or before the day the bank opened.[9]

---

6. For the plan, see Morris, "Plan for Establishing a National Bank, with Observations," *Morris Papers,* 1:66–74.

7. *Journals,* 20:546–48.

8. Robert Morris to Benjamin Franklin, 14 July 1781, *Morris Papers,* 1:295–96, is typical of the promotional effort. See Diary, 30 and 31 October and 1 November 1781, in ibid., 3:118–22; Thomas Fitzsimons, "State of Facts Respecting the National Bank," John J. Maitland Family Papers, Fitzsimons, Meade, and Cook Section, Fitzsimons Folder, HSP.

9. Ferguson, *Power,* 136; Robert Morris to the President of the Congress, 21 June 1781, in *Morris Papers,* 2:161–62; Diary, 4 July 1781, in ibid., 2:220–21; *Journals,* 17:542, 548–50; 20:688–89; *Pa. Packet,* 19 and 27 June 1780; Stock Ledger, I, Bank of North America, Bank of North America Papers, Box 6-D, HSP. Morris's efforts were not limited to the investors in

Again, Morris stepped into the breach. When a French loan of $470,000 materialized, he invested more than half in the bank and announced that the organization of the bank would immediately proceed. On the appointed day, the directors were elected. By January 1, 1781, some $280,000 had been collected: $254,000 from the French loan and a mere $24,000 from the private sector. Even though the required $400,000 capital had not been raised, Morris and the directors applied for the charter.[10]

This time Congress was reluctant. The doubts planted by the minority, who had pointed out that nothing in the Articles of Confederation gave Congress the power to grant charters, bore fruit. Congress appointed a committee to negotiate with the Financier and the directors of the bank. Morris and the directors pressed aggressively ahead and reached a compromise. Congress would grant the charter, but the states would be asked to pass laws legalizing the grant.[11]

The act of incorporation provided that the Bank of North America would be a corporation with full legal standing. It would have a seal and exist "for ever after." The bank would have twelve directors, one of whom would be the bank president. They would have the power to create bylaws and regulations, issue dividends, and appoint necessary staff. The charter permitted the corporation "to have, purchase, receive, possess, enjoy and retain Lands, Rents, Tenements, Hereditaments, Goods, Chattles and Effects." Finally, the capital could be expanded to a munificent $10,000,000.[12]

The charter was extraordinarily generous. Beyond the assertion that nothing in the charter could contravene the laws and constitutions of the

---

the Bank of Pennsylvania. Samuel Osgood of Massachusetts recalled that Robert Morris had invited him to a meeting whose purpose was to elect the bank's directors. When he arrived, Osgood found his name in nomination. Willing and Morris wanted a director who was not a Philadelphian. When Morris learned Osgood did not have money to purchase shares, the Financier promptly lent it to him. Samuel Osgood to John Lowell, 13 November 1781, in Smith, ed., *Letters of Delegates*, 18:196–98.

10. Ferguson, *Power*, 136; Diary, 1 November 1781, *Morris Papers*, 3:121–22; Thomas Fitzsimons, "State of Facts Respecting the National Bank," Maitland Family Papers, Fitzsimons, Meade, and Cook Section, Fitzsimons Folder; Stock Ledger, I, Bank of North America, Bank of North America Papers, Box 6-D.

11. Diary, 27–29 December 1781, *Morris Papers* 3:446–48, 452–53, 462–63; Virginia Delegates to Benjamin Harrison, 8 January 1782, and Virginia Delegates to Edmund Pendleton, 8 January 1782, *Madison Papers*, 4:18–19, 22–23; Ver Steeg, *Morris*, 84–87.

12. Circular to the Governors of the States, 8 January 1782, *Morris Papers*, 3:507–8; Ordinance of Congress Incorporating the Bank of North America, 11 December 1781, in ibid., 508–11; *Journals*, 21:1187–91.

various states, it contained almost no restraints. In fact, the charter contained no limits on the kind of business the bank could engage in, and did not require the bank to do business with the government. Bank notes were not mentioned. No provision for government regulation was included, although the enabling legislation allowed the Financier to examine the cash account and the bank notes and look at the bank's books on a daily basis.[13]

Congress also approved the board of directors, which consisted mostly of wealthy Philadelphia merchants. The only exceptions were Samuel Osgood, a resident of Boston, who was in town as a representative to the Congress, and James Wilson, a Philadelphia lawyer. Nine of the group were Pennsylvania Republicans, and at least five had been business associates of Morris. Thomas Willing, who had been the senior partner in Morris's mercantile firm and the Financier's dearest friend, was chosen president.[14]

Located on Chestnut Street, the bank opened on January 7, 1782. While the fledgling institution organized itself, a number of states complied with Congress' request and passed enabling legislation. Between January and May, Rhode Island, Connecticut, Massachusetts, New York, North Carolina, and New Jersey acted. In February, President Willing petitioned the Supreme Executive Council of Pennsylvania for an act of incorporation. The request wound its way leisurely through the legislative mills and came up for debate at the end of March.[15]

When the bill was presented, several amendments were offered. A motion limiting the life of the charter to seven years was defeated 42 to 12. Another, preventing the bank from buying and selling land, was defeated by a closer margin, 35 to 21. At the end of the day a last-minute rider was offered, providing that the General Assembly of 1789, or any following year, be granted the power "to alter, amend, or repeal this act." This adroit maneuver almost worked—the margin of defeat was only three votes, 27 to 24. The earlier motion limiting the charter to seven years had failed because it had appeared to be hostile to the bank, but actually the intent had been to protect the Assembly's

13. Ordinance of Congress Incorporating the Bank of North America, 11 December 1781, *Morris Papers*, 3:508–11; Plan for Establishing a National Bank with Observations, in ibid., 1:67.

14. Ver Steeg, *Morris*, 3–4, 230 n. 16; J. Wilson, "Bank of North America," 3–4.

15. *Morris Papers*, 2: 181–82 n. 6; Hammond, *Banks and Politics*, 50–51; Lewis Jr., *History of the Bank*, 36–37, 44; 21, 23, 25, and 26 February and 12 and 25 March 1782, *Pa. Min.*, 567, 572, 578, 591, 602.

prerogative. The amended rider made this clear and nearly passed; it failed because the majority believed that "the charter of the bank must necessarily be always within the power of the house" and that it was therefore not necessary to assert the power.[16]

A few of the assemblymen who supported the rider explained their position in the minutes. Most opposed the charter because they saw it as a threat to the authority of the house and the community. One cause of the danger was the absence of a time limit. History has taught us, they warned, that "all perpetuities are . . . dangerous." They cited the entailed estates of the English barons that had almost allowed them to "enslave the kingdom." In their estimation, the bank's ability to increase its capital to the "enormous" sum of $10,000,000 exacerbated the danger. Such an immense sum of money would translate into power and lead to the establishment of a "dangerous aristocracy." Governmental power was the only protection for the republic. Therefore, they concluded, the Assembly must have the power to "alter, amend or repeal" the charter. The minority also opposed the grant of incorporation because they felt that the "bank [was] entirely for the private advantage and the emolument of the subscribers, and we know of no reason why they should have an established monopoly in this business, from which the government can have no advantage."[17]

The minority's final argument raises a number of questions about the nature and purpose of corporate charters. Corporations are state-created entities. Their life begins when a charter is issued and ends when it expires, and they have clearly defined charters that specify their duties and powers. Corporations are entitled to own and sell property, which legally belongs to the corporation and not to its members. As a result, shareholders are immune from debts incurred in the name of the corporation. Finally, charters might grant privileges, such as a monopoly, the right of eminent domain, or a tax exemption. They might even delegate some of the sovereign power. In the case of banks, as James Willard Hurst notes, charters conferred the power to "issue promises to pay (bank notes), which the law would permit to circulate as a medium of exchange."[18]

16. 25 March 1782, *Pa. Min.*, 602–23, 605–7, 610–11; Carey, ed., *Debates and Proceedings*, 14.

17. 1 April 1782, *Pa. Min.*, 649.

18. Bruchey, "Historical Development," 525; Davis, *Essays*, 1:5; Friedman, *History*, 166. For the quotation, see Hurst, *Legitimacy*, 20 (see also 19–22); Seavoy, "Public Service Origins," 31.

Incorporation conferred a number of advantages, the most important of which was the ability to own property in the name of an organization with potentially unlimited existence. This made it easier to defend both the property and the organization in court. The second advantage was the fact that the organization was designed for a specific purpose and that it limited demands of time and energy on the shareholders.[19]

Colonial Americans were familiar with the corporate form because a great many cities, towns, villages, and boroughs had been incorporated. Even more common were ecclesiastical charters and charters for schools and colleges. A wide range of benevolent organizations had also been chartered, including institutions to care for poor ministers and their families, libraries, fire-fighting companies, and hospitals. The rarest colonial corporation was one created for business purposes. Pennsylvania only had two: The Free Society of Traders was incorporated in England in 1682, and a century later (1768) The Philadelphia Contributionship for the Insuring of Houses from Loss by Fire was chartered.[20]

Almost all colonial corporate charters had been issued to institutions that served important public services. After Independence, innovative state legislatures began issuing charters to businesses that also furthered public purposes. James Willard Hurst notes, "almost all of the business enterprises incorporated here in the formative generation starting in the 1780s were chartered for activities of some community interest." Between 1780 and 1801, 317 separate business corporations were chartered. Almost two-thirds of them were granted to improve inland transportation facilities. Thirty-four commercial banks, thirty-two water companies, thirty-two insurance companies, and four companies to erect and maintain docks were also chartered. Less than 4 percent of the grants went to general-purpose private enterprises.[21]

The concerns of the minority in the Assembly can best be understood in the light of this background. Like most Americans, their view of corporations were conditioned by their reading of the European past and by their own experience. From Europe they had inherited the assumption that acts of incorporation should be granted only for important public purposes, and the colonial experience reinforced the associa-

---

19. Hurst, *Legitimacy*, 26–29; Seavoy, "Public Service Origins," 31.

20. Davis, *Essays*, 1:75, 78, 81–84, 86–89, 95–96, 96 n. 2, 100–101; Seavoy, *Origins*, 12–13, 20–21, 35 n. 30; Seavoy, "Public Service Origins," 41–50, 50 n. 44; Friedman, *History*, 166.

21. Bruchey, *Enterprise*, 205–6; Hurst, *Legitimacy*, 15, 17.

tion between corporations and public service. The mere fact that the Bank of North America was asking for a corporate charter meant that one of the standards used in reviewing the request would be its public utility.[22]

Thus, although a comfortable majority in the Pennsylvania Assembly supported the bank as a war measure, it was inevitable that some would be disturbed at the proposal that a group of private entrepreneurs be singled out and lent state support. The grant of a charter in perpetuity to private investors whose primary aim was profits, along with the grant of what was at the moment a monopoly, resonated with fears long trumpeted by Republican writers. They had long warned about the danger of a "money power," about those who sought to control money and use it to corrupt the nation. In 1781, in the midst of a difficult war, these fears failed to elicit significant support. It is also noteworthy that the legislative minority did not vilify the occupation of commercial banking—the first concerns were about the new institution's corporate status.

An analysis of the Assembly's roll calls reveals that only 12 percent voted consistently against the bank. Given that the Assembly was divided almost evenly between the Constitutionalists and Republicans, the widespread support for the bank was impressive. In the light of later developments, it is worth noting the absence of a sectional pattern in the voting. The bank had support all over the state.[23]

The Assembly debates did not attract public interest. Local newspapers were silent on the subject; pamphleteers did not rush into print with missives for or against the proposal. Patriotism, the exigencies of war, and widespread ignorance about the nature of commercial banking explain the silence.

Charter in hand, the bank turned to the problem of establishing itself as a going concern. For a short while it was not clear whether the enterprise would succeed. The bank remained undercapitalized; as late

22. Seavoy, "Public Service Origins," 31–33; Hurst, *Legitimacy*, 1–11.
23. The list of elected representatives and the roll calls are in 1 April 1782, *Pa. Min.*, 500–501, 602–3, 605, 610. The percentages include only the fifty-nine assemblymen who voted; fifteen did not vote. For a more detailed discussion of the proceedings in the General Assembly in particular, and the bank war in general, see Rappaport, "Sources," 25–28; "An Act to Incorporate the Subscribers to the Bank of North America," in Mitchell and Flanders, eds., *Statutes at Large*, 10:406–8. See also the companion legislation, "An Act for Preventing and Punishing the Counterfeiting of the Common Seal, Bank Bills and Bank Notes of the President, Directors and Company of the Bank of North America and for Other Purposes Therein Mentioned," in ibid., 10:383–84.

as a year after the bank had opened, only 269 shares had been purchased, by 99 people. Even worse, many of the investors were slow to come up with the promised funds. Not until August 30, 1783, well after the war had ended, was the subscription completed. Furthermore, bank notes did not circulate in New York and Hartford in 1782. To make matters worse, the government was forced to borrow most of the money it had invested, thereby depleting the capital stock and forcing the directors to pressure customers to accept bank notes instead of specie.[24]

Part of the problem was that no one knew anything about commercial banking or about the use of the corporate form in a commercial enterprise. Thomas Willing later recalled that when they had undertaken to establish the bank the business appeared to be "a pathless wilderness." Besides avoiding bad loans, the directors had to concern themselves with counterfeit bank notes and with managing the accounts of hundreds of depositors. Deposits were a puzzle; the directors did not know how to handle them. Even though many customers made frequent deposits and wrote dozens of checks each month, the bank neither charged customers for the privilege of depositing nor offered interest to attract deposits.[25]

Nevertheless, matters went relatively well from the beginning. In early February, Isaac Wharton, a Philadelphia merchant, reported optimistically to a business correspondent:

> Such is the Stability and Credit of the Bank, that, its Notes as receivd without any hesitation in all payments—whether public or private. . . . Besides the Aids recd from publick Monies deposited in it—most of our wealthy Merchants send Cash there as to be a Place of the greatest Security. . . . The Directors

24. Thomas Fitzsimons, "State of Facts Respecting the National Bank," Maitland Family Papers, Fitzsimons, Meade, and Cook Section, Fitzsimons Folder; "Draft of Petitions to the Legislature Citing the History and Services of the Bank" in folder entitled "18 Documents pertaining to the attempt in 1812 to secure a recharter for the Bank," Bank of North America Papers, Box 6-C; Stock Ledger, Bank of North America, in ibid., 6-D; Alexander Hamilton to Robert Morris, 21 and 28 September 1782, Robert Morris to Alexander Hamilton, 5 October 1782, *Hamilton Papers*, 3:169–71, 177–79; Lewis Jr., *History of the Bank*, 41–42; Ver Steeg, *Morris*, 116–17; "Early Records of the Bank of North America," *Morris Papers*, app. 1, 7:797 and 817–18 n. 13.

25. "Letter of Thomas Willing, of Philadelphia, to William Phillips and Five Others in Boston, January 6, 1784," in Gras, *Massachusetts*, 210 and 209–12; Doerflinger, *Vigorous Spirit*, 298, 302; Rappaport, "First Description," 665 and 661–67.

being calm, judicious Men, well experienced in Business, who have Staked their Reputations & [illegible] for its Safety—they will not Suffer more Notes to be issued than what they can at any time answer.[26]

Locally, bank notes circulated at par almost from the day the bank opened. In April, Pelatiah Webster commented that bank notes were "as good as cash here." Philadelphians were confident that as Morris was both "guardian of the public revenues, and of the interests of the bank" he would "be careful to draw from the latter no more than he is absolutely enabled to replace by the former." They were correct. Robert Morris and his assistant Gouverneur Morris labored to ensure the bank's survival. They helped write the bylaws and influenced virtually every aspect of the business. Known as "The Financier," Robert Morris asked the states to accept bank notes as payment for taxes, and in April convinced the French to deposit military funds in the bank. The following spring, "the bank was apparently saved from another suspension of discounting by the arrival of specie imported by Robert Morris and deposited in the bank." Through skillful manipulation, the Financier kept the bank notes from the parts of the country where they had depreciated, and thereby created a demand for them. Soon they were as good as specie everywhere.[27]

By the fall of 1782 the stockholders were celebrating their "present flourishing situation and flattering prospects." A year later President Willing's correspondence told a glowing story: "Our success increases daily. Our circulation is widely extended. Customers are above 700— and our weekly rects [sic] and payments one Million at least." Reports that foreign investors were interested added to the excitement. The dividends of 8¾ percent in 1782 and 14½ percent in 1783 seemed to assure success.[28]

26. Isaac Wharton to Nathaniel Shaw Jr., February 9, 1782, in Anderson, "Vote of Confidence," 57 and 48–59.

27. 30 April 1782, Pelatiah Webster Ciphering Book, HSP; Charles Pettit to General Greene, 14 February 1782, in Hinkels, *Extraordinary Collection,* 78–79; Charles Pettit to General Greene, 23 August 1781, Charles Pettit Correspondence, Greene Papers, CL; Diary, 30 April 1782, *Morris Papers,* 5:82–83 and n. 3, 83; Robert Morris to Alexander Hamilton, 5 October 1782, *Hamilton Papers,* 3:177–79; Ferguson, *Power,* 138–39; Lewis Jr., *History of the Bank,* 42–44; Ver Steeg, *Morris,* 116; Riesman, "Money," 142–43; John Taylor Gilman to Mesheck Weare, 3 July 1782, P. Smith, ed., *Letters of Delegates,* 18:620–21; Connecticut Delegates to Jonathan Trumbull Sr., 29 July 1782, in ibid., 673–75.

28. Minutes and Letterbook, Bank of North America, 14 November 1782, Bank of North

The bank was also useful to the government. Robert Morris insisted that "without the establishment of the national bank the business of the Department of Finance could not have been performed." He was right. The Financier borrowed $450,000 in both 1782 and 1783. Advances during his tenure totaled some $1,200,000. Bank notes enabled Morris to anticipate revenues and continue cash payments without depleting the nation's limited supplies of specie. In addition, the bank made possible a larger and better provisioned army. Morris could have added that state governments and patriotic groups also received aid. The bank advanced $80,000 to Pennsylvania to meet a congressional requisition, and $22,000 to a group of merchants to fit out a warship. Maryland and Delaware also received small loans.[29]

Certainly, the bank was a fiscal tool vastly superior to what had existed before, but it had limits. The imposing $1,200,000 in advances was largely composed of small loans that were repaid rapidly. In addition, the loans made to the government varied between only $50,000 and $165,000 above the government's investment.[30]

America Papers; Thomas Willing to William Bingham, 12 September 1783, Provincial Delegates, 1:5, HSP; William Bingham to Thomas Willing, 14 October and 29 December 1783, William Bingham Papers, HSP. The bank's dividends are in Lewis Jr., *History of the Bank* (folio ed.), vol. 2, app. 8, 313 (this valuable work is in the Bank of North America Papers).

29. Carey, ed., *Debates and Proceedings*, 49; Diary, 12 November 1781, *Morris Papers*, 3:172–73; Diary, 17 January 1782, in ibid., 4:58; Morris, *Statement of Accounts*; Robert Morris, "An Historical Account of the Bank," Bank of North America Papers; Thomas Fitzsimons, "State of Facts Respecting the National Bank," Maitland Family Papers, Fitzsimons, Meade, and Cook Section, Fitzsimons Folder; Minute Books, Supreme Executive Council, RG 27, 5:348–49, PSA; Lewis Jr., *History of the Bank*, 48–50; Ver Steeg, *Morris*, 116; "Early Records of the Bank of North America," in *Morris Papers*, app. 1, 7:800 and 820 notes 26 and 27.

30. Ferguson, *Power*, 137; Elliot, *Funding System*, 2, 91–92. Using Morris's statements, Elliot calculated the bank's dealings with the government as follows:

Date	Credit	Debit	Amt. Owed Bank
1782			
April	$252,918	$300,000	$ 47,082
July	252,918	400,000	147,082
October	253,394	400,000	146,606
1783			
January	53,394	100,000	46,606
April	53,394	100,000	46,606
July	—	129,800	129,800
October	—	164,781	164,781

On 1 January 1784 the debt was discharged.

Although the bank had lent little more to the government than it had invested, what it did lend placed a severe strain on the bank's capital reserve. Between January and June, Morris negotiated a series of loans that totaled $400,000. Each was for six months, and when they fell due they were renewed and rediscounted. The first two loans, for $100,000, were renewed and rediscounted a second time. When the rest of the loans came due at the end of 1782, the government had made no progress at repayment.[31]

The bank's directors were unhappy with the situation. Before peace negotiations had gotten under way, the directors had begun extricating the corporation from its relationship with the government. In the spring and summer, Morris was told that the bank would not make advances or discounts until some of the debts were cleared up. They did not carry out the threat, but the directors' concerns increased and they demanded bank shares in lieu of payment. An agreement was hammered out, and on December 14, 1782, Morris transferred 500 shares worth $200,000 to the bank. Before the year's end the Financier paid off another $100,000; on this occasion he used his own credit. The remainder of the government's shares were turned over to the bank in April 1783 as part of a settlement that included payment of a Pennsylvania debt (an unpaid warrant Morris had discounted at the bank). This completed the transformation of the corporation from a quasi-public business to a private business.[32]

This time, private investors stepped forward. When the bank first opened, only fifty-six subscribers had been willing to risk their capital; they purchased 120 shares for $48,000. A year later on January 1, 1783, as the government unloaded its stock, the number of subscribers rose to ninety-nine, and they held 269 shares worth $107,600. By July the number of subscribers went up to 111 and their shares increased to 536, worth $214,000. That month the directors announced a dividend of 6½ percent, and the remaining stock sold quickly. Willing happily wrote to his son-in-law, William Bingham:

31. Discount Ledger, 7 January 1782 to 6 February 1783, Bank of North America Papers; Morris, *Statement of Accounts*. Morris paid for the bank's services. The cost was about $29,719 more than the earnings from the bank dividends. See "Early Records of the Bank of North America," in *Morris Papers*, app. 1, 7:798 and 818 n. 14.

32. Robert Morris, "An Historical Account of the Bank," Bank of North America Papers; Diary, 23 May 1782, in *Morris Papers*, 5:242, 243 n. 7; Diary, 3 and 12 September 1782, in ibid., 6:305, 365; Diary, 24 December 1782, in ibid., 7:201–3; app. 1, "Early Records of the Bank of North America," ibid., 7:797–99 and 818–19 nn. 15–22; Lewis Jr., *History of the Bank*, 48; *Morris*, 178.

I exerted myself with success to save yours in the Scramble. Expresses came even from N York, and the run was too quick even for me to provide, so as to obtain one share more than my original for myself—however! I am happy to have contributed in conjunction with you and others, to the establishing such a degree of confidence in our New Establishment.[33]

Despite the "expresses" from New York City, most of the new investors were Philadelphians. Ninety-nine of the 145 stockholders, or 68.3 percent, were locals. They owned 648 of 992 shares, or 65.3 percent of the capital stock. The list of owners has been described as a "roll call of the prominent members of the Philadelphia mercantile community." Many of the out-of-town investors were, like Jeremiah Wadsworth, from the procurement network that had operated out of Robert Morris's Office of Finance during the war.[34]

The speed of the transformation of this quasi-public corporation is striking. When the bank had opened its doors on January 7, 1782, Congress was the largest stockholder and an important customer. In sixteen short months the Bank of North America had become a privately owned corporation doing relatively little business with the government. The shift occurred as the war was winding down; the Yorktown campaign ended before the bank opened. In February and March, Parliament moved to withdraw from the war and begin peace negotiations, and the preliminary Articles of Peace were signed on November 30, 1782.

But the directors of the bank had been unhappy about the relationship between the government at least as early as the previous May. There were at least two reasons for the rapid transformation of the relationship between the bank and Congress. The first has to do with the economic situation of Congress. Congressional finances were in disarray, and future prospects were bleak. When it began to appear that Congress might not be able to repay the money the bank had advanced—money that exceeded the congressional investment—the directors of the bank

33. Thomas Fitzsimons, "State of Facts Respecting the National Bank," Maitland Family Papers, Fitzsimons, Meade, and Cook Section, Fitzsimons Folder; Thomas Willing to William Bingham, 12 September 1783, Provincial Delegates, 6:5; Lewis Jr., *History of the Bank* (folio ed.), II, app. 8; Stock Ledger, I, Bank of North America, Bank of North America Papers, Box 6-D.

34. Ferguson, *Power,* 137 n. 31; Lewis Jr. *History of the Bank,* 32–35; List of Stockholders, First Ledger, Bank of North America, Bank of North America Papers, Box 6-D; Stock Ledger, Bank of North America, Bank of North America Papers, Box 6-D; Wilson, "Bank of North America," 3–4.

were faced with an unpleasant situation, and they solved their problem by demanding that Morris turn over the government's stock. He did, and the Bank of North America severed its ties with the government.

The fact that this transformation occurred raises questions about the motives of Robert Morris and his friends. Everyone agrees that the bank was part of an effort to shore up "the financial integrity of the United States government after the collapse of 1780–1781," but scholars disagree about Morris's ultimate purpose. Some believe that the Financier was more interested in strengthening Congress at the expense of the states than he was in shoring up the financial integrity of Congress. Complicating the analysis is Morris's strategy of using the private sector, in the guise of his own credit and the new bank, to rescue the national government, and at the same time using the bank to strengthen the mercantile sector.[35]

Statements by Robert Morris explaining the purpose of the bank are opaque. His circular advertising the bank explains that the bank would strengthen the national and state governments by acting as their fiscal agent, and that by providing an effective circulating medium it would also stimulate the "internal and external Commerce of North America." Finally, the circular explains that the bank would be "infinitely useful to the Traders in every state in the union."[36]

Even though Robert Morris had sold the bank to Congress and the nation as a fiscal tool necessary for the survival of the nation and useful to the commercial sector, it is likely that he had additional motives. His appointment rested not only on the fiscal and political ability he had demonstrated while serving in Congress but also on his success as a merchant. Those who treat him simply as a nationalist political leader ignore his class and local interests. In a speech he made some years later, Robert Morris recalled: "Though the old government had no idea of a bank, the commercial men of the province had: and I, as a merchant, laid the foundation of one [bank]; and established a credit in Europe for that purpose. From the execution of this design, I was prevented only by the revolution." It appears that plans for the bank grew out of local entrepreneurial concerns. The charter Morris wrote and got approved reminds us that Congress did not create a quasi-public corporation. In

35. Doerflinger, *Vigorous Spirit,* 296–97; Ferguson, *Power,* ch. 6, esp. 142–45. Riesman suggests that Morris and his group hoped the bank would also stabilize the social structure against democratic forces (Riesman, "Money," 142–56).

36. Robert Morris, "Circular to the Governors of the States," *Morris Papers,* 3:507–8.

fact, the bank had no legal responsibility to the government, Morris and Congress had created a private commercial bank.[37]

The manner in which the bank was created lends credence to this interpretation. The plan was submitted only three days after Morris accepted the position as superintendent of finance, but months passed before the rest of his program emerged. During his early days in office, he floundered. Some four and a half months after assuming office, Morris admitted to a friend that he could give him neither the details of the situation nor any remedies, because "I have not yet sufficiently obtained the one nor matured the other."[38]

The most reasonable explanation is that the bank, initially, was not part of a comprehensive nationalist program. This does not mean the bank did not play an important role in Robert Morris's plans for the nation. It did. It simply suggests that his motives were more complex and that his plans were less clearly formulated than has generally been recognized.

The entrepreneurial ambitions of Robert Morris and his allies were thwarted by the tie to the government. Discounts were increasing rapidly, and dividends were large. Loans and discounts to the government stretched the specie reserve and limited the business the bank could offer the private sector. Similarly, the government's possession of a large block of stock siphoned off dividends from the now-eager investors. Once peace was ensured and nationalist obligations were satisfied, the way was paved for the directors and for Morris to further their business ambitions.[39]

The procedures and regulations that governed the operation of the new bank clearly reveal the intention to establish a private commercial bank whose "raison d'être" was to earn profits for its owners through short-term discounts. That these procedures and regulations were implemented well before the bank had withdrawn from its relationship with Congress tells us a great deal about the hopes and intentions of the bank's founders.

37. Carey, ed., *Debates and Proceedings*, 37. See also Robert Morris to Benjamin Franklin, 7 January 1782, *Morris Papers*, 3:503; Rappaport, "Sources," 18–19.

38. Rappaport, "Sources," 20–21; Robert Morris to John Jay, 7 July 1781, *Morris Papers*, 1:250–51; Ver Steeg, *Morris*, 69.

39. This was not a conspiracy. Morris's motives were simply more complex than has been recognized. Previous discussions have not paid enough attention to the fact that Morris was a Philadelphia merchant. See Rappaport, "Sources," 17–21. For the point of departure for this interpretation, see Hammond, "Long and Short Term Credit," 79–103.

The organization created by the bylaws was simple. Power was concentrated in the hands of twelve directors who were elected annually by the stockholders, and the directors, in turn, chose a president from among their own number. The president and directors could hire and fire all necessary personnel and make any rules that did not violate the bylaws. [40]

Unlike the charter, the bylaws spelled out the nature of the business quite clearly. A "capital stock" of $400,000 in specie would be collected, and with the approval of the stockholders the stock could be expanded. The directors were empowered to use the capital as a reserve and to issue bank notes that would be redeemable in specie. Article 15 laid out the discounting policy: The directors could "discount Bills of Exchange, Promissory Notes, and other personal obligations, that have no more than Sixty days to run, at a rate not exceeding 12 pcent pmonth [*sic*], provided there shall be two or more persons of approved credit engaged for the Payment." There was no requirement that the bank lend to the government, the bank would do business with Congress and the state governments only if it chose to. [41]

The bylaws did impose one significant restriction: The new bank would not engage in either domestic or foreign commerce, it would not buy or sell any commodities "except in bullion, gold or silver, public funds," land, and its produce and goods mortgaged but not claimed. Thus, the bank would not compete with merchants. The institution's profits were designed to come from credit operations—primarily from discounting mercantile paper. [42]

Contemporary comments support the view that the bank functioned as a service institution for merchants. John Wilson, the bank's accountant, wrote to his former employer Joseph Pemberton describing the nature of the bank's business. He reported that "Bills and notes" are discounted for sixty days or less at a rate of 6 percent a year if the "drawer and payer are good and the latter lives in the city." He went on to say: "One person is allowed to discount only a moderate sum, that a greater number may be accommodated." It is, wrote Wilson, "from this business of discounting" that "the profits to the Bank must arise."[43]

40. The bylaws are in Minutes and Letterbook, Bank of North America, 4 November 1782, Bank of North America Papers; "Early Papers of the Bank of North America," *Morris Papers*, app. 1, 7:802–5.

41. Minutes and Letterbook, Bank of North America, 14 November 1782. Discounts are loans for which the interest is deducted before receiving the loan.

42. Minutes and Letterbook, Bank of North America, 14 November 1782.

43. Rappaport, "First Description," 665–66.

Wilson's description of the bank was corroborated by Charles Pettit, a local merchant and stockholder. Pettit wrote to a friend:

> The Bank will not advance money ordinarily for more than 30 Days—it must be an act of official Grace & Favor if they exceed it, & 60 Days is the outside—to obtain an advance from them, there must be two Persons of good Credit in this Town or within their Reach, answerable for the Repayment as Drawers, Indorsers or acceptors and they consider anything more than 1000 Dollars to one man, as a large advance, be the Security ever so good. It is not therefore as a Thing of Course that Money can be taken up at the Bank.

He went on to warn: "Any Person who pushes for large Sums, or is forward Chiefly in getting Cash from the Bank by as many Channels as he can, will be marked & perhaps suspected. A Man who is tenacious of his Credit will therefore be cautious in his use of it."[44]

Pelatiah Webster, a Philadelphia merchant, an investor in the Bank of North America, and an essayist, offered the best contemporary analysis of banking. He described a bank as "a large repository of cash, deposited under the direction of proper officers . . . for the purpose of establishing and supporting a great and extensive credit." Once established, the capital reserve will "support the credit of double or treble its amount in bank-bills." In addition to expanding the supply of credit, bank notes provided a valuable supplement to the money supply; their convertibility made them "as good as cash." A bank, Webster concluded, was "a sort of mercantile institution, or at least has such a close connexion with the whole mercantile interest, that it will more naturally and properly fall under the direction of merchants, than any other sort of men."[45]

An examination of the bank's ledger supports Webster's view. In its first year, between January 7, 1782, and February 6, 1783, when the bank was presumably a public institution, the bank made 2,335 loans worth $2,420,688. Of this, Congress received 137 loans, 6 percent of the total number of loans, worth $673,334, or 28 percent of the dollar amount loaned. Congress was charged the same rate, 6 percent, as

44. Charles Pettit to General Greene, 23 July 1783, Charles Pettit Correspondence, Greene Papers, CL. See also Robert Morris to John Wendell, 23 March 1782, *Morris Papers*, 4:453–54; Francisco Rendon's Memorandum on the Finances of the United States, in ibid., 616–17.

45. Webster, *Essay on Credit*; Webster, *Political Essays*, 433.

everyone else. The only significant exceptions made in the government's favor were a few unusually large loans made for long periods of time. Congress borrowed for as long as six months and had the loans renewed and rediscounted.[46]

The bulk of the bank's loans not only went to the private sector, but for the most part went to residents of Philadelphia. During the period under study, 2,198 loans were made to private firms and individuals, Philadelphians received 73 percent of these loans, and other Americans got at least 13 percent. Foreigners received an insignificant 2.5 percent.

Most of the borrowers were merchants, accounting for 68 percent of the loans and a striking 73 percent of the dollars lent. No other occupational group was such a large portion of the bank's business. Manufacturers, with a bit less than 2 percent of the loans made and less than 2 percent of the dollar amount, were the second-largest group of borrowers. Most of the remaining loans were divided between retailers, captains, professionals, government officials, and gentlemen, who got more than 7 percent of the loans made and a bit less than 5.5 percent of the dollars lent.

It is not surprising that women were not regular customers. They received only ten loans—a minuscule 0.45 percent of all of the loans made and only 0.55 percent of the dollar amount. On the other hand, the economic elite did quite well. Among those who have been identified as members of Philadelphia's economic elite, eighty-seven, or 19 percent, used the bank. Members of this group received 493, or 21 percent, of the loans made to nongovernment borrowers. The dollar amount of their loans was $373,282—15 percent of the total; and their average size was $757.

In fact, loans to the elite were even more concentrated than these numbers suggest. Half of all loans going to the elite were granted to eight men and mercantile firms, and all were rich merchants, owning bank stock, except Biddle and Hollingsworth. Two or three were

46. For the analysis of the Discount Ledger, 7 January 1782, through 6 February 1783, Bank of North America, Bank of North America Papers, see Appendix A. For sources and methodology used to analyze the bank's discount ledger, see Appendix B. Doerflinger's study of the bank's business is reasonably consistent with these conclusions. Looking at account holders in 1784–85 and at discounters in 1790–91, he finds that merchants predominated, especially among active users of the bank. When retailers and gentlemen, some of whom were former merchants, are included in the calculations, the dominance is even clearer (*Vigorous Spirit*, 303–5).

directors of the bank or their brothers, and all were allies of Robert Morris.[47]

The duration of the loans made provides additional support for the view that the Bank of North America was a business institution servicing Philadelphia merchants. From January through May, loans averaged forty-five days in length, but during the rest of the year they shrank to only twenty-nine days. This pattern was most suitable, of course, for merchants.

Like its customers, the bank operated through a network of friends and kin. Shareholders received 37 percent of the loans made and 36 percent of the dollars. The dollar amount loaned to nonshareholders was virtually the same, but the average loan to shareholders was $1,022 while the average loan to nonshareholders was only $650. The favored status of shareholders and friends emerges even more clearly if we look at the nonshareholders. Borrowers who were related to, or friends with, or had business ties to shareholders got loans that averaged $746. Customers with no discernible ties to the owners made loans averaging $621. Their loans were 20 percent smaller than borrowers with ties to the shareholders, and 39 percent smaller than those issued to the bank's owners. Furthermore, shareholders and their intimates got about 50 percent of the bank's loans and some 45 percent of the dollar amount of all loans. If we look at only the loans made in the private sector, the in-group got 53 percent of the loans and a munificent 63 percent of the dollars.

Close connections between merchants and banks have an ancient pedigree. Virtually every large-scale, complex, traditional society that had an important mercantile community practiced some form of banking, and in each such society banks and merchants were intimately linked. Moreover, commercial banking, a relatively recent innovation, grew directly out of the development of the bill of exchange and the specialized trade in these bills. Italian merchants were responsible for these innovations in the thirteenth century. Slowly—the process took more than 400 years—the bills became fully negotiable. When they were, it was possible for merchants to avoid barter, settle books face-to-face, and make payment in bullion.[48]

Bankers rationalized their business practices in ways that revealed

47. The men and firms are Meredith & Clymer, George Meade, Haynes & Crawford, Levi Hollingsworth, Thomas Fitzsimons, John Donnaldson, Tench Coxe, Clement Biddle.

48. Kindleberger, *Financial History*, ch. 3.

their close ties to commerce. Like merchants, they had a faith in specie, and that manifested itself in the insistence on a specie reserve and on the convertibility of bank notes into specie. Bankers believed that loans on commercial paper, or "real bills," were safe because they were used to purchase real things, or commodities that could be possessed by the bank and sold if necessary. The loans were also believed to be self-liquidating, because mercantile transactions created income that could be used to pay off loans.[49]

The differences between the Bank of North America and the other establishments that composed the Philadelphia business community were striking and important. These differences manifested themselves in form, operation, and spirit. The bank emerged in an economy characterized by small-scale, unspecialized organizations. Owner-operated economic units—frequently partnerships—dominated. Business and work relationships were infused with personal and social motives, and the pace of economic and social life was leisurely.

This economic portrait reflected realities in Philadelphia and in the countryside. Mercantile firms carried on a wide range of economic activities. Their main activity was exporting and importing, but merchants also acted as money lenders, dealt in foreign exchange, underwrote insurance, provided business information and advice, rented space in their warehouses, owned ships and engaged in the carrying trade, invested in land, and a variety of manufacturing activities that included flour-milling, iron production, distilling, and shipbuilding. This diversity was mandated by the small-scale and dispersed character of available markets, by the desire to keep their capital working, by primitive transportation and communication technologies, and by the absence of ancillary business services. Prudence mandated scattered, small-scale investments.

In addition, economic life moved at a leisurely pace; deals took months and sometimes years to complete. Family and personal needs and friendships, as well as business concerns, appeared in account ledgers and influenced hiring practices and business networks. The small size of the mercantile community in Philadelphia reinforced the importance of interpersonal relations. Slow turnover and scattered, small-scale investments combined with the emphasis on personal relationships to minimize tendencies toward maximization.

The contrast between the Bank of North America and the rest of the

49. Redlich, "Mercantilist Thought," 107–16; Redlich, *Moulding,* 1–12.

business community could hardly be more extreme. The bank was a large, specialized corporation with a capital stock that dwarfed the resources of even the wealthiest mercantile firms. While the bank was owner-operated, ownership and the power to control (micro-manage) policy was sundered. The corporate structure was impersonal, and this impersonality was one of the most important characteristics of the new institution.

When stockholders disagreed with the policies of the directors, the gap between ownership and control would become clear. The consequences of impersonality were also demonstrated to the bank's customers as they became familiar with the operating rules of the new institution. These rules, especially the time limit on discounts and the requirement of punctual repayment, resemble the impersonality of modern bureaucratic procedures. In addition, the insistence on speed and punctual repayment were at variance with contemporary business practices and morality, which were shaped by the slow pace of life and the intermingling of social and business relations.

As the utility of the bank became clearer, merchants felt compelled to obtain and maintain a line of credit at the bank. Failure to do so might mean the difference between success and failure. When their dependence became clear, many merchants began to fear that the economic independence they so valued in their striving to be good Republican citizens was threatened.

The advent of commercial banking in Pennsylvania had a number of important consequences. As we shall see, the Bank of North America had an impact on the conduct of business and on the larger economy. The bank and the other banks that followed played a pivotal role in the development of money markets. They increased the supply and use of money and the speed with which it circulated. Banks facilitated commercial interactions, strengthened the mercantile community, and furthered consumerism and commercialization.

As commercialization increased, so did its impact on social relations. To the extent that the evolution of markets and market-oriented behavior was important to the development of capitalism, it seems clear that the Bank of North America and commercial banking, in general, played a significant role in the transformation.[50]

50. A literal reading of the Marxist definition of capitalism might note that bankers are not directly involved in the process of production and that credit does not necessarily cause changes in the relations of production, but this is too rigid. Because banks expand both markets and commercial relations, they should be seen as instruments of transformation.

7

The Seeds of War

The successful establishment of the Bank of North America had unforeseen results. The 14½ percent dividend suggested to most of the stockholders that more stock should be issued. The desire for expansion was strengthened by the postwar boom and its flood of foreign imports. This led to a rapidly growing demand for credit that the bank encouraged but could not fully satisfy. Announcements appeared in the local press that the January stockholder meeting would consider an expansion of the capital.[1]

While the bank was engaged in expansion, a series of events threatened its success and its survival. Two weeks after the 14½ percent dividend had been declared, a movement to organize a second bank was launched by a group of wealthy local merchants who were dissatisfied with some of the bank's business practices and eager to earn profits for themselves. A number of these entrepreneurs were shareholders in

---

1. *Pa. Gazette,* 19 and 26 November 1783; John Chaloner to Jeremiah Wadsworth and John Church, 4 and 28 January 1784, Chaloner and White Letterbook; 23 January 1782 to 9 November 1784, Chaloner and White MSS, HSP; Minutes and Letterbook, 12 January 1784, Bank of North America, Bank of North America Papers; Lewis, *History of the Bank,* 51; McDonald, *Formation,* 44–45; Rappaport, "Sources," 46–50.

the Bank of North America, but they were not members of the controlling group.[2]

Announcements proclaiming the creation of a new bank, the Bank of Pennsylvania, appeared in the newspapers on January 21, 1784. In ten days the necessary capital had been raised, directors were elected, and a constitution was drawn up. The new bank's constitution resembled that of the Bank of North America with two exceptions. Tax collectors were not obliged to accept notes of the new bank, and state officials were substituted for national officials. The Speaker of the Assembly, the Chief Justice, and the President of the Council would have the right to inspect the books of the bank.[3]

Having completed the initial stage of their organization, the directors of the new institution petitioned the Assembly for a charter. All signs pointed to speedy compliance with this request when the Bank of North America asked to be heard in opposition. The legislature agreed and scheduled hearings.[4]

Like the party system, the Assembly's procedures encouraged public participation. Hearings focused public attention, educated, legitimated participation, and increased conflict. As people came to understand their class, religious, and ethnic needs and identities, they entered the political arena, and when they did so they found themselves pitted against other individuals who were also acting in their own interests. The Assembly and the parties acted like modern "centers"—that is, they served as institutionalized focal points for the interaction and conflict of classes and status groups.

The hearings were open to the public and attracted large audiences. Gouverneur Morris and James Wilson spoke for the old bank, while Jared Ingersoll, William Bradford, Jonathan D. Sergeant, and Miers

2. The dividends were announced in the *Pa. Gazette*, 7 January 1784, and in the *Pa. Packet*, 6, 8, and 24 January 1784; John Chaloner to Jeremiah Wadsworth and John Church, 14 February 1784, Jeremiah Wadsworth Papers, CHS; John Chaloner to Philip Schuyler, 2 February 1784, Chaloner and White Letterbook; Cooke, *Tench Coxe*, 87–88; Rappaport, "Sources," 50–54.

3. *Freeman's Journal*, 21 January 1784; *Pa. Gazette*, 21 January 1784; John Chaloner to Philip Schuyler, 2 February 1784, Chaloner and White Letterbook; *Pa. Packet*, 31 January and 7 February 1784; Thomas Wistar to Caspar Wistar, 15 May 1784, Henry Goddard Leach Collection, Wistar Section, HSP; John Chaloner to Alexander Hamilton, 2 February 1784, *Hamilton Papers*, 3:504–5.

4. *Pa. Min.*, 10, 24, 26, and 28 February 1784, 123–24, 149, 154, 156–57; Edward Burd to J. Yeates, 4 March 1784, in Walker, ed., *Burd Papers*, 130–31; John Chaloner to Jeremiah Wadsworth and John Church, 4 March 1784, Wadsworth Papers.

Fisher were the advocates for the new. The discussions generated considerable heat. Gouverneur Morris opened with a suggestion that the applicants were Tories and impugned the Quaker backers of the new bank with the same brush, but after being strongly rebuked by Sergeant he abjectly apologized. In turn, Miers Fisher apparently directed anti-Semitic remarks at the Bank of North America and its Jewish supporters. As tempers rose, the exchange spilled over into the local press.[5] When they turned to the main thrust of their argument, Morris and Wilson insisted that a single bank could do a safer and more effective job of banking than two or several because its capital stock would be larger. The strength derived from this position, they correctly suggested, would allow the bank to issue more loans than it would in a competitive situation.[6]

The most damaging thrust made by those speaking for the Bank of Pennsylvania was that the Bank of North America was a monopoly. Over and over they raised the specter of monopoly and unchecked power. Ingersoll contended that monopolies were "an abridgment of the Rights of Freemen," and Sergeant sounded a similar note when he angrily raised the question of equal access: "Are we to be denied the Privileges of Citizens and turned out of Doors?"[7]

This line of attack was particularly damaging to the Bank of North America. In the heightened political climate of the 1780s, fears of conspiracy and factionalism, and aristocrats and monopolists, were rampant. People seeking special privileges seemed to be everywhere, and many feared that if they were successful it would destroy the Republic. A newspaper article by "Septimus," which appeared a scant week before the Assembly hearings, gave voice to these fears.

Septimus argued that the old bank's opposition to the proposed charter was part of a broad attack on freedom by the "ruling junto" who wanted to "raise themselves to power" and create a new constitution that would destroy "that equal liberty so dear to all men, who are not great men." The Bank of North America, he insisted, was an

5. Thomas Wistar to Casper Wistar, 15 May 1784, Leach Collection, Wistar Section. For the exchange in the press, see "A Jew Broker," *Independent Gazeteer,* 13 March 1784; and "Spectator," in ibid., 20 March 1784.

6. The most fruitful source for the hearings is James Wilson, Before Committee of Assembly, 2 March 1784, James Wilson Papers, II, HSP. These are notes Wilson took at the hearings to help him prepare his rebuttal. See also Edward Burd to J. Yeates, 4 March 1784, in Walker, ed., *Burd Papers,* 130–31; Thomas Wistar to Caspar Wistar, 15 May 1784, Leach Collection, Wistar Section; Rappaport, "Sources," 56–68.

7. James Wilson, Before Committee of Assembly, 2 March 1784, Wilson Papers, II.

"abomination," an "unholy temple in which the clean and unclean, the Jews and Gentiles, the Christians and Infidels" are joined "together without any other principles to direct them, than the love of filthy lucre!" Septimus feared that the old bank hoped to control all the money and credit in the state. Their real goal was to see "all power . . . centered in the hands of one man and his creatures." Should the public accept the views of Septimus and the advocates of the Bank of Pennsylvania and come to see the Bank of North America as a dangerous monopoly, the institution would indeed be in trouble.[8]

The most effective speaker in favor of the proposed bank was Miers Fisher, who insisted that another bank was needed because the old one had simply been unable to meet the demand for discounts: "We have heard [that the Bank of North America has not satisfied] one third part of all applications" for discounts. The Quaker lawyer also criticized the old bank for practicing favoritism and punctuality. While promptness and regularity were necessary, the Bank of North America had enforced them "with too much violence."[9] Fisher's charges can be read in several ways. First of all, the Philadelphia lawyer was representing a group of businessmen who wanted to establish another commercial bank. Had they succeeded, they undoubtedly would have adopted the same policy regarding punctuality and regularity. Fisher probably knew this and was most likely indulging in a bit of "pragmatic" oratory. Complaints of favoritism and "violent" punctuality reappeared with increasing regularity. Fisher had touched upon an issue of some merit.

Even though the Bank of North America's defenders ignored the charges of favoritism and excessive punctuality on this occasion, they are worth commenting on. After all, everyone involved in commerce labored to build up networks of friends with whom they dealt. Similarly, it seems at least a little odd that a lawyer defending merchants and other investors would complain about insistence that debtors honor their obligations. Why was the bank singled out? Apparently, a substantial portion of the public, including local merchants and lawyers, did not see the bank as just another business. In fact, the bank was judged by different standards, standards that were not applicable to aspiring citizens scrambling in their own self-interest.

Despite the silence of the Bank of North America's defenders, the charges of unfair business practices rankled. A few years later Robert

8. *Freeman's Journal,* 25 February 1784.
9. James Wilson, Before Committee of Assembly, 2 March 1784, Wilson Papers, II.

Morris complained that such charges were "extraordinary" precisely because they originated from the general public. If the bank's stockholders complained, he asserted, there would be grounds for concern. After all, "the directors are accountable only to them." The bank, he reminded the public, was "private property."[10]

The explanation for these complaints and the singling out of the bank lies partly in the newness of commercial banking and in the difference between the bank and the other business enterprises in Philadelphia. The Bank of North America was a wealthy and powerful monopoly that was attempting to create a new niche in the economy. While the community was comfortable with the phenomenon of mercantile notes, the bank was a veritable moneymaking machine.

Its size also marked it as different. There was simply no comparison between the scale of the operations of an individual merchant and that of the bank. Finally, its operating procedures differed dramatically from traditional practice. The insistence on punctuality gave the bank's procedures an impersonal aura. These rules ignored the vagaries of the marketplace and the needs of individuals and appeared to be at variance with the slow pace of economic life and the mix of economic and social motives.

But more was involved. Robert Morris's complaint makes clear that some were unhappy precisely because the directors of the Bank of North America treated the bank as if it were simply private property. Because the people making these complaints were not frontiersmen or farmers but sober Philadelphia merchants, they are particularly noteworthy.

Two points should be made here. First, although the Bank of North America was a corporation, it was a private enterprise, but unlike other businesses the bank was endowed with the prestige, legal backing, and power of the state. It is therefore not surprising that significant elements of the public would hold it to different standards. Many saw corporations as public service institutions and demanded standards of fairness and equality of treatment that would not be appropriate if applied to individual businessmen. Viewed in this light, the complaint about favoritism makes a good deal of sense. Second, the imposition of cold and impersonal "market" standards on moneylending upset many people. Lending and borrowing, like all economic relations, were understood to involve more than a simple contractual relationship. Reciprocal concerns, as well as

10. Carey, ed., *Debates and Proceedings*, 36.

an understanding of the vagaries of time, were also involved. Pennsylvania was not simply noncapitalist, it was also a good deal less commercial than has been realized.

The leisurely pace of life in general, and business in particular, affected all social relations and institutional arrangements. In this context it seems appropriate to reverse Robert E. Mutch's assertion that "market relations were not so pervasive as to determine social relations." Actually, noncapitalist, traditional social relations and values were so pervasive and important that they frequently determined economic relations.[11]

The last speaker before the General Assembly was the bank's counsel, James Wilson, who predictably did not believe that the creation of a second bank would have any good consequences. The dispersal of bank capital would only make both banks more vulnerable to runs on their reserves, he said, and competition between banks would confuse the public and discourage investment. This gloomy prognosis set the stage for a proposal. All problems could be avoided if the two banks would merge "under the mediation of the Legislature."[12]

The proposal for a merger was not the only proposal Wilson made. The directors took an ill-fated step and authorized Wilson to offer the state two loans: $200,000 to help meet a congressional requisition and $300,000 to establish a loan office. According to President Willing, $300,000 would "be lent on Mortgage in the manner formerly used in the loan Office, and be repaid by Installments in five years, the last sum to be advanced in the course of next Summer, if our Subscription fills up, or in proportion as it may fill up."[13]

The bank's leadership did not believe their petition would be granted. Thomas Willing called an emergency stockholders' meeting and announced that he expected the new bank would be granted a charter. The directors were especially disturbed that many of the bank's depositors were investing in the new bank, and they were embarrassed because shares of the new bank were being purchased with bank notes

11. Mutch, "Yeoman and Merchant," 280.

12. James Wilson, The Case of the Two Banks—Notes, Wilson Papers, ii. All the early banks tried to achieve monopolies; see Klebaner, *Commercial Banking*, 3–7.

13. Thomas Willing to Sharp Delany, Minutes and Letterbook, Bank of North America, 5 March 1784, Bank of North America Papers; John Chaloner to Alexander Hamilton, 25 March 1784, *Hamilton Papers*, 3:524–25; John Chaloner to Wadsworth and Church, 25 March 1784, Chaloner and White Letterbook; "Liberty," *Freeman's Journal*, 10 March 1784; Rappaport, "Sources," 66–67.

and, as they were presented for redemption, the capital reserve was shrinking alarmingly.[14]

As they would in the Assembly, the directors proposed to meet the threat by merging with the new institution. They suggested expanding the sale of bank stock and lowering the price to new investors. The deal was proposed and accepted, and the petition for a new charter was withdrawn from the legislature. The Bank of North America had successfully defended its monopoly. Another result of the merger was that most of the city's leading merchants were now shareholders. Robert Morris's bank had been transformed into "the bank of the merchant community as a whole."[15]

If the problems of February and March were caused by profits, the bank would soon be tested by adversity. That spring, Pennsylvania was hit by a full-scale commercial crisis. The first hints of trouble cropped up in early March. Personal letters from this period are filled with complaints about the balance of trade, an outflow of specie, bankruptcies, and a shortage of money. The reasons are not hard to find. As the war ended Dutch, French, and British imports flooded into Pennsylvania. Thomas M. Doerflinger calculates that "the total influx in 1783 and 1784 was roughly twice as great as the largest importations for two consecutive years before the Revolution (1771 and 1772)." Foreign markets contracted at the same time. When the bubble burst, imports stopped arriving. "The city's imports from areas other than the West Indies fell by 75 percent between 1784 and 1786–1787." Between 1784 and 1790 at least sixty-eight merchants went bankrupt. Prices fell, credit was scarce, and local industries, like shipbuilding, suffered.[16]

In this economic climate, the Bank of North America was forced to limit and then stop discounting, which made the credit market even

14. John Chaloner to Jeremiah Wadsworth and John Church, 1 March 1784, Wadsworth Papers; Schwartz, "Beginning," 419. For the announcement of the meeting, see *Pa. Packet*, 26 February 1784.

15. John Chaloner to Jeremiah Wadsworth and John Church, 1 and 21 March 1784; Charles Pettit to Joseph Reed, 18 April 1784, MSS of Joseph Reed, xi, NYHS; *Pa. Min.*, 16 March 1784, 186; Doerflinger, *Vigorous Spirit*, 300.

16. For the quotes, see Doerflinger, *Vigorous Spirit*, 244, 246. Doerflinger offers the best modern treatment of the economic troubles; see ibid., 244–48, 262–67. See also Jensen, *New Nation*, 184–91; Kaminski, "Paper Politics," 1–22. For representative letters, see Alexander Hamilton to John Church, 25 March 1784, *Hamilton Papers*, 3:522; William Seton to Alexander Hamilton, 27 March 1784, in ibid., 526–27; John Chaloner to Wadsworth and Church, 3 April 1784, Chaloner and White Letterbook; John Chaloner to Peter Colt, 14 April 1784, Chaloner and White Letterbook; Robert Morris to Tench Tilghman, 10 and 30 April 1784, Robert Morris Papers, NYPL.

worse. "The bank," noted Charles Pettit, "diminished the Quantity of Circulation by contracting its discounts latterly and many People Depending perhaps too much on that mode of Payment are greatly distressed."[17]

Even though the bank was a victim of the same debilitating crunch that was afflicting the whole community, its failure to carry on business as usual aroused deep hostility. One outraged merchant complained:

> The Bank has Stopped discounting by which means many of our Merchants and Traders have Suffered much. Those who had experienced the convenience of the Bank heretofore are much distress'd as they had a wright to expect from their former punctuality in taken up their Notes when they became due to expect to rase Mony that way again, Many where Supplyd who had no great Capittal but would redeam their Notes by geting their Friends Notes to redeam their own—The Bank by not discounting has interely put a Stop to many of this Clase—Our Vendues are very frequent and the largest I ever saw in the City owing to the people's being pushed so exceedingly for Mony.

A resident of Philadelphia, the writer was the brother of a shareholder in the stillborn Bank of Pennsylvania. His belief that businessmen "had a wright to expect" support from the bank because of their previously circumspect behavior was probably widespread.[18]

Buffeted by forces beyond their control, Pennsylvanians predictably lashed out at the bank. One angry merchant, Peter Kuhn, proclaimed that it was the bank "which has in no small degree deranged us and [we] have solemnly protested against putting ourselves in future into their power as we will rather be content with one-half the business then be subject to so much anxiety."[19]

Peter Kuhn's complaints—the belief that discounting was an earned "wright" rather than a privilege granted by the bank, Fisher's complaints about favoritism, and "too much violence" in punctuality—reveal that part of the business community felt that the bank was violating traditional values and norms. Like the rest of the population, merchants and lawyers mixed family, friendship, and economics, strove for independence, and feared monopolies. They expected neighbors and the people

17. Charles Pettit to General Greene, 6 March 1784, Charles Pettit Correspondence.
18. Barth Wistar to Caspar Wistar, 8 April 1784, Leach Collection, Wistar Section.
19. Dated 18 November 1783, quoted in Bezanson et al., *Prices*, 301.

they did business with to conform to these traditional social usages and when it became clear that the bank would not, their concerns intensified.

As Philadelphians were struggling to come to terms with the new bank, an economic crisis transformed the situation. Hints of trouble can be discerned in the early spring of 1784. In March and April an increasing number of letters had complaints about the balance of trade, an outflow of specie, a shortage of money, and bankruptcies. Philadelphia's mercantile community was hard hit. In the next few years, more than sixty firms went bankrupt. Some of these traders were marginal, but some of the great mercantile houses also went under. [20]

Fueled by hard times, public concerns intensified, and the General Assembly was pressed to act. On March 18 an assemblyman rose and proclaimed: "The inhabitants of this state have been drained of almost all the ready money, . . . by which means the people are much distressed; and in order to relieve, as far as possible, the land holders in this state, there ought to be a Loan-Office established." Before it acted on this proposal, the Assembly tried a different tact. Recalling James Wilson's recent offer of a loan of $300,000 "to be lent on Mortgage in the manner formerly used in the loan office," the Assembly approached the bank and asked for loan of $200,000 to be used to set up a loan office. [21]

The loan office was Pennsylvania's land bank. It antedated the Bank of North America by almost sixty years, having been created in the early 1720s when the provincial economy was suffering from serious economic problems. The Assembly hoped that paper emissions would stimulate recovery, provide an effective circulating medium, help debtors, and promote economic development. At the heart of the plan was a state-run General Loan Office, empowered to emit paper money and lend it in the form of relatively small long-term loans at 5 percent simple interest to owners of land and houses. The paper was made legal tender. [22]

20. Alexander Hamilton to John Church, 25 March 1784, *Hamilton Papers*, 3:522; William Seton to Alexander Hamilton, 27 March 1784, in ibid., 526–27; John Chaloner to Wadsworth and Church, 3 April 1784, Chaloner and White Letterbook; John Chaloner to Peter Colt, 14 April 1784, in ibid.; Robert Morris to Tench Tilghman, 10 and 30 April 1784, Morris Papers, NYPL. The best modern treatment of the business cycle is Doerflinger, *Vigorous Spirit*, 261–67.

21. *Pa. Min.*, 18 March 1784, 190; John Chaloner to Jeremiah Wadsworth, 25 March 1784, Chaloner and White Letterbook; John Chaloner to Alexander Hamilton, 25 March 1784, Chaloner and White Letterbook; Barth Wistar to Caspar Wistar, 8 April 1784, Leach Collection, Wistar Section; McDonald, *American Republic*, 48.

22. Thayer, "Land Bank System," 152–55; Yoder, "Paper Currency," 23–24, 231–33;

Started in 1723, the loan office continued without interruption until 1764. Between 1723 and 1754–55 the Assembly issued some £85,000, backed by land and houses. The exigencies of global warfare forced a change in the system: pressured by Parliament, Pennsylvania emitted more than £550,000 in only five years, but unlike the earlier emissions, which were supported by land and property, these were backed by future taxes.[23]

The system, then, was essentially a legal-tender paper currency issued and administered by provincial rather than county officials. The paper was circulated by lending it in small amounts varying between £12 and £200 to property owners; payments were in equal installments. When the loan office received the payments, that money was loaned out again. The security required was twice the value of land and/or triple the value of houses. Mary M. Schweitzer established that "of 3,111 loans for which we have records, only 55, or less than 2 percent, were for more than £100. The average loan was for £64.13s." Although the loans were small their duration was long, ranging from eight to sixteen years, and the interest charged—5 percent—was below rates prevailing in the private sector.[24]

The funds were carefully dispersed throughout the province. Each county was allotted funds and instructed to make the money available. Anyone with a "clear title had to be given a loan." That point is important—friendships or well-placed relatives were not necessary. As a result, many of those who could not normally hope to receive loans in the private sector received them at the loan office.[25]

The loan office offered its services to a wide spectrum of Pennsylvanians. As Schweitzer makes clear, the overwhelming majority of the borrowers were small-property owners—farmers and artisans. The former accounted for just under 67 percent, and the latter were just over 24 percent of the borrowers. Among the remaining borrowers (9 percent) were found a sprinkling of laborers, esquires, merchants, surveyors, teachers, clerks, ministers, physicians, lawyers, artists, spinsters, widows, and a variety of retailers. Because the average loan was for £64, the average recipient owned land worth £128. In at

Lester, "Currency Issues," 76–79, 91–92; and the important Schweitzer, *Custom*, 115–30, 135.

23. Yoder, "Paper Currency," 48–51, 96–100, 113–18, 282–86.

24. Kaminski, "Paper Politics," 74–78; Shepherd, *History*, 412–14; Schweitzer, *Custom*, 129, 128–30, 149–51; Yoder, "Paper Currency," 232.

25. Schweitzer, *Custom*, 147, 151; Shepherd, *History*, 412.

least one county—Chester—those who received loans were generally "among the upper one-fifth of wealth holders."[26]

It is not surprising that in a society with an important class of petty-commodity producers with a producer mentality, most of the loans furthered investment rather than consumption. Typically, farmers used the loans to improve or build " 'good English meadow,' orchards, fences, outbuildings, stone houses, [and] stone barns." They were used to help build mills, iron foundries, and ships as well. Investments were also made in slaves, indentured servants, apprenticeships, and cattle.[27]

The loan office was an astonishingly versatile institution. As John Dickinson noted, its primary purpose was to make it possible for those with "very small fortunes . . . to purchase and cultivate land, which is of so much consequence in settling new countries, or to carry on some business, that without such assistance they would be incapable of managing: For no private person would lend money on such favourable terms." Moreover, the money flowed from the loan recipients "into other hands, encreases consumption, raises the prices of commodities, quickens circulation, and communicating a vigour to all kinds of industry, [and] returns . . . [to] the borrowers."[28]

In addition, the loan office proved to be an important source of public revenue. The interest raised by the land bank was the single largest source of public revenues in the province until the French and Indian War. Revenue from the loan office provided about half the operating expenses for the province during the period of its existence and allowed the government to exist without direct taxes until the French and Indian War. Morever, loan office notes were issued to combat economic downturns and proved to be extraordinarily effective supplements to the money supply. According to Richard A. Lester, "the price level in Pennsylvania was more stable during the fifty years following the first Colonial currency issue in 1723 than the American price level has been during any succeeding fifty-year period."[29]

The record of the land bank with regard to safety was excellent. The

26. Schweitzer, *Custom*, 129, 152–61. Apparently tenants were able to use the loan office to buy land; ibid., 152–54. See also Kaminski, "Paper Politics," 74–78; Thayer, "Land Bank System," 155.

27. Schweitzer, *Custom*, 161–63.

28. Dickinson, "Late Regulations," 1:220.

29. Yoder, "Paper Currency," 290–300; Thayer, "Land Bank System," 157; Ferguson, "Currency Finance," 169, 170–72; Lester, "Currency Issues," 114–15. Ironically, the proprietor's resistance to the loan office limited the emissions and was a major cause of the stability and value of the paper.

loan office records of 1763 reveal that only £1,555 of all the loans made since 1723 was still outstanding. At the same time, however, the performance on promptness was poor. Between 1731 and 1739 the unpaid principal grew to one-fifth of the whole. This remained constant until 1752, when war worsened the situation. Eventually the books were balanced. Permissiveness, of course, was consistent with the general purpose of the land bank—the provision of cheap, long-term credit to farmers and artisans. As a result, the administrators of the system did not insist on promptness.[30]

The proper balance between the public sector and private sector has always been an issue in American politics. What is fundamentally different about the seventeenth and eighteenth centuries is that the weight of popular opinion was strongly on the side of public action. An example of this is the enormous popularity of the loan office. Almost everyone agreed with Joseph Pemberton, a Philadelphia merchant, that "paper currency hath proved of singular services in advancing the interest of all parties." The only real debate over the system before the 1780s occurred when it was first proposed in 1722. Only the proprietors consistently opposed the loan office, and this heightened its popularity. There is simply no doubt that Governor Thomas Pownall's laudatory estimation reflected the majority's view: "There never was a wider or better measure; never one better calculated to serve the uses of our encreasing country."[31]

The loan office had been created because private capital markets were inadequate. Urban money rarely filtered into the countryside in the form of loans, and when it did the amounts were too small to satisfy the demand. Rural lenders were similarly unable to satisfy the need. The solution was found in the public sector.

Both the land bank and the Bank of North America were attempts to improve capital markets, but beyond this they had little in common. The two institutions grew out of the needs of different social classes and carried with them different belief systems. If commercial banking was rooted in the mercantile community, then land banking grew out of the needs of small-scale petty-commodity producers (independent farmers and artisans). The former placed its faith in specie, the latter in land and "real" property. Commercial banks were designed to earn profits by

30. Yoder, "Paper Currency," 255–79; Thayer, "Land Bank System," 157.
31. Pownall, *Administration*, 1:188; Proud, *History*, 2:152–70; Thayer, "Land Bank System," 146.

offering short-term credit to merchants, while the loan office was a government agency whose main functions were to provide the public with a circulating medium and the producers with cheap long-term credit. Enhancing the land bank's popularity was its success as a painless source of public revenue. The purposes of the land bank and the values it promoted were consistent with and supportive of the widespread distribution of property and skills that characterized Pennsylvania's social structure.

The loan office acted to strengthen and develop family farms and other small-scale family enterprises throughout the province. As an institution, it embodied the belief that the good citizen strove for "competence, independence and morality" by improving families' ability to provide for themselves. At the same time, the use of the power of the state to help families reflected and strengthened norms of neighborliness and reciprocity. The example of the loan office heightened the public's expectation that the Bank of North America would be a public service institution. As the nature of commercial banking became clear, the contrast with the land bank also served to heighten public resentments.[32]

Thomas Willing and the directors were appalled by the request from the General Assembly for a loan of $200,000 to establish a loan office. They had offered a loan at a time when the bank was doing well and future prospects were bright, but in the midst of an economic panic they simply would not hear of it. They reminded the Assembly that the offer had been conditional on the success of the subscription but that it was not doing well. Unhappy with the fix they had gotten themselves into, the directors added another condition. They asserted that "when trade came into its proper channells," and they "had devised proper and sufficient Securities," they would be happy "to gratify the People of the Country."[33]

The directors of the bank were not exaggerating. The second subscription was doing poorly, and as late as June 2 more than 1,500 shares had not been disposed of. The reason is not difficult to uncover: The

32. For the suggestion that antibanking is rooted in the conflict between land banking and commercial banking, see the seminal essay of Fritz Redlich, "Mercantilist Thought," and his *Moulding*, 1:1–12.

33. John Chaloner to Jeremiah Wadsworth and John Church, 25 March 1784, Chaloner and White Letterbook; John Chaloner to Jeremiah Wadsworth and John Church, 25 March 1785, Wadsworth Papers; Barth Wistar to Caspar Wistar, 8 April 1784, Leach Collection, Wistar Section.

bank suffered from the same economic ills that plagued everyone else. Its specie reserves were depleted as some depositors withdrew specie and sent it abroad to pay off debts, and bankruptcies hurt too. The directors sharply reduced discounts in March; only those who already had "bills due in the Bank and could not otherwise be punctual in payment" were able to have their notes discounted, and even they were limited to a maximum of two-thirds of the amount due. The decline in the bank's fortunes was reflected in the value of its stock, which fell from $525 to $400 a share. [34]

The response of the Bank of North America disturbed the legislators, who inquired whether the bank would "give a Credit to money which the Legislature might make on the plan above mentioned." This suggestion was also firmly rejected. The angry assemblymen pointedly noted that they had the power to act without the bank's cooperation. [35]

A bill to issue $50,000 of paper money to be lent on land was quickly proposed, and the measure, which was popular, passed easily. Its provisions passed by margins that varied from 41–16 to 38–19. The only exception was a clause making the paper legal tender, which was narrowly rejected, 27 to 25. To support the value of the bills, they were made receivable at par in specie at all land offices for land purchased in Pennsylvania. Even though proponents of the bill had a clear majority, the measure was not brought before the house for the third and final vote—probably because the Assembly was busy dealing with other issues, such as the Test Acts and the College of Pennsylvania. The bill was held over until the next session. [36]

Faced with an economic crisis and a loan office, the future of the bank seemed bleak. The unfavorable balance of trade and the subsequent outflow of specie made it appear that an institution that depended on a specie reserve could not survive. Everyone assumed that bank notes could not coexist with paper money and that if the paper were issued the bank would be forced to "shut and divide stock." Although the Assembly had not made the notes legal tender, neither the bank nor the mercantile community was comforted. It was widely believed that the next Assembly would take the fatal step. [37]

34. John Chaloner to Jeremiah Wadsworth and John Church, 3 April 1784, Chaloner and White Letterbook; John Chaloner to Jeremiah Wadsworth and John Church, 3 April 1784, Wadsworth Papers; Doerflinger, *Vigorous Spirit,* 269.

35. John Chaloner to Jeremiah Wadsworth and John Church, 25 March 1784, Wadsworth Papers.

36. *Pa. Min.*, 31 March 1784, 218–19, 226–27, 229–35, 239–40, 242–43, 245–46.

37. John Chaloner to Jeremiah Wadsworth and John Church, 3 April 1784, Wadsworth

The bank's concerns are understandable. Everyone remembered the devastating wartime inflation, and in their first commercial crisis the directors' primary responsibility was to maintain the confidence of their stockholders and customers. Bankers and merchants unhappily understood that the recent boom of imports had stretched credit beyond prudent limits. Should they be forced to accept the loan office notes on a par with specie, they feared a run on the bank's specie reserve. The historical success of the loan office notwithstanding, the bank's directors absolutely refused to moderate their opposition.[38]

In fact, it is highly unlikely that the bank would have cooperated with the loan office even if hard times had not made its position precarious. In a newspaper article published February 3 in the *Pennsylvania Packet,* Gouverneur Morris made this clear. Writing anonymously as "An American," he bluntly stated that no one should be deceived by "the idea that this bank (or any other) can minister *directly* to the views of those who desire to borrow on landed security." No sensible man will trust his funds where that practice prevails. Morris tried to soften the blow by suggesting that the bank would make credit more plentiful and therefore indirectly aid "the landholder." In this vein, he also suggested that a few years of peace might restore "the confidence lost by paper money during the war."[39]

When the next Assembly resumed consideration of the bill to create a loan office, the bank moved to defeat it. The bank's president offered to furnish $300,000 in bank notes at 6 percent to a public loan office. The notes would be convertible on demand, and once returned to the loan office they would be retired. President Willing's proposal also required that the Assembly pass a special impost tax to raise $300,000 and support the bank notes. The Assembly rejected the suggestion. Faced with an economic crisis, the majority were not willing to experiment or consider additional taxation.[40]

At the end of 1784, the bank's prospects were no longer promising. Willing confessed that he had lost his optimism because of the "Spirit . . . in this State very unfavorable to any institution however commodious or

---

Papers; John Chaloner to Peter Colt, 22 May 1784, Wadsworth Papers; Jeremiah Wadsworth to John Chaloner, 24 October 1784, Chaloner and White MSS.

38. The best general discussion of the bank's reaction is Doerflinger, *Vigorous Spirit,* 267–70.

39. The article was mainly an attack on the attempt to establish the Bank of Pennsylvania. Elizabeth Nuxoll of the Morris Papers identified the writer.

40. Edward Burd to J. Yeates, 25 August 1784, in Walker, ed., *Burd Papers,* 132; Thomas Willing to George Gray, 24 August 1784, Minutes and Letterbook, Bank of North America, Bank of North America Papers; *Pa. Min.,* 24 August 1784, 294–96, 358–59.

beneficial it may be." He was correct: The bank's future was in jeopardy. Although the storm had not yet broken, the stage was set for America's first bank war.[41]

A newspaper article by "Philopatria," published in the spring, presaged the direction the assault would take. The author was fearful of the bank's power. The coalition between the two banks had increased the power of the survivor too much, it was now a threat to the government. In a healthy government, Philopatria insisted, "particular regard and attention ought to be given to preserve the different interests of the body politic, to grant equal indulgencies to the members that compose it, in order that like a well regulated machine, it may move on smoothly, and no jealousies arise, that one branch is favored more than another."[42]

Philopatria feared that if a loan office were not opened the power of the Bank of North America would grow so great that "the landed interest must fall prey" to it. Certainly, he admitted, the bank has been useful, but only to those living in Philadelphia, whereas the loan office would spread its credit throughout the whole state. That was the crucial distinction: one institution would benefit the few, and the other would aid the larger community.[43]

The danger facing the bank was clear. It had pursued its interests in too heavy-handed a fashion. The "clubbish" discount policy, while understandable as a business tactic, had alienated members of the Philadelphia mercantile community. Opposition to the Bank of Pennsylvania, which was also understandable, increased these concerns. The bank's policies made it easy to see the institution as a selfish faction. Furthermore, its enormous size and monopolistic position always made it possible to perceive the bank as a money power and a possible threat to the Republic.

Beyond these potential problems is the fact that the bank had a corporate charter. Fears of the bank's charter had surfaced as early as the Assembly debates of 1781, and they would continue to reappear over the course of the bank war. These concerns were directed at the charter rather than at commercial banking. In the heightened political atmosphere of post-Revolutionary America, a great deal of energy went into sorting out exactly what Republicanism meant. Many people felt that charters threatened freedom, and George Bryan's views are repre-

41. Thomas Willing to Tench Tilghman, 24 March 1784, Willing, Morris, Swanwick Records, Folder 4, Box 1, MG 134, PSA.
42. *Freeman's Journal*, 14 April 1784.
43. Ibid.

sentative. Bryan believed that "the purpose of the revolution was to preserve representative government" and that although corporations were useful in Europe they were not needed in America. Corporations contradicted "the spirit of the Pennsylvania government."[44]

The belief that corporations were dangerous to republics was widespread and had real power. When the City of Philadelphia applied for a charter in 1781, 1783, and 1785, the Assembly refused to act. Not until 1789 did the Republicans finally grant Philadelphia a charter. Part of the reason for the delay was that there were more-urgent issues facing the Assembly. Nevertheless, anticorporate sentiment made the proposal controversial.[45]

When fifty-four people signed a petition supporting a charter for Philadelphia in 1781, "Agricola" [George Bryan] mounted a counterattack in the *Pennsylvania Gazette*. Because the French have a powerful king, they might find corporations "useful counterweight[s]," but Pennsylvania was not France. He insisted:

> In a democratic republic like ours, they [corporations] tend to split the state at large into lesser States, each having powers to make its own ordinances. They serve to combine the inhabitants for purposes of a local nature, and at the same time occasion parties in the cities and towns concerning measures and leaders, of trifling or no importance, to the neglect, and perhaps general neglect of the general concerns of the nation.

Thus, Agricola feared that incorporating Philadelphia would fragment Pennsylvania and inflame "the jealousy which the country people are so apt to entertain of us town people."[46]

In such a social context, if the Bank of North America ever appeared to thwart the will of the majority, an attack on the institution was all but inevitable. To many Pennsylvanians the bank's opposition to paper money and to a loan office was exactly the sort of evidence needed to trigger a political assault.

44. George Bryan, Read in the Society, 28 August 1783, Bryan Papers; Maier, "Revolutionary Origins," 51–77.

45. Brunhouse, *Counter-Revolution,* 152–54, 184–85, 220–21; Teaford, *Municipal Revolution,* 62–63, 65–69, 71–72, 74.

46. Agricola, *Pa. Gazette,* 13 June 1781. Also on the question of the Philadelphia charter: a petition to the General Assembly, 4 September 1783, reprinted in Hazard, ed., *Register,* 2:327; and "On Incorporations," *Pa. Herald,* 2 and 6 September 1786.

Reinforcing these concerns was a growing awareness and understanding of the Bank of North America. During 1784 the nature of the bank became clear to everyone: The main function of commercial banks was to provide short-term discounts to merchants. Moreover, bank notes were convertible into specie and therefore seemed to be incompatible with a state-issued legal-tender paper money.

As the public clarified its perceptions of the bank, and as the bank's mode of operation, function, and power grew clearer, it became apparent that the bank might clash with popular feelings on several other grounds. The bank's militant espousal of private enterprise upset those who believed that a single-minded pursuit of wealth was morally reprehensible and alienated those who believed that charters of incorporation should be granted only for public purposes. This belief was strengthened by the region's long and happy experience with the public loan office—a very different "bank" that was the embodiment of a public utility. Legal tradition and historical experience fused together to create a widespread expectation that banking should involve public service rather than private profits. These feelings were held by a broad spectrum of merchants, lawyers, farmers, and artisans.

The bank's opposition to the paper money and to the land bank injected a class and geographical basis into the traditionalist reaction against the bank. Rural elements—especially petty-commodity producers—were enraged at the bank's stand. Suffering from hard times, farmers saw the bank's lobbying against the paper money and the land bank as a direct challenge to their economic and class interests. The fact that the bank was owned and operated by wealthy merchants who ran it as a mercantile service institution focused the class animus of the farmers. In addition, the location of the bank in the regional metropolis made it all but inevitable that urban-rural tensions would be entwined with the class differences.

To further complicate matters, the proposal for paper money and the land bank came from the Constitutionalists. When the Bank of North America opposed the loan office, it was inevitable that the Constitutionalists would take umbrage. Because Robert Morris and the directors of the bank were prominent Republicans, the party lineup was preordained. Thus, the tensions surrounding the bank almost automatically involved regions, parties, and social classes.

Like ripples spreading from a stone dropped into still waters, the establishment of the Bank of North America had an impact on Pennsylvania's social structure. The fledgling institution caused a series of changes within the mercantile community and upset the balance of power between merchants and farmers, and between city and countryside.

The size and power of the bank was responsible for much of this dislocation, and so was its organizational structure. The bank was a prototypically modern organization. It had a single purpose and it functioned bureaucratically. In purpose and form the bank was an early and disturbing step toward modernity. When Pennsylvanians came to understand the bank and its impact, a traditionalist revolt erupted. As passions rose, people turned to the Assembly, where the issue was dealt with by the Constitutionalist and Republican parties.

8

Destroying the Monster

Hard times came and galvanized political change. Class consciousness was strengthened and tempers rose. Interest in politics increased, as did party activity. The politics of 1785 provides a perfect example of the interconnectedness of class, party, and public policy.

The 1784 fall elections resulted in a clear-cut victory for the Constitutionalists. Their power had been on the increase since 1783 and peaked in 1785–86. By this time the leadership of the Constitutionalists had changed. For the most part, the early leaders had passed from the scene. The electoral losses in Philadelphia, city and county, had weakened the party's urban elite. As a result, in 1785, westerners like John Smilie and Robert Whitehill emerged as party leaders, and, along with urban merchants like Charles Pettit, they constituted a revamped leadership. Having reduced the Republicans to an impotent minority, the Constitutionalists were free to enact their program.[1]

Economics was on everybody's mind. First on the agenda was the depression. To the Constitutionalists and their constituents this meant a loan office and issuing paper money. The public debt—state and

1. Brunhouse, *Counter-Revolution,* 156, 164, 190.

national—was second. More than one-third of the national debt was held by citizens of Pennsylvania. A broad bipartisan coalition favored action to help them. Finally, the Bank of North America was marked for liquidation. The issues were interconnected, and all had national and local implications.[2]

It is significant that neither party was particularly concerned about the needs and desires of the urban artisans. Like everyone else, artisans were hurt by the economic crisis. The flood of British imports after the war, and the wall erected by British mercantilism, had hurt them badly. Almost immediately, they raised a cry for a protective tariff. Both parties would eventually listen, but in 1784 and 1785 other priorities took precedence. The Constitutionalists were dominated by their rural wing, and the Republicans were still locked into their desire for free trade. In time, the Constitutionalists were moved by political considerations to support a tariff and the Republicans supported a national tariff. Reduced to interest-group politics, artisans were not major political players in 1785.[3]

As the 1780s progressed, it became clear that Congress would not win the power to tax. Public creditors organized to protect their interests. Constitutionalists like Charles Pettit, Blair McClenachan, and Jonathan Sergeant joined with Republicans like William Bingham and Benjamin Rush. Working in and out of the Assembly, these men were the driving force behind the funding bill of 1785.[4]

Although the Constitutionalists were determined to aid the public creditors, they worried that such a course of action might anger their rural and artisanal followers, who were unhappy at the prospect of paying taxes to aid well-to-do creditors. Adroitly, they tied the funding bill to the sale of public lands and a land bank.

The funding bill provided for an issue of £150,000 in paper money; two-thirds of that, or £100,000, would be used to pay the interest charges on the state and national debt. To placate the merchants and the growing sentiments for hard money, the paper was made legal tender for government obligations but *not* for private transactions. The paper—which was supported by new taxes and the sale of unappropriated public lands—would be retired in annual amounts of £20,000,

---

2. Ibid., 169.

3. Doerflinger, *Vigorous Spirit*, 261–67; Olton, *Artisans*, 90–107; Schultz, *Republic*, 93–101.

4. Brunhouse, *Counter-Revolution*, 131–34, 170; Arnold, "Political Ideology," 208–9; Baumann, "Democratic-Republicans," 44–45; Ferguson, *Power*, 221–30.

and the remaining £50,000 would establish the land bank. Borrowers could get between £25 and £100 for eight years at 6 percent interest. For collateral, borrowers were required to mortgage land or houses for triple the value of the loan. To be eligible, applicants had to own property worth £75.[5]

Charles Pettit, who boasted about "My funding Plan," formulated the bill. A prominent Philadelphia merchant and a leading Constitutionalist, Pettit owned large numbers of public certificates. The funding plan offered something to everybody. Farmers, merchants, land speculators, public creditors, paper advocates, and hard-money advocates all had reasons for supporting the bill. The big winners were the public creditors and speculators, because the bill made it possible to use the interest payments to purchase state lands. Since the securities were available at a discount and it was possible to pay for them with notes from the loan office, where public securities were accepted at par, alert investors could make substantial profits.[6]

The paper money was the most controversial element in the bill. Even though the paper was backed by taxes and was not legal tender for private transactions, the Philadelphia mercantile community remained unalterably opposed. Memories of the recent and disastrous wartime inflation were too fresh, "and their financial condition [was] too precarious for them to do otherwise."[7]

Merchants called a mass meeting to protest the paper money. "Money being the grand instrument of commerce, and the measure of value, it is an indispensible condition of its own value that its own value be determined and known." Only specie would do. Experience since the Revolution, they insisted, has made it clear that governments do not always have the "power to give to paper money this indispensible property of gold and silver."[8]

The meeting selected a committee of twelve merchants to petition the Assembly to strike the paper from the bill, five of whom were directors of the bank. Even at this late hour the bank refused to quiet

5. Ferguson, *Power,* 228–30; McDonald, *Formation,* 49–51; Arnold, "Political Ideology," 211–13; Baumann, "Democratic-Republicans," 45–46; Kaminski, "Paper Politics," 50–53, 84 n. 6; Mitchell and Flanders, eds., *Statutes,* 40:454–86, 560–72.

6. McDonald, *Formation,* 51–52; Charles Pettit to General Greene, 23 March 1785, Pettit Correspondence.

7. Doerflinger, *Vigorous Spirit,* 269.

8. "The Representation of the Merchants and Traders of the City of Philadelphia," *Pa. Gazette,* 2 March 1785.

its resistance to paper money, but the voices of doubt never attracted a significant following. The need was too great and the bill was too popular. It passed, 47 to 18.[9]

Having issued paper money, created a loan office, supported the public creditors, and opened state lands to speculators, the Constitutionalists moved against the bank. The fact that it was created and run by prominent Republicans had always made it a potential political target. The timing of the attack was determined by the onset of hard times and the bank's opposition to the paper money and the land bank. As George Bryan noted, "the contention will be whether our Paper Credit shall be that of a bank or of the public."[10]

The opening shot in America's first bank war was a petition advocating repeal of the bank's charter. It was carried in the newspapers on February 23, 1785, and reached the Assembly early the next month. The petition made three charges: first, that the bank caused a shortage of money because wealthy individuals had invested in the bank and were no longer lending to the public; second, that the bank was "able to give preference in trade by advances of money to their particular favorites . . . [so] as to destroy that equality which ought to take place in a commercial country"; third, that the bank did not permit the government to issue a legal-tender paper money.[11]

Unaccountably, President Willing and the directors ignored the petitions. Even though Willing had expressed concern in 1784 about the growing hostility to the bank, he airily dismissed the petitions. In a letter to his son-in-law, William Bingham, he mentioned them, then confidently asserted that if the bank simply stood its ground its obvious utility would "baffle all opposition."[12]

While the directors baffled the opposition by doing nothing, the petitions arrived and were sent to a committee, which deliberated for two days before reporting in favor of repealing the charter. The committee claimed that the bank was attracting foreign investment, and then raised the specter of foreign control. The committee also asserted

9. Ibid.; Brunhouse, *Counter-Revolution*, 170.
10. George Bryan to William Augustus Atlee, 23 June 1785, Peter Force Misc. Papers, LC.
11. *Freeman's Journal*, 23 February 1785; *Pa. Evening Herald*, 23 February 1785; *Pa. Min.*, 9 March 1785, 233; Rappaport, "Sources," 93–95.
12. Thomas Willing to William Bingham, 12 March 1785, Bingham Papers. Willing's denseness is difficult to fathom. Toward the end of the Assembly's proceedings, despite all the evidence to the contrary, he was able to "believe they'll drop the attack before the end of the Session." Willing to William Bingham, 29 August 1785, in Balch, ed., *Willing Letters*, 112.

that paying dividends to foreigners would send specie out of the region and cause local shortages. But the most dangerous charge the committee made was that the bank constituted a money power that threatened equality and the survival of the Republic. In the eyes of the committee,

> the accumulation of enormous wealth in the hands of a society, who claim perpetual duration, will necessarily produce a degree of influence and power, which cannot be entrusted in the hands of any sett [*sic*] of men, whatsoever, without endangering the public safety. . . . We have nothing in our free and equal government capable of balancing the influence which this bank must create, and we see nothing which in the course of a few years, can prevent the directors of the bank from governing Pennsylvania. Already we have felt its influence indirectly interfering in the measures of the legislature. Already the house of assembly, the representatives of the people have been threatened, that the credit of our paper currency will be blasted by the bank; —and if this growing evil continues, we fear the time is not very distant, when the bank will be able to dictate to the legislature, what laws to pass and what to forbear.[13]

The most interesting new issue raised by the petitions and the committee report was the complaint about foreign investment. On the surface it made little sense to complain that the bank was draining specie out of the region by attracting foreign investment. Even though the bank's defenders would have a lot to say about the utility of foreign capital as an aid to economic development, the charge was damaging. Concerns about foreign control intensified fears of the money power.

When the first sale of bank stock ended in July 1783, some 67 percent of the stock was held by Pennsylvanians; other Americans held another 30 percent. If we count as "foreigners" Americans who were not from the Quaker state—a position many Pennsylvanians took—then a significant 33 percent of the bank's owners were "foreigners." When the second subscription was completed in the spring of 1786, other Americans had purchased 27.8 percent and Europeans had acquired

---

13. *Pa. Min.*, 23 and 25 March 1785, 240–43, 249; *Pa. Gazette*, 30 March 1785; *Pa. Packet*, 29 March 1785; John Chaloner to Jeremiah Wadsworth, 25 March 1785, Wadsworth Papers; Rappaport, "Sources," 96–98.

13.1 percent—a grand total of almost 41 percent. Pennsylvanians' holdings had declined to 59.1 percent.[14]

Politically and symbolically, connecting the bank to foreigners made a good deal of sense. The bank was so different from other organizations that it appeared alien to many Pennsylvanians. Similarly, while the bank's defenders would find it easy to refute the charge that the rich were no longer lending to the public because they were investing in the bank, the defense missed the point. The expression of anger at the rich made sense as an expression of class resentment about the changes being made by the bank in the areas of class and community relations.

The central core of truth in the charges made by the committee was that the bank opposed the paper money and the land bank. Because these charges were factually correct, they lent credence to the perception of the bank as a dangerous, aristocratic money power. The fact that the bank had aggressively defended its monopoly in 1784 also intensified these concerns. Finally, the bank's "special" corporate privileges upset those who saw corporations as public service institutions and reinforced the view of the bank as an aristocratic institution. The specter of a money power had been raised by a small minority as early as 1782, during the initial discussion over the bank's charter. It reappeared when the Bank of Pennsylvania applied for a charter, and it reappeared repeatedly in the course of the bank war.

The social reality that gave these charges their meaning and significance was rural Pennsylvania's egalitarian social structure. In their families, associations, and neighborhoods, and in their religious and political institutions, Pennsylvanians were encouraged to participate. These participatory impulses were tied to an economy in which property and skills were widely disseminated and neighborly and reciprocal social relations played a major role. The result was an egalitarian orientation in which equality would be defended both ideologically and as existential reality.

During the Assembly's discussion of the committee report in favor of revoking the bank's charter, the ubiquitous Charles Pettit emerged as the bank's defender. He unsuccessfully moved to postpone the debate, and then tried to substitute "alter and amend" for "repeal." The urban, mercantile wing of the Constitutionalist Party was not committed to the

---

14. For the shareholders, see Stock Ledger, I, Bank of North America, Bank of North America Papers, Box 6-D; Lewis Jr., *History of the Bank* (folio ed.), 2:273–77, 279–301; Carey, ed., *Debates and Proceedings*, 94–95.

destruction of the bank, but they had to compromise with the rural wing of the party. In effect, they traded assumption for a loan office and the destruction of the bank.[15] The voting on Pettit's proposals was not close. The Constitutionalist majority rejected them 40 to 17. Then the report was voted on and accepted by a similarly lopsided margin, and the committee was instructed to bring in a bill.[16]

Constitutionalists were thrilled at the popularity of their attack. They believed that the bank itself was largely responsible for its plight: The "opposition to the second bank, . . . to the funding, or money bill etc., etc., were all foolish interferences & provocations." It is not surprising that Republicans blamed the prevailing spirit of "party and faction." Francis Hopkinson, a Republican lawyer who held a few shares of bank stock, explained the attack on the grounds that the Constitutionalists "hated Mr. Morris personally and because the Directors were not under their influence."[17]

Lurking behind the Republican belief that the attack on the bank was "merely" a Constitutionalist ploy was a powerful sense of class and status. Republicans were contemptuous of the Constitutionalists, describing them as "Country Wiseacres" and "scum." They were haunted by a fear that the majority had designs on the property of the rich. Charles Thomson worriedly wrote to his wife:

> The principles of the report are alarming & strike at all property. . . . The people are not settled down to their condition. Those that have suddenly got wealth or power are grasping at more. Those that have neither are pressing for them not by virtue & the fair deeds and honest paths of industry and frugality, but by knavery and tricking. So that till some have their deserts and others are reduced to their former insignificancy I expect little else but confusion.[18]

By now even Thomas Willing understood that something more than pious hopes were needed. He wrote to James Wilson, serving in

15. *Pa. Min.*, 25 March 1785, 254–55; Baumann, "Democratic-Republicans," 52–55.

16. *Pa. Min.*, 25 March 1785, 254–55.

17. George Bryan to William Augustus Atlee, 29 March 1785, William Atlee Papers, LC; Francis Hopkinson to Thomas Jefferson, 28 September 1785, in *Jefferson Papers*, 8:562.

18. Charles Thomson to Hannah Thomson, 6 April 1785, *PMHB*, 25 (1901), 430–31; Benjamin Fuller to Robert Totten, 21 April 1785, Fuller Letterbook, HSP. For similar comments, see William Bingham to Thomas Willing, 29 April 1785, Bingham Papers; Robert Morris to Tench Tilghman, 29 March 1785, Morris Papers, NYPL; Francis Hopkinson to Thomas Jefferson, 20 April 1785, in *Jefferson Papers*, 8:99.

Congress, and directed him to take whatever course of action might help the bank. Another director contacted the Dutch ambassador, Pieter Johan Van Berckel, and suggested that he could protect his investment by speaking to members of Congress. The ambassador followed this advice and spoke to Samuel Osgood, who promised action. The bank also launched a propaganda campaign, and Wilson was hired to write a pamphlet. President Willing promised his correspondents that the pamphlet was only the beginning; "Other Fugitive & Weekly pieces, will directly follow to suit the people at large."[19]

Summer turned into fall, and the Assembly prepared to act on the bill revoking the charter, but when the bank asked to be heard in its defense, the Assembly was amenable. Wilson was chosen to speak for the bank, and Jonathan Sergeant for repeal of the charter.[20]

If we date the beginning of the debate on the merits of the bank from the surfacing of the petitions against the bank, the discussions gripped the attention of the public for about two years. Legislative hearings occurred before packed galleries, and the outpouring of newspaper articles and pamphlets are evidence of the depth of these concerns. The bank war provides a clear illustration of Pennsylvania's political system at work. Political parties representing social classes and status groups interacted in the legislature, which functioned like a modern "social center." Politicians used petitions and other devices of the associational system, and also the press, to mobilize supporters, to magnify popular concern, and to educate the public. At the same time, the outpouring of propaganda reveals an assumption that popular support could be created.

The presence of a focal point—an institutional nexus—in which opposing groups were encouraged to defend their interests, and the existence of effective integrative networks that politicized and involved the public, resulted in an intensification of political conflict and, at the same time, an improved potential to contain and manage conflict within the system.

James Wilson appeared before the Assembly to defend the bank,

19. Thomas Willing to James Wilson, 12 May and 1 and 22, September 1785, Minutes and Letterbook, Bank of North America Papers; Van Berkel to Thomas Fitzsimons, 29 August 1785, Case S, Box 22, Simon Gratz Autograph Collection; Thomas Willing to William Bingham, 29 August 1785, in Balch, ed., *Willing Letters*, 112.

20. Unless otherwise noted, the following discussion of the debate between Wilson and Sergeant is based on James Wilson, The Opinion of Counsel 1785 and Wilson's Rebuttal, Wilson Papers, II; *Pa. Evening Herald*, 7 and 8 September 1785; and Rappaport, "Sources," 103–17.

arguing that the bank was not responsible for the shortage of money plaguing the state. The real causes, insisted the bank's counsel, were the depreciation of the continental dollar and the enormous expense of the Revolutionary War, the postwar buying spree with its resultant export of specie, and the tremendous opportunities to invest in America.

Wilson was in fine fettle as he demonstrated that foreign investment was beneficial rather than dangerous. Any enlargement of America's capital stock would help expand local business and should therefore be encouraged. Foreign capital had helped Americans turn a wilderness into a productive province. But the heart of the matter—the real basis for the objections to the bank—insisted Wilson, was simply the newness of the institution. The same thing had happened when the Bank of England was chartered. Many had feared that the bank would become a monopoly and engross the nation's wealth, but time had quieted these fears.

This was a genuine insight. Had Wilson and the bank's directors fully grasped its implications and adopted a more conciliatory stance, the bank might have had an easier time. Instead, the bank's defenders defended it belligerently against every attack, treating critics with contempt. Thus, when Wilson dealt with the Assembly's threat to revoke the charter, he thundered that it would amount to an action without forfeiture, crime, or trial. Instead of spreading soothing balm, he concluded that even English despots like Charles and James had not dared to revoke charters without trials.[21]

Wilson then turned to two widely held ideas that had hurt the bank. The first was that the existence of the bank "prevents loans on legal interest." He cogently pointed out that the high rates had been produced by the shortage of funds, a shortage caused by wartime expenses, the postwar export of specie, and the tremendous opportunities to invest in the New World. Never before has a nation been blessed with "so many lucrative ways of employing money, . . . purchasing lands—speculating in certificates and other securities—and in improvements."

Second, Wilson dealt with the concern that the bank's paper could not coexist with the state's paper. Because he and the bank's directors still believed that the allegation was correct, his handling of the issue was not effective politically. According to Wilson, the real problem was not

21. Wilson's full argument is not carried by the *Pa. Evening Herald*, but the coverage of Sergeant's rebuttal makes it possible to reconstruct his argument. An examination of Wilson's soon-to-be published pamphlet, "Considerations," also helped.

the bank notes but rather a lack of public confidence in the state's paper money. The reason for this lack of confidence was that loan office notes were not convertible into silver and gold. Wilson knew his cure—making the loan office notes convertible into specie—was neither acceptable nor practical. Convertibility was subversive of the principles of land banking and in practical terms was beyond the means of the government.

On the following day, the counsel for the petitioners opposed to the bank made his appearance. Jonathan Sergeant appealed to the fears of those in the rural areas and stressed the conflict between the bank and the region's farmers. In the past, he recalled, our farmers were dependent on the loan office because "99 out of 100" did not have the money to purchase tools and livestock. The loan office enabled them to raise the required funds by pledging their land, and the system allowed farmers, and along with them the whole community, to prosper. But now the loan office could not function effectively because its notes could not compete with bank notes, which were convertible on demand and loaned only for short periods of time. As a result, bank notes were more valuable than loan office notes, which were backed by land and taxes and were granted for as long as sixteen years. "[So long] as there is a bank we will never have a state paper money."

To make matters worse, the bank's profits were so high that it was impossible to borrow at the legal rate. Sergeant was not sure exactly what the bank's profits were, although estimates as high as 16 percent were common. Because the legal interest rate was 6 percent, who would be foolish enough to lend to farmers at the legal rate?

Returning to his major theme, Sergeant insisted that the loan office was the only way out of the present economic morass: He said, "[We need] loans to the farmers to enable them to improve and cultivate the country. Can they derive this assistance from the bank? No—The bank is calculated to accommodate persons in want of money for a short time—and the sphere of its operations is confined to Philadelphia."

Because the stake in the bank war was the future shape of money markets, it is not surprising that class interests played such a prominent role in the struggle. Both sides believed the conflict was rooted in a fundamental difference of interest. Reality, of course, was more complex. In many ways, the economic activities of farmers and merchants were complementary—merchants exported farm produce and provided manufactured goods for the rural population. The conflict between farmers and merchants over the future of Pennsylvania's money markets is a perfect illustration of the fact that the primary vectors of class struggle in the last third of the eighteenth century did not involve exploitative relations of production. Classes jockeyed to improve their position in the market.

Shifting his attack, Sergeant argued that because the bank damaged agriculture and encouraged cheap imports, the region's mechanics were hurt by high food prices and foreign competition. The bank and its exorbitant profits also discouraged private investors from investing in internal improvements. Sergeant was careful to point out that the danger transcended economics. By encouraging usury and enforcing prompt payment, he argued, the bank was threatening traditional values and morality. When a person had a note due at the bank, he had to pay on time "or his character, fortune, and everything near or dear were lost. Let him give what interest he would, his note must be taken up, or his credit blasted—this made even the most opulent tremble—the more hollow a man's circumstances were, the more studiously must he avoid the danger of having his character tarnished." Such a requirement for prompt payment forced people to borrow and find co-signers. Eventually, a "current of bankruptcy" ruined some borrowers, leaving their friends and neighbors to pay the debt. In this atmosphere usury flourished. How else could one explain the prevailing interest rates of 5 to 10 percent? It was "no longer a question with many of how to E A R N money, but of how to G E T it, by any means, however iniquitous."

Building to a rhetorical climax, Sergeant roared: "Consistent with the duty I owe my country, I cannot behold this dreadful engine working such horrid mischiefs without raising my voice aloud, and crying out to you — e x t e r m i n a t e   t h e   b a n k! —It ruins our manufactures, beggars our mechanics, and totally retards our agriculture."

Sergeant's rhetoric was overblown, but so was Wilson's—recall his suggestion that revoking the charter would be an act worthy of European tyrants. Part of the reason the rhetoric was so excited is that the issue at hand was genuinely important; the shape of the future was at stake.

Shaken by the turn of events, and aware that the charter would be revoked, the bank's defenders made a vain, last effort to placate their foes. Wilson rose and announced that he had been authorized to promise that in order to give the loan office money a fair chance the bank would not issue any notes payable to the bearer for one year, or reissue any that were brought in. If anything short of destruction would satisfy the foes of the bank, Wilson hoped that this offer would accomplish it.[22]

22. *Pa. Evening Herald,* 14 September 1785.

Having listened, the Assembly voted. Given the solid Constitutionalist majority, the issue was never in doubt. The margin on the five important votes varied from 41 to 18, to 47 to 21. Only Chester, York, Bedford, and Washington counties and the City of Philadelphia supported the bank. What a reversal! Three and a half years before, when the bank had been chartered, there had been little opposition to the new institution anywhere in the state.[23]

While the Assembly was busy revoking the bank's charter, the issue was the subject of lively debate in the local press. In 1784, seven people wrote seven newspaper articles. The following year, nineteen people wrote twenty-three articles and another three had pamphlets published. In just two years, then, twenty-nine people wrote thirty-three articles and pamphlets. Republicans wrote one more pamphlet, but the two sides had the same number of correspondents and the same number of newspaper articles.[24]

Aware of the public's interest, the local press carried detailed reports on the Assembly's proceedings. The petitions advocating repeal of the bank charter were carried in several newspapers, as was the committee report that supported the petitions. Mathew Carey even printed almost verbatim accounts of the debate between Wilson and Sergeant, as well as the last-minute offer to have the bank sharply curtail its activities for a year in his *Pennsylvania Evening Herald.*

Among those criticizing the bank, Colbert's was the clearest, most logical, and most perceptive voice in 1785. His analysis was built around the polar opposites of equality and aristocracy. He contended:

> Equal liberty and equal privileges are the happy effect of a free government. . . . A popular government (that is a genuine republic) holds out *this equality* to its citizens; . . . in this consists its excellence. The unequal or partial distribution of public benefits within a state creates distinctions of interest, influence, and power, which lead to the establishment of an aristocracy, the very worst species of government.[25]

23. *Pa. Min.*, 25 March, 4 April, and 10 September 1785, 254–56, 285–86, 367–68.

24. See Appendix C for a listing of the English-language newspaper articles and pamphlets published during the bank war. For a detailed discussion of the public debate of 1785, see Rappaport, "Sources," ch. 5.

25. Colbert, "Strictures on the Bank and on a Paper Currency," pt. 1, *Pa. Packet,* 31 March 1785.

It was the duty of free people to guard against all possible encroach-ments, and because equality already existed in Pennsylvania, change was dangerous and the bank was a threat. In its present form, warned Colbert, the Bank of North America "was destructive to the freedom of the state." That point was important and would reappear again and again in the debate. Constitutionalists wanted to preserve liberty that they believed already existed.

Colbert worried that "only a handful of our citizens were aided by the bank" and noted correctly that the bulk of the loans were confined to Philadelphia and were made to wealthy merchants. Occasionally the bank lent to young merchants who could provide good endorsers—that is, rich, Philadelphia merchants—and to a few farmers and mechanics living in or near the city. The only other beneficiaries of the institution were the stockholders.

Even worse, the bank's directors had complete control over whom they lent to and were under no obligation to explain their decisions. They were totally free of all governmental restraint. The result was that the directors could arbitrarily limit the benefits of the bank to a small clique. Suppose the directors were evil or were the subjects of a foreign power we were at war with. What recourse, Colbert asked, would we have?

Underlying Colbert's argument is a genuine insight, that economic power has political dimensions. We have created, he warned in a phrase that appeared repeatedly in discussions of corporations, a *"government within a government."* The bank was an "aristocratical faction, an oligarchical junto" that will rule through a "system of favoritism."

The argument derived from the Whig emphasis on the mixed or balanced constitution. Colbert saw the world through lenses that magni-fied the dangers of unchecked power. His analysis can be reduced to a fear that the bank could control access to credit, a power he cogently pointed out had political implications.

The economic argument offered by the bank's critics was simple and less effective. They insisted that the bank had worsened the balance of trade and hindered agriculture. "Philadelphiensis" believed that banks were useful only in commercial nations, and then only as long as the balance of trade was favorable. America was likely to remain agricultural because of its huge land mass and small population. As a result, labor would remain expensive, manufacturing would be unprofitable, and imports would exceed exports. American specie would therefore be siphoned off, and our farmers would be hurt by a shortage of circulating medium. Because the bank encouraged imports, it would worsen the situation.[26]

As a remedy, the bank's critics offered two solutions: first, a ritual appeal to Republicanism, which, they insisted, was essential to promote "oeconomy" and to suppress "luxury, indolence and false credit"; second, and more important, the creation of a loan office, which, if "confined within moderate limits and well funded," said Philadelphiensis, would "answer all the valuable purposes of specie" and satisfy our need for credit.[27]

When they discussed what to do with the erring corporation, these writers differed from the Constitutionalist legislators. Only one of the seven advocated revoking the charter—the rest saw some merit in the institution and limited themselves to suggesting charter revisions. They wanted to limit the duration and size of the charter and to give the Assembly the right to renew it. It is significant that these proposals came close, at least in spirit, to those made during the legislative discussions by Constitutionalist Charles Pettit. As the charter was being revoked, the terms of a possible compromise were being hammered out.[28]

Defenders of the bank mounted a spirited campaign. Stressing the bank's contribution to the state's monetary system, they correctly contended that the bank facilitated the circulation of money—increasing the quantity of money and providing a superior circulating medium. Their heaviest ammunition was aimed at the charge that the bank was responsible for a shortage of money, to which they repeatedly responded by insisting that the real culprit was the call for paper money, which led to hoarding. Alluding to the recent inflation, Gouverneur Morris contended that money was scarce because many merchants had been ruined by the "payment of their debts in paper greatly depreciated." As a result, merchants had refused to lend, out of a "well grounded apprehension that [when due] it will not be re-paid."[29]

Friends of the bank defended foreign investment. Gouverneur Morris

26. Philadelphiensis, *Freeman's Journal*, 19 January 1785. See also Anon., *Remarks on a Pamphlet*.

27. Philadelphiensis, *Freeman's Journal*, 19 January 1785; *Remarks on a Pamphlet*; Colbert, "Strictures on the Bank and on a Paper Currency," pt. 2, *Pa. Packet*, 1 April 1785.

28. *Remarks on a Pamphlet*; Colbert, "Strictures on the Bank and on a Paper Currency"; Philadelphiensis, *Freeman's Journal*, 19 January 1785.

29. Artemon, *Pa. Gazette*, 16 February 1785; A Pennsylvanian, "To the People of Pennsylvania," *Pa. Packet*, 29 March 1785; A.B., *Pa. Gazette*, 6 April 1785; An Old Banker, in ibid., 30 March 1785; Wilson, "Considerations," 143–44; Morris, "Address on the Bank," 446.

impatiently dismissed concerns that foreign investors might dominate the bank and that the payment of dividends out of the state hurt the local economy. He insisted that the need for capital was so acute that there was no other choice. Following the lead of James Wilson, Morris noted that development in America had always utilized foreign credit. While debt had disadvantages, he said, ours had transformed "a wilderness . . . into beautiful cultivation. From the discovery of America to the present hour, we have been paying interest for what we owe the other side of the Atlantic. Our debt and our prosperity have gone hand in hand."[30]

The bank's defenders were especially anxious to refute the charge that the bank had dried up the sources of credit that farmers had traditionally used. They were on sure ground. Gouverneur Morris provided the most complete rebuttal. He argued that those who had invested in the bank would not normally lend to Pennsylvania's farmers. The shareholders included foreigners and residents of other states, small stockholders with minimal resources, and more-substantial export-import merchants who needed capital to finance their own mercantile operations. Supporters of the bank could have strengthened their argument by showing that private capital markets had never been adequate for farmers' needs. Of course, that was the reason the loan office had been created in the first place, and predictably most of the bank's defenders carefully avoided the subject.[31]

In his forthright manner, Gouverneur Morris put his finger squarely on the problem. The bank's assailants, he noted, have complained that the bank impeded the circulation of bills of credit, but "paper can only circulate on a par with specie, from a general belief that it is equal to specie. The faith makes the thing." Bank notes were worth more because they were redeemable in specie on demand. If the bank accepted the state's paper, however, it would be forced to exchange the paper for specie. Since the public did not accept the paper at equal value, why should the bank?[32]

Attempts to rebut the widespread concerns about the bank were an interesting mix of strength and weakness. Economic analysis was generally effective, but the absence of plausible attempts to deal with the portrait of the bank as a dangerous money power was noticeable.

30. Morris, "Address on the Bank," 450–53.
31. Ibid., 445–46. See also An Old Banker, *Pa. Gazette,* 30 March 1785; "A Friend to the Trading and Landed Interests of Pennsylvania," *Pa. Gazette,* 4 May 1785.
32. Morris, "Address on the Bank," 457. See also Artemon, *Pa. Gazette,* 16 February 1785.

When they did attempt a reply, the results were often laughable. One writer suggested that even if the bank did try to abuse its powers it could dominate only Philadelphia and its environs. Considering the size of Pennsylvania, he thought, that would not be too bad. The weak performance of the bank's defenders on this point can be attributed to the fact that they accepted their opponents' charges. The bank was a powerful institution, and it was having a visible impact on the economic, political, and social spheres. Reality stood in the way of obfuscation.[33]

Once the bank's friends turned to other issues, their performance improved. The most important question facing them was the wisdom and legality of the Assembly's act of revocation. The subject was a painful one, and the response of Gouverneur Morris was uncharacteristically timid. He asked whether there were any limits at all to the power of the legislature, and if not, if the Assembly could destroy the bank, then all private property was in jeopardy. Therefore, concluded Morris, even if the bank were a "pernicious" institution, it was not prudent to revoke the charter. Morris's obvious difficulty—his emphasis on prudence and moderation—came from his belief that revocation was legal.[34]

James Wilson was made of sterner stuff. In his pamphlet "Considerations, on the Power to Incorporate the Bank of North America," he offered a brilliant if politically unwise defense of the right of Congress to issue charters. This was a difficult proposition to defend. The Articles of Confederation clearly stated that the states retained their "sovereignty, freedom, and independence, and every power, jurisdiction, and right" that is not *"expressly* delegated to the United States." Nowhere in the Articles was Congress expressly given the right to issue charters of incorporation. On the face of it, it seemed obvious that Congress had no such power.[35]

Wilson refused to retreat. He pointed to the rights and powers that grew out of the "union of the whole." The general power, he explained, came into operation over issues that single states were not competent to handle. The territories, the creation of new states, paper money, and foreign relations were such issues.[36] Using Blackstone as his authority, Wilson discussed the bank and the subject of charters. According to the common law, the executive had the power to issue charters, and because Congress possessed the executive power the

33. *Pa. Gazette,* 1 June 1785.
34. Morris, "Address on the Bank," 438–39.
35. Wilson, "Considerations," 130–31.
36. Ibid., 131–33.

bank's charter was legal. Furthermore, Congress had this power because "the object of this institution could not be reached without the
exertion of the combined sovereignty of the union."[37]

While brilliant, Wilson's argument did not strike a responsive chord,
and if anything was a liability in the debate. But this was not the case
when Wilson turned to the more important question of the right of the
state legislature to revoke charters. The question was particularly
disturbing to the bank's defenders, because they accepted the legality
of the Assembly's action.

Wilson's rejoinder was clever, and it also pointed to a way around this
obstacle. "It may be asked," he began, "has the state power over her
own laws?" This was the critical point, which he refused to concede.
The basis of Wilson's argument was a distinction between types of laws.
He argued that some laws dealt with the property of a few individuals,
while others affected groups of people and some touched every citizen.
In form they were all similar: They "are all passed in the same manner,
are all clothed in the same legislative formality, and are all equally acts"
of the Assembly. Yet, despite these superficial similarities, Wilson
contended that the Assembly did not have the same power of repeal
over both types of law.[38]

When an action of the legislature touched on the rights and property
of every citizen, Wilson asserted that no conflict existed because the
Assembly represented all the people. However, this was not the case
when laws affected individuals, groups of citizens, and corporations. In
these cases

> two parties are instituted, and two distinct interests subsist.
> Rules of justice, of faith, and of honor must, therefore, be
> established between them: for if interest alone is to be viewed,
> the . . . [corporation] must always lie at the mercy of the
> community. Still more different is the case in regard to a law, by
> which an estate is vested or confirmed in an individual: if, in this
> case the legislature may, at discretion, and without any reason
> assigned, devest [sic] or destroy his estate, then a person seized
> of an estate in fee simple, under legislative sanction, is in truth,
> nothing more than a solemn tenant at will.

37. Ibid., 134.
38. Ibid., 138.

Wilson concluded: "Whenever the objects and makers of an instrument
. . . are not the same, it [the law] is to be considered as a compact" and
attempts by the government to change or revoke the agreement must
apply judicial rules of "accusation," "hearing," "proof," and "forfeiture."
Because the Assembly had not followed this procedure, Wilson concluded, the property rights of the bank had been violated.[39]

The analogy between a charter of incorporation and a compact, or
contract, enabled Wilson to make a convincing case that the bank's
property rights were being violated, and this in turn made it possible for
the bank to develop a counterattack based on a defense of property
rights. The Lockean compact theory, on which Wilson was building,
legitimated government in terms of the protection of private property,
and it was of no small moment that this theory had been at the heart of
the argument for independence.[40]

Thus, if the bank's critics could hurl epithets of monopoly and
aristocracy and draw on widespread concerns about corporate grants,
Wilson had found a way to attach the cause of the bank to the banners
of legality, private property, and, in the political rhetoric of the era,
liberty and independence. The following year, Tom Paine would translate Wilson's argument into language that everyone could understand
and place it at the center of the bank's defense.

Originally, when the General Assembly had chartered the bank it had
done so for patriotic reasons. Only a tiny minority had raised concerns,
but by 1784 events had legitimated their fears. On the broadest level,
the bank war was a traditionalist reaction. The Bank of North America
was a new kind of organization—specialized, powerful, and wealthy. It
was, moreover, one of the first private enterprises to receive a public
charter, and it was a monopoly. The rigorous discipline the bank
imposed on its customers seemed too commercial and unacceptably
impersonal. It offended many in the urban commercial community as
well as many of those from rural areas because the discipline violated
the norms and values of a social system that had a leisurely pace of life
and intense concerns about reciprocity. Above all, what made the bank
so fearsome was its alien nature and enormous power.

Opposition to the bank inevitably raised the chimera of class warfare,
for a number of reasons. First, the issues involved—the loan office and
the bank—were directly tied to the economic interests of the region's

39. Ibid., 138–39. The same idea had been suggested by Candid, *Pa. Gazette*, 6 April 1785.
40. Ely, *Guardian*, 27–38, 64–66.

farmers and merchants. Second, the men who ran the bank were not simply Philadelphia merchants, but were also prominent members of the regional upper class. As the bank war unfolded, the conflict inevitably involved upper and lower elements of the stratification system. Much of the talk of "aristocracy" and "equality" stemmed from this aspect of the conflict.

The fact that issues of class were translated into legitimate political activity tells us a great deal. Pennsylvania had a remarkably open and responsive political system that made it astonishingly easy for citizens, even the rural masses, to make demands on the central political institutions of the state. The events of 1785 clearly demonstrate this. The other side of this openness is that the upper class simply could not control the political agenda. They were unable to stop the attack on the bank or to prevent the Assembly from repealing the bank's charter.

The bank war also demonstrates how easily and quickly the needs of the various social classes could be translated into party programs and then into public policy. This responsiveness grew out of the participatory norms and institutions that were key elements of the social fabric, as well as out of the simplicity of the social structure. The associational system's flexibility combined with the widespread possession of property and skill to empower large numbers of people. Simple farmers, as well as people like Robert Morris, were secure in the knowledge that their actions made a difference.

An important consequence of the ability of the political system to deal with class tensions was that the imperatives of class were harnessed to the needs and imperatives of party. The process of translating class conflict into party conflict involved reformulating the issues into the broad concerns of public policy that could be defended by party leaders.

Those attacking the bank argued that revocation of the charter would promote justice, prosperity, and the general welfare. Building their case on the virtues of and economic centrality of agriculture and small-scale production, they advocated a land bank and portrayed the Bank of North America as an aristocracy and a threat to liberty and republican virtue.

Conversely, the friends of the bank labored to convince the public that the bank promoted prosperity. They were hard-pressed to defuse the central thrust of the critics, that the bank furthered commercialization and was a threat to equality, but James Wilson provided the necessary strategy with his argument that the charter was a form of property and that its destruction violated due process and property rights. This enabled Republicans to use the language and logic of

Whiggery to remind the public of the relationship between property and liberty. In this fashion, the class interests that provoked the bank war were reformulated into party platforms, and economic interests were transmuted into concerns about the general welfare and defenses of liberty and justice.

9

The Bank Reborn

As everyone anticipated, the loss of the charter at the height of a major business contraction endangered the bank. It was widely believed that the corporation would have to close, and to make matters worse, a bitter internal corporate struggle broke out. In the crisis the directors prevailed, retaining their positions, holding the bank together, and winning a new charter.

The position of the bank was serious. In 1784 the cash account of the bank was approximately $59,570,000, but a year later it dropped to $37,000,000—a decline of approximately 39 percent. Dividends slipped from 14 percent to 6 percent in 1785 and remained at that level until 1788. The market price of bank shares reflected the decline. When the bank had been doing well, its shares were in demand and sold well above par, but now they sold at a discount—when any buyers could be found. The bottom was reached in the early spring of 1786, when shares sold at 8 percent below their face value. Finally, loss of the charter raised the frightening possibility that investors would be liable for the debts of the bank.[1]

---

1. Lewis Jr., *History of the Bank*, 66–67; McDonald, *Formation*, 53; Platt, "Wadsworth,"

In order to appreciate the seriousness of the situation, it is necessary to say a word about the bank's business. Because the business was so new and the business climate of the 1780s was so troubled, the directors were much more conservative in their operation than anyone had expected them to be. Discounts had to be approved by the entire board of directors, and a unanimous vote was required. As a result, "the value of outstanding [bank] notes during the 1780s" was equal to "about $364,200," which meant that the bank supported a note issue of only about 50 percent "of its paid in capital."[2]

If the discount policy was conservative, the dividend policy adopted by the bank was aggressive. But this policy was also based on fear. The directors paid large dividends—8¾ percent and 14½ percent in 1782 and 1783—in order to maintain the value of the bank's stock and to keep investors interested. The policy was successful, but it had negative consequences. Because almost all the profits were paid "to the stock-holders as dividends," little was left to reinvest in the bank's capital stock. Clearly the bank's directors saw the institution as fragile, and losing the charter compounded their concerns.[3]

Although everyone connected with the bank was in jeopardy, the position of out-of-state investors was especially unenviable. Investing simply to earn profits, they owned 891 shares, or 40 percent of the bank's stock.

While all investors desire profits, additional motives, like loyalty to place and group, entrepreneurial pride, status, and the expectation that ownership would make it easier to obtain discounts, encouraged Philadelphians to invest in the bank, and then to defend it when it came under attack. All the options facing out-of-state investors were unpleasant. Because the stock was selling below par, they would lose money if they tried to sell, and if a large block of stock appeared on the market they would get even less. Of course, if they did not sell and the bank failed, they would get nothing.[4]

Jeremiah Wadsworth, a resident of Hartford, Connecticut, and the

152; Thomas Willing to Tench Tilghman, 19 April 1786, Willing, Morris, Swanwick Records, Box 1, PSA; John Swanwick to Tench Tilghman, 10 January 1786, in ibid.; Robert Morris to Thomas R. Tilghman, 2 July 1786, Morris Papers, NYPL; Thomas Willing to Pieter Johan Van Berckel, William Denning, Sampson Fleming, William Edgar, and John Barker Church, 13 June 1786, Stockholders Minutes, Bank of North America, Bank of North America Papers.

2. Doerflinger, *Vigorous Spirit*, 302–3.

3. Ibid., 301.

4. Lewis Jr., *History of the Bank*, 67; Carey, ed., *Debates and Proceedings*, 94–95.

bank's largest stockholder, attended the January stockholders' meeting. He hoped to have the stockholders pass a resolution instructing the directors to go to court to find out if the "laws of Pennsylvania still acknowledge the Bank of North America as a corporate body."[5] Arriving in Philadelphia before the meeting, Wadsworth and Robert Morris met together several times. Wadsworth made it clear that he and the people he represented were unhappy with the directors. They were especially troubled by what they believed were unwise loans and by the frequency with which discounts had been suspended.[6]

The first complaint referred specifically to James Wilson, whose indebtedness to the bank was close to $100,000. Wilson's privileged position—his debt was well beyond any reasonable estimation of his assets, and the directors had repeatedly extended the length of the loans—also troubled local investors. Considering the stockholders' exposed position regarding liability, this was no small matter. The second complaint had less merit. When the directors suspended discounts, they did so to protect the bank's capital reserve. While the tension between the safety of an enterprise and the drive to maximize profits is inevitable, entrepreneurs are necessarily more concerned with safety than are investors.[7]

After a private meeting with Robert Morris, Wadsworth smugly reported that Morris had "softened down much." At the stockholders' meeting a motion to test the act repealing the charter in court was passed, as was a motion to wind up the business of the bank if the case were lost. But it soon became clear that the directors had no intention of going to court or winding down the business. Thomas Willing let it be known that he found the prospect of asking the courts to sit in judgment on the action of the legislature exceedingly disagreeable. The reason was not difficult to determine. Willing and Morris knew that they would lose in court.[8]

5. Pieter Johan Van Berckel, William Edgar, Sampson Fleming, William Denning, and Alexander Hamilton (for John Barker Church) to Jeremiah Wadsworth, 3 January 1786, in *Hamilton Papers*, 3: 643–45.

6. Jeremiah Wadsworth to Alexander Hamilton, 9 January 1786, in ibid., 645–46; John Barker Church to Alexander Hamilton, 5 April 1786, in ibid., 657; Platt, "Wadsworth," 152–55; John Chaloner to Jeremiah Wadsworth, 7 October 1785, Wadsworth Papers.

7. Schwartz, "Attempt," 212 n. 4; Jeremiah Wadsworth to Alexander Hamilton, 9 January 1786, in *Hamilton Papers*, 3:646.

8. Jeremiah Wadsworth to Alexander Hamilton, 9 January 1786, in *Hamilton Papers*, 3:646; John Swanwick to Tench Tilghman, 10 January 1786, Willing, Morris, Swanwick Records, Box 1; Thomas Willing to Pieter Johan Van Berckel et al. (see note 1 above); John Chaloner to

The recent proceedings of the Council of Censors, the state's supreme constitutional body, had made it absolutely clear that no relief could be found in the courts. The Council existed to ensure that the Assembly did not "add to, alter, abolish, or infringe any part of" the Constitution of 1776. Popularly elected and meeting every seven years, the Council could declare legislation unconstitutional and could call for a constitutional convention. Meeting in 1784, the Council heard a petition from the old College of Pennsylvania. The college claimed that an act of the legislature changing their charter was unconstitutional. While the majority of the Council agreed that the Bill of Rights of the Constitution of 1776 protected liberty and property from legislative interference, they rejected the claim.[9]

The Council of Censors ruled that corporations "which are the creatures of society" were not exempt from legislative actions. Suppose a corporation became "dangerous"? They refused to "concede, that a charter obtained perhaps by fraud or imposition . . . cannot be altered or repealed by any succeeding general assembly." Ominously, the Council illustrated by pointing to the bank. "Should the Bank of North America, or any other corporation, become a monster of weight and influence" it might overawe the Assembly. They believed the danger in Pennsylvania was especially great because the constitution did not provide a powerful executive to check corporations. Without the power of legislative restraint, the people's only recourse to an oppressive corporation would be revolt.[10]

The warning was clear, and the bank's directors had no desire to go to court. Morris and the directors had simply outmaneuvered the opposition. They understood that Wadsworth and the people he represented were reluctant to sell their stock so long as they risked a substantial loss, so they promised anything to retain control. Once elected, they ignored their promises and pursued their own plans.

At the very moment the directors were committing themselves to reviving the charter, the political pendulum began to swing in their favor. The year 1785 marked the peak of the Constitutionalists' for-

---

Jeremiah Wadsworth, 21 November 1785, and 19 March and 23 April 1786, Wadsworth Papers; McDonald, *Formation*, 56.

9. "Constitution of Pennsylvania, 1776," 227; Pennsylvania, *Constitutional Convention*, 117–23; Brunhouse, *Counter-Revolution*, 77–79; Rappaport, "Sources," 81–83.

10. Pennsylvania, *Constitutional Convention*, 121–22.

tunes—in the next few years the Republicans gained victory after victory.[11]

The failure of the Constitutionalists was largely due to the party's stance on the Test Acts. These measures created a permanent reservoir of animosity and eventually doomed the party. Moreover, the party's rural base made it difficult to build and maintain strong ties to the artisanal and mercantile communities. The Constitutionalists were aware of their problems. They began dismantling the Tests, and they passed a protective tariff but were unable to save themselves.[12]

Perhaps because they began as the opposition party, the Republicans were more flexible in their efforts at coalition building. They were also right on a number of issues, such as price-fixing and the Tests. The fact that the party's leadership was recruited largely from the regional upper class was also helpful, as was the party's stance on private property and the rights of individuals.

The Morris-Willing plan to revive the bank's charter involved a sophisticated combination of political action and propaganda. Recognizing the need to improve the bank's image, the directors agreed to receive the £150,000 in state paper money for deposits, and they honored drafts by depositors. So extensive did the business become that the bank was forced to hire a clerk to handle it. The only thing the bank did not do was exchange the paper for gold as it did its own notes. It also refused to accommodate the loan office paper, an exception that was typical of its intransigence on that subject.[13]

In the October 1785 elections, Robert Morris, Thomas Fitzsimons, and George Clymer ran on the Republican ticket and won Assembly seats. No one mistook the bank's involvement. Morris, of course, was the individual most responsible for the creation and survival of the institution, Fitzsimons was a director of the bank, and Clymer, a close political ally of Morris, owned stock.[14]

Bolstered by the elections, Morris happily predicted: "Our bank will not be dissolved at all, but on the contrary it will derive Strength, Confidence & credit from the opposition it has met with." His excessive optimism was probably due to the slow mails, which delayed the news

---

11. Brunhouse, *Counter-Revolution*, 190–93, 202.

12. Ibid., 172–73, 179–82; Baumann, "Democratic-Republicans," 57–58; Ireland, "Ratification," 189–92; Olton, "Philadelphia Artisans," 225, 262–65, 286–300, 307–11, 315, 325–26.

13. Lewis Jr., *History of the Bank,* 55; Carey, ed., *Debates and Proceedings,* 58, 119.

14. Brunhouse, *Counter-Revolution,* 176–77, 338.

of the election results in the west. An arduous road still lay ahead. Although the October elections signaled a change in the political climate, the house was still controlled, albeit by a much narrower margin, by the Constitutionalists. [15]

A lull occurred while Willing and Morris shored up their position within the bank. After winning reelection at the January stockholders meeting, the directors asked Delaware for a charter. Soon the city abounded with rumors that the bank would move unless a new charter was forthcoming. Nothing could have been further from the truth; the bank had no intention of leaving Philadelphia for the hinterland. The application was a not-so-subtle way of applying pressure to the recalcitrant legislature. [16]

At the very moment Willing and Morris were turning the screw, they unleashed a petition campaign. Everyone was impressed by the impact last year's antibank petitions had on public opinion, and the bank determined to use the same tool. Beginning in early March, the Assembly was flooded with petitions. [17]

Using James Wilson's argument, the petitions insisted that the principles of impartial justice and private property had been violated by revocation. They also complained that no attempt had been made to investigate the validity of the charges leveled against the bank. Admitting that repeal was legal, the petitioners insisted that the house had departed from the spirit of the constitution and acted injudiciously. [18]

Embarrassed, the Constitutionalist majority created a committee to deal with the question. The new committee found that the committee that had reported in favor of revoking the charter had not visited the bank. The present committee did so, and it is not surprising that they found the directors to be cooperative. The committee also lauded the petitioners, whom they portrayed as "the most respectable amongst us, men who from their intercourse and conditions in life must be supposed best experienced in the effects good or bad, produced by the operations of the bank." After due deliberation, they concluded that the previous

15. Robert Morris to Thomas R. Tilghman, 4 February 1786, Morris Papers, NYPL; John Chaloner to Jeremiah Wadsworth, 18 October 1785, Wadsworth Papers; Brunhouse, *Counter-Revolution*, 176–79.

16. Davis, *Essays*, 2:43; Lewis Jr., *History of the Bank*, 67–69. For the charter, see *Pa. Packet*, 6 March 1786.

17. Lewis Jr., *History of the Bank*, 69. For the petitions, see *Pa. Min.*, 3 March 1786, 184–87. For the petition campaign, see ibid., 4, 6, 7, 9, 15, and 24 March 1786, 193, 195, 198, 201, 210, 242.

18. *Pa. Min.*, 3 March 1786, 184–87.

petitions and report were based on preconceived ideas and motivated by a punitive spirit. They advocated repeal of revocation.[19]

The committee report completed the development of the argument offered by the friends of the bank. The process had been initiated by James Wilson when he appeared as counsel for the bank before the Assembly in 1785. The barrage of newspaper articles and pamphlets appearing that year explored most of the avenues open to the defense. Although the emphasis shifted in 1786 and 1787, little new ground was broken. The bank's defenders insisted that the charter should not have been revoked, and they were particularly critical of the procedures used during revocation. In its final form, the argument they formulated insisted that the bank was a boon to the economy and that the Constitutionalists had acted injudiciously and illegally.

A week after the committee reported, the Assembly began a full-scale debate on the bank, which by then had become one of the most exciting and divisive issues of the decade. Agitation had been going on for almost a year and a half, and it climaxed in 1786. Keenly aware that public attention was riveted on the bank, the legislature set aside four full days for a debate. Tom Paine reported that he had never seen "such crowded audiences as attended the house during the four days the debate lasted."[20]

The debate began at the end of March. Both sides spent a deal of time discussing the committee report of March 1785, which had advocated repeal of the charter. The Constitutionalists had been embarrassed by the accusation that they had acted injudiciously, and the Republicans pressed their advantage. The general question of charters and whether or not they might be repealed, and of the economic impact of the bank, also provided the occasion for a series of lively exchanges.[21]

William Robinson Jr., a Republican and a member of the recent committee that had recommended reinstating the charter, spoke first. Using Wilson's argument, he focused on the legality of repeal. Robinson noted that the Assembly had many different types of power and acted

19. Lewis Jr., *History of the Bank*, 69–70; Carey, ed., *Debates and Proceedings*, 10; *Pa. Min.*, 15, 24 March 1786, 210, 235; *Pa. Gazette*, 29 March 1786; John Chaloner to Jeremiah Wadsworth, 26 March 1786, Wadsworth Papers.

20. *Pa. Min.*, 29, 30, and 31 March and 1 April 1786, 242–48; Common Sense, *Pa. Packet*, 4 April 1786, reprinted in Paine, *Complete Writings*, 1:417.

21. By far the best source for the debate is Carey, ed., *Debates and Proceedings*. See also Hammond, *Banks and Politics*, 54–60; Wilson, "Bank of North America," 16–23; and the detailed Rappaport, "Sources," 158–91.

in different capacities, and that when it granted charters it acted in an executive capacity; the ability to pass laws was, of course, the legislative power. The two powers were quite different. The former bestowed privileges on a few individuals, the latter had an impact on the whole community.[22]

Because repeal constituted an exercise of judicial power, Robinson insisted, the Assembly had exceeded its powers. Even though the house had some judicial power, it did not have jurisdiction in cases involving property. In such cases the constitution guaranteed jury trials. Since charters were property, they could not be revoked by legislative action. They could be terminated by courts only if the corporation violated the terms of the grant. Robinson concluded, therefore, that the Assembly's action was illegal.

There were problems with this argument. Everybody knew that Blackstone believed Parliament had the power to revoke charters, and the history of that august body was filled with examples of its doing so. Robinson anticipated this thrust. He asserted that these precedents were not applicable because the American and British constitutions were different. In Great Britain, acts of Parliament had the same weight as the constitution, while in America the constitution was distinct from and superior to the government. Moreover, to protect individual freedom in America, power was distributed among the branches of government. Should these principles be violated, Robinson warned, "by one branch of government passing beyond the bounds which separate it from the other, liberty cannot long exist."

This was the weakness the Republicans were eager to exploit. Confident about the correctness of their economic arguments, they hammered away at the idea that the Constitutionalists had acted injudiciously and improperly when they repealed the charter. The portrayal of the charter as a form of property allowed friends of the bank to make the Lockean connection between private property and liberty. If the public came to accept this linkage, reinstating the charter would be easier.

On the whole, the bank's defenders made excellent use of their opportunity. Robert Morris and his allies discussed the commercial, financial, and political issues associated with the bank and its charter, and the Financier bore the brunt of the load. An energetic figure—by turns merchant, real-estate operator, financier, banker, and politician

22. Carey, ed., *Debates and Proceedings*, 11–13.

(national and local)—Morris addressed the Assembly several times; on one occasion he gave a bravura performance that lasted almost an entire day. His unique combination of status, energy, knowledge, and intelligence made him a formidable advocate. When the defense finished, the public had a clearer idea of what a commercial bank was, how it operated, and why it was necessary, and as the public's understanding grew, some of the fear subsided. This was the most important consequence of the debate.[23]

Robert Morris and the Republicans did not hold the field unopposed. Constitutionalists like John Smilie, Robert Whitehill, and especially the redoubtable William Findley, provided formidable opposition. Trying to stem the tide, they responded to the Republican critique. Troubled by the argument that charters were property and therefore sacrosanct, they responded that the rights of the people were paramount.

Smilie noted that society's definition of "sacred" was subject to change. Americans had once believed that monarchy was sacred, but that was now an absurd idea, he said. He insisted that the viability of particular charters had to be judged by their utility:

> Charters are rendered sacred, not because they are given by the assembly, or by the parliament—but by the objects for which they are given. If a charter is given in a favour of a monopoly, whereby the natural and legal rights of mankind are invaded, to benefit certain individuals, it would be a dangerous doctrine to hold that it could not be annulled. All the natural rights of the people, as far as is consistent with the welfare of mankind, are secured by the constitution. All charters granting exclusive rights, are a monopoly on the great charter of mankind. The happiness of the people is the first law.

In other words, the function of government is to protect the people's rights, and if a charter infringes on those rights the charter would have to go. This was a version of Jefferson's dictum that the earth belonged to the living.[24]

Smilie gloried in excitement. While discussing the committee report

23. For the heart of the Republican case, see ibid., 22–58, 80–83, 94–95, 100–105, 119. In the course of the debates, Thomas Fitzsimons made an interesting speech in which he rejected the balance-of-trade argument in favor of free trade. This was one of the few examples of free trade liberalism to appear in the whole debate over the bank. See ibid., 100–102.

24. Ibid., 22.

that advocated repeal of the charter—a report he helped write—he unleashed pandemonium with the remark that, unlike the Republicans, the Constitutionalists had no private stake in the bank. Later, Smilie seized on the Republican committee's reference to the "respectable" character of those who petitioned in favor of the bank. Everyone understood, he sneered, that respectable meant wealthy. Angrily Smilie retorted: "This is holding out an aristocratical idea. An honest man's the noblest work of God."[25]

Gordon Wood perceptively links attacks on "great men," like Smilie's, to class animus. He notes that the westerners focused on the propensity of the elite to portray themselves as disinterested gentlemen in the Republican mold. Enraged by this portrayal, which left them playing parochial country bumpkins, the Constitutionalists "hammered home one basic point: the supporters of the bank were themselves interested men. They were directors or stockholders in the bank, and therefore they had no right in supporting the rechartering of the bank to pose as disinterested gentlemen promoting the public good."[26]

The thrust hurt. Robert Morris was the main target of the attack. He had heard the charges before and would hear them again. Frustrated, Morris asked Findley why "if wealth be so obnoxious" he was "so eager in pursuit of it." The retort missed the target. Findley and Smilie and their allies were trying to establish that "Morris and his patrician Philadelphia crowd were no different from them, were no more respectable than they were. Such would-be aristocrats simply had 'more money than their neighbors.'"[27]

That was indeed the point, and William Findley made it eloquently and cogently. His appearance was an important development in Pennsylvania politics. Everyone regarded him highly. Even Robert Morris—despite or perhaps because he was severly pummeled by Findley in the debate—announced that he had "great respect" for Findley's ability, candor, and intelligence. A self-educated Irish immigrant "who affected large white beaver hats," Findley worked as a weaver and a teacher. During the Revolution he served as a militia captain and then moved west. The owner of a 250-acre farm, Findley was primarily a professional politician. Aside from his political gifts, he is important because

25. Ibid., 21.
26. Wood, "Interests," 97.
27. Ibid., 97 and 97–100.

he used his talents to speak for rural Pennsylvania, especially the small producers.[28]

Findley refused to allow the Republicans to control the debate. Impatiently, he dismissed criticisms of the report of 1785 and the behavior of that Assembly. What mattered was whether the principles behind repeal were sound, and Findley believed they were:

> All governments being instituted for the good of the society to which they belong, the supreme legislative power of every community necessarily possesses a power of repealing every law inimical to the public safety. But the government of Pennsylvania being a democracy, the bank is inconsistent with the bill of rights thereof, which says, that government is not instituted for the emolument of any man, family, or set of men. Therefore, this institution being a monopoly, . . . is inconsistent with not only the frame but the spirit of our government.[29]

Findley's strength was his ability to root his analysis in the social fabric. Other critics had argued that the bank was a monopoly and was therefore inconsistent with democracy. Findley went beyond this and insisted that the bank threatened "our habits—our manners," which "countenance long credits" and "slow methods for recovering debts." Moreover, "our estates, both real and personal [are divided] more equally among our heirs, than the laws and habits of any other country." Unhappily, this equality left Pennsylvania defenseless. "We are so equal in wealth, power, &c. that we have no counterpoise sufficient to check or control an institution of such vast influence." Pennsylvania had "no wealthy companies of merchants incorporated—no hereditary nobles" and no royal prerogative that might withstand the enormous power and "boundless charter" of the bank.[30]

If the bank's power was dangerous to the republic, so was its wealth. The wide distribution of property we enjoy "operates as many checks" and protects the public. But in the Bank of North America we have a corporation chartered forever with a huge capital designed to increase

28. Carey, ed., *Debates and Proceedings*, 86. See also ibid., 100; "William Findley," *DAB*, 6:385; Schram, "Findley"; Burrows, *Gallatin*, 187; Charles Pettit to James Hutchinson, 18 December 1785, James Hutchinson Papers, APSL.
29. Carey, ed., *Debates and Proceedings*, 65 and 64–75, 121–30.
30. Ibid., 65, 124.

wealth. Because it has a single purpose, all "principles of honour [and] generosity" become irrelevant, and the bank is led to "continually increase its dimensions and influence" until finally it will "engross all the wealth, power, and influence of the state."[31] Findley concluded with an emotional flourish, proclaiming:

> We are one great family: and the laws are our common inheritance. They are general rules, and common in their nature. No man has a greater claim of special privilege for his £100,000 than I have for my £5. No. The laws are a common property. . . . This house will not—this house has no right, no constitutional power to give monopolies of legal privilege—to bestow unequal portions of our common inheritance on favourites.[32]

That was the most powerful and cogent attack launched against the bank. Findley had made the alien nature of the Bank of North America starkly clear. Its mode of operation, size, wealth, power, and corporate privileges set the bank apart. Equally important was his attack on the bank because it was created with "the sole purpose" of creating wealth for its owners. A stronger indication of the noncapitalist orientation of the petty-commodity producers of rural and western Pennsylvania can hardly be imagined.

Another part of Findley's presentation is worth commenting on. Findley charged that the Assembly had abused the public trust by granting permanent, legal privileges to a few individuals, when those privileges were "our common inheritance." He worried that a "wanton assembly may parcel out the commonwealth into little aristocracies, and so overturn the nature of our government without remedy."[33]

Similar concerns had surfaced before. Sometimes in muted tones and sometimes stridently, Pennsylvanians had attacked the bank as an aristocracy. The charge appeared as early as 1782, when the bank applied for a charter, and it reappeared in every subsequent public discussion of the bank. The accusation had been made by Jonathan Sergeant in his defense of the Bank of Pennsylvania, and it surfaced in the proceedings of the Council of Censors and in the petitions and committee report of 1785. In addition, the charge appeared repeatedly

31. Ibid., 66.
32. Ibid., 130.
33. Ibid., 65.

in newspaper articles and pamphlets. It was, in fact, one of the most serious charges leveled against the bank.

Part of the reason the bank was identified with the aristocracy was the fact that it enjoyed permanent, legal privileges and was also a monopoly. But more was involved. When the accusation was made, it was invariably done in the context of its opposite, "equality." Someone would charge that the bank was a dangerous aristocracy that threatened to destroy the degree of equality necessary in a republic. The difficulty in making sense of this is that equality has at least three meanings. It can refer to legal equality, free and equal access to a resource or service, or identity of condition.

When Republicans talked about equality they always meant legal equality, and almost always free and equal access to markets and other resources or services. Some Constitutionalists, especially the urban, mercantile-professional wing of the party, used the word the same way the Republicans did. When the petitions of 1785 complained that the bank destroyed "that equality which ought to take place in a commercial country" because it could deny its services to some, they clearly meant legal equality and free and equal access—in this case to the bank's credit. Colbert's talk of "equal liberty and equal privilege" had the same meaning.

But Findley and his rural constituents meant something else. When Findley spoke about equality, it was equated with democracy. And, as he made clear, democracy meant more than "the spirit of the government." It also meant the division of "our estates" and "wealth and power." In other words, to Findley and the people he represented, democracy was social and economic as well as legal and political.

It is no accident that western politicians like William Findley were spokesmen for this point of view. They represented its main constituency: petty-commodity-producing farmers and artisans. These men had no desire to weaken or destroy the institution of private property; they were not levelers. They were motivated by a dislike of "great men" and a related fear of "an excessive accumulation of wealth."

Small producers feared great wealth because they believed it would degrade the "human soul" and destroy a social order they cherished. They were suspicious of powerful governments and cities, with their wealthy merchants and bankers. Politically they espoused equality, democracy, and localism. Many of those who raised the cry against the bank wanted to protect and conserve a social order that was, in the words of "Atticus," "remarkable for the equal distribution of its property" and the similarly remarkable "equal system of its laws."[34]

The birth of what Saul Cornell calls "plebian populism" is a complex and largely unstudied subject. In Revolutionary Pennsylvania, the existence of a large, prosperous class of independent, small-scale farmers and artisans engaged in petty-commodity production was the key to its appearance, and the economic and social life of this class was strongly influenced by patterns of reciprocity and neighborly exchange. These men and their representatives feared the bank for what it was, for the present it threatened, and for the future it represented.[35]

Generally, discussions of ideology and world views assume that the spread of ideas is from the top down. Reality is more complex. Because the great bulk of Pennsylvania's population was rural, and because most families had property, tools, and skills, they developed a constellation of shared hopes, desires, and norms that reflected and defended their reality.

At the same time, the process of creating hopes, desires, and norms was repeated in urban communities. Although the urban and rural worlds differed in significant ways, they also had a good deal in common. The wide distribution of property and the striving for independence, along with a shared sense of participatory "citizenship," gave a substantial portion of the population of Revolutionary Pennsylvania, urban and rural, a sense of belonging to a common universe. This is why many urban artisans, professionals, and merchants found rural fears of "aristocracy" meaningful, and why so many of them joined the fray against the bank to protect the equality that was so necessary in a republic.

Eventually, the time allotted for debate ended. The Assembly proceeded to vote on a proposal to revoke the repeal of the bank's charter, and predictably party lines held firm. The Constitutionalists won by a margin of 41 to 27. The committee report favorable to the bank was rejected by the same margin, but the Republican effort had not been wasted. The Republicans had gained an opportunity to present their case to the public and had made good use of the public forum.[36]

The heightened interest in the bank and its charter was reflected in the press rooms and print shops of Philadelphia. In 1786 and the first three months of 1787, twenty-six writers contributed six pamphlets and

34. Atticus, "Letter the Fourth," *Pa. Packet,* 28 June 1786.
35. Cornell, "Aristocracy Assailed."
36. *Pa. Min.,* 1 and 7 April 1786, 147–48, 164–65; John Chaloner to Jeremiah Wadsworth, 2 April 1786, Wadsworth Papers.

at least thirty-one newspaper articles—a significant increase in output over the previous year.[37] The number of probank writers declined to seven, but the appearance of Tom Paine in their ranks more than compensated for the decline. The gifted and energetic propagandist produced a long pamphlet and nine newspaper articles. Like Pelatiah Webster's fine "Essay on Credit," which also appeared in 1786, and the speeches Morris and Fitzsimons made in the Assembly debates, Paine's *Dissertations on Government* was intended to educate the public.[38]

Paine launched a ferocious attack against the Constitutionalists, and especially the committee that had advocated repealing the charter. Paine noted caustically that the committee had claimed that the bank banished large sums of money from the state while at the same time accumulating huge amounts of specie in its vaults. Apparently, there were "two enormous sums of specie. . . . One enormous sum going out, and another enormous sum remaining."[39]

Even though he used humor to embarrass his opponents, and artfully crafted phrases to win converts, Paine was a serious writer. Like most of the Republicans, he built his analysis around Wilson's distinction between an act of the Assembly that affected everyone and an act that affected specific groups or individuals. Because it was written like a legal brief, Wilson's pamphlet was difficult to comprehend. Moreover, his insistence that the congressional charter was sufficient by itself was out of step with public opinion. Paine dropped the impolitic remarks about congressional power and effectively popularized the more useful parts of the barrister's analysis.[40]

Once he established that the charter was a contract and could therefore be voided only in the courts, Paine was faced with an uncomfortable dilemma. He was unhappy with his own conclusion, especially with the clause in the charter that established the bank forever. Like Jefferson, Paine believed that future generations should be free to shape their own lives. They had the same rights as citizens of the 1780s and would "not admit any assumed authority of ours to encroach upon the system of their day." Aware that there was a

37. See Appendix C.
38. Webster, "Essay on Credit." As the title indicates, Webster was laying out as clearly as he could the nature of a commercial bank. Fitzsimons was also among the many who tried to explain banking; see Carey, ed., *Debates and Proceedings*, 104–5.
39. Paine, *Complete Writings*, 1:394.
40. For Paine and the bank, see Foner, *Paine*, 197–203; Rappaport, "Sources," 198–207; King, "Paine in America," 354–62.

contradiction between arguing that a legislative act could not be voided and that every generation had to be free to make its own laws, Paine suggested a constitutional amendment to limit all legislative acts to thirty years.[41]

The contradiction was especially painful for Paine. One of the moving forces behind the writing and adoption of Pennsylvania's radical constitution of 1776, he had become disillusioned with its constitutional and political theory and with his former friends. The bank war precipitated Paine's shift, and symbolized, to him, the failure of the Constitution of 1776. Earlier, Paine had hoped that whatever factions existed would "unite and agree in the general principle of good government." Like many of his contemporaries, he was deeply upset by the unexpected appearance of political parties and the intense animosities of "normal" politics. He not only broke with his former allies but also rejected the unicameral legislature.[42]

Paine offered an interesting version of the bank's defense. He contended that the bank was opposed by an alliance of four groups: frontiersmen, western politicians, eastern usurers, and speculators. It was in the west, said Paine, that we first heard the complaint that "a Bank is of no use." Western agriculture was so primitive that it could not produce enough to sell, and as a result farmers wanted developmental capital and strongly supported the loan office. The west produced not only the mass base for a move to destroy the bank but also the leaders. Referring scornfully to Findley and Smilie as "obscure promotors," Paine insisted that they opposed progress and prosperity because they were afraid they would lose their influence and power: "Their sphere of importance was that of general poverty, and their hopes depended on its duration."[43]

The westerners were supported by eastern usurers who opposed the bank because it thwarted their "avarice" by discounting at the legal rate of 6 percent. Cooperating with the usurers were a group of speculators who had speculated in the public debt. They had attempted to form a rival bank, the Bank of Pennsylvania, and when that enterprise failed they joined the attack against the bank.[44]

Like the Republicans, the Constitutionalists generated considerable

41. Paine, *Complete Writings*, 1:395–97.
42. Ibid., 409–10.
43. Ibid., 423–27, 433, 436–37.
44. Ibid.

excitement in the local press. An anonymous poet portrayed the bankers as following a rule or ruin policy.

> Nor laws nor reason can prevent
> The *Bankers,* on their plans intent;
> The well-trained'd pack pursue;
> Resolv'd to rule, or crush the State,
> They mingle in the loud debate
> With Int'rest full in view. [45]

A clever humorist styled "Machiavel" suggested that the impending reestablishment of the bank offered an opportunity to improve the state's government. His fervent hope was that

> in time the influence of the Bank will gain such ascendency in the councils of the State as to put an end to that rivalry of interests which some people seem to be apprehensive of. Then, instead of being rivals for power, the governments of the State and of the Bank . . . both will be under the direction of the same will. And then will the State be wisely governed, for the rulers will be men of wisdom.

At that point, Machiavel reflected happily, it would be appropriate to alter the constitution. The bank, of course, provided an excellent model. Like the bank, we should allow plurality of voting for the wealthy, which "would prevent factious men from getting into power" and "save the common people from the trouble and expense of attending elections."[46]

At least seven writers defended revocation. Like their Republican opponents, they had little new to add to the discussion. They still blamed the bank for worsening the balance of trade, draining specie from the countryside to the city, creating a shortage of money, and generally hurting the interests of agriculture. They also insisted that the bank had destroyed the government's credit. Finally, the bank was depicted as a corrupter of Republican virtue and a dangerous faction.[47]

The most important development in the public discussions of 1786

45. "On a Late Political Hunting Match," *Freeman's Journal,* 25 April 1787.

46. Machiavel, in ibid., 3 January 1787.

47. Amicus, *Pa. Herald,* 13 December 1786; Patriot, *Freeman's Journal,* 7 February 1787; Atticus, "Letter the Second," *Pa. Packet,* 8 May 1786; Anon., "On a Late Political Hunting Match," *Freeman's Journal,* 25 April 1787. See also Appendix C of this book.

and 1787 was the growing strength of a body of moderate opinion. Appearing first in 1785, this current of thought helped create the climate for a successful compromise. Like the friends of the bank, the moderates had no doubts about the value of the institution. So strong was the defense of commercial banking offered by the moderates that at first glance some of their essays appear to be Republican tracts, but like the opponents of the bank they were critical of the original charter.

Tench Coxe, the most important of the moderate writers, believed that "several extreme dangers" had been ignored when the bank had been created. Like the Constitutionalists, Coxe and other moderates felt the corporation was so powerful that it posed a threat to "our form of government." The moderates combined a Republican awareness of the bank's utility and a Constitutionalist sensitivity to the danger inherent in the bank's power.[48]

Coxe's appearance as a moderate was an important event in the bank war. The scion of a prestigious Philadelphia family that had produced a number of political and mercantile luminaries, Coxe was related to the Francises, the Willings, the Binghams, the Shippens, the Mifflins, the Chews, and the Burds—the "cream" of the colonial upper class. His career encompassed typical upper-class activities. Coxe was a successful merchant, and active in prison reform and abolition circles as well. An energetic and effective writer, he is best remembered for his later advocacy of American manufacturing. By the mid-1780s Coxe had recovered from his Toryism and was launching what would be a successful political career. He also held shares in the bank. Socially prominent, wealthy, experienced in commerce and banking, well read in politics and economics, he could not be ignored or dismissed as a crank. His three pamphlets on the bank lent prestige to the cause of reform.[49]

The moderates advocated limiting the capital and duration of the charter, restricting the business to trading notes and specie, and limiting the number of notes the bank might issue. These proposals offered a viable solution to the bank war. Once enacted, they allowed both sides to feel that some of their fears had been allayed and some of their needs satisfied. Although the directors of the bank were unhappy with the proposed limitations, they offered the bank what it needed most: legal sanction and government protection. On the other hand, the prospect

48. An Independent Citizen, *Pa. Herald,* 13 December 1786; Coxe, *Further Thoughts,* 14; Rappaport, "Sources," 211–15.

49. Cooke, *Tench Coxe,* 11, 92–93; "Tench Coxe," *DAB,* 2:448–49.

of strong government regulation and charter revision appeased some of those who feared the power of the bank.[50]

When the bank war erupted, it had done so because a broad spectrum of the public had seen the bank's opposition to paper money and the land bank as an attack on their class interests. Almost immediately, the struggle shifted into the political sphere. Eventually, the differences between Constitutionalists and Republicans were resolved by modifying the bank's charter. In this circular fashion, class antagonisms were defused and at least partly ameliorated by party politics.

Further blurring class lines is the fact that party politics is quintessentially the politics of coalition. In this endeavor, the Republicans were more successful than the Constitutionalists in attracting support. Republicans were able to build a stable following in Philadelphia, in the larger towns, and among the rural elements situated within the economic orbit of Philadelphia. In this more commercial zone, farmers and artisans, as well as merchants and professionals, were receptive to the political appeal of the old upper class. Many of those living in the Philadelphia trading area, then, ignored their class interests and voted Republican for a variety of ideological, economic, political, and social reasons. On the other hand, Constitutionalist strength centered in the hinterland, and in that region there was a closer fit between the imperatives of class and the other factors that impelled action. This congruence was a source of strength in the west and a source of weakness in the more diverse east.

In the 1786 fall elections, the Republicans emerged triumphant. The elections were decided in the eastern counties, which the Republicans swept. On most issues the Republicans could count on 36 votes and the Constitutionalists 29. When the House was called to order, Robert Morris, George Clymer, and Thomas Fitzsimons proudly presented themselves as the victorious candidates from Philadelphia.[51]

Moving swiftly, the friends of the bank pressed for action, and the house was almost immediately presented with a petition on behalf of the bank, which was sent to a committee that reported in favor of a new charter. The committee also suggested putting limits on the size of the capital and the duration of the charter. Punctuating the appointment of the committee and the reading of its report were two attempts by

---

50. Amicus, *Pa. Packet*, 28 February 1787; Coxe, *Further Thoughts*, 14.

51. Brunhouse, *Counter-Revolution*, 190–93; *Pa. Min.*, 2 November 1786, 4, 11; John Chaloner to Jeremiah Wadsworth, 30 October 1786, Wadsworth Papers.

Fitzsimons to present a bill that would have revived the original charter. These moves failed, and Fitzsimons supported the report.[52]

Predictably, Constitutionalists believed that the limits proposed in the report were not strong enough. William Findley shrewdly raised two issues. He was concerned that those who managed "unbounded wealth" would monopolize the sale of public land when the government disposed of its western landholdings. He also wondered why the bank was so eager to renew its charter: Was there a "secret reason" behind the demand? Was the bank close to bankruptcy? Findley asked the directors to open up the bank's books.[53]

Robert Morris rose to answer Findley. He explained that the charter was needed because it provided security to investors and stockholders by punishing fraud committed by the directors and counterfeiting by criminals. Morris also noted that corporate status meant that the bank could sue and be sued. Last and most important, the charter clarified the issue of liability. If a suit were instituted against the bank, who would be liable? If the bank's president signed a note and refused to pay, would it "bind me, Robert Morris, because I hold a share in the bank stock? I am a stockholder to-day, but not to-morrow; and how is the [injured] party to prove that I had any share or interest during the term of his transactions? There are no articles of copartnership. . . . This cannot be; the thing is too unjust in itself."[54]

Morris then responded to Findley's suggestion that the bank might monopolize the state's public domain. The Financier chose to argue that it was impractical and that the job of the directors was to use the bank's capital and credit to make short-term loans and to divide and distribute the dividends every six months. With neither the capital nor profits available to invest in land, the accusation was simply unfounded.[55]

Morris and the friends of the bank were justifiably irritated with Findley for raising this charge since it had no foundation in fact. Because they had a high regard for his ability, they must have suspected that he was playing the demagogue. Still, Findley's accusation touched a raw

52. *Pa. Min.*, 16, 22, and 29 November and 13 December 1786, 38–39, 46, 54, 76. The petition was also published in *Pa. Herald*, 9 December 1786. For the committee report, see ibid., 30 December 1786; and Wilson, "Bank of North America," 26–27; *Pa. Herald*, 25 November and 2 December 1786.

53. *Pa. Herald*, 30 December 1786.

54. Ibid., 3 January 1787.

55. Ibid.

nerve. The argument made more sense emotionally than the facts the friends of the bank could martial, and ultimately the charter included a clause prohibiting the bank from buying land.

Finally the vote was held. Republicans presented a solid front and the report passed 33 to 28. The voting followed a sectional pattern. Twenty-six of the votes in favor of the bank were cast by assemblymen from the eastern and southeastern parts of the state, while twenty-two of the votes against the bank came from the west and the north. This sectional pattern was in sharp contrast to the earlier votes chartering the bank and repealing the charter, when support and opposition to the bank were widespread.[56]

A few scattered votes did not fit the sectional pattern. York, a western county, voted for the bank, while Berks and Dauphin counties, in the east, opposed it. Moreover, such western notables as Hugh Brackenridge and John Cannon were advocates of the bank. The Assembly also received petitions from four eastern and southern counties and the City of Philadelphia against the new charter. Nevertheless, a sectional pattern predominated. Fully 79 percent of the votes on both sides of the aisle followed a sectional pattern.[57]

The sectional pattern underscores the presence of socioeconomic elements in the bank war. Merchants joined with farmers and independent artisans who operated in the larger Philadelphia region to support the bank, while those who lived outside or on the fringes of the trading area constituted the core of the opposition to the institution. Those living in the periphery of Philadelphia's hinterland lived a life that was significantly less commercial and were more concerned with defending communities that were integrated along bonds of family and reciprocal exchange.

William Findley was the spokesman for these people. He addressed their fears of the urban upper class and their desire to protect an egalitarian social structure. As he had the previous year, Findley attacked the bank as a corrupting influence. What was it, he asked, that explained the different manners shown by the English and the Swiss? They were both Republican. The answer was that the English had a vast and growing commerce and had become "dissipated, extravagant

56. *Pa. Min.*, 13 December 1786, 76–78; *Pa. Herald*, 6 January 1787. See also the voting maps in Brunhouse, *Counter-Revolution*, 323–24; Ireland, "Ratification," 202–5.

57. Ireland, "Ratification," 202–5; 26 of the 33 pro votes, or 78.78 percent, and 22 of the 28 negative votes, or 78.57 percent, followed a sectional pattern.

and vicious," while the Swiss had "little or no commerce, and . . . their manners had remained truly Republican."[58]

Read in this light, Findley's concern that the bank might monopolize the western lands was an expression of the fear that the bank and the commercialization it was intensifying threatened their world. The most spectacular economic development of the 1780s was the expansion of the mercantile sector. The Bank of North America was both a cause and a result of this expansion. It was a convenient symbol of the dreams and power of the mercantile upper class, who wanted to make Philadelphia the Amsterdam of America. And that was precisely the vision that frightened western populists who wanted to protect and strengthen their own utopian vision of America as the home of free and independent, small-producer citizens.

This interpretation is supported by what the friends and enemies of the bank had to say in defense of their positions. The Assembly debates and the flood of propaganda that flowed from the print shops provide us with eloquent explanations of the bank war. What emerges from the torrent of words is that the participants believed that the bank war was primarily a conflict between agriculture and commerce. The policy question that triggered the conflict was the farmers' demand for a loan office and the bank's adamant resistance to it. The sectional pattern revealed in the Assembly's roll calls marks the translation of the battle from the realm of class to the realm of politics.

Once the bank became a political issue, it necessarily became part of the party battles that were at the heart of the politics of the 1780s. As Owen Ireland has shown, there was a close correlation between voting on the bank and voting on other questions, such as the Test Acts. When the bank became a party issue, the balance between the parties would determine the future of the bank.[59]

Having accepted the report, the Assembly turned to the problem of establishing the duration of the new charter and the limits to be imposed on the bank. The Republican majority approved a charter that incorporated the Bank of North America for fourteen years and limited the capital to a maximum of $2,000,000. The bank was forbidden to own real estate or to trade in anything except public funds, specie, and bills of exchange; exceptions were made for land and goods taken as collateral. Should the bank be caught engaging in commerce, it would

---

58. *Pa. Herald,* 30 December 1786.
59. Brunhouse, *Counter-Revolution;* Main, *Political Parties,* ch. 7; Ireland, "Ratification."

be liable for three times the amount of goods it had bought. The charter also enabled the bank to sue and be sued in a court of law. If one of its officers was found guilty of stealing or embezzling bank property, he would be punished for grand larceny. Finally, the charter made provision for twelve directors and a president and gave them the authority to govern the bank in accordance with its own bylaws. The bylaws, of course, could not be contrary to the laws of the province, and they had to be deposited with state authorities.[60]

The directors were jubilant. They had survived a deadly attack on their business and had emerged stronger from the struggle. Still, the victory was not total. Morris remained unhappy about the idea that the government had a right to revoke charters and regulate corporations. This principle was as abhorrent to the Financier as it was precious to the majority of the state's citizens.

If the friends of the bank were joyful, its enemies were not. One woefully reported: "Well then the Bank is reestablished, and we may sit down and groan under its Baneful Influence. Had the Friends to equal liberty had a few more such men as Finley [*sic*] in the House, this Monster never would again have raised its Head." The battle was over. Commercial banking had secured a foothold in the American economy, and western populists were left a grievance.[61]

60. For the resolves, see *Pa. Min.*, 17 and 28 December 1786, 84–85, 101–5; *Pa. Herald*, 17 January 1787; Rappaport, "Sources," 232–38. For the charter, see "An Act to Revive the Incorporation of the Subscribers to the Bank of North America," Mitchell, ed., *Pa. Statutes*, 3:412–16; Brunhouse, *Counter-Revolution*, 196–97; Thomas Willing to William Bingham, 15 March 1787, Hampton L. Carson Collection, Thomas Willing Papers, HSP; John Chaloner to Jeremiah Wadsworth, 31 March 1787, Wadsworth Papers.

61. Joseph Hart to George Bryan, 2 January 1787, Bryan MSS.

Afterword

As the 1780s ended, the stresses and strains caused by the Revolution eased and Pennsylvanians began to deal more comfortably with the creation of a new world. In this environment, it is possible to discern signs of modernity and capitalism. At the same time, the last third of the eighteenth century can also be seen as the time when a preindustrial, noncapitalist, traditional social order flourished. These views are not contradictory. What we have in Pennsylvania is the simultaneous maturing of one social order and the birth of another.

Revolutionary Pennsylvania was not in the throes of the transformations that mark modern societies; the pace of change was slow. That point is crucial. People were not subject to constant specialization or to fragmenting of social roles and organizations. Single-purpose organizations, large and small, bureaucratic and nonbureaucratic, were not prominent in the social structure. The major integrative systems were families, neighborhoods, classes, ethnic groups, churches, and the associational system that was neither modern nor traditional. Finally, conflict in the region was not caused by the pulsations of system transformation, but instead grew out of traditional disasters like war and disease and social tensions stemming from religious, ethnic, racial, and class tensions.

Moreover, while capitalism had made inroads, it was not dominant. Markets existed, and the desire to own private property, especially land, was deeply rooted. Business and money were important, and the process of commercialization, as exemplified by the establishment of the Bank of North America was well under way.

Despite this, and despite the fact that a large percentage of the population owned property, markets did not systematically organize or drive the economy, and market values were not important to a substantial portion of the population—and alien to many. Neighborhood networks, borrowing and barter, and community labor-sharing loomed large in the lives of Pennsylvanians. These institutions were given meaning by a constellation of noncapitalist values that included reciprocity, neighborliness, and a striving for independence.

Even where business flourished and markets were important, as in urban areas and the nearby hinterland, many farmers, merchants, and artisans were worried and appalled by the commercialization the bank represented. On the whole, the business sector and the practices and values associated with it resembled the world of the traditional merchant more than it did that of the modern, capitalist businessman.

But what about the signs of change that did exist? Should we view them as tentative steps toward capitalism and modernization? Can we see in the establishment of the Bank of North America part of the beginning of an institutional "take-off" into social change and transformation?

The answer appears to be yes. The bank was a prototypical modern organization—large, highly specialized, and bureaucratic in its rules and operating procedures if not in its internal organizational structure. The bank also furthered the spread of business rationality and depersonalized and fragmented social roles. Slowly up to 1816, and more rapidly afterward, one can follow the spread of a modern organizational mode and the specialization that was an integral part of it, from the money markets out into the larger economic sphere and into the other institutional spheres. In this sense the establishment of the bank can be seen as an early step in the onset of social transformation.

Moreover, the bank and the banking system that quickly developed stimulated the use of money and furthered the development and spread of markets and market-oriented behavior. In fact, the spread of banking was one aspect of the process of commercialization and consumerism that was discernible well before the appearance of a capitalist economy and society. These developments—the establishment of the Bank of North America, the spread of money markets, and consumerism—were part of the complex process of capitalist development.

Exploring this enormously difficult subject has been one of the central chores of modern social science since early in the nineteenth century. In the case of America, during the last third of the eighteenth century the process of transformation had barely begun. The establishment of the bank was an important step in the creation of a system of financial intermediaries that would mobilize capital for entrepreneurial purposes.

Later developments in the creation of markets were even more important. Preeminent among them were the building of an integrated national market and the strengthened ties between the eastern seaboard and Europe ushered in by the transportation revolution of the nineteenth century. Market expansion, of course, was not a new phenomenon. Early modern merchants, soldiers, politicians, and missionaries had gone a long way toward creating a global market well before the settlement of Pennsylvania. But the construction of steamboats, canals, railroads, and telegraph lines ushered in a new age. The nineteenth century was the century of market expansion par excellence. The process occurred within Europe and between Europe and its posses- sions, and between Europe and the rest of the world.

The transformation of the class system was also a crucial element of the emergence of capitalism. In the middle of the eighteenth century, Pennsylvania's class system was composed of indentured servants, apprentices, slaves, petty-commodity producers, commercial farmers (owners and tenants), laborers, merchants, and artisans. A few occupa- tional groups, including professionals, millers, and artists, were present, as were wealthy "gentlemen."

The key groups in this amalgam were the merchants, the commercial farmers, and the petty-commodity producers—farmers and artisans. All wanted private property, but petty-commodity producers were not ideologically or materially committed to capitalism. The world views of the merchants and the commercial farmers would prove to be compatible with capitalism, but in the 1780s this could not be fully realized. Finally, because merchants did not control production they were both a perfect complement to petty-commodity producers and weak leaders in the transition to capitalism.

Slaves and servants aside, each class was engaged at least nominally in the sale of goods and services, and it was the location of each class in the marketplace that determined its relationship to the other classes. At the same time, because the economy was not capitalist and because market values were not universally accepted, market relations did not shape behavior as fully as relations of production would in the nineteenth century.

By the end of the eighteenth century, signs of change were notice- able. Slavery was rapidly waning, and wage labor was slowly becoming more common. The employer-employee relationship and the class system that derived from it took on a new significance in the 1820s after the emergence of the factory system. Along with the new classes came new social relations that were characterized by functional interdependence and conflict. The capitalist stratification system and the social relations that characterized it did not fully dominate in the northeast until the second half of the nineteenth century.

The political sphere also poses complex analytic problems for an evolutionary framework. Social classes and class conflict carried out through political parties in a polity characterized by a high degree of participation gave the political arena a modern aura, and that polity was remarkably open to the initiatives of individuals. Nevertheless, the apparent modernity of Pennsylvania's polity is largely illusory. Two of the social classes—merchants and artisans—were traditional, while the majority of the region's farmers were petty-commodity producers and were neither traditional nor modern. Finally, the political arena in which they struggled was shaped by the associational system, with its related norms and values.

Other traditional societies, such as classical Greece and Rome, had participatory political systems and political parties. Social classes, political parties, and participatory politics were not sufficient to create an institutional and moral order that generated social transformation. Not until the appearance of paid political organizers and propagandists, and the bureaucratic organizational forms of the second party system did political organization come to have an unmistakably modern quality. Furthermore, the second generation of parties emerged after economic development, the formation of modern classes, and modernization had clearly begun. In fact, parties were an important part of the rapid social change that was so apparent after the War of 1812.

If there was no direct connection between the two party systems, the social structure that had emerged in Pennsylvania by the 1770s did play an important role in easing the transition to a modern political order. The extraordinarily open nature of the political system meant that integrating the great bulk of the citizenry into the central political institutions of the state was largely accomplished before the onset of modernization, a development whose importance can hardly be overstated.

The public debate on the merits of the bank offers a striking example of the openness and participatory nature of Pennsylvania politics. The general public eagerly filled the Assembly's galleries for debates on such abstruse topics as banks, money, and corporations. Between 1784 and early 1787, fifty-five people wrote seventy English-language newspaper essays and pamphlets about the bank. This openness is one reason that political development and modernization in Pennsylvania and America, outside of the South, has been so much less disruptive than in many portions of the world.

Still, although American modernization has been comparatively easy, it has not been free of pain. In fact, the very political openness that eased the development of a modern polity also created serious problems. The independent artisans and land-owning farmers injected an enduring populist strain into America's heritage. Because they look backward to a past they were happy with, American populists have always been traditionalists. They have been strong advocates of democracy and powerful opponents of capitalism and modernization.

While America has not suffered from Luddite attacks on technology, the nineteenth and twentieth centuries were troubled by a variety of traditionalist movements, many of which stem from America's first crusade against commercial banking. In particular, the fear of an aristo-cratic (corporate) money power entered the political mainstream in the 1780s. Giving this fear lasting relevance was a past that included a Republican revolt versus monarchy and a historical present involving a traditional, egalitarian, and noncapitalist social structure.

Although its appearance would change, the fear of an aristocratic money power never quite vanished. It reappeared in Antifederalism and in the rhetoric of the urban labor radicals of the late 1820s, who proclaimed against monopolists and speculators in their struggle to protect small-shop owners and independent farmers. In the following generation, similar arguments were used by Andrew Jackson and his followers against the Second Bank of the United States.[1]

Everyone recalls the dramatic battle between President Jackson and the Second Bank of the United States. In what is probably the most famous veto in American history, Jackson attacked the bank in a manner that recalls the antibanking rhetoric of the 1780s. His deepest concern was that the bank was distorting and endangering the social fabric by destroying what we would call legal equality and what he called "equal protection":

1. For the bank war, see Remini, *Jackson;* Myers, *Jacksonian Persuasion;* Hammond, *Banks and Politics.*

Equality of talents, of education, or of wealth can not be produced by human institutions. In the full enjoyment of the gifts of Heaven and the fruits of superior industry, economy, and virtue, every man is equally entitled to protection by law; but when the laws undertake to add to these natural and just advantages artificial distinctions, to grant titles, gratuities, and exclusive privileges, to make the rich richer and the potent more powerful, the humble members of society—the farmers, mechanics, and laborers—who have neither the time nor the means of securing like favors to themselves, have a right to complain of the injustice of their Government.[2]

President Jackson's followers made similar points. About a year and a half earlier, Senator Thomas Hart Benton attacked the bank because it was "too great and powerful to be tolerated in a government of free and equal laws." The bank was authorized to own the enormous sum of $90,000,000, its notes were legal tender, it had the power to control the state banks, and it had "the federal government for a partner." "To whom," Benton asked, "is all this power granted? To a company of private individuals, many of them foreigners." This power was centralized in one city and in one bank, controlled by a small number of men, some of them foreigners, with a charter that granted "a prolonged existence." Senator Benton feared that the bank would therefore become "the absolute monopolist of American money." As presently constituted, he warned, the bank is permitted "to hold real estate, receive rents, and retain a body of tenantry. This privilege is hostile to the nature of our republican government. . . . Monopolies and perpetual succession are the bane of republics."[3]

Other Jacksonians attacked the bank because it had a corporate charter. Theodore Sedgwick Jr. argued that charters were grants of "exclusive privilege" because they give to a few men the opportunity to make profits, or some "other gains from which the mass of . . . citizens are excluded." He concluded that every corporate grant destroys equal rights and is therefore "wholly adverse to the principle of our institutions."[4]

2. Andrew Jackson, "Veto of the Bank Renewal Bill," 10 July 1832, in Heffner, ed., *Documentary History,* 99 and 94–100.

3. Senator Thomas Hart Benton, "The Mischiefs of a National Bank," in *Annals of America,* 5: 430–36.

4. Theodore Sedgwick Jr., "What Is a Monopoly?" in Blau, ed., *Social Theories,* 222.

Fiery William Leggett saw the bank as a harbinger of a new aristocracy. America was being divided into two parties—one of them "for a
popular government; the other for an aristocracy." The former is
primarily composed of farmers, artisans, laborers, and "other producers
of the middling and lower classes"; the latter consists of the "consumers, the rich, the proud, [and] the privileged." The aristocratic party
wants nothing more than to "monopolize the advantage of the Government, to hedge themselves round with exclusive privileges and elevate
themselves at the expense of the people."[5]

While everyone recalls the war against the Second Bank of the United
States, fewer recall the aftermath. By 1852 there were no private,
incorporated commercial banks in the organized territories of Minnesota
and Oregon, in the District of Columbia, and nine of the thirty-one
states—Arkansas, California, Florida, Illinois, Iowa, Texas, Wisconsin,
Indiana, and Missouri. Two of these states—Indiana and Missouri—had
state-controlled banking monopolies, and the constitutions of most of
these states explicitly forbade commercial banking. When the territory
of Wisconsin was organized in 1836, its charter carefully stipulated that
every corporate charter granted in the territory, even those given to
churches, should make it clear that the grant did not allow banking.[6]

After the Civil War, commercial banks remained controversial. It is
not surprising that farmers remained in the vanguard of the attack. The
great rural protest movements of the 1880s and 1890s continued the
onslaught. The Agricultural Wheel, the Farmers' Alliance, and the
People's Party demanded abolition of private, corporate, commercial
banks and advocated a variety of government programs in their stead.[7]

Over time, the protests broadened. As the urban and industrial
transformations created a new world, outraged consumers, small businessmen, laborers, intellectuals, and urban reformers joined the farmers. Rural protesters reached out for new ideas and new allies, and
antibanking was fused to antimonopoly. The violent eruptions of 1877
are indicative of the change. Entire communities, urban and rural,
turned out to attack and loot railroad property. What remained constant
was the fear and resentment against wealthy and powerful corporations.
In the twentieth century, as local, state, and national governments grew

5. William Leggett, "Democratic Editorials," in ibid., 66–68.
6. Hammond, *Banks and Politics,* 605, 612–14, 617–18. See also Shade, *Banks or No
Banks;* Sharp, *Jacksonians Versus Banks.*
7. Hicks, *Populist Revolt;* Goodwyn, *Democratic Promise.*

in size, especially during the Cold War, antibureaucratic and antistatist impulses grew in importance.[8]

These social and political movements represent an indigenous American traditionalism. American traditionalists are haunted by the specter of a world that once existed and has been lost. In Pennsylvania this vision was asserted and defended by William Findley and his allies, and once expressed it never disappeared. Egalitarian traditionalism took root in the culture and became a resource for later generations.

8. Theorelli, *Antitrust Policy;* Piott, *Anti-Monopoly Persuasion,* 7–17, 22, 153–54; Ware, *Labor Movement.*

Appendixes

Appendix A:
Analysis of the Discount Ledger of the Bank of North America, January 7, 1782, to February 6, 1783

Table 1. Overview of the Discount Business

	No. of Loans	% of Loans	Dollar Amt. Loaned	% of Amt. Loaned	Avg. Amt. Loaned	Avg. Interest Charged	Avg. Length of Loans
Government	137	6%	$673,334	28%	$4,915[a]	6%	—
Shareholders	854	37	873,210	36	1,022	6	—
Nonshare-holders	1,344	57	874,124	36	650	6	—
Total	2,335	100	2,420,668	100	1,037	6	33 days[b]

SOURCE: Discount Ledger of the Bank of North America.

[a] Includes a small loan to South Carolina.

[b] For January through May (5 months) the average length is 45; for June through February 6 (+8 months) the average length is 29 days. A few large loans to the government deviated from this pattern: they were for $100,000 (6 months).

Table 2. Lending Policy: Shareholders vs. Nonshareholders

	No. of Loans	Amt. Loaned	Avg. Amt. Loaned	% Smaller Than Average $ Amt. of Shareholder Loan
Shareholders	854	$873,210	$1,022	—
Nonshareholders				
In group[a]	304	226,881	746	27.0
Out group[b]	1,040	647,243	622	39.0
Total	1,344	874,124	650	34.6
Shareholders				
& in group	1,158	1,100,091	905	—

SOURCE: Discount Ledger of the Bank of North America.

[a] The "in group" is comprised of nonshareholders who have family or close social ties, or business or political affiliations, with shareholders.

[b] The "out group" is comprised of nonshareholders who have no close ties, personal or business, to shareholders.

Table 3. Lending Policy: Gender

Female[a]	
No. of loans	9
Amount loaned	$3,736
Avg. loan	$415
Male	
No. of loans	2,188
Amount loaned	$1,737,701
Avg. loan	$790

SOURCE: Discount Ledger of the Bank of North America.

NOTE: Government loans are not included in this table.

[a] One loan to Elizabeth Rutledge for $5,892 was not included in the above calculations because of its unrepresentative nature.

Table 4. Lending Policy: Geographical Distribution

A. Home Address

	No. of Loans	% of Loans	Amt. Loaned	% $ Amt. of Loans	Avg. Loan
Phila.	1,603	73.0	$1,223,379	70.0	$ 763
Pa.	40	1.8	35,182	2.0	880
N.Y.	94	4.3	118,541	6.8	1,261
N.J.	2	0.1	1,398	0.1	699
Conn.	6	0.3	11,491	0.7	1,915
Mass.	2	0.1	1,700	0.1	850
Va.	37	1.7	57,351	3.2	1,550
S.C.	8	0.4	3,253	0.2	407
Canada	3	0.1	1,280	0.1	427
Europe	27	1.2	41,574	2.4	1,540
Other	376	17.1	252,185	14.4	671

B. Business Address

	No. of Loans	% of Loans	Amt. Loaned	% $ Amt. of Loans	Avg. Loan
Phila.	1,785	81.30	$14,381,182	82.30	$ 805
Pa.	21	1.00	23,717	1.40	1,129
N.Y.	46	2.10	47,346	2.70	1,029
N.J.	1	0.04	266	0.02	266
Conn.	—	—	—	—	—
Mass.	2	0.09	1,700	0.09	850
Va.	3	0.10	1,488	0.09	496
S.C.	—	—	—	—	—
Canada	—	—	—	—	—
Europe	—	—	—	—	—
Other	339	15.40	234,635	13.40	692

C. Home and Business Address

	No. of Loans	% of Loans	Amt. Loaned	% $ Amt. of Loans	Avg. Loan
Phila.	1,607	73.0	$1,221,309	70.0	$ 760
Other	591	27.0	526,025	30.0	890

SOURCE: Discount Ledger of the Bank of North America.

NOTE: Government loans are not included in this table.

Table 5. Lending Policy: Occupation

	No. of Loans	% of Loans	Amt. Loaned	% $ Amt. of Loans	Avg. Loan
Merchant	1,490	67.80	$1,276,329	73.00	$ 857
Captain	15	0.70	5,765	0.30	351
Mariner	1	0.10	267	0.02	267
Plantation owner	2	0.10	933	0.05	467
Retail	57	2.60	19,872	1.10	349
Artisan and/or manufacturer	42	1.90	—	1.80	733
Professional	25	1.10	28,521	1.60	1,141
Gentleman	36	1.60	29,279	1.70	813
Government official	41	1.90	17,110	1.00	417
Other	489	22.20	338,966	19.40	693

SOURCE: Discount Ledger of the Bank of North America.

Appendix B:
A Note on the Metholodology Used to Analyze the Discount Ledger of the Bank of North America, January 7, 1782, to February 1783

Of the 409 nongovernment individuals and firms whose names appear in the seventy-six pages of the Discount Ledger of the Bank of North America, 260, or 63.6 percent, could be identified. Consequently, the statistics developed in Tables 4 and 5 of Appendix A must be used with some caution. Luckily, however, when the number of loans is considered the situation is less dire. In Table 4, section A, the home addresses of those making 17.1 percent of the loans, and in Section B the business addresses of 15.4 percent, could not be found. Similarly, in Table 5 the occupations of those making 22.2 percent of the loans could not be determined. These limitations are real and should be noted. Even more uncomfortable to anyone who tries to construct statistical data is the "guess factor" that enters into the process: Which John Smith is he? Anyone using these statistics should not be misled by the exact nature of the numbers and percentages created.

The most useful primary sources for this study were volume 16 of the third series of the *Pennsylvania Archives,* which replicates the tax assessments for Philadelphia for 1782, and Francis White's *Philadelphia Directory* of 1785. Other useful sources were the list of contributors to the Bank of Pennsylvania printed in the *Pennsylvania Packet,* June 25, 1780, and the list of men who signed the Address of the Republican Society, found in the *Pennsylvania Packet,* March 25, 1779.

Information about individuals was also culled from a wide variety of sources. The most important Roland M. Baumann, "The Democratic-Republicans of Philadelphia: The Origins, 1776–1797" (Ph.D., Pennsylvania State University, 1970); Stephen Brobeck, "Changes in the

Composition and Structure of Philadelphia Elite Groups, 1756–1790"
(Ph.D., University of Pennsylvania, 1973); Robert L. Brunhouse, *The
Counter-Revolution in Pennsylvania 1776–1790* (Harrisburg, Pa.:
PHMC, 1971); L. H. Butterfield, ed., *Letters of Benjamin Rush*, 2
vols. (Princeton, N.J.: Princeton University Press, 1951); John Hugh
Campbell, *History of the Friendly Sons of St. Patrick and of the Hibernian
Society for the Relief of Emigrants from Ireland: March 17, 1771–March
17, 1892* (Philadelphia: Hibernian Society, 1892); George W. Corner,
ed., *The Autobiography of Benjamin Rush: His "Travels Through Life"
Together with His Commonplace Book for 1789–1813* (Princeton, N.J.:
Princeton University Press, 1948); Elizabeth Forman Crane, ed., *The
Diary of Elizabeth Drinker*, 3 vols. (Boston: Northeastern University
Press, 1991); Thomas M. Doerflinger, "Commercial Specialization in
Philadelphia's Merchant Community, 1750–1791," *BHR*, 57 (Spring
1983): 20–49; Rezin Fenton Duvall, "Philadelphia's Maritime Commerce
with the British Empire, 1783–1789" (Ph.D., University of Pennsylva-
nia, 1960); Robert A. East, *Business Enterprise in the American Revolu-
tionary Era* (Gloucester, Mass.: Peter Smith, 1964); E. James Fergu-
son, John Catanzariti, Elizabeth M. Nuxoll et al., eds., *The Papers of
Robert Morris, 1781–1784* (Pittsburgh: University of Pittsburgh Press,
1973–); Robert James Gough, "Towards a Theory of Class and Social
Conflict: A Social History of Wealthy Philadelphians, 1775 and 1800"
(Ph.D., University of Pennsylvania, 1977); Lawrence Lewis, Jr., *History
of the Bank of North America*, 2 vols., folio ed. (Philadelphia: Lippincott
& Co., 1888); Joseph R. Rosenbloom, *A Biographical Dictionary of Early
American Jews: Colonial Times through 1800* (Lexington: University of
Kentucky Press, 1960); Richard Alan Ryerson, *The Revolution Is Now
Begun: The Radical Committees of Philadelphia, 1765–1776* (Philadel-
phia: University of Pennsylvania Press, 1978).

Appendix C:
English-Language Newspaper Articles and Pamphlets on the Bank of North America Published in Philadelphia, 1784–1787

(A) refers to anti-bank; (M) refers to moderate; (P) refers to pro-bank.

		Freeman's Journal
1784	(A)	Septimus, February 25.
	(A)	Philopatria, April 14.
1785	(A)	Philadelphiensis, January 19.
	(A)	———, March 2. This is a reply to Artemon in the *Pennsylvania Gazette*, February 16.
	(A)	———, April 6. Another reply to Artemon, ibid.
	(A)	Mirror, October 5.
1786	(A)	Anon., March 2. This is a satirical piece.
	(A)	Plain Sense, March 29.
	(A)	Amicus, December 13.
1787	(A)	Machiavel, January 3.
	(A)	Patriot, February 7.
	(A)	Independent, February 28.
	(A)	"On a Late Political Hunting Match," April 25. This is a satirical poem.

		Independent Gazeteer
1784	(A)	A Mechanic, March 13.
1785	(A)	Anon., A Customer, June 4.
	(P)	Editorial, September 3.
	(P)	A Pennsylvanian, December 24.
1787	(A)	A Fellow Citizen, February 28.

Pennsylvania Gazette

1784	(P)	S.G., "Queries Humbly Submitted to the Serious Consideration of the Legislature of Pennsylvania," August 4.
1785	(P)	Artemon, February 16.
	(P)	———, March 16.
	(P)	A Gazer On, March 30. This is a satirical piece.
	(P)	An Old Banker, March 30.
	(P)	A Philadelphia Country Farmer, April 6.
	(P)	A.B., June 1.
	(P)	"Considerations of the Bank of North America," September 7.
	(P)	Anon., September 21. This is a satirical piece.
	(P)	Thomas Paine, "To the Printers of the Pennsylvania Gazette," *Common Sense,* December 21. This is an April 19 letter on the Bank to Thomas Fitzsimons.
1786	(P)	A Friend to the Farmer, and the Bank, March 22.
	(P)	Nestor, July 19.
	(P)	Common Sense, "Number V: On the Affairs of the State," September 20.
	(P)	A Friend to the Prosperity of Both Sides of the Susquehanna, "To Messeurs Hall & Sellers," November 29.

Pennsylvania Herald

1786	(A)	Amicus, December 13.
	(M)	An Independent Citizen, December 13.
1787	(M)	A Citizen, February 24.

Pennsylvania Mercury and Universal Advertiser

1784	(A)	A Mechanic, October 1.
	(A)	A Citizen, December 10.
1785	(P)	Crito, April 1.
	(P)	Editorial, April 29.
	(A)	A Republican, November 4.

Pennsylvania Packet

1784	(A)	A Friend to Liberty, October 9.
1785	(A)	Dr. Price, "Of Trade, Banks, and Paper Credit," March 7.

(P) A Pennsylvanian, "To the People of Pennsylvania," March 29.

(A) Colbert, "Strictures on the Bank and on a Paper Currency, Part I," March 31.

(A) ———, "Strictures on the Bank and on a Paper Currency, Part II," April 1.

1786 (P) *Common Sense*, "For the Pennsylvania Packet & Daily Advertiser," March 25.

(P) ———, "For the Pennsylvania Packet & Daily Advertiser," March 28.

(A) Plain Sense, March 29.

(P) Thomas Paine, "To the Printers," *Common Sense*, April 4.

(P) ———, "To the Printers," *Common Sense*, April 7; also in the *Pennsylvania Gazette*, April 12.

(P) Common Sense, "Number III: To the Public," April 20.

(A) Atticus, "Letter the First," April 25.

(A) ———, "Letter the Second," May 8.

(A) ———, "Letter the Third," May 22.

(P) Common Sense, "Number IV: On the Advantages of a Public Bank," June 20; also in the *Freeman's Journal*, June 21.

(A) Atticus, "Letter the Fourth," June 28.

(P) Common Sense, "Number IV," November 7; also in the *Pennsylvania Gazette*, November 8.

(P) Several of the Stockholders of the Bank, "To the Printers of the Pennsylvania Packet & Daily Advertiser," December 20.

(P) "Faction Detected by the Evidence of Facts," December 22.

1787 (M) Amicus, February 28.

(P) Common Sense, "Number VII: Addressed to the Opposers of the Bank," March 6; also in the *Pennsylvania Gazette*, March 7.

Pamphlets

1785 (A) Anon., *Remarks on a Pamphlet Entitled "Considerations on the Bank of North America"* (Philadelphia, 1785).

(P) Gouverneur Morris, *An Address on the Bank of North*

America, An Address Made to the Representatives in the Assembly Vs. Abolition of the Charter and in Defense of the Bank (Philadelphia, 1785).

(P)   James Wilson, *Considerations, on the Power to Incorporate the Bank of North America* (Philadelphia, 1785).

1786   (A)   William Barton, *The True Interest of the United States, and Particularly of Pennsylvania Considered: With Respect to the Advantages Resulting from a State Paper Money: With Some Observations on the Subject of a Bank, and on Agriculture, Manufactures and Commerce* (Philadelphia, 1786).

(M)   Tench Coxe, *Thoughts Concerning the Bank of North America; with Some Facts Relating to Such Establishments in Other Countries, Respectfully Submitted to the Honorable General Assembly of Pennsylvania, by One of Their Constituents* (Philadelphia, 1786); also in the *Pennsylvania Packet,* December 6, 1786.

(M)   ———, *Cool Thoughts on the Subject of the Bank, Addressed to the Honorable the Representatives of the Freemen of the Commonwealth of Pennsylvania in General Assembly* (Philadelphia, 1786).

(M)   ———, *Further Thoughts Concerning the Bank, Respectfully Submitted to the Honorable General Assembly of Pennsylvania, by One of Their Constituents* (Philadelphia, 1786); also in *Pennsylvania Packet,* December 22, 1786.

(P)   Thomas Paine, *Dissertations on Government: The Affairs of the Bank; and Paper Money* (Philadelphia, 1786).

(P)   Pelatiah Webster, *An Essay on Credit: In Which the Doctrine of Banks is Considered, and Some Remarks Are Made on the Present State of the Bank of North America* (Philadelphia, 1786).

NOTE: Thomas Paine contributed at least eleven newspaper essays to the bank war, including an anonymous brief note in the *Pennsylvania Packet,* November 29, 1786; (compare this note with the letter to Daniel Clymer, September 1786, in Foner, ed., *Paine,* 1255–57). Not included among the eleven newspaper essays is Paine's introduction of a reprint of an essay from Rhode Island attacking paper money, Common Sense, "For the Pennsylvania Packet & Daily Advertiser," *Pennsylvania Packet,* August 21, 1786, and it does not include the pamphlet he wrote.

The author of the vitriolic attack on Thomas Paine (Atticus, *Pennsylvania Packet,* April 25, May 8 and 22, and June 28) was probably the Constitutionalist politician John Smilie. See David Freemen Hawke, *Paine* (New York, 1974), 157.

Bibliography

I. Primary Sources

Manuscript Collections

American Philosophical Society Library. Philadelphia.
  Hutchinson, James. Papers.
  Peale, Charles Willson. "Autobiography." Typescript, Part I.
Clements Library. Ann Arbor, Michigan.
  Pettit, Charles. Correspondence, Greene Papers.
Connecticut Historical Society. Hartford, Connecticut.
  Wadsworth, Jeremiah. Papers.
Historical Society of Pennsylvania. Philadelphia.
  Bank of North America Papers:
    Discount Ledger, 7 January 1782 to 6 February 1783.
    "Draft of Petitions to the Legislature Citing the History and Services of the
      Bank." In folder entitled "18 Documents Pertaining to the Attempt in 1812
      to Secure a Recharter for the Bank," Box 6-D.
    First Ledger, Bank of North America, Box 6-D.
    Minutes and Letterbook, Bank of North America.
    Stockholders Minutes, Bank of North America.
    "Stock Ledger, I, Bank of North America," Box 6-D.
  Bingham, William. Papers.
  Bryan, George. Papers.
  Carson, Hampton L. Collection. Thomas Willing Papers.
  Chaloner & White. Letterbook, 1782–84.
  Chaloner and White MSS.
  Dreer, Ferdinand J. Collection.
  Fitzsimons, Thomas. "State of Facts Respecting the National Bank." John J.
    Maitland Family Papers, Fitzsimons, Meade, and Cook Section, Fitzsi-
    mons Folder.
  Fuller Letterbook.

Gratz, Simon. Collection.
Grubb Collection.
Leach, Henry Goddard. Collection. Wistar Section.
Pemberton Papers. Volume 36.
Provincial Delegates.
Rush, Benjamin. Papers.
Society Collections.
Wallace Papers. Volumes 1 and 4.
Wayne, Anthony. Manuscripts.
Webster, Pelatiah. Ciphering Book.
Wilkinson, James. Papers.
Wilson, James. Papers. Volumes 2 and 3.
Library of Congress. Washington, D.C.
Atlee, William Augustus. Papers.
Force, Peter. Miscellaneous Papers.
New York Historical Society. New York City.
Reed, Joseph. Manuscripts.
New York Public Library. New York City.
Morris, Robert. Papers.
Pennsylvania State Archives. Harrisburg, Pennsylvania.
General Correspondence Section of the Sequestered John Nicholson Papers, MG96.
Office of the Comptroller General. New Loan Accounts, 1776–95. Volumes A, B, C, and D.
Records of the General Assembly. Boxes No. 1 and 2.
Supreme Executive Council. Minutes Books. Record Group 27, V.
Willing, Morris, Swanwick Records. Folder 4, Box 1', MSS. Group 134.
Rutgers University Library Manuscript Section. New Brunswick, New Jersey.
Capner-Exter-Hill Family Papers, Correspondence, etc. Burr Family Papers, Sebrig Family Papers, Flemington, N.J., etc.
West Chester Historical Society. West Chester, Pennsylvania.
Sugar, John. Diary, 1793–1801.

Government Publications

Allen, Andrew Hussey, ed. *Documentary History of the Constitution of the United States, 1786–1870.* Vol. 4. Washington, D.C.: Department of State, 1905.
"Constitution of Pennsylvania, 1776." In *Constitutions of Pennsylvania, Constitution of the United States,* ed. John H. Fertig and Frank M. Hunter, 221–39. Harrisburg, Pa., 1916.
Hazard, Samuel, ed. Pennsylvania Archives. First series, vols. 1–12; second series, vols. 1–19. Philadelphia, 1852–56.
Historical Statistics of the United States: Colonial Times to 1957. Washington, D.C., 1960.
Pennsylvania. *Pennsylvania Minutes of the General Assembly of the Commonwealth of Pennsylvania.* Sessions 6–14. Philadelphia, 1781–90.
Pennsylvania Constitutional Convention, 1776. The Proceedings Relative to Calling the Conventions of 1776 and 1790. The Minutes of the Convention That Formed the Present Constitution of Pennsylvania Together with the Charter to William

Penn. The Constitution of 1776 and 1790. And a View of the Convention of 1776 and the Council of Censors. Harrisburg, Pa., 1825.
United States. *Journals of the Continental Congress, 1774–1789.* Washington, D.C., 1912.

Newspapers

Freeman's Journal, or North-American Intelligencer. 1784–87.
Independent Gazeteer, or the Chronicle of Freedom. 1786, 1787.
Pennsylvania Evening Herald and American Monitor. 1785, 1786.
Pennsylvania Gazette. 1780–87.
Pennsylvania Packet. 1781–87.

Pamphlets

Barton, William. *The True Interest of the United States, and Particularly of Pennsylvania Considered: With Respect to the Advantages Resulting from a State Paper Money: With Some Observations on the Subject of a Bank, and on Agriculture, Manufactures and Commerce.* Philadelphia, 1786.
Coxe, Tench. *Cool Thoughts on the Subject of the Bank, Addressed to the Honorable the Representatives of the Freemen of the Commonwealth of Pennsylvania.* Philadelphia, 1786.
————. *Further Thoughts Concerning the Bank, Respectfully Submitted to the Honorable General Assembly of Pennsylvania, by One of Their Constituents.* Philadelphia, 1786.
————. *Thoughts Concerning the Bank of North America; with Some Facts Relating to Such Establishments in Other Countries, Respectfully Submitted to the Honorable General Assembly of Pennsylvania, by One of Their Constituents.* Philadelphia, 1786.
Morris, Gouverneur. "An Address on the Bank of North America." In vol. 1 of *The Life of Gouverneur Morris With Selections From His Correspondence & Miscellaneous Papers. Detailing Events in the American Revolution, the French Revolution, And in the Political History of the United States,* ed. Jared Sparks, 437–65. Boston, 1832, 1785.
Morris, Robert. *A Statement of the Accounts of the Superintendent of Finance, 1781–1784.* Philadelphia, 1785.
Paine, Thomas. "Dissertations on Government: The Affairs of the Bank, and Paper Money." In vol. 1 of *The Complete Writings of Thomas Paine,* collected and edited by Philip S. Foner, 367–414. New York, 1945.
Remarks on a Pamphlet Entitled "Considerations on the Bank of North America." Philadelphia, 1785.
Webster, Pelatiah. *An Essay on Credit: In Which the Doctrine of Banks is Considered, and Some Remarks Are Made on the Present State of the Bank of North America.* Philadelphia, 1786.
————. *Political Essays on the Nature and Operation of Money, Public Finances and Other Subjects. Published During the American War, and Continued up to the Present Year, 1791.* Philadelphia, 1791.
Wilson, James. "Considerations, on the Power to Incorporate the Bank of North America." In *Selected Political Essays of James Wilson,* ed. Randolph G. Adams, 125–49. New York, 1930.

Published Primary Sources

Balch, Thomas, ed. *Letters and Papers Relating Chiefly to the Provincial History of Pennsylvania, With Notices of the Writers.* Philadelphia, 1855.

Balch, Thomas Willing, ed. *Willing Letters and Papers.* Philadelphia, 1922.

Benton, Thomas Hart. "The Mischiefs of a National Bank." In *The Annals of America,* vol. 5, 430–36. Chicago, 1976.

Biddle, James S., ed. *Autobiography of Charles Biddle, Vice-President of the Supreme Executive Council of Pennsylvania, 1754–1821.* Philadelphia, 1883.

Blau, Joseph L., ed. *Social Theories of Jacksonian Democracy: Representative Writings of the Period 1825–1850.* New York, 1954.

Bordley, John Beale. *Essays and Notes on Husbandry and Rural Affairs.* Second edition, with additions. Philadelphia, 1801.

Boyd, Julian P., et al., eds. *The Papers of Thomas Jefferson.* Princeton, N.J., 1950–.

Bryan, Samuel. "Samuel Bryan to George Bryan, 3 November 1785." Letter. *PMHB* 42 (1918): 286–87.

Butterfield, L. H., ed. *Letters of Benjamin Rush.* 2 vols. Princeton, N.J., 1951.

Carey, Mathew. *Autobiography.* Research Classics 1. Brooklyn, N.Y., 1942.

———, ed. *Debates and Proceedings of the General Assembly of Pennsylvania on the Memorials Praying a Repeal or Suspension of the Law Annulling the Charter of the Bank.* Philadelphia, 1786.

Chastellux, Marquis de. *Travels in North America; in the Years 1780, 1781, and 1782.* Translated and edited with introduction and notes by Howard C. Rice. 2 vols. Chapel Hill, N.C., 1963.

Cheyney, Thomas. "Thomas Cheyney, Esq. of Thornbury 1796 to Relatives in England." In *History of Chester County, Pennsylvania with Genealogical and Biographical Sketches,* 339. Philadelphia, 1881.

Corner, George W., ed. *The Autobiography of Benjamin Rush: His "Travels Through Life" Together with His Commonplace Book for 1789–1813.* Princeton, N.J., 1948.

Dickinson, John. "The Late Regulations . . . Respecting the British Colonies on the Continent of America Considered, in A Letter from a Gentleman in Philadelphia to His Friend in London." In vol. 1 of *The Writings of John Dickinson, 1764–1774,* ed. Paul L. Ford. Philadelphia, 1885.

Duane, William, ed. *Extracts from the Diary of Christopher Marshall, Kept in Philadelphia and Lancaster During the American Revolution, 1774–1781.* Albany, N.Y., 1877.

Ferguson, E. James, John Catanzariti, Elizabeth M. Nuxoll, et al., eds. *The Papers of Robert Morris, 1781–1784.* 7 vols. Pittsburgh, 1973–.

Foner, Philip S., ed. *The Complete Writings of Thomas Paine.* 2 vols. New York, 1945.

Hazard, Samuel, ed. *The Register of Pennsylvania Devoted to the Preservation of Facts and Documents, and Every Other Kind of Useful Information Reflecting the State of Pennsylvania.* Philadelphia, 1828.

Heffner, Richard D., ed. *A Documentary History of the United States.* Fifth edition. New York, 1991.

Hinkels, Stan V. *An Extraordinary Collection of Historical Documents and Other Important Letters and Documents.* Catalog no. 1290. Philadelphia.

Hutchinson, William T., Robert A. Rutland, et al., eds. *The Papers of James Madison.* Chicago, 1962–.

Johnson, C. B. [pseudonym for Robert H. Rose]. *Letters from the British Settlement in Pennsylvania.* Philadelphia, 1819.

Littell, John Stockton, ed. *Memoirs of His Own Time, with Reminiscences of the Men and Events of the Revolution by Alexander Graydon.* Philadelphia, 1846.

Mitchell, James T., and Henry Flanders, eds. *The Statutes at large of Pennsylvania from 1682 to 1801.* Harrisburg, Pa., 1906.

————, comp. *The Statutes at Large of Pennsylvania, 1682–1801.* 17 vols. Harrisburg, Pa., 1896–1915.

Pennsylvania Archives, Series I, 1664–1790. Edited by Samuel Hazard. 12 vols. Philadelphia, 1852–56.

Pownall, Thomas. *Administration of the Colonies.* 2 vols. London, 1764.

Rutherford, John. "Notes on the State of New Jersey Written August, 1786." In vol. 1 of *Proceedings of the New Jersey Historical Society,* second series, 79–89. Newark, N.J.

Schoepf, Johann David. *Travels in the Confederation, 1783–1784.* Translated and edited by Alfred J. Morrison. 2 vols. New York, 1968.

Smith, Paul H., ed. *Letters of Delegates to Congress, 1774–1789.* Washington, D.C., 1991.

Syrett, Harold C., Jacob E. Cooke, et al., eds. *The Papers of Alexander Hamilton.* New York, 1961–87.

Thomson, Charles. "Charles Thomson to Hannah Thomson, 6 April 1785." *PMHB* 25 (1901): 430–31.

————. "The Thomson Papers." In *Collections of the New York Historical Society for the Year 1878,* 218–19. New York, 1878.

Walker, Lewis Burd, ed. *The Burd Papers.* Private printing (130 copies), 1899.

Watson, John. "An Account of the First Settlement of the Township of Buckingham and Solesbury in Bucks County, Pennsylvania with Remarks on the Advance of Improvement in Agriculture, Etc. MDCCCIV." In vol. 1 of *Memoirs of the Historical Society of Pennsylvania.* Philadelphia, 1864.

II. Secondary Materials

Abbott, Richard H. "The Agricultural Press Views the Yeoman, 1819–1859." *AH* 42 (January 1968): 35–48.

Abrams, Philip. *Historical Sociology.* Ithaca, N.Y., 1982.

Adams, Jane H. "The Decoupling of Farm and Household: Differential Consequences of Capitalist Development on Southern Illinois and Third World Family Farms." *CSSH* 30 (July 1988): 453–82.

Adams, Willi Paul. *The First Constitutions: Republican Ideology and the Making of the State Constitutions in the Revolutionary Era.* Translated by Rita Kimber and Robert Kimber. Foreword by Richard B. Morris. Chapel Hill, N.C., 1980.

Alberts, Robert C. *The Golden Voyage: The Life and Times of William Bingham, 1752–1804.* Boston, 1969.

Alexander, Jeffrey C. "Durkheim's Problem and Differentiation Theory Today." In *Social Change and Modernity,* ed. Hans Haferkamp and Neil J. Smelser, 180–204. Berkeley and Los Angeles, 1992.

————. "Introduction—Differentiation Theory: Problems and Prospects." In *Differentiation Theory and Social Change: Comparative and Historical Perspectives,* ed. Jeffrey C. Alexander and Paul Colomy, 1–15. New York, 1990.

————. "Introduction." In *Neofunctionalism,* ed. Jeffrey C. Alexander and Jonathan Turner, 7–18. Beverly Hills, Calif., 1985.

──── . "Neofunctionalism and Modern Sociology." In *The Renascence of Sociological Theory*, ed. Henry Etzkowitz and Ronald Glassman, 267–75. Itasca, Ill., 1991.

Alexander, John K. "The Fort Wilson Incident of 1779: A Case Study of the Revolutionary Crowd." *WMQ* 31 (October 1974): 589–612.

──── . *Render Them Submissive: Responses to Poverty in Philadelphia, 1760–1800*. Amherst, Mass., 1980.

Althusser, Louis, and Etienne Balibar. *Reading "Capital."* London, 1970.

Ammerman, David. *In the Common Cause: American Response to the Coercive Acts of 1774*. New York, 1974.

Anderson, James D. "Thomas Wharton, 1730/31–1784: Merchant in Philadelphia." Ph.D. diss., University of Akron, 1977.

──── . "A Vote of Confidence: Isaac Wharton and the Bank of North America." *PH* 49 (January 1982): 48–59.

Anderson, Perry. *Lineages of the Absolutist State*. London, 1974.

Anderson, Robert T. "Voluntary Associations in History." In *VAR, 1973*, ed. David Horton Smith, 9–28. Lexington, Mass., 1973.

Arbuckle, Robert D. *Pennsylvania Speculator and Patriot: The Entrepreneurial John Nicholson, 1757–1800*. University Park, Pa., 1975.

Arnold, Douglas McNeill. "Political Ideology and the Internal Revolution in Pennsylvania, 1776–1790." Ph.D. diss., Princeton, N.J., 1976.

Ashmead, Henry Graham. *History of Delaware County, Pennsylvania*. Concord, Pa., 1968, 1884.

Bailyn, Bernard. "Communications and Trade: The Atlantic in the Seventeenth Century," *JEH* 13 (Fall 1953): 378–87.

──── . *The Ideological Origins of the American Revolution*. Cambridge, Mass., 1967.

Ball, Duane Eugene. "The Process of Settlement in Eighteenth Century Chester County, Pennsylvania: A Social and Economic History." Ph.D. diss., University of Pennsylvania, 1973.

Baltzel, E. Digby. *Puritan Boston and Quaker Philadelphia*. Boston, 1982.

Bauman, Richard. *For the Reputation of Truth: Politics and Conflict Among the Pennsylvania Quakers*. Baltimore, 1971.

Baumann, Roland M. "The Democratic-Republicans of Philadelphia: The Origins, 1776–1797." Ph.D. diss., Pennsylvania State University, 1970.

Baxter, W. T. "Accounting in Colonial America." In *Studies in the History of Accounting*, ed. A. C. Littleton and B. S. Yamey, 272–87. Homewood, Ill., 1956.

Becker, Laura L. "Diversity and Its Significance in an Eighteenth-Century Pennsylvania Town." In *Friends and Neighbors: Group Life in America's First Plural Society*, ed. Michael Zuckerman, 196–221. Philadelphia, 1982.

Beeman, Richard R. "Deference, Republicanism, and the Emergence of Popular Politics in Eighteenth-Century America." *WMQ* 49 (July 1992): 401–30.

Beer, Samuel. "The Comparative Method and the Study of British Politics." *CP* 1 (October 1968): 19–36.

Bell, Whitfield J., Jr. "The Federal Procession of 1788." *NYHSQ* 47 (January 1962): 18–29.

Bendix, Reinhard. "Tradition and Modernity Reconsidered." *CSSH* 9 (April 1967): 292–346.

Berg, Harry D. "Merchants and Mercantile Life in Colonial Philadelphia, 1748–1763." Ph.D. diss., State University of Iowa, 1940.

──── . "The Organization of Business in Colonial Philadelphia." *PH* 10 (July 1943): 157–77.

Berger, Brigitte. *Societies in Change: An Introduction to Comparative Sociology.* New York, 1971.

Berger, Peter L., and Brigitte Berger. *Sociology: A Biographical Approach.* Second edition. New York, 1975.

Bernstein, Henry. "Capitalism and Petty Commodity Production." *SA* 20 (December 1986): 11–27.

Berthoff, Rowland, and John Murrin. "Feudalism, Communalism, and the Yeoman Freeholder: The American Revolution Considered as a Social Accident." In *Essays on the American Revolution,* ed. Stephen G. Kurtz and James H. Hudson, 256–88. New York, 1973.

Beynon, Huw. "Class and Historical Explanation." In *Social Orders and Social Classes in Europe Since 1500: Studies in Social Stratification,* ed. M. L. Bush, 230–49. New York, 1992.

Bezanson, Anne, et al. *Prices and Inflation During the American Revolution: Pennsylvania, 1770–1790.* Philadelphia, 1951.

Bidwell, Percy Wells, and John T. Falconer. *History of Agriculture in the Northern United States.* New York, 1941.

Blau, Peter M. "Parameters of Social Structure." In *Approaches to the Study of Social Structure,* ed. Peter M. Blau, 220–53. New York, 1975.

———. "Structures of Social Positions and Structures of Social Relations." In *Theory Building in Sociology: Assessing Theoretical Cumulation,* ed. Jonathan H. Turner, 43–59. Beverly Hills, Calif., 1989.

Bockelman, Wayne L. "Local Government in Colonial Pennsylvania." In *Town and Country: Essays on the Structure of Local Government in the American Colonies,* ed. Bruce C. Daniels, 216–37. Middletown, Conn., 1978.

Bockelman, Wayne L., and Owen S. Ireland. "The Internal Revolution in Pennsylvania: An Ethnic-Religious Interpretation." *PH* 61 (1974): 125–59.

Bonami, Patricia. "The Middle Colonies: Embryo of the New Political Order." In *Perspectives on Early American History,* ed. Alden T. Vaughan and George A. Billias, 63–92. New York, 1973.

Bonnell, Victoria E. "The Uses of Theory, Concepts, and Comparison in Historical Sociology." *CSSH* 22 (April 1980): 156–73.

Bottomore, T. B. *Classes in Modern Society.* New York, 1968.

———. *Sociology: A Guide to Problems and Literature.* Second edition. New York, 1972.

———. "Structure and History." In *Approaches to the Study of Social Structure,* ed. Peter M. Blau, 159–71. New York, 1975.

Boylan, Anne M. "Women in Groups: An Analysis of Women's Benevolent Organizations in New York and Boston, 1797–1840." *JAH* 71 (December 1984): 497–517.

Braverman, Harry. *Labor and Monopoly Capital: The Degradation of Work in the Twentieth Century.* New York, 1974.

Breen, T. H. "An Empire of Goods: The Anglicization of Colonial America, 1690–1776." *Journal of British Studies* 25 (October 1986): 467–99.

Brenner, Robert. "The Social Basis of Economic Development." In *Analytic Marxism,* ed. John Roemer, 23–53. New York, 1986.

Bridenbaugh, Carl. *Cities in Revolt: Urban Life in America, 1743–1776.* New York, 1955.

———. *The Colonial Craftsman.* Chicago, 1950.

———. "Press and Book in Eighteenth Century Philadelphia." *PMHB* 65 (January 1941): 1–30.

Bridenbaugh, Carl, and Jessica Bridenbaugh. *Rebels and Gentlemen: Philadelphia in the Age of Franklin.* New York, 1942.

Brobeck, Stephen. "Changes in the Composition and Structure of Philadelphia Elite Groups, 1756–1790." Ph.D. diss., University of Pennsylvania, 1973.

———. "Revolutionary Change in Colonial Philadelphia: The Brief Life of the Proprietary Gentry." *WMQ* 33 (July 1976): 410–34.

Bronner, Edwin B. "Village into Town, 1746–1791." In *Philadelphia: A 300-Year History,* ed. Russell F. Weigley. New York, 1982.

Brophy, Alfred L. "Law and Indentured Servitude in Mid-Eighteenth Century Pennsylvania." *Willamette Law Review* 28, no. 69 (1991): 69–126.

Brown, Richard D. "The Emergence of Urban Society in Rural Massachusetts, 1760–1820." *JAH* 61 (June 1974): 29–51.

———. *Modernization: The Transformation of American Life, 1600–1865.* New York, 1976.

Brubaker, Rogers. *The Limits of Rationality: An Essay on the Social and Moral Thought of Max Weber.* Boston, 1984.

Bruchey, Stuart. "Economy and Society in an Earlier America." *JEH* 47 (June 1987): 299–320.

———. *Enterprise: The Dynamic Economy of a Free People.* Cambridge, Mass., 1990.

———. "The Historical Development of the Corporation in the United States." In vol. 6 of *Encyclopædia Britannica,* 525–28. Chicago, 1963.

———. *Robert Oliver, Merchant of Baltimore 1783–1819.* Baltimore, 1956.

Brunhouse, Robert L. *The Counter-Revolution in Pennsylvania, 1776–1790.* Harrisburg, Pa., 1942, 1971.

Buck, Solon J., and Elizabeth Hawthorn Buck. *The Planting of Civilization in Western Pennsylvania.* Pittsburgh, 1939.

Buell, Richard, Jr. "The Committee Movement of 1779 and the Formation of Public Authority in Revolutionary America." In *The Transformation of Early American History: Society, Authority, and Ideology,* ed. Michael Kammen, James A. Henretta, and Stanley N. Katz, 151–69. New York, 1991.

Buley, R. Carlyle. *The Old Northwest: Pioneer, 1815–1840.* 2 vols. Indianapolis, Ind., 1950.

Burke, Peter. *History and Social Theory.* Ithaca, N.Y., 1992.

Burns, Rex. *Success in America: The Yeoman Dream and the Industrial Revolution.* Amherst, Mass., 1976.

Burrows, Edwin G. *Albert Gallatin and the Political Economy of Republicanism.* New York, 1986.

Bushman, Richard L. "American High-Style and Vernacular Cultures." In *Colonial British America: Essays in the New History of the Early Modern Era,* ed. Jack P. Greene and J. R. Pole, 345–83. Baltimore, 1984.

———. "Massachusetts Farmers and the Revolution." In *Society, Freedom, and Conscience: The American Revolution in Virginia, Massachusetts, and New York,* ed. Richard M. Jellison, 77–124. New York, 1976.

———. " 'This New Man': Dependence and Independence, 1976." In *Uprooted Americans: Essays to Honor Oscar Handlin,* ed. Richard L. Bushman et al., 79–124. Boston, 1979.

Butler, Jon. "A Spiritual Tower of Babel: Shifting Structure and Functions of Religious Diversity in Colonial Pennsylvania." Unpublished paper presented at a conference at the University of Pennsylvania, 1982.

Buttel, Frederick H., Olaf F. Larson, and Gilbert W. Gillespie Jr. *The Sociology of Agriculture*. New York, 1990.

Cabeen, Francis A., von. "The Society of the Sons of Saint Tammany of Philadelphia." *PMHB* 26 (April 1902): 7–24.

Calvert, Peter. *The Concept of Class: An Historical Introduction*. New York, 1982.

Carp, E. Wayne. *To Starve the Army at Pleasure: Continental Army Administration and American Political Culture, 1775–1783*. Chapel Hill, N.C., 1984.

Case, Robert P. *Prosperity and Progress: Concord Township, Pennsylvania, 1683–1983*. 2 vols. Concord, Pa., 1983.

Chambers, William Nesbet. "Parties and Nation-Building in America." In *Nation and State Building in America: Comparative Historical Perspectives*, ed. J. Rogers Hollingsworth, 88–113. Boston, 1971.

———. "Party Development and Party Action: The American Origins." *HT* 3, no. 1 (1963): 91–120.

———. "Party Development and the American Mainstream." In *The American Party Systems: Stages of Political Development*, ed. William Nesbet Chambers and Walter Dean Burnham, 3–32. New York, 1967.

———. "Politics in the Early American States." *RAH* 1 (December 1973): 499–503.

Chandler, Alfred D., Jr., Stuart Bruchey, and Lewis Galambos, eds. *The Changing Economic Order: Readings in American Business and Economic History*. New York, 1968.

Clark, Christopher. *The Roots of Rural Capitalism: Western Massachusetts, 1780–1860*. Ithaca, N.Y. 1990.

Clark, Ronald. *Benjamin Franklin: A Biography*. New York, 1983.

Clemens, Paul G. E., and Lucy Simler. "Rural Labor and the Farm Household in Chester County, Pennsylvania, 1750–1820." In *Work and Labor in Early America*, ed. Stephen Innes, 106–43. Chapel Hill, N.C., 1988.

Cmiel, Kenneth. "Destiny and Amnesia: The Vision of Modernity in Robert Wiebe's *The Search for Order*." *RAH* 21 (June 1993): 352–68.

Cochran, Thomas C. *Business in American Life: A History*. New York, 1972.

———. *Pennsylvania: A Bicentennial History*. New York, 1978.

Cockcroft, James D., Andre Gunner Frank, and Dale Johnson, eds. *Dependence and Underdevelopment: Latin America's Political Economy*. Garden City, N.Y. 1972.

Cole, Arthur H. *Business Enterprise in Its Social Setting*. Cambridge, Mass., 1959.

———. "The Tempo of Mercantile Life in Colonial America." *BHR* 33 (Autumn 1959): 277–99.

Coleman, James. "The Development Syndrome: Differentiation—Equality—Capacity." In *Crises and Sequences in Political Development*, ed. Leonard Binder et al., 73–100. Princeton, N.J., 1971.

Collins, Randall. *Weberian Sociological Theory*. New York, 1986.

Colomy, Paul. "Conclusion: Revisions and Progress in Differentiation Theory." In *Differentiation Theory and Social Change: Comparative and Historical Perspectives*, ed. Jeffrey C. Alexander and Paul Colomy, 464–95. New York, 1990.

———. "Recent Developments in the Functionalist Approach to Change." In *Neofunctionalist Sociology*, ed. Paul Colomy, 289–308. Brookfield, Vt., 1990.

———. "Uneven Differentiation and Incomplete Institutionalization: Political Change and Continuity in the Early American Nation." In *Differentiation Theory and Social Change: Comparative and Historical Perspectives*, ed. Jeffrey C. Alexander and Paul Colomy, 119–62. New York, 1990.

Cooke, Jacob E. *Tench Coxe and the Early Republic.* Chapel Hill, N.C., 1978.

Cornell, Saul. "Aristocracy Assailed: The Ideology of Backcountry Anti-Federalism." *JAH* 76 (March 1990): 1148–72.

Cox, Jonathan-Peet. "Woodworkers in Allentown: Salisbury Township, and Whitehall Township, Pennsylvania, 1753–1805: A Study in Community and Craft." M.A. thesis, University of Delaware, 1982.

Craib, Ian. *Modern Social Theory: From Parsons to Habermas.* Brighton, Sussex, 1984.

Crone, Patricia. *Pre-Industrial Societies.* Cambridge, Mass., 1989.

Crowther, Simeon J. "The Shipbuilding Industry and the Economic Development of the Delaware Valley, 1681–1776." Ph.D. diss., University of Pennsylvania, 1970.

Culbertson, John Newton. "A Pennsylvania Boyhood: An Affectionate Memoir of Rural Life a Century Ago." *American Heritage* 18 (December 1966): 81–88.

Dalton, George. "Economic Theory and Primitive Society." *AA* 63 (February 1961): 1–25.

——. "Introduction." In *Economic Development and Social Change: The Modernization of Village Communities,* ed. George Dalton. New York, 1971.

Danhof, Clarence. *Change in Agriculture: The Northern United States, 1820–1870.* Cambridge, Mass., 1969.

Dauer, David E. "Colonial Philadelphia's Inter-Regional Transportation System: An Overview." *REHC* 2 (Fall 1977): 1–16.

Davis, Joseph Stancliffe. *Essays in the Earlier History of American Corporations.* 2 vols. New York, 1965.

Degler, Carl. *Out of Our Past: Forces That Shaped Modern America.* Revised edition. New York, 1970.

Diamondstone, Judith M. "The Government of Eighteenth-Century Philadelphia." In *Town and Country: Essays on the Structure of Local Government in the American Colonies,* ed. Bruce C. Daniels, 238–63. Middletown, Conn., 1978.

Dobb, Maurice. *Studies in the Development of Capitalism.* Revised edition. New York, 1963.

Doddridge, Joseph. *Notes on the Settlement and Indian Wars of the Western Parts of Virginia and Pennsylvania from 1763–1783, inclusive, together with a Review of the State of the First Settlers of the Western Country. With a Memoir of the Author by His Daughter Narcissa Doddridge.* Pittsburgh, 1912.

Doerflinger, Thomas M. "Commercial Specialization in Philadelphia's Merchant Community, 1750–1791." *BHR* 57 (Spring 1983): 20–49.

——. "Farmers and Dry Goods in the Philadelphia Market Area, 1750–1800." In *The Economy of Early America: The Revolutionary Period, 1763–1790,* ed. Ronald Hoffman et al., 166–95. Charlottesville, Va., 1988.

——. *A Vigorous Spirit of Enterprise: Merchants and Economic Development in Revolutionary Philadelphia.* Chapel Hill, N.C., 1986.

Dorfman, Robert. *The Price System.* Englewood Cliffs, N.J., 1965.

DuPlessis, Robert S., and Martha C. Howell. "Reconsidering the Early Modern Economy: The Cases of Leiden and Lille." *PP* 94 (February 1982): 49–84.

Durkheim, Emile. *The Division of Labor in Society.* Glencoe, Ill., 1960.

Duvall, Rezin Fenton. "Philadelphia's Maritime Commerce with the British Empire, 1783–1789." Ph.D. diss., University of Pennsylvania, 1960.

East, Robert A. *Business Enterprise in the American Revolutionary Era.* Gloucester, Mass., 1964.

------. "The Business Entrepreneur in a Changing Colonial Economy, 1763–1795." *JEH* 6 (1946): 16–27.

Egnal, Marc. "The Changing Structure of Philadelphia's Trade with the British West Indies." *PMHB* 99 (April 1975): 156–79.

------. "The Economic Development of the Thirteen Continental Colonies, 1720–1775." *WMQ* 32 (April 1975): 191–222.

Eicholtz, Hans L. "The Economic Education of William Findley: Banking and Finance, 1780 to 1820." Unpublished paper presented at the SHEAR Conference, 1992.

Eisenstadt, S. N. "Breakdowns of Modernization." *EDCC* 12 (July 1964): 345–67.

------. "Modernization and Conditions of Sustained Growth." *WP* 16 (1963–64): 576–94.

------. *Modernization: Protest and Change.* Englewood Cliffs, N.J., 1966.

------. "A Reappraisal of Theories of Social Change and Modernization." In *Social Change and Modernity,* ed. Hans Haferkamp and Neil J. Smelser, 412–29. Berkeley and Los Angeles, 1992.

------. "Social Change, Differentiation and Evolution." *ASR* 29 (1964): 375–86.

------. "Studies of Modernization and Sociological Theory." *HT* 13, no. 3 (1974): 225–52.

------. *Tradition, Change, and Modernity.* New York, 1973.

------. "Transformation of Social, Political, and Cultural Orders in Modernization." *ASR* 30 (October 1965): 659–73.

Eisinger, Chester E. "The Freehold Concept in Eighteenth-Century American Letters." *WMQ* 4 (January 1947): 42–59.

Eldersveld, Samuel J. *Political Parties in American Society.* New York, 1982.

Elliot, Jonathan. *The Funding System of the United States and of Great Britain with Some Tabular Facts of Other Nations Touching the Same Subject.* Executive Documents, 28th Cong., 1st sess., 1843–44. Washington, D.C., 1845.

Ellis, Frank. *Peasant Economics: Farm Households and Agrarian Development.* New York, 1988.

Ellis, Richard, and Aaron Wildavsky. "A Cultural Analysis of the Role of Abolitionists in the Coming of the Civil War." *CSSH* (January 1990): 89–116.

Ellsworth, Lucius F. "The Philadelphia Society for the Promotion of Agriculture and Agricultural Reform, 1785–1793." *AH* 42 (July 1968): 189–99.

Elster, Jon. "Three Challenges to Class." In *Analytical Marxism,* ed. John E. Roemer, 141–61. Cambridge, Mass., 1986.

Ely, James W., Jr. *The Guardian of Every Other Right: A Constitutional History of Property.* New York, 1992.

Epstein, Leon D. *Political Parties in Western Democracies.* New York, 1967.

Etzkowitz, Henry, and Ronald Glassman. "Introduction." In *The Renascence of Sociological Theory,* ed. Henry Etzkowitz and Ronald Glassman, 1–64. Itasca, Ill., 1991.

Evans, Peter B., and John D. Stephens. "Development and the World Economy." In *Handbook of Sociology,* ed. Neil J. Smelser, 739–73. Beverly Hills, Calif., 1988.

Faragher, John Mack. *Sugar Creek: Life on the Illinois Prairie.* New Haven, Conn., 1986.

Ferguson, E. James. "Currency Finance: An Interpretation of Colonial Monetary Practices." *WMQ* 10 (April 1953): 153–80.

------. *The Power of the Purse.* Chapel Hill, N.C., 1961.

Finley, M. I. *Ancient Slavery and Modern Ideology.* New York, 1980.

Fletcher, Stephen W. *Pennsylvania Agriculture and Country Life, 1640–1840*. Harrisburg, Pa., 1950.

Foner, Eric. *Free Soil, Free Labor, Free Men*. New York, 1970.

———. *Tom Paine and Revolutionary America*. New York, 1976.

Forbes, Susan. "Quaker Tribalism." In *Friends and Neighbors: Group Life in America's First Plural Society*, ed. Michael Zuckerman, 145–73. Philadelphia, 1982.

Foster, Joseph S. *In Pursuit of Equal Liberty: George Bryan and the Revolution in Pennsylvania*. University Park, Pa., 1994.

Fraser, L. M. *Economic Thought and Language*. London, 1937.

Friedman, Lawrence M. *A History of American Law*. New York, 1973.

Friedmann, Harriet. "Family Enterprises in Agriculture: Structural Limits and Political Possibilities." In *Agriculture: People and Policies*, ed. Philip Lowe and Michael Winter, 41–59. London, 1986.

———. "World Market, State, and Family Farm: Social Basis of Household Production in the Era of Wage Labor." *CSSH* 20 (October 1978): 545–86.

Fullam, W. Ross. "The Farm Account Book as an Economic Instrument in Orange County, 1790–1840." M.A. Thesis, New York College at Oneonta, 1972.

Galeski, Boguslaw. *Basic Concepts of Rural Sociology*. Translated by H. C. Stevens. London, 1972.

Geib, George Winthrop. "A History of Philadelphia, 1776–1789." Ph.D. diss., University of Wisconsin, 1969.

Gerth, H. H., and C. Wright Mills, eds. and trans. *From Max Weber: Essays in Sociology*. New York, 1958.

Giddens, Anthony. *Capitalism and Modern Social Theory: An Analysis of the Writings of Marx, Durkheim, and Max Weber*. New York, 1971.

———. *The Class Structure of the Advanced Societies*. New York, 1975.

Giddens, Anthony, and David Held. "Introduction: Class Places and Class Boundaries." In *Classes, Power, and Conflict: Classical and Contemporary Debates*, ed. Anthony Giddens and David Held, 93–100. Berkeley and Los Angeles, 1982.

Giere, Ronald N. *Explaining Science: A Cognitive Approach*. Chicago, 1988.

Gilbert, Daniel R. "Patterns of Organization and Membership in Colonial Philadelphia Club Life, 1725–1755." Ph.D. diss., University of Pennsylvania, 1952.

Goodman, David, and Michael Redclift. "Capitalism, Petty Commodity Production, and the Farm Enterprise." In *Agriculture: People and Policies*, ed. Philip Winter and Michael Winter, 20–40. London, 1986.

Goodwyn, Lawrence. *Democratic Promise: The Populist Mind in America*. New York, 1976.

Gough, Robert James. "Towards a Theory of Class and Social Conflict: A Social History of Wealthy Philadelphians, 1775 and 1780." Ph.D. diss., University of Pennsylvania, 1977.

Gras, N. S. B. *The Massachusetts First National Bank of Boston, 1784–1934*. Cambridge, Mass., 1937.

Grew, Raymond. "More on Modernization." *JSH* 14 (Winter 1980): 179–87.

Grubb, Farley. "Immigrant Servant Labor: Their Occupational and Geographic Distribution in the Late Eighteenth-Century Mid-Atlantic Economy." *SSH* 9 (Summer 1985): 249–75.

———. "The Long-Run Trend in the Value of European Immigrant Servants, 1654–1831: New Measurements and Interpretations." *REH* 14 (1992): 167–240.

——. "Servant Auction Records and Immigration into the Delaware Valley, 1745–1831: The Proportion of Females Among Immigrant Servants." *Proceedings of the American Philosophical Society,* 133, no. 2 (1989): 154–69.

Habermas, Jürgen. "Modernity—An Incomplete Project." In *Interpretive Social Science: A Second Look,* ed. Paul Rabineau and William M. Sullivan, 141–56. Berkeley and Los Angeles, 1987, 1979.

Hadenius, Axel. *Democracy and Development.* New York, 1992.

Hahn, Steven. "The 'Unmaking' of the Southern Yeomanry: The Transformation of the Georgia Upcountry, 1860–1890." In *The Countryside in the Age of Capitalist Transformation: Essays in the Social History of Rural America,* ed. Steven Hahn and Jonathan Prude, 179–204. Chapel Hill, N.C., 1985.

Halpern, Manfred. "The Rate and Costs of Political Development." *AAAPSS* 358 (March 1965): 20–28.

——. "The Revolution of Modernization in National and International Society." In *Issues in Comparative Politics: A Text with Readings,* ed. Robert J. Jackson and Michael B. Stein, 39–60. New York, 1971.

——. "Toward Further Modernization of the Study of New Nations." *WP* 17 (October 1964–65): 157–81.

Hammond, Bray. *Banks and Politics in America from the Revolution to the Civil War.* Princeton, N.J., 1957.

——. "Long and Short Term Credit in Early American Banking." *QJE* 49 (November 1934–35): 79–103.

Hanna, William, Rev. *History of Green County, Pennsylvania. Containing an Outline of the State from 1682, Until the Foundation of Washington County in 1781.* 1882.

Hanson, Norwood Russell. *Patterns of Discovery: An Inquiry into the Conceptual Foundations of Science.* London, 1971.

Haritos, Rosa, and Ronald Glassman. "Emile Durkheim and the Sociological Enterprise." In *The Renascence of Sociological Theory,* ed. Henry Etzkowitz and Ronald Glassman, 69–97. Itasca, Ill., 1991.

Harper, R. Eugene. "The Class Structures of Western Pennsylvania, 1783–1790." Ph.D. diss., University of Pittsburgh, 1969.

——. "Town Development in Early Western Pennsylvania." *Western Pennsylvania Historical Magazine* 71 (January 1988): 3–26.

Harre, Rom. "The Constructive Role of Models." In *The Use of Models in the Social Sciences,* ed. Lyndhurst Collins, 16–25. Boulder, Colo., 1976.

——. *The Philosophies of Science: An Introductory Survey.* New York, 1972.

Harrington, Virginia. *The New York Merchant on the Eve of the Revolution.* New York, 1935.

Harrison, David. *The Sociology of Modernization and Development.* Boston, 1988.

Harrison, John. *Marxist Economics for Socialists: A Critique of Reformism.* London, 1978.

Hart, Keith. "Barter." In *The New Palgrave: A Dictionary of Economics,* ed. John Eatwell, 196–98. New York, 1985.

Hawke, David. *In the Midst of a Revolution: The Politics of Confrontation in Colonial America.* Philadelphia, 1961.

Hays, Samuel P. "Introduction: The New Organizational Society." In *Building the Organizational Society: Essays on Associational Activities in Modern America,* ed. Jerry Israel, 1–15. New York, 1972.

Headlee, Sue. *The Political Economy of the Family Farm: The Agrarian Roots of American Capitalism.* New York, 1991.

Heilbroner, Robert L. *The Economic Problem*. Third edition. Englewood Cliffs, N.J., 1972.

Henderson, H. James. "Constitutionalists and Republicans in the Continental Congress." *PH* 36 (April 1969): 119–44.

———. *Party Politics in the Continental Congress*. New York, 1974.

Henning, D. C. "The German Settler and Farmer of the Early Days Along the Blue Mountains from 1750 to the Beginning of the Nineteenth Century." In *Publications of the Historical Society of Schuylkill County: "Tales of the Blue Mountains,"* vol. 3, 19–34. Pottsville, Pa., 1911.

Henretta, James. "Families and Farms: Mentalite in Pre-Industrial America." *WMQ* 35 (January 1978): 3–32.

———. "The Transition to Capitalism in America." In *The Transformation of Early American History: Society, Authority, and Ideology,* ed. Michael Kammen, James A. Henretta, and Stanley N. Katz, 218–38. New York, 1991.

Hesse, Mary. "Models Versus Paradigms in the Natural Sciences." In *Use of Models in the Social Sciences,* ed. Lyndhurst Collins, 1–15. Boulder, Colo., 1976.

Hicks, John D. *The Populist Revolt: A History of the Farmers' Alliance and the People's Party*. Omaha, Neb., 1931.

Hindess, Barry, and Paul Q. Hirst. *Pre-Capitalist Modes of Production*. London, 1975.

Hindle, Brooke. *David Rittenhouse*. Princeton, N.J., 1964.

Hirsch, Susan E. *Roots of the American Working Class: The Industrialization of Crafts in Newark, 1800–1860*. Philadelphia, 1978.

Hodges, Richard. *Primitive and Peasant Economic Markets*. New York, 1988.

Hodgkin, Thomas. *African Political Parties*. London, 1961.

Hoebel, E. Adamson, and Everett L. Frost. *Cultural and Social Anthropology*. New York, 1976.

Hood, Adrienne Dora. "Organizational Extent of Textile Manufacturing in Eighteenth-Century, Rural Pennsylvania: A Case Study of Chester County." Ph.D. diss., University of California at San Diego, 1988.

Hubka, Thomas C. "Farm Family Mutuality: The Mid-Nineteenth Century Maine Farm Neighborhood." In *The Farm,* ed. Peter Benes, 13–23. Boston, 1988.

Hummel, Charles F. *With Hammer in Hand: The Dominy Craftsmen of East Hampton, New York*. Charlottesville, Va., 1968.

Humphrey, Caroline. "Barter and Economic Disintegration." *Man* 20 (March 1985): 48–72.

Huntington, Samuel. "The Change to Change: Modernization, Development, and Politics." *CP* 3 (April 1970–71): 283–322.

———. *Political Order in Changing Societies*. New Haven, Conn., 1968.

Hurst, James Willard. *The Legitimacy of the Business Corporation in the United States, 1780–1970*. Charlottesville, Va., 1970.

Hutson, James, *Pennsylvania Politics: The Movement for Royal Government and Its Consequences*. Princeton, N.J., 1972.

Illick, Joseph E. *Colonial Pennsylvania: A History*. New York, 1976.

Ireland, Owen S. "The Ethnic-Religious Dimension of Pennsylvania Politics, 1778–1779." *WMQ* 30 (July 1973): 423–48.

———. "Political Development in Pennsylvania Legislative Behavior and Political Parties in the Confederation, 1776–1790." Unpublished essay.

———. "The Ratification of the Federal Constitution in Pennsylvania." Ph.D. diss., University of Pittsburgh, 1966.

————. *Religion, Ethnicity, and Politics: Ratifying the Constitution in Pennsylvania.* University Park, Pa., 1995.

Jaffee, David. *Levels of Socio-Economic Development Theory.* New York, 1990.

Jensen, Arthur L. *The Maritime Commerce of Colonial Philadelphia.* New York, 1966.

Jensen, Joan M. "Churns and Butter Making in the Mid-Atlantic Farm Economy, 1750–1850." *REHC* 5, no. 2–3 (1982): 60–100.

Jensen, Merrill. *The New Nation: A History of the United States During the Confederation, 1781–1789.* New York, 1950.

Johnstone, Paul H. "On the Identification of the Farmer." *RS* 5 (March 1940): 32–45.

Jones, Alice Hanson. "Wealth Estimates for the American Middle Colonies, 1974." *EDCC* 18 (July 1970).

Kahn, Joel S. "Marxist Anthropology and Peasant Economics: A Study of the Social Structure of Underdevelopment." In *The New Economic Anthropology,* ed. John Clammer, 110–37. New York, 1978.

Kaminski, John Paul. "Paper Politics: The Northern State Loan-Offices During the Confederation, 1783–1790." Ph.D. diss., University of Wisconsin, 1974.

Kelly, Kevin D. "The Independent Mode of Production." *RRPE* 11 (Spring 1979): 38–48.

Kimball, Solon T. "Rural Social Organization and Co-Operative Labor." *AJS* 55 (July–May 1949–50): 38–49.

Kindleberger, Charles P. *A Financial History of Western Europe.* Boston, 1984.

King, Anthony. "Political Parties in Western Democracies." *Polity* 2 (Winter 1969): 112–41.

King, Arnold Kimsey. "Thomas Paine in America, 1774–1787." Ph.D. diss., University of Chicago, 1951.

Klebaner, Benjamin J. *American Commercial Banking: A History.* Revised, enlarged, and updated version of his earlier *Commercial Banking in the United States: A History* (1974). Boston, 1990.

Klein, Randolph Shipley. *Portrait of an Early American Family: The Shippens of Pennsylvania Across Five Generations.* Philadelphia, 1975.

Kocka, Jürgen. "Theories and Quantification in History." *SSH* 8 (Spring 1984): 169–78.

Krooss, Herman E. *American Economic Development: The Progress of a Business Civilization.* Englewood Cliffs, N.J., 1966.

Krooss, Herman E., and Charles Gilbert. *American Business History.* Englewood Cliffs, N.J., 1972.

Krooss, Herman E., and Martin A. Blyn. *A History of Financial Intermediaries.* New York, 1971.

Kulikoff, Allan. *The Agrarian Origins of American Capitalism.* Charlottesville, Va., 1992.

————. "The Transition to Capitalism in Rural America." *WMQ* 1 (January 1989): 120–44.

Landes, David S., and Charles Tilly, eds. *History as Social Science.* Englewood Cliffs, N.J., 1971.

Lane, Frederick C. "Meanings of Capitalism." *JEH* 29 (March 1969): 5–12.

Lanier, Gabrielle Milan. "Samuel Wilson's Working World: Builders and Building in Chester County, Pennsylvania, 1780–1827." Ph.D. diss., University of Delaware, 1989.

La Palombra, Joseph, and Myron Weiner, eds. *Political Parties and Political Development.* Princeton, N.J., 1966.

Laurie, Bruce. *Working People of Philadelphia, 1800–1850.* Philadelphia, 1980.

Lawson, Kay. *The Comparative Study of Political Parties.* New York, 1976.

Leach, Edmund R. "Social Structure: The History of the Concept." In *IESS* 14: 482–89. New York, 1968.

Leiserson, Avery. *Parties and Politics: An Institutional and Behavioral Approach.* New York, 1958.

Lemon, James T. *The Best Poor Man's Country: A Geographical Study of Early Southeastern Pennsylvania.* Baltimore, 1972.

———. "Early Americans and Their Social Environment." *Journal of Historical Geography* 6, no. 2 (1980): 115–31.

———. "Household Consumption in Eighteenth-Century America and Its Relationship to Production and Trade: The Situation Among Farmers in Southeastern Pennsylvania." *AH* 41 (January 1967): 59–70.

———. "A Rural Geography of Southeastern Pennsylvania in the Eighteenth Century: The Contributions of Culture, Inheritance, Social Structure, Economic Conditions, and Physical Resources." Ph.D. diss., University of Wisconsin, 1964.

———. "Spatial Order: Households in Local Communities and Regions." In *Colonial British America: Essays in the New History of the Early Modern Era,* ed. Jack P. Greene and J. R. Pole, 86–122. Baltimore, 1984.

Lemon, James T., and Gary B. Nash. "The Distribution of Wealth in Eighteenth-Century America: A Century of Change in Chester County, Pennsylvania, 1693–1802." In *Class and Society in Early America,* ed. Gary B. Nash, 166–88. Englewood Cliffs, N.J., 1970.

Lester, Richard A. "Currency Issues to Overcome Depressions in Colonial Pennsylvania, 1723 and 1729." In *New Views on American Economic Development,* ed. Ralph L. Andreano, 73–118. Cambridge, Mass., 1965.

Levy, Marion J., Jr. *Modernization and the Structure of Societies: A Setting for International Affairs.* Princeton, N.J., 1966.

Lewis, Lawrence, Jr. *A History of the Bank of North America: The First Bank Chartered in the United States.* Philadelphia, 1888.

———. *History of the Bank of North America.* Folio edition. 2 vols. Philadelphia, 1888.

Loehr, Rodney C. "Farmers' Diaries: Their Interest and Value as Historical Sources." *AH* 12 (October 1939): 313–25.

———. "Self-Sufficiency on the Farm." *AH* 26 (April 1952): 37–41.

Lowie, Robert H. *Social Organization.* New York, 1948.

Lydon, James G. "Philadelphia's Commercial Expansion, 1720–1739." *PMHB* 91 (October 1967): 401–18.

Maier, Pauline. "The Revolutionary Origins of the American Corporation." *WMQ* 50 (January 1993): 51–77.

Main, Jackson Turner. *Political Parties Before the Constitution.* Chapel Hill, N.C., 1973.

Mandel, Ernest. *An Introduction to Marxist Economic Theory.* New York, 1970.

Martin, James Kirby, and Mark Edward Lender. *A Respectable Army: The Military Origins of the Republic, 1763–1789.* Arlington Heights, Ill., 1982.

Martin, Shirley A. "Craftsmen of Bucks County, Pennsylvania, 1750–1800." M.A. thesis, University of Delaware, 1956.

Marx, Karl. *Capital: A Critique of Political Economy.* Edited and translated by Samuel Moore and Edward Aveling. 3 vols. New York, 1967.

———. *Economic and Philosophic Manuscripts of 1844 and the Communist Manifesto.* Translated by Martin Milligan. Buffalo, N.Y., 1988.

McCusker, John J., and Russell R. Menard. *The Economy of British North America, 1607–1789.* Chapel Hill, N.C., 1985.

McDonald, Forrest. *The Formation of the American Republic, 1776–1790.* Baltimore, 1965.

McKendrick, Neil, et al. *The Birth of a Consumer Society: The Commercialization of Eighteenth-Century England.* Bloomington, Ind., 1982.

McMillan, Wheeler. *Ohio Farm.* Columbus, Ohio, 1974.

Mendres, Henri. *The Vanishing Peasant: Innovation and Change in French Agriculture.* Translated by Jean Lerner. Cambridge, Mass., 1970.

Merrill, Michael. "The Anticapitalist Origins of the United States." *Review* 13 (Fall 1990): 465–97.

———. "Cash Is Good to Eat: Self-Sufficiency and Exchange in the Rural Economy of the United States." *RHR* 7 (Winter 1977): 42–71.

———. "Self-Sufficiency and Exchange in Early America: Theory, Structure, Ideology." Ph.D. diss., Columbia University, 1986.

Michel, Jack. "In a Manner and Fashion Suitable to Their Degree: A Preliminary Investigation of the Material Culture of Early Rural Pennsylvania." *REHC* 5, no. 1 (1981): 1–83.

Miller, Richard G. *Philadelphia, the Federalist City: A Study of Urban Politics, 1789–1801.* Port Washington, N.Y., 1976.

Mooney, Patrick H. *My Own Boss? Class, Rationality, and the Family Farm.* Boulder, Colo., 1988.

Morris, Cynthia, and Irma Adelman. *Comparative Patterns of Economic Development, 1850–1914.* Baltimore, 1988.

Moss, Roger William, Jr. "Master Builders: A History of the Colonial Philadelphia Building Trades." Ph.D. diss., University of Delaware, 1972.

Murrin, John. "Political Development." In *Colonial British America: Essays in the New History of the Early Modern Era,* ed. Jack P. Greene and J. R. Pole, 408–56. Baltimore, 1984.

Mutch, Robert E. "The Cutting Edge: Colonial America and the Debate About Transition to Capitalism." *Theory and Society* 9, no. 6 (1980): 847–64.

———. "Yeoman and Merchant in Pre-Industrial America: Eighteenth-Century Massachusetts as a Case Study." *Societas* 7 (Autumn 1977): 279–302.

Myers, Marvin. *The Jacksonian Persuasion.* New York, 1960.

Nash, Gary B. "Artisans and Politics in Eighteenth-Century Philadelphia." In *The Origins of Anglo-American Radicalism,* ed. Margaret Jacob and James Jacob, 162–82. Boston, 1984.

———. *Quakers and Politics: Pennsylvania, 1681–1726.* Princeton, N.J., 1968.

———. "The Social Evolution of Preindustrial American Cities, 1700–1820: Reflections and New Directions." *Journal of Urban History* 13 (February 1987): 115–45.

———. "The Transformation of Urban Politics, 1700–1765." *JAH* 60 (December 1973): 605–32.

———. "Up from the Bottom in Franklin's Philadelphia." *PP* 77 (November 1977): 57–83.

————. *The Urban Crucible: Social Change, Political Consciousness, and the Origins of the American Revolution.* Cambridge, Mass., 1979.

————. "Urban Wealth and Poverty in Pre-Revolutionary America." *JIH* 6, no. 4 (1976): 545–84.

Nash, Gary B., and Jean Soderlund. *Freedom by Degrees: Emancipation in Pennsylvania and Its Aftermath.* New York, 1991.

Nash, Manning. *Primitive and Peasant Economic Systems.* San Francisco, 1966.

Neale, Walter C. "The Market in Theory and History." In *Trade and Market in the Early Empires: Economics in History and Theory,* ed. Conrad M. Arensberg, Karl Polanyi, and Harry W. Pearson, 357–72. Glencoe, Ill., 1957.

Neilly, Andrew H. "The Violent Volunteers: A History of the Volunteer Fire Departments of Philadelphia, 1736–1871." Ph.D. diss., University of Pennsylvania, 1959.

Newby, Howard. "The Deferential Dialectic." *CSSH* 17 (1975): 139–64.

Northrup, Ric. "Decomposition and Reconstruction: A Theoretical and Historical Study of Philadelphia Artisans, 1785–1820." Ph.D. diss., University of North Carolina, 1989.

Oaks, Robert F. "Big Wheels in Philadelphia: Du Simitiere's List of Carriage Owners." *PMHB* 95 (July 1971): 351–62.

Olton, Charles S. *Artisans for Independence: Philadelphia Mechanics and the American Revolution.* Syracuse, N.Y., 1975.

————. "Philadelphia Artisans and the American Revolution." Ph.D. diss., University of California at Berkeley, 1968.

————. "Philadelphia's Mechanics in the First Decade of Revolution, 1765–1775." *JAH* 59 (1972–73): 311–26.

Osterud, Nancy Grey. *Bonds of Community: The Lives of Farm Women in Nineteenth-Century New York.* Ithaca, N.Y., 1991.

Papineau, David. "Ideal Type and Empirical Theories." *British Journal of the Philosophy of Science* 27 (1976): 136–46.

Parker, Peter J. "The Philadelphia Printer: A Study of an Eighteenth-Century Businessman." *BHR* 40 (1966): 24–46.

Parkin, Frank. "Social Stratification." In *A History of Sociological Analysis,* ed. Tom Bottomore and Robert Nisbet, 599–632. New York, 1978.

Perkins, Edwin J. *The Economy of Colonial America.* New York, 1980.

Piott, Steven L. *The Anti-Monopoly Persuasion: Popular Resistance to the Rise of Big Business in the Midwest.* Westport, Conn., 1985.

Platt, John. "Jeremiah Wadsworth: Federalist Entrepreneur." Ph.D. diss., Columbia University, 1955.

Plumb, Henry Blackman. *History of Hanover Township Including Sugar Notch, Ashley, and Nanticoke Boroughs and Also a History of Wyoming Valley in Luzerne County, Pennsylvania.* Wilkes-Barre, Pa., 1885.

Pocock, J. G. A. "Machiavelli, Harrington, and English Political Ideologies in the Eighteenth Century." In *Politics, Language, and Time: Essays on Political Thought and History,* 104–47. New York, 1973.

Polanyi, Karl. *The Great Transformation: The Political and Economic Origins of Our Time.* New York, 1944.

Porpora, Douglas V. "Four Concepts of Social Structure." *JTSB* 19 (June 1989): 195–211.

Porter, Glen, and Harold C. Livesay. *Merchants and Manufacturers: Studies in the Changing Structure of Nineteenth-Century Marketing.* Baltimore, 1971.

Potter, J. "The Colonial Period." In *Population in History,* ed. D. V. Glass and D. E. C. Eversley, 636–46. London, 1965.

Presthus, Robert. *The Organizational Society: An Analysis and a Theory.* New York, 1962.

Price, Jacob M. "Economic Function and the Growth of American Port Towns in the Eighteenth Century." *Perspectives in American History* 8 (1974): 121–86.

Proud, Robert. *The History of Pennsylvania.* 2 vols. Philadelphia, 1797–98.

Quimby, Ian M. "Apprenticeship in Colonial Philadelphia." M.A. thesis, University of Delaware, 1963.

Rakove, Jack N. *The Beginnings of National Politics: An Interpretive History of the Continental Congress.* Baltimore, 1979.

Rappaport, George David. "The First Description of the Bank of North America." *WMQ* 33 (October 1976): 661–67.

———. "The Sources and Early Development of the Hostility to Banks in Early American Thought." Ph.D. diss., New York University, 1970.

Rasmusson, Ethel E. "Capital on the Delaware: The Philadelphia Upper Class in Transition, 1789–1801." Ph.D. diss., Brown University, 1962.

———. "Democratic Environment—Aristocratic Aspirations." *PMHB* 90 (April 1966): 155–82.

Reddy, William M. "The Concept of Class." In *Social Orders and Social Classes in Europe Since 1500: Studies in Social Stratification,* ed. M. L. Bush, 13–25. New York, 1992.

Redlich, Fritz. "Mercantilist Thought and Early American Banking." In *Essays in American Economic History: Eric Bollman and Studies in Banking,* 107–30. New York, 1944.

———. *The Moulding of American Banking: Men and Ideas,* Part I, 1781–1840. New York, 1947.

Remini, Robert. *Andrew Jackson and the Bank War.* New York, 1967.

Reynolds, Lloyd G. "The Spread of Economic Growth to the Third World, 1850–1980." *Journal of Economic Literature,* 21 (September 1988): 941–80.

Riesman, Janet. "Money, Credit, and Federalist Political Economy." In *Beyond Confederation: Origins of the Constitution and American National Identity,* ed. Stephen Botwein, Richard Beeman, and Edward C. Carter, 128–61. Chapel Hill, N.C., 1987.

———. "The Origins of American Political Economy, 1690–1781." Ph.D. diss., Brown University, 1983.

Risch, Erna. "Immigrant Aid Societies Before 1820." *PMHB* 60 (January 1936): 15–33.

Ritzer, George. *Sociological Theory.* New York, 1992.

Roosevelt, Frank. "Part I: Controversies in Economic Theory—Cambridge Economics as Commodity Fetishism." *Review of Radical Political Economics* 7 (Winter 1975): 1–29.

Ross, Earle D. "Retardation in Farm Technology Before the Power Age." *AH* 30 (January 1956): 11–18.

Rosswurm, Steven. *Arms, Country, and Class: The Philadelphia Militia and "Lower Sort" During the American Revolution, 1775–1783.* New Brunswick, N.J., 1987.

Roth, Guenther. "The Genesis of the Typological Approach." In *Scholarship and Partnership: Essays on Max Weber,* 253–65. Berkeley and Los Angeles, 1971.

Rothenberg, Winifred B. *From Market-Places to a Market Economy: The Transformation of Rural Massachusetts, 1750–1850.* Chicago, 1992.

―――. "The Market and Massachusetts Farmers, 1750–1855." *JEH* 41 (June 1981): 283–314.

Rothermund, Dietmar. *The Layman's Progress: Religious and Political Experience in Colonial Pennsylvania, 1740–1770.* Philadelphia, 1961.

Rowe, Gail Stuart. "Power, Politics, and Public Service: The Life of Thomas McKean, 1734–1817." Ph.D. diss., Stanford University, 1969.

Roxborough, Ian. "Modernization Theory Revisited: A Review Article." *CSSH* 30, no. 4 (October 1988): 753–61.

Rule, John. "The Property of Skill in the Period of Manufacture." In *The Historical Meanings of Work,* ed. Patrick Joyce, 99–118. New York, 1987.

Ryerson, Richard Alan. "Political Mobilization and the American Revolution: The Resistance Movement in Philadelphia, 1765 to 1776." *WMQ* 31 (October 1974): 565–88.

―――. "Portrait of a Colonial Oligarchy: The Quaker Elite in the Pennsylvania Assembly, 1729–1776." In *Power and Status: Officeholding in Colonial America,* ed. Bruce C. Daniels, 106–35. Middletown, Conn., 1986.

―――. "Republican Theory and Partisan Reality in Revolutionary Pennsylvania: Towards a New View of the Constitutionalist Party." In *Sovereign States in an Age of Uncertainty,* ed. Ronald Hoffman and Peter J. Albert, 95–133. Charlottesville, Va., 1982.

―――. *The Revolution Is Now Begun: The Radical Committees of Philadelphia, 1765–1776.* Philadelphia, 1978.

Sabia, Daniel R., Jr., and Jerald T. Wallulis, eds. *Changing Social Science: Critical Theory and Other Critical Perspectives.* Albany, N.Y., 1983.

Salinger, Sharon. "Artisans, Journeymen, and the Transformation of Labor in Late Eighteenth-Century Philadelphia." *WMQ* 40 (January 1983): 62–84.

―――. "Colonial Labor in Transition: The Decline of Indentured Servitude in Late Eighteenth-Century Pennsylvania." *Labor History* 22 (1981): 165–91.

Sanderson, Stephen K. *Social Evolutionism: A Critical History.* Cambridge, Mass., 1990.

Saunders, Jennings B. *Evolution of Executive Departments of the Continental Congress, 1774–1789.* Gloucester, Mass., 1935.

Scharf, Thomas J., and Thomas Westcott. *History of Philadelphia, 1607–1884.* 3 vols. Philadelphia, 1884.

Schlesinger, Arthur M. *The Colonial Merchants and the American Revolution, 1763–1776.* New York, 1918.

―――. *Paths to the Present.* New York, 1949.

Schmidt, Herbert G. *Agriculture in New Jersey: A Three-Hundred-Year History.* New Brunswick, N.J., 1973.

―――. *Rural Hunterdon: An Agricultural History.* New Brunswick, N.J., 1945.

Schram, Callista. "William Findley in Pennsylvania Politics." M.A. thesis, University of Pittsburgh, 1936.

Schultz, Ronald. *The Republic of Labor Philadelphia Artisans and the Politics of Class, 1720–1830.* New York, 1993.

―――. "The Small-Producer Tradition and the Moral Origins of Artisan Radicalism in Philadelphia, 1720–1810." *PP,* 127 (May 1990): 84–116.

Schumpeter, Joseph A. *History of Economic Analysis.* New York, 1954.

Schwartz, Anna Jacobson. "An Attempt at Synthesis in American Banking History." *JEH* 7 (November 1947): 208–17.

————. "Beginning of Competitive Banking in Philadelphia, 1728–1809." *JPE* 55 (1947): 417–31.

Schweitzer, Mary. *Custom and Contract: Household, Government, and the Economy in Colonial Pennsylvania.* New York, 1987.

————. "Elements of Political Economy in the Late Eighteenth Century: The Backcountry of Pennsylvania and the Shenandoah Valley of Virginia." Unpublished paper delivered at the seminar of the Philadelphia Center for Early American Studies, 1990.

Scott, Alison MacEwen, ed. "Rethinking Petty Commodity Production," *SA* 20 (December 1986).

Seavoy, Ronald E. *The Origins of the American Business Corporation, 1784–1855: Broadening the Concept of Public Service During Industrialization.* Westport, Conn., 1982.

————. "The Public Service Origins of the American Business Corporation." *BHR* 52 (Spring 1978): 30–60.

Sellers, Charles Coleman. *The Artist of the Revolution: The Early Life of Charles Willson Peale.* Hebron, Conn., 1939.

————. *Charles Willson Peale.* New York, 1969.

————. *The Market Revolution: Jacksonian America, 1815–1846.* New York, 1991.

Shade, William Gerald. *Banks or No Banks: The Money Issue in Western Politics.* Detroit, 1972.

Shaeffer, John N. "Public Consideration of the 1776 Pennsylvania Constitution." *PMHB* 98 (October 1974): 415–37.

Shammas, Carole. "How Self-Sufficient Was Early America?" *JIH* 13 (1982): 247–72.

Shanin, Teodor, ed. *Peasants & Peasant Society.* Second edition. New York, 1987.

Sharp, James Roger. *Jacksonians Versus Banks: Politics in the States After the Panic of 1837.* New York, 1970.

Shefter, Martin. "Party and Patronage: Germany, England, and Italy." *Politics and Society* 7, no. 4 (1977): 403–52.

Shepherd, James, and Gary M. Walton. *Shipping, Maritime Trade, and the Economic Development of Colonial North America.* London, 1972.

Shepherd, William R. *History of Proprietary Government in Pennsylvania.* New York, 1896.

Shils, Edward. "Centre and Periphery." In *The Logic of Personal Knowledge: Essays Presented to Michael Polanyi on His Seventieth Birthday, 11th March 1961,* 117–30. Glencoe, Ill., 1961.

————. "Deference." In *Social Stratification,* ed. John Archer Jackson, 104–32. Cambridge, 1968.

Shiner, L. E. "Tradition/Modernity: An Ideal Type Gone Astray." *CSSH* 17 (April 1975): 245–52.

Shorter, Edward. "The History of Work in the West: An Overview." In *Work and Community in the West,* ed. Edward Shorter, 1–33. New York, 1973.

Shultz, James. "The Voluntary Society and Its Components." In *VAR: 1972,* ed. David Horton Smith et al., 25–38. Lexington, Mass., 1972.

————. "Voluntary Associations, II: Sociological Aspects." In *IESS* 16:362–78. New York, 1968.

Simler, Lucy. "The Landless Worker: An Index of Economic and Social Change in Chester County, Pennsylvania, 1750–1820." *PMHB* 114 (April 1990): 163–99.

———. "Tenancy in Colonial Pennsylvania: The Case of Chester County." *WMQ* 43, no. 4 (October 1986): 542–69.

Simmons, Ossie G. *Perspectives on Development and Population Growth in the Third World.* New York, 1988.

Singleton, Gregory H. "Protestant Voluntary Associations and the Shaping of Victorian America." In *Victorian America,* ed. Daniel Walker Howe, 47–58. Philadelphia, 1976.

Sjoberg, Gideon. *The Preindustrial City: Past and Present.* New York, 1960.

Skocpol, Theda. "Bringing the State Back In: Strategies of Analysis in Current Research." In *Bringing the State Back In,* ed. Dietrich Rueschmeyer, Peter B. Evans, and Theda Skocpol, 3–37. New York, 1985.

Smelser, Neil J. "From Structure to Order." In *The Social Fabric: Dimensions and Issues,* ed. James F. Short Jr., 33–38. Beverly Hills, Calif., 1986.

———. "Mechanisms of Change and Adjustment to Change." In *Industrialization and Society,* ed. Bert F. Hoselitz and Wilbert Moore, 32–54. Mouton, 1963.

———. "Social Structure." In *Handbook of Sociology,* ed. Neil J. Smelser, 103–29. Beverly Hills, Calif., 1988.

Smith, Barbara Clark. *After the Revolution: The Smithsonian History of Everyday Life in the Eighteenth Century.* New York, 1985.

Smith, Billy G. "Inequality in Late Colonial Philadelphia: A Note on Its Nature and Growth." *WMQ* 41 (October 1984): 629–45.

———. *The "Lower Sort": Philadelphia's Laboring People, 1750–1800.* Ithaca, N.Y., 1990.

Smith, Carole A. "Reconstructing the Elements of Petty Commodity Production." *SA* 20 (December 1986): 29–46.

Smith, Constance, and Anne Freedman. *Voluntary Associations: Perspectives on the Literature.* Cambridge, Mass., 1972.

Smith, David C. "Middle Range Farming in the Civil War Era: Life on a Farm in Seneca County, 1862–1866." *New York History* 48 (October 1967): 352–69.

Smith, Gavin. "Reflections on the Social Relations of Simple Commodity Production." *JPS* 13 (October 1985): 99–108.

So, Alvin Y. "Class Struggle Analysis: A Critique of Class Structure Analysis." *SP* 34, no. 1 (1991): 39–59.

———. *Social Change and Development.* 1990. Newbury Park, Calif., 1990.

So, Alvin Y., and Muhammad Hikam. " 'Class' in the Writings of Wallerstein and Thompson." *SP* 32, no. 4 (1989): 453–67.

Sorauf, Frank J. *Party Politics in America.* Second edition. Boston, 1972.

Stavenhagen, Rondolfo. *Social Classes in Agrarian Societies.* Translated by Judy Adler Hellman. Garden City, N.Y., 1975.

Studenski, Paul, and Herman E. Krooss. *Financial History of the United States.* New York, 1952.

Sumner, William Graham. *The Financier and the Finances of the American Revolution.* 2 vols. New York, 1891.

Suppe, Frederick, ed. *The Structure of Scientific Theories,* with a critical introduction. Urbana, Ill., 1974.

Sztompka, Piotr. *The Sociology of Social Change.* Cambridge, Mass., 1993.

Tatum, George B. *Philadelphia Georgian: The City House of Samuel Powel and Some of Its Eighteenth-Century Neighbors.* Middletown, Conn., 1976.

Teaford, Jon C. *The Municipal Revolution in America: Origins of Modern Urban Government, 1650–1825.* Chicago, 1976.

"Tench Coxe." In *DAB* 2:448–49. New York, 1928–80.

Thayer, Theodore. "An Eighteenth-Century Farmer and Pioneer: Sylvanus Seeley's Early Life in Pennsylvania." *PH* 35 (January 1968): 45–63.

———. "The Land Bank System in the American Colonies." *JEH* 13 (1953): 145–59.

———. *Pennsylvania Politics and the Growth of Democracy, 1740–1776*. Harrisburg, Pa., 1953.

Theorelli, Hans. B. *The Federal Antitrust Policy*. Baltimore, 1955.

Thompson, E. P. "The Moral Economy of the English Crowd in the Eighteenth Century." *PP* 50 (February 1971): 76–136.

Thompson, Peter John. "A Social History of Philadelphia's Taverns, 1683–1800." Ph.D. diss., University of Pennsylvania, 1989.

Throne, Mildred. " 'Book Farming' in Iowa, 1840–1870." *Iowa Journal of History* 49 (April 1951): 117–42.

Tipps, Dean C. "Modernization Theory and the Comparative Study of Societies: A Critical Perspective." *CSSH* 15 (March 1973): 199–225.

Tiryakian, Edward A. "Typologies." In *IESS* 16:177–86. New York, 1968.

Tolles, Frederick B. *Meeting House and Counting House: The Quaker Merchants of Colonial Philadelphia, 1682–1763*. New York, 1948.

———. "Town House and Country House: Inventories from the Estate of William Logan, 1976." *PMHB* 82 (October 1958): 397–410.

Tully, Alan. "Ethnicity, Religion, and Politics in Early America." *PMHB* 107 (October 1983): 491–536.

———. "Quaker Party and Proprietary Policies: The Dynamics of Politics in Pre-Revolutionary Pennsylvania, 1730–1775." In *Power and Status: Officeholding in Colonial America*, ed. Bruce C. Daniels, 75–105. Middletown, Conn., 1986.

———. *William Penn's Legacy: Politics and Social Structure in Provincial Pennsylvania, 1726–1755*. Baltimore, 1977.

Turner, Jonathan H. "Ideographic vs. Nomothetic Explanation: A Comment on Porpora's Conclusion." *JTSB* 13 (October 1983): 273–80.

Ulrich, Laurel Thatcher. " 'A Friendly Neighbor': Social Dimensions of Daily Work in Northern Colonial New England." *Feminist Studies* 6 (1980): 392–405.

———. "Housewife and Gadder: Themes of Self-sufficiency and Community in Eighteenth-Century New England." In *"To Toil the Livelong Day,"* ed. Gail Broneman and Mary Beth Norton, 21–34. Ithaca, N.Y., 1987.

Van Doren, Carl. *Benjamin Franklin*. New York, 1938.

Van Voorhis, John S. *The Old and the New Monongahela*. Pittsburgh, 1893.

Ver Steeg, Clarence. *Robert Morris: Revolutionary Financier*. Philadelphia, 1954.

Waggoner, Priscilla. "Producers and Participants: Women in the Rural German Culture of Eighteenth-Century Pennsylvania." Unpublished paper delivered at the 41st Conference in Early American History and Culture, Millersville State College, Millersville, Pa., 1981.

———. "Women in the Household Economy of Eighteenth- and Nineteenth-Century Pennsylvania." Unpublished paper.

Walton, Joseph S. "Nominating Conventions in Pennsylvania." *AHR* 2 (January 1897): 262–78.

Walzer, John F. "Colonial Philadelphia and Its Backcountry." *Winterthur Portfolio* 7 (1972): 161–73.

———. "Transportation in the Philadelphia Trading Area, 1740–1775." Ph.D. diss., University of Wisconsin, 1968.

Ware, Alan. *Citizens, Parties, and the State: A Reappraisal.* Princeton, N.J., 1987.
Ware, Alan, ed. *Political Parties: Electoral Change and Structural Response.* New York, 1987.
Ware, Norman J. *The Labor Movement in the United States, 1860–1895: A Study in Democracy.* New York, 1929.
Warner, Keith W. "Major Conceptual Elements of Voluntary Associations." In *VAR: 1972,* ed. David Horton Smith et al., 71–80. Lexington, Mass., 1972.
Warner, Sam Bass, Jr. *The Private City: Philadelphia in Three Periods of Its Growth.* Philadelphia, 1968.
Warriner, Charles K. "Levels in the Study of Social Structure." In *Continuities in Structural Inquiry,* ed. Peter M. Blau and Robert K. Merton, 179–90. Beverly Hills, Calif., 1981.
Weber, Max. *Economy and Society: An Outline of Interpretive Sociology.* Edited by Guenther Roth and Claus Wittich. 3 vols. New York, 1968.
Weiman, David F. "Families, Farms, and Rural Society in Preindustrial America." *REH,* suppl. no. 5 (1989): 255–77.
Welsh, Peter C. "The Brandywine Mills: A Chronicle of an Industry, 1762–1816." *DH* 7 (1956): 17–36.
———. "Merchants, Millers, and Ocean Ships: The Components of an Early American Industrial Town." *DH* 7 (1957): 319–36.
Wharton, Clifton R., Jr. "Subsistence Agriculture: Concepts and Scope." In *Subsistence Agriculture and Economic Development,* ed. Clifton R. Wharton Jr., 12–22. Chicago, 1969.
Wiarda, Howard. "Rethinking Political Development: A Look Backward over Thirty Years, and a Look Ahead." *Studies in Comparative International Development* 24 (Winter 1989–90): 65–82.
Wiebe, Robert. *The Search for Order, 1877–1920.* New York, 1967.
Willer, David, and Murray Webster, Jr. "Theoretical Concepts and Observables." *ASR* 35 (1970): 748–57.
Wilson, Janet. "The Bank of North America and Pennsylvania Politics, 1781–1787." *PMHB* 66 (January 1942): 3–28.
Wolf, Stephanie Grauman. *Urban Village: Population, Community, and Family Structure in Germantown, Pennsylvania, 1683–1800.* Princeton, N.J., 1976.
Wood, Gordon S. *The Creation of the American Republic, 1776–1787.* Chapel Hill, N.C., 1969.
———. "Interests and Disinterests in the Making of the Constitution." In *Beyond Confederation: Origins of the Constitution and American National Identity,* ed. Stephen Botwein, Richard S. Beeman, and Edward C. Carter, 69–112. Chapel Hill, N.C., 1987.
Wood, Jerome H. *Conestoga Crossroads: Lancaster, Pennsylvania, 1730–1790.* Harrisburg, Pa., 1979.
Worsley, Peter. *The Third World.* Chicago, 1964.
Worsley, Peter, et al. *The New Introducing Sociology.* Third edition. New York, 1987.
Wright, Gavin. *The Political Economy of the Cotton South: Households, Markets, and Wealth in the Nineteenth Century.* New York, 1978.
Yoder, Paton Wesley. "Paper Currency in Colonial Pennsylvania." Ph.D. diss., Indiana University, 1941.
Zemsky, Robert. "American Legislative Behavior." *ABS* 16 (May–June 1973): 675–94.

Index

Affleck, Thomas, 21
abolition society, 72
African Methodist Episcopal Church, 73
Africans, 44, 72
Agricola, 175. *See also* Bryan, George
Alexander, Jeffrey C., 55–56
alienation, 9–10, 32
Allen, William, 122, 124
American Philosophical Society, 73, 96, 124
An American, 173. *See also* Morris, Gouverneur
Anderson, Perry, 10
Anglicans, 14, 46, 63, 82, 93, 122, 123, 124, 126
antibanking, 53, 62, 79–80, 127, 138, 145, 161–63, 166–67, 170–71, 171 n. 32, 173–77, 182–85, 196–98, 209–12, 214, 219–21, 227–30. *See also* aristocracy; bank war; corporations, fear of; equality; money power; monopoly
apprentices, 13, 14, 16, 21, 28, 60, 116. *See also* labor; markets
aristocracy, fear of, 5, 143, 190–91, 196–97, 208–12, 227–30. *See also* bank war
artisans (craftsmen, mechanics). *See also* labor; markets; Schultz, Ronald
   as businessmen, 20–21, 130
   community of, 21–22
   craft skills, 21
   leisure activities, 115–16
   maximization and, 22–23

mechanics committee, 118
Patriotic Society, 118
political goals, 117–19, 133–34, 180, 209–12, 217
scale of production, 22
small producer tradition, 116–17
as a social class, xi–xii, 112, 115–19, 133–34
ascription, social, 7, 41–42, 66–67, 68, 109–10, 113, 114, 131–32
Ashton, Samuel, 29
Association for Southwark for Suppressing Vice and Immorality, 72
associational system, xii, 74–79, 96, 106, 107, 109, 117, 123–24, 132–33, 138, 186, 197, 223. *See also* integration
Atticus, 211–12
Attmore, Caleb, 21

Bache, Richard, 97
Bank of North America, xii, 31, 42, 49, 53, 62, 65, 79–80, 105, 108, 121, 127, 128, 130, 134, 138, 140, 145, 157–58, 159, 160, 161, 163–66, 167, 170, 171, 172, 174, 176–77, 180, 196, 197, 201, 202, 209–10, 220, 223, 224. *See also* banking; markets: capital; Morris, Robert
   board of directors, 140 n. 9, 142
   business of, 199–200
   by-laws, 152–53
   charter revision (1786–87), 216–19, 220–21

the Continental Congress and, 139–42
establishing the business, 145–47, 149, 159
loan office, opposition to, 181–82
Office of Finance, relations with, 148–49, 149 n. 31, 150–51
Pennsylvania charter debate (1782), 142–43, 145, 145 n. 22
state charters, 142, 204
subscription: first, 140–41, 145–46, 149–50, 183; second, 171–72, 183–84
bank notes (bills), 140, 142, 143, 147, 148, 153, 154, 156–57, 164–65, 172, 173, 176, 179, 181, 182, 185, 187–88, 193, 196
Bank of Pennsylvania
in 1780, 140
in 1784, 159–65, 166, 174, 184, 210, 214
bank war, 53, 62, 65, 75, 79–80, 95, 106, 115, 128, 130, 197–98, 219, 220. See also antibanking; aristocracy; corporations; equality; monopoly
attack on the bank, 182–85, 188–89, 190–92, 207–12, 214–15, 226–30
defense of the bank, 185–88, 192–96, 204–8, 213–14
moderate opinion, 192, 215–17
banking, 156–57, 173. See also markets: capital
private, 12, 30–31, 131
commercial, 31, 49, 49, 127, 138, 144, 145, 146, 151–56, 158, 163, 170–71, 174, 176, 207, 221
Baptists, 64
barter, 30, 31, 32, 35–38, 131, 224. See also bees; exchange networks; reciprocity
Bayard, John, 95, 102, 103
Bedford, John, 22
bees (frolics), 33–35, 38–39, 224. See also barter; exchange networks; reciprocity
Beef-Stake Clubbe, 71
Bettering House, 73
Biddle, Charles, 30, 104
Biddle, Clement, 155
Biddle, Edward, 30, 86
bills. See bank notes
bills of credit (exchange), 153, 157
Bingham, William, 124, 125, 149, 180, 216
Blackstone, Sir William, 206
Bottomore, Tom, 67

Boyd, Major Alexander, 89
Brackenridge, Hugh, 219
Bradford, William, 98, 160
Brobeck, Stephen, 124, 126
Brunhouse, Robert L., 92–93, 103
Bryan, Arthur, 104–5
Bryan, George, 85, 95, 98, 103, 104, 104 n. 65, 125, 129, 175, 182. See also Agricola
Bryan, Samuel, 102, 104–5
Bruchey, Stuart, 13, 61
Bull, Colonel John, 89
Burd, James, 34
Bushman, Richard L., 122

Cadwallader, John, 125
Cannon, James, 82, 96, 97, 103, 118, 119
capitalism, 223–26, 56, 60, 134, 158. See also capitalist commodity exchange; consumer revolution; markets; maximization
British capitalism, 42, 61, 131
definitions of: entrepreneurial, 5–6, 7; market, 6–8; Marxist, 8–10, 10 n. 21, 158 n. 50
transition debate, 3–5, 41, 224–25
capitalist commodity exchange, 9–10, 33
capitalist mode of production, 9
Carey, Matthew, 105, 190
Catholics, 64
centers, modern social, 52–54, 91, 138, 160, 186. See also integration
Chambers, William Nesbet, 94, 105–6
Chew, Benjamin, 97, 216
China Emporium, 48
City Tavern, 12
Clark, Christopher, 41
Clemens, Paul, 37
Clymer, George, 97, 125, 129, 203, 217
Cochran, Thomas C., 12
Colbert, 190–91, 211
Cole, Arthur H., 14
College of Pennsylvania, 172, 202
College of Philadelphia, 73, 84, 103, 106
Colomy, Paul, 56
Colony in Schuylkill, 69, 123
commercial crisis (1784), 165–67, 179
Committee for Improving the Condition of Free Blacks, 72
Committee of Privates, 78, 82, 89, 118–19, 133

Committee on Public Finance, 139
committee report, 1785 (General Assembly), 182–84, 190, 207–8, 209, 210, 213
committees of correspondence, 74–75, 75 n. 39, 77, 98, 106. *See also* associational system
Considerations, on the Power to Incorporate the Bank of North America, 194–96, 205–6, 213. *See also* corporations; Wilson, James
Constitution of 1776, 81–85, 90, 91, 132
Constitutional Society (Party), xiii, 78, 98, 101, 103, 105, 106, 107, 145, 176, 177, 179, 182, 185, 190, 191, 202, 203, 204, 205, 208, 211, 212, 216, 217–18. *See also* political parties; Whig Society
   as a coalition, 127–28, 180
   leadership of, 125–26
   formation of, 84–90, 95–98
   style and progams, 90–91
consumer revolution, 23–25, 48, 112–13, 131, 138, 158, 163–64, 170, 189, 197–98, 219, 220, 224. *See also* capitalism
Cooper, Direk, 21
Cordwainers Fire Company, 70
Cornell, Saul, 212
corporations. *See also* Blackstone, Sir William; *Considerations, on the Power to Incorporate the Bank of North America*
   for business, 144
   City of Philadelphia, 65–66, 84, 175
   colonial charters, 144
   fear of, 142–43, 145, 163, 174, 184, 190–91, 202, 207, 216, 227–29
   as private property, 162–63, 195–96
   and public service, 144–45, 163, 171
cottagers, 15, 27–28. *See also* labor; markets
Council of Censors, 202, 210
Coxe, Tench, 102, 104, 105, 216
county government, 65
craftsmen. *See* artisans
Crage, William, 29

Darwin, Charles, xiii–xiv
Davis, Jacobus, Jr., 36
Degler, Carl, 4
de Kadt, Maarten, 9
Delameter, Jacob, 36
Dickinson, John, 102, 124, 125, 169

Doddridge, Joseph, 35
Doerflinger, Thomas M., 25, 120 n. 37, 121 n. 38, 128, 155 n. 46, 165, 165 n. 16, 167 n. 20
Durkheim, Emile, 49–52. *See also* functionalism; neo-Durkheimianism; Parsons, Talcott
Dutch, 44

Eisinger, Chester E., 113–14
Eisenstadt, S. N., 52–54, 56, 70
elective affinities, 79, 111
Englishmen, 14, 34, 44, 126
Episcopalians, 73
equality, 82–83, 114, 163, 182, 184, 209–12, 227–30. *See also* antibanking; bank war; corporations: fear of; farmers: as a class; Findley, William; petty-commodity producers
Ewing, James, 102
Ewing, Rev. John, 95, 125
exchange. *See* bills of credit
exchange networks, 4, 29, 31, 32, 33, 35–39, 60–61, 68–69, 73, 113–14, 212, 219, 224. *See also* barter; bees; reciprocity
exploitation, 112–13
export-import. *See* merchants

Faulk, William, 29
farmers, xi, 4, 14–17, 20, 21, 22–23, 26, 39, 40–41, 130, 225. *See also* petty-commodity producers
   agricultural surplus, 19–20
   as businessmen, 14–17, 20, 130
   as a class, 113–14, 133–34, 209–12, 217
   as maximizers, 20
   and self-sufficiency, 17–18
Faulkner, Captain Ephrain, 89
financial intermediaries, 30 n. 84, 31, 225
Findley, William, 125, 207–11, 214, 218, 219–20, 221, 230
First Company of the Philadelphia Militia Artillery, 88
First Troop of Philadelphia Cavalry, 124
Fisher, Miers, 160–62, 166. *See also* Bank of Pennsylvania: in 1784
Fitzsimons, Thomas, 203, 207 n. 23, 213, 217–18
flax, 23
Fort Wilson riot, 78, 88–89, 107

Fox, Sherwood, 70
Franklin, Benjamin, 30, 70–71
Free Society Society of Traders, 144
French Society, 72
Frenchmen, 14, 44, 126, 147
Friendly Sons of Saint Patrick, 72, 99
Friends of Equal Liberty, 101
Friends of the Young Sort, 123
frolics. *See* bees
functionalism, 137. *See also* Durkheim,
    Emile; neo-Durkheimianism; Parsons,
    Talcott
funding bill (1785), 180–82

Gentlemen of the British Society, 72
German Society of Philadelphia, 72, 73
Germans, 14, 27, 35, 44, 77, 82
Gloucester Hunting Club, 123
government, weakness of, 64–66
Governor's Club, 123
Graydon, Alexander, 91
Grew, Raymond, 55

Hahn, Steven, 38
Hall, John, 34
Halpern, Manfred, 52
Hamble, Alisha, 37
Hancock, Thomas, 12
Hand-in-Hand Fire Company, 69, 124
Hanna, Rev. William, 35
Hannum, John, 100
Hartley, Thomas, 100
Henretta, James, 41
Hibernia Company, 70
Hibernian Club, 72
Holiday, John, 21
Hollingsworth, Levi, 155
Hopkinson, Francis, 69, 104, 125, 185
Humphrey, Joshua, 28
Huntington, Dr. James, 89, 98, 125, 126
Huntington, Samuel, 95
Hurst, James Willard, 143, 144

ideal type, xv–xvi, 50, 54, 56, 92
indentured servitude, 27, 60, 72, 225. *See
    also* labor; markets: labor
Independent Constitutional Ticket, 101
inflation, 87–88
Ingersoll, Jared, 97, 126, 160–61
institutionalization, 92–93, 92 n. 35

insurance, 30. *See also* markets: capital
integration, 51, 52–54, 57, 60–61, 67, 68,
    79, 132, 223. *See also* associational sys-
    tem; Durkheim, Emile; social structure
Ireland, Owen, 87, 106, 107, 220
Irish, 14, 23, 70, 126

James Coffee House, 48
Jefferson, Thomas, 207, 213
Jews, 14, 161, 162
Jockey Club, 123
Junto (Leather Apron Club), 70

Kennedy, Robert, 21
Kuhl, Frederick, 125
Kuhn, Peter, 166
Kulikoff, Alan, 41

labor. *See also* apprentices; bees; exchange
    networks; indentured servitude; mar-
    kets: labor; reciprocity; slavery
  mobility, 28–29
  rural, 33–39
  urban, 28–29
  wage labor, 27–28
land bank. *See* loan office
Lawrence, Thomas, 69
Lawson, Kay, 93–94
Leather Apron Club. *See* Junto
Leiserson, Avery, 92
Lemon, James T., 19
Lenin, Vladimir I., 110–11
Lester, Richard A., 169
Library Company, 71
Library Tavern, 48, 71
Livesay, Harold C., 59
Lloyd, Peter Z., 102
loan office (land bank), 31, 82, 115, 127, 164,
    167–71, 172, 173, 174, 175, 176,
    180–82, 187–88, 189, 192, 193,
    196–97, 203
Locke, John, view of property, 196, 205–6
Logan, Dr. George, 105, 106
London Coffee House, 12
loyalty oaths. *See* Test Acts
Lutherans, 70

Machiavel, 215
Magdalen Society, 72
Main, Jackson Turner, 106

markets, 112, 113, 116, 119, 120, 127, 157, 158, 188–89, 191, 200, 211. *See also* capitalism
capital, 30–31, 170–71, 188, 193, 224–25
definition of, 7
expansion of, 224–25
export markets, 46–47, 59–60
flax, 23
labor, 26–29, 225–26
land, 26
limits of, 58–59, 157, 224
lumber, 25 n. 70
product, 7, 23–25, 131
retail, 23–25
Marshall, Alfred, 7
Marshall, Christopher, 76, 101
Marx, Karl, 8–10, 49, 51, 56, 111
Masonic Lodges, 71
Matlock, Timothy, 89, 90, 95, 103, 118
maximization. *See also* capitalism; Weber, Max
artisans and, 22–23
definition of, 6
farmers and, 20, 23
merchants and, 12–14, 22–23
McClean, Archibald, 85
McClenachan, Blair, 180
McKean, Thomas, 95, 126
mechanics. *See* artisans
Mechanics Committee, 77, 118, 133
Mechanical Society, 77, 98
Mennonites, 64, 104
merchants (export-import), 66, 116, 117, 118, 142, 146, 153–54, 156, 158, 166, 167, 173, 191, 192, 193, 209, 211–12. *See also* upper class
as businessmen, xi–xiii, 10–14, 22–23, 41, 47–48, 59, 120–21, 130, 157
community of, 13–14, 41, 120–25, 157, 167, 176–77, 181
goals, political and social, 125–27, 180–82, 217, 219, 220
kinship networks, 13–14, 67
maximization and, 12–14, 22–23
production, control of, 32–33, 47, 59
as a social class, 41, 112, 120–25, 128–30, 133, 188–89, 196–97, 225
Merrill, Mike, 36, 41
Mifflin, Thomas, 89, 97, 102, 124, 216
militia association, 64, 71, 77–78, 89–90, 95,

98, 103, 107, 118–19, 132, 139. *See also* Committee of Privates; Fort Wilson riot
mode of production, 8–9, 9 n. 16
modernization, xi–xii, 48–49, 51–57, 60, 61, 177, 223–27. *See also* Eisenstadt, S. N.; system transformation
critique of, 54–55
money power, 145, 161–62, 174, 183–84, 191, 193–94, 209–10, 227–30. *See also* antibanking, aristocracy; monopoly
monopoly, fear of, 143, 145, 161–62, 164 n. 12, 166, 174, 187, 196, 207, 209–11, 220, 227–30. *See also* antibanking, aristocracy, money power
Moore, William, 95, 102, 125, 126
Moravians, 73
Moravian Collegium Musicum, 73
Morgan, Benjamin, 29
Morris, Gouverneur, 147, 160, 161, 173, 192–94. See also *An American*
Morris, Robert, 88, 97, 124, 125, 129, 142, 150, 156, 162–63, 176, 201–2, 203, 204, 206–7, 208, 213, 217, 218, 221. *See also* Bank of North America; Bank of Pennsylvania: in 1780; Office of Finance
Bank of North America, origins of, 151–52
as Financier, 139, 141, 147, 148, 149, 151
Mount Regale Fishing Company, 71
Muhlenberg, Frederick, 102
Mutch, Robert E., 31–33, 164

Nash, Gary, 28, 29
Neale, Walter C., 7
neo-Durkheimianism, 55–56. *See also* Durkheim, Emile; functionalism; Parsons, Talcott
Neutrals. *See* Tories
Nicholson, John, 100, 104, 106
night watch, 66
nonjurors, 101, 104. *See also* test acts
Norris, Isaac, 29

Office of Finance (Department), 139, 150, 148, 150. *See also* Morris, Robert
Orpheus Club, 73
Osgood, Samuel, 140 n. 9, 142, 186

Paine, Thomas, 76, 82, 89, 96, 102, 103, 118, 129, 196, 205, 213–14

paper money, 88, 126–27, 167, 172, 173, 175, 176, 179–82, 187–88, 193
Parsons, Talcott, 51, 56
Patriotic Association, 96, 97 n. 46
Patriotic Society, 77, 98, 118, 133
Peale, Charles Willson, 89, 90, 96, 102, 104, 125
Pemberton, Joseph, 153, 170
Penn, John, 97
Pennsylvania, 47. See also government, weakness of; militia; Quakers; social classes; social structure
    changes in, 137–38
    churches, 63–64
    farmers, 113–15
    state, 63
Pennsylvania Hospital, 72, 124
Perkins, Edwin J., 20
petitions. See political parties: petitions
Pettit, Charles, 95, 124, 125, 126, 154, 166, 179, 180–81, 184, 192
petty-commodity producers, xi–xii, 39–41, 130–31. See also farmers
    political goals, 114–15, 133, 209–12, 220
    as a social class, 112, 113–15, 133–34, 225–26
Philadelphia, 34, 46, 48, 59–60, 68–69
Philadelphia Contributorship for the Insurance of Homes by the Loss of Fire, 144
Philadelphia Corporation, 65–66
Philadelphia Dancing Assembly, 71, 123
Philadelphia Dispensary for the Medical Relief of the Poor, 72
Philadelphia Society for Alleviating the Miseries of Public Prisons, 72
Philadelphia Society for the Encouragement of Manufactures and the Useful Arts, 99
Philadelphia Society for the Promotion of Agriculture and Agricultural Reform, 73, 124
Philadelphia Society for the Relief of Distressed Prisoners, 73
Philadelphia Society of Ancient Bretons, 72
Philadelphiensis, 191–92
Philopatria, 174
piracy, 46–47
Plumstead, William, 69
Polanyi, Karl, 8
Pole, Edward, 98
political parties, xii, 85, 87, 109, 132, 138,
    160, 179, 214, 217, 220, 226. See also Chambers, William Nesbit; Constitutional Society; Lawson, Kay; Quaker Party; Republican Society
    activists, 104–5
    caucuses, 101
    committees, use of, 98–99
    coordinators, 99–100
    creation of, 95–98
    defined, 90–95
    elections, 106
    elections, disputed, 103, 107
    general assembly, organization of, 102
    labels, 101, 101 n. 60
    patronage, 103, 106, 107
    petitions, 75, 86, 88, 93, 98, 99, 100, 102, 103, 104, 106, 107, 117, 140, 181, 182–83, 186, 190, 210, 211, 219
population, 44, 48–49, 57–58
populism, 106, 212, 220, 221, 227–30
Porter, Glen, 59
Powel, Samuel, III, 119–20
Pownall, Gov. Thomas, 170
Presbyterians, 14, 46, 75, 77, 78, 126, 132
price-fixing campaign, 87–90, 98, 107, 203
proprietary elite, 124

Quaker Party, 63, 76–77, 82, 114–15, 117–18
Quakers, 14, 46, 47, 63–64, 73, 76–77, 78, 81–82, 93, 104, 124, 161, 162
Queen Charlotte Company, 70

reciprocity, 7–8, 8 n. 13, 33, 36–38, 49, 59, 68, 113–14, 163–64, 196. See also bees; exchange networks
Reed, Joseph, 90, 95–96, 102, 103, 125
relations of circulation, 113
Republican Society (party), 99, 101, 103, 104, 105, 106, 108, 132, 142, 145, 176, 177, 180, 182, 185, 190, 203, 205, 208, 209, 211, 212, 216, 217–18, 219, 219 n. 57. See also political parties
    coalition, 87, 128
    formation of, 84–90, 97
    leadership, 125–26,
    style and programs, 84–91, 126–27
Rittenhouse, David, 86, 89, 96, 97, 103, 125
Roberdeau, Daniel, 98, 125
Robinson, William, Jr., 205–6

Roosevelt, Frank, 8
Rothenberg, Winifred, 41
rural isolation, 17
Rush, Benjamin, 69, 97, 99, 102, 104, 106,
    116, 125, 180
Ryerson, Richard Allan, 75

Saint Andrew's Society of Philadelphia, 72
Saint Thomas African Church, 72
Schultz, Ronald, 116–17. *See also* artisans
Schultze, Christopher, 100
Schumpeter, Joseph A., 5–6, 14
Schweitzer, Mary M., 168
Scots, 44, 72
Scots-Irish, 14, 44, 77, 82
Scott, James, 22
self-sufficiency. *See* farmers: self-sufficiency;
    petty-commodity producers
Sellers, Nathan, 116
Septimus, 161–62
Sergeant, J. D. (Jonathan Dickinson), 95,
    100, 102, 103, 125, 126, 160, 161, 180,
    186, 188–89, 210
Shils, Edward, 52–53
Shippen, Edward, 124, 216
Shippen, Polly, 123
Shoemaker, Samuel, 69
Shultz, James, 79
Simler, Lucy, 37
Sjoberg, Gideon, 60
slavery, 26–27, 29, 30, 33, 42, 61, 64, 227.
    See also markets: labor
Smedley, William, 15, 16, 21, 31, 41,
Smilie, John, 179, 207–8, 214, 243 (App. C)
Smith, Barbara Clark, 35–36, 37
Smith, Billy, 120 n. 37, 121 n. 38
Smith, Jonathan Bayard, 125
So, Alvin Y., 111
social classes, xii. *See also* artisans; exploita-
    tion; farmers; merchants; petty-com-
    modity producers; proprietary elite; re-
    lations of circulation; upper class
  class struggle, 10, 133, 160, 179, 184,
    188–89, 196–98, 208–9, 211–12, 219,
    220, 223, 225
  definition of, 110–11
  formation, 8, 10, 225–26
  in Pennsylvania, 66–67, 112–24, 133–34,
    138, 176
social formation, 9

social structure, xi–xii, 43, 56, 57, 60–61,
    78–79. *See also* associational system;
    Durkheim, Emile; functionalism; mod-
    ernization; Parsons, Talcott; social
    classes; status groups; stratification;
    voluntary associations
  changes in, 137, 226–27
  in Pennsylvania, 49, 67–69, 130–34,
    176–77, 196, 209–12, 219, 220
  social simplicity, 67–68
Society for the Relief of Poor Decayed Mas-
    ters of Ship Carpenters, 73
Society of Ancient Britons, 69
Sons of Saint George, 72
Sons of Saint Tammany, 68, 72, 78, 96,
    98, 132
Sombart, Werner, 5
specialization, 48, 50–52, 57, 58, 60–61, 68,
    132–33, 223, 224. *See also* integration,
    modernization, social structure
state debt, assumption of, 106, 126, 127,
    179–82
status groups, 111–12, 121, 160, 186. *See
    also* social class; stratification
stratification, 44–46, 109, 111, 112, 123. *See
    also* social class
structural differentiation, 49–50, 51, 131. *See
    also* Durkheim, Emile; Eisenstadt, S.
    N.; integration; modernization; special-
    ization
Supreme Executive Council, 83, 88, 95–96,
    104, 106, 142
Swanwick, John, 124
Swayne, Hannah, 37, 39–40
Swayne, Samuel. *See* Swayne, Hannah
Swedes, 44
system transformation, 52, 60–61, 131, 224.
    See also Eisenstadt, S. N.; moderniza-
    tion; structural differentiation

Test Acts (loyalty oaths), 75, 76, 84, 86–87,
    99, 100, 104, 106, 108, 127, 132, 172,
    203, 220. *See also* nonjurors
Thayer, Theodore, 91–93
theory, xiii–xvi, xv n. 6
  antitheory, xiii–xv
  definition of, xv
  theoretical explanation, xv, 5 n. 6
Thomson, Charles, 74, 185
Thompson, Peter, 48

Tilghman, James, 97
Tocqueville, Alexis de, 43
Tories, 61, 75, 81, 85, 86, 87, 88, 89, 90,
    97, 98, 106, 108, 132, 161, 216
transportation, 17, 19, 25–26, 46, 131
Tully, Allan, 74, 120 n. 36
typology. See ideal type

Union Fire Company, 71
University of Pennsylvania, 95, 124
University ticket, 101
upper class, 119, 26–27, 134, 203, 216, 217,
    220. See also social class; stratification
    and the bank war, 197, 208
    composition, 120–21, 121 n. 38
    country seats, 121–22, 123
    Philadelphia, 120, 120 n. 36, 120 n. 37
    and the Revolution, 124–25
    as a ruling class, 128–30

Van Berckel, Johan, 186
voluntary associations, xi. See also associa-
    tional system; social structure
    definition of, 69–70, 69 n. 20, 79
    in history, 79
    and nonvoluntary institutions, 77–78
    in Philadelphia, 68–69, 71–73, 117, 132–33
    in rural areas, 73–74

Wadsworth, Jeremiah, 105, 150, 200–201
Wardens of the Watch, 66
Warder, Jeremiah, 105
Warner, Sam Bass, Jr., 20
Washington, George, 123, 139
Wayne, General Anthony, 99, 100, 104
Weber, Max, 5, 6, 7, 49, 51, 56, 79, 111, 129
Webster, Pelatiah, 102, 129, 147, 154, 213
Welsh, 44, 69, 72
Wharton, Isaac, 146–47
Wharton, Thomas, 13
Whig Association, 78, 98
Whig Society, 96–98
Whitehill, Robert, 179, 207
Willing, Thomas, 69, 97, 119, 124, 125, 142,
    146, 147, 149–50, 164, 171, 173–74,
    182, 182 n. 12, 185–86, 201–2, 203,
    204, 216
Wilson, James, 78, 89–90, 97, 102, 125, 129,
    142, 160, 161, 164, 167, 185–87, 189,
    194–98, 201, 204–6, 213
Wilson, John, 105, 153
Wilson, Samuel, 37
Wood, Gordon, 84–85, 208
Wright, Henry Clark, 115

Yates, Jaspar, 99
Young, Dr. Thomas, 96, 97, 118

Zane, Isaac, 29